DRIVING INNOVATION

INTELLECTUAL PROPERTY STRATEGIES FOR A DYNAMIC WORLD

Michael A. Gollin

Partner, Venable LLP
Adjunct Professor, Georgetown University
McDonough School of Business

CAMBRIDGE
UNIVERSITY PRESS

CAMBRIDGE UNIVERSITY PRESS
Cambridge, New York, Melbourne, Madrid, Cape Town, Singapore,
São Paulo, Delhi, Dubai, Tokyo

Cambridge University Press
32 Avenue of the Americas, New York, NY 10013-2473, USA

www.cambridge.org
Information on this title: www.cambridge.org/9780521701693

First published 2008

A catalog record for this publication is available from the British Library

Library of Congress Cataloging in Publication data

Gollin, Michael A.
Driving innovation: intellectual property strategies for a dynamic
world / Michael A. Gollin.
   p.   cm.
Includes bibliographical references and index.
ISBN-978-0-521-87780-0 (hardback)
ISBN-978-0-521-70169-3 (pbk.)
1. Intellectual property.   I. Title
K1401.G65   2008
346.04′8–dc22   2007025090

ISBN 978-0-521-87780-0 Hardback
ISBN 978-0-521-70169-3 Paperback

Transferred to digital printing 2010

DRIVING INNOVATION

Driving Innovation reveals the dynamics of intellectual property (IP) as it drives the innovation cycle and shapes global society. The book presents fundamental IP concepts and practical legal and business strategies that apply to all innovation communities, including industry, nonprofit institutions, and developing countries. How does IP balance the exclusive rights of innovators with public demand for access to their innovations? How can organizations manage IP strategically to meet their goals? How do IP strategies play out on the global stage? The answers draw on the author's broad experience, news headlines, and precedent-setting lawsuits relating to patents, trademarks, copyright, and trade secrets – from biotechnology to the open source movement. General readers and students will welcome the lively overview of this complex topic, while executives and practitioners can gain new insights and valuable approaches for putting ideas to work, navigating within or changing the global IP system to expand innovation.

Michael A. Gollin is a law partner at Venable LLP and a faculty member at the Georgetown University McDonough School of Business. He obtained his bachelor's degree in biochemical sciences from Princeton University and a master's degree (*Diplom*) in zoology and molecular biology from the University of Zurich, where he was a Swiss National Foundation Fellow. He received his law degree from Boston University School of Law in 1984, where he was a Tauro Scholar and Liacos Scholar and received the Faculty Award. He became a patent attorney and has worked in law firms in Boston, New York, and (since 1990) in Washington, DC, where he represents corporations and nonprofits.

Mr. Gollin teaches strategic management of intellectual property at Georgetown University. He has held many appointed and elected positions, and in 2002 he launched Public Interest Intellectual Property Advisors (PIIPA), a pro bono service for developing country clients. He has coauthored two books: *Biodiversity Prospecting* and *Innovations in Ground Water and Soil Cleanup: From Concept to Commercialization* and has published and presented about 100 law review articles, papers, and speeches. He has been interviewed by National Public Radio, Fox News Channel, *Time* magazine, and Bloomberg News on intellectual property issues.

To my family

Contents

Foreword

Innovation is the creative lifeblood of every country. One of my proudest accomplishments as a United States Senator was to help promote innovation in my country by bringing about the passage of the Bayh-Dole Act of 1980. The Bayh-Dole Act gave universities ownership and control of government-funded inventions that are balanced by restrictions to ensure that the public would benefit from the research. The resulting system has borne fruit beyond my dreams over the past 25 years. The law tapped into a basic truth – that society can benefit from creativity only if a properly balanced legal and institutional framework is in place to drive innovation forward. In particular, a special framework is required to bring publicly funded innovations out into the commercial marketplace so they are broadly accessible. Without such a framework, government-owned inventions gathered dust. With the right system, the benefits of academic creativity have washed across the globe in the form of new medicines, foods, materials, and information technology.

In this book, Michael Gollin explores the same fundamental concept – the process by which individual creativity leads to social progress is one that requires careful balancing of private control with public access, within an elaborate infrastructure of intellectual property. The intellectual property system has grown and changed over the centuries through legal reforms as well as business and technical innovation. Moreover, globalization has brought us to a time when creativity and innovation have an impact on everyone, rich and poor, in every nation. Intellectual property affects that process in important and complex ways, and we need a guide to help us understand it. This book fills that need. This book outlines the rise of intellectual property into a system that drives innovation in corporations and universities, in artists' studios and farmers' fields, around the world. It also offers practical strategies for working within the system to foster innovation, and some guidance on standards for reforming the system to maintain the balance so crucial to society, the balance between private control and public access.

This book can help us follow such strategies to keep the engine of innovation going and the orchard growing, so individuals can work together in creative communities to find new ideas, develop them into products, and bring them out into the marketplace, until they are broadly available.

Without the necessary knowledge and skills, we fail, the brakes go on, and the trees come down.

Those of us who care about innovation know that we need to keep an eye on the big picture – including international and national intellectual property laws and public funding – while also working to support the individual creative and entrepreneurial acts that, together, lead to the benefits of innovation. I am pleased to introduce you to this book because it will help you do both. It is also a good read, with many stories that simplify the complex topic with clear examples and illustrations based on the author's extensive practical experience. Enjoy it.

The Honorable Birch Bayh
United States Senator 1963–1981

Preface

I wrote this book with the goal of helping people understand our intellectual property system as a human endeavor, a social and economic force that drives innovation, a manifestation of creativity and trade, a sometimes crude balance between exclusivity and access, and a topic worthy of study, teaching, learning, and practice. My hope is that such understanding can lead people from crude generalities about what's good or bad about the system, toward more productive pursuits like how to make it work better.

Writing the book has also helped me understand the larger significance of my work as a patent attorney, in a global context, along the arc of history. Since finishing law school in 1984, my career has involved helping clients put their ideas to work, mainly pharmaceutical, biotechnological, and other industrial companies and universities from the U.S., Europe, and Japan, by obtaining patents, registering trademarks, licensing rights, and arguing about them in court. I learned to see intellectual property law as the invisible infrastructure of innovation, underlying most of modern society. I also spent a few years practicing environmental law and saw firsthand how the promise at the leading edge of innovation can lead to problems at the trailing edge, and I have long been disturbed by that contradiction.

Since about 1990, I have had the opportunity to see how intellectual property affects widely different communities around the world – participating in negotiations about biodiversity between Fijian villagers and a pharmaceutical company, cross-legged on straw mats drinking kava kava with tribal officials; waiting for the generator to kick on each time there was a power outage during a presentation to plant breeders and other agricultural researchers in Nigeria; working with researchers in developing countries suffering from malaria and subject to military unrest, authoritarian oversight, and lack of funds; witnessing the contrast between technology haves and have-nots, side by side in India; marveling at how the most modern genomic sequencing technology can help traditional herdsmen in Kenya cure their livestock.

My broad interest in the impacts of innovation on our global community led me into writing, teaching, and public service. These activities have allowed me to go beyond the practice of law (with its fierce duty to individual clients and attention to minute detail), so that I could look for larger truths. I developed an intellectual property curriculum for professionals in developing countries and used it in India, Kenya, Tanzania, Cote d'Ivoire, Nigeria, Syria, and elsewhere. Since 2000, I have taught IP management to MBA students at Georgetown University with co-professor Leo Jennings, and I am no longer surprised at how quickly they go from not knowing a trademark from a copyright to producing a comprehensive report on the intellectual property of a selected major corporation, giving sound management advice that may not even have occurred to executives within the company. I continue to learn concepts and strategies from established masters, clients, colleagues, and students around the world.

The global need for practical assistance with intellectual property matters has led me to take on pro bono projects. In 2002, to fill that need, I founded a nonprofit organization that helps developing country organizations find IP professionals who can represent them on a volunteer basis. That organization, Public Interest Intellectual Property Advisors (PIIPA, www.piipa.org), is based on the conviction that all people, regardless of their sophistication and financial means, should have the benefit of good counsel on how IP issues affect them, and how they can use IP principles to help them meet their own goals.

Writing this book, then, was a logical extension of such activities, a way to extract fundamental concepts and dynamics of intellectual property, to outline practical strategies that organizations can use in managing it, and to convey the stakes involved in the ongoing policy debates about reforming the IP system around the world.

Acknowledgments

John Berger saw the book concealed in my original proposal and patiently encouraged me to complete it. My law school professor Michael Baram introduced me to John, and for 25 years has mentored me in the law and beyond. My father, Prof. Richard Gollin, diligently edited the manuscript, expecting nothing but clear ideas and precise language. Others helped edit, including my wife, Jill Dickey, and my mother, Prof. Rita Gollin.

I am particularly grateful to my co-professor Leo Jennings, whose fresh approach to IP management and legal issues always keeps me on my toes. Leo's ideas are most apparent in Part Three, which roughly tracks the course that we first taught in 2000. Our Georgetown MBA students contributed ideas, too.

For crucial guidance at the formative proposal stage, I thank my brother-in-law Stephen Marshak, Adam Bellow, Richard Razgaitis, the originator of patent strategies Stephen Glazier, Scott Turow, Richard Zacks, Madison Bell, John Barton, and Michael Lyon, who also helped edit. Mark Lerman and Dan Armstrong provided valuable insights about innovation in drama and classical music. Graham Dutfield, Simon Best, Scott Miller, Mike Polacek, Anil Gupta, Geoff Tansey, and brother Jim Gollin all shared their perspectives. Other ideas were inspired by clients, including the University of California, the J. Craig Venter Institute, and the Bill & Melinda Gates Foundation.

Historical materials regarding Venice were helpfully provided by Cesare Bosman and colleagues at the patent firm of Studio Torta, and by the Archives of the City of Venice, and hieroglyphic help came from Serge Rosmerduc of the Université Paris 8. Katherine Boyle enthusiastically helped with more modern references.

Thanks to my partners at Venable for encouraging and supporting my efforts to finish this book, in particular Birch Bayh (the indefatigable advocate for public-private partnerships for innovation), Bill Coston, Marina Schneller, Clif McCann, Josh Kaufman, and Zayd Alathari (who created early versions of some of the figures); to librarian Nassim Mohammed; and to my assistant Shana Stiles for endless efforts to keep everything running.

My experience with Public Interest Intellectual Property Advisors has proved the importance of making innovation work for everybody. A portion of proceeds from this book will go to PIIPA. I thank my fellow board members, the international advisory committee, volunteers, and donors for supporting that mission (including the Fogarty Center of the U.S. NIH, the Smithsonian Institution, Rockefeller Foundation, UK Department for International Development, the Ford Foundation, and WIPO). Special thanks to PIIPA colleagues Dick Wilder, Chuck McManis, Josh Sarnoff, Roy Widdus, Rota Khanna, Tzen Wong, Ben Prickril, and Michael Davitz for their frank and helpful input.

My dear wife, Jill, has given unwavering love and support from the beginning and accepted my countless absences from family activities, as have my children, Natasha (who helped design the cover), Max (who helped with the bibliography), and Julia. For putting us up and putting up with us at the Old House, UK, where much of this was written, thanks to Rachel and Adrian Besancon and Ben and Claire.

There are countless others who contributed to the ideas and words included here, including many unnamed clients and friends. And acknowledgments in advance to those who send comments to be taken up in the second edition. Thanks to all!

Abbreviations

AIDS	Acquired immunodeficiency syndrome
ARIPO	African Regional Intellectual Property Organization
ATCC	American Type Culture Collection
AUTM	Association of University Technology Managers
CBD	Convention on Biological Diversity
CDA	Confidential disclosure agreement
CGIAR	Consultative Group on International Agricultural Research
CIPIH	Commission on Intellectual Property Rights, Innovation, and Public Health
CIPR	Commission on Intellectual Property Rights
CTM	Community Trade Mark (Europe)
DMCA	Digital Millennium Copyright Act
EPO	European Patent Office
FAO	Food and Agriculture Organization (UN)
FDA	US Food and Drug Agency
FED. CIR.	U.S. Court of Appeals for the Federal Circuit
FTC	US Federal Trade Commission
FTO	Freedom to operate
HIV	Human immunodeficiency virus
IARC	International Agriculture Research Centre
ICANN	Internet Corporation for Assigned Names and Numbers
ICARDA	International Centre for Agricultural Research in the Dry Areas
ICC	International Chamber of Commerce
ICRISAT	International Crop Research Institute for the Semi-Arid Tropics
ILRI	International Livestock Research Institute
IP	Intellectual property
IPCC	Intergovernmental Panel on Climate Change
IPGRI	International Plant Genetic Resources Institute (Bioversity)
IPO	Intellectual Property Owners Organization
ITPGR	International Treaty on Plant Genetic Resources for Food and Agriculture
MTA	Material transfer agreement
NCI	U.S. National Cancer Institute
NDA	Nondisclosure agreement
NIH	U.S. National Institutes of Health
NPV	net present value

OAPI	African Intellectual Property Organization
PCT	Patent Cooperation Treaty
PD	Public domain
PIIPA	Public Interest Intellectual Property Advisors
PIPRA	Public Sector Intellectual Property Resource for Agriculture
PVPA	Plant Variety Protection Act
RIM	Research in Motion
TIGR	The Institute for Genomic Research (J. Craig Venter Institute)
TK	Traditional knowledge
TRIPS	Agreement on Trade-Related Aspects of Intellectual Property Rights
UN	United Nations
UPOV	International Union for the Protection of New Varieties of Plants
U.S.	United States
U.S.C.	United States Code
USPTO	United States Patent and Trademark Office
WARDA	West Africa Rice Development Association (African Rice Center)
WHO	World Health Organisation
WIPO	World Intellectual Property Organization
WTO	World Trade Organization

The Invisible Infrastructure of Innovation

Intellectual property (IP) is the invisible infrastructure of innovation. Intellectual property rights are a source of hidden wealth worth trillions of dollars, and they impose hidden costs on the same scale. The rules of intellectual property range from confusing to nearly incomprehensible, and the professional practitioners who manage these rights sometimes seem to belong to a secret society. Many of those who use the intellectual property system, or oppose it, have hidden agendas. This book reveals those secrets, and helps readers grasp how the system works and how they can make it work for them.

Tensions about intellectual property are no surprise. Fights over intellectual property issues are increasingly tumbling out of obscurity and into public view on the global stage, in international organizations, national legislatures, boardrooms, and courtrooms.

- Pharmaceutical companies promote stronger patents to stimulate innovation, while patient advocates around the world seek greater access to patented drugs.
- Tropical nations demand that anyone who removes biological materials must ask permission and pay for the privilege, while researchers from the north complain that the "greenhouse door" is being slammed closed.
- The Canadian makers of the ubiquitous Blackberry device claim they were "bullied" into a $600M settlement by NTP, a small U.S. company with no products on the market. With its new wealth, NTP takes on Palm and others.
- The United States pushes China to stop the rampant piracy of software and movies, while others debate whether stronger enforcement of copyright in developing countries only benefits foreign businesses.
- Multinational media publishers promote tighter control over distribution of music and video works on the Internet, while open source software and open access science thrive.

Intellectual property surrounds us. You may be standing in a bookstore, or sitting with this book at home, in your office, in a library, or a classroom. Or you may be reading an excerpt on a computer screen, accessed through the Internet. Intellectual property helped give you these options. For example, the computer embodies decades of continuous innovation. Invisible and hidden within the computer are countless intellectual property rights that serve as the infrastructure of that innovation. The monitor, the hard drive, the keyboard, the printer, and the cabling each are the subject of numerous patents on electronic circuits, materials, and mechanical structures. The software programs used to write this book, edit it, and print it,

1

and make it readable on a computer screen, embody layers of copyrights as well as trade secrets. Different vendors have branded the computer and its components with trademarks (e.g., DELL, INTEL, and SEAGATE). The hardware may be built in Korea, and the software may have been written in India.

Once you start to pay attention, you see that the same invisible infrastructure exists in the clothes you wear, the medicine you take, the books and entertainment you enjoy, your car, your home, the food you eat, and the energy you consume.[1] In the blood coursing through your veins, patented medicines may protect you from diseases.

Nutrients from breakfast also circulate in your blood – perhaps the residue of branded products sold internationally, like CHEERIOS® cereal, DUNKIN'® donuts, and STARBUCKS® coffee, or bread from a bakery known locally. Your clothes, too, bear trademarks – perhaps ARMANI®, if you are wealthy, or a less expensive brand sold at WALMART®, – and could have been made by complex computer-driven textile equipment having patented machinery and copyright protected software, or by poor laborers in developing countries using designs created in Europe or the United States.

The newspaper you read this morning (in print or on line) probably included reports about war, with its advanced destructive military technologies, and features about the latest sports results, blockbuster movie, and hit song. There may be stories about a new drug, the ongoing disputes between rich and poor countries about world trade and the balance of power, and public budgets for scientific research and the arts. Advertisements for electronic devices, foods, beverages, and clothing abound. All of this is driven by the forces of innovation and intellectual property.

How did intellectual property – in the modern form of patents, copyrights, trade secrets, and trademarks – arise? How did these rights flow together into the computer on your desk, and into, on, and around your own body? What role does intellectual property play in driving engineers, scientists, and creative talent to generate such remarkable innovations? How does intellectual property serve as a social force that drives and nurtures creativity, or blocks its benefits, in so many spheres?

Intellectual property remains a "black art," understood by few while influencing many. To shed light on that dark topic, this book provides a dynamic view of intellectual property – how it arises, grows, and flows, how it shapes global society, and how society shapes it over time. This book is directed to people who want to learn how intellectual property shapes our world, to understand the controversies over intellectual property, and more importantly to use their knowledge to help them meet their own goals.

All of us – creative individuals, inventors, authors, business people, and curious people everywhere, in corporations, academia, nongovernmental organizations, and government agencies, in rich and poor countries – can learn the fundamental concepts, dynamics, and strategies of intellectual property. We can apply this

---

[1] "Intellectual Property in Everyday Life – A Virtual Tour" (World Intellectual Property Organization 1999), available at http://www.wipo.int/about-ip/en/athome.htm, accessed December 31, 2006.

understanding to find new meaning in our surroundings, and new strategies that will best help us achieve our goals.

NEED FOR A SHARED FRAMEWORK

Globalization, innovation, and good leadership are universally recognized as driving forces in society, given the accelerating pace of technological change; the rise of a "knowledge economy;" the tightening interdependence of markets, technology, and culture; and the growing disparity between global haves and have-nots. It should be self-evident that intellectual property is a key to understanding the dynamics of global innovation, but it has not received the comprehensive attention it deserves.

Most books about intellectual property are written narrowly for a specialized audience. These include legal treatises, textbooks, and policy books typically opposing intellectual property rights and advocating change. Business management books on intellectual property generally focus on the benefits of IP management for U.S. industries, not its larger role in the global economy and public institutions.

The lack of broad attention to intellectual property's central role in innovation may derive from the extreme legal, economic, and technical complexity of the topic, and a lack of education about its fundamental concepts. A shared global conceptual framework would help innovators, authors, leaders, and ultimately society. Business people, management experts, and lawyers could avoid costly mistakes. Economists, academics, policy makers, and lobbyists could reconsider unhelpful simplistic polarized positions opposed to or in favor of the present system, and instead present more practical suggestions. If these people could gain an understanding of the duality of intellectual property and its role in driving the innovation cycle, society would benefit, and so would they. As one critic said:

> Global accounts of recent trends in intellectual property constitute the greatest gap in the literature. The provincialism, the Americanism, of the field is deeply troubling. Almost all of the books on the subject are written for and about America. In a global information age (and book market) this makes no sense.[2]

This book begins to fill that gap by providing a brief but comprehensive account of the fundamental IP concepts and dynamics that apply broadly to all communities throughout the world – including industry, nonprofit institutions, and developing countries.

Surprisingly, despite the excruciating complexity of the field, people can quickly learn the basic tools they need to understand what intellectual property is, why it is important in their lives, and how they can use this knowledge to further their own pursuits, or just to become better informed citizens.

The audience for this book includes anyone interested in innovation, and how intellectual property encourages, channels (or stifles), and puts innovation to work. That includes innovators and people who work with innovation – lawyers, business people, academics, and policy makers, in rich and poor countries, whether or not

---

[2] Siva Vaidhyanathan, "Celestial Jukebox: the paradox of intellectual property," *The American Scholar* (Spring 2005), p. 131.

they have any experience with intellectual property, and regardless of their nationality and profession. It includes practitioners concerned with entrepreneurship, scientific research, technical and cultural innovation, and other creative endeavors around the world, as well as academics and policy analysts concerned with innovation and globalization. It also includes business students and business people in all industries (publishing, biotechnology, computer science, manufacturing, finance, entertainment, and service industries), and a broader range of academics, government officials, intellectual property and business lawyers, law students, nonprofit entrepreneurs, history buffs, and more.

OVERVIEW OF THEMES AND CONTENT

This book presents the big picture, focusing on fundamental concepts and practical strategies, meaning those that are relevant in three very different global communities: industry, nonprofit organizations, and developing countries. Likewise, the book emphasizes concepts and strategies that are common to all types of intellectual property – trade secrets, patents, trademarks, and copyright. These fundamentals are illustrated with a broad range of examples of how intellectual property shapes our world, drawn from personal experience, recent and older lawsuits, books, articles, and news stories. The topics are diverse, including genetic engineering, pharmaceuticals, nanotechnology, electronics, Internet distribution of entertainment and media, and the open source movement. This comprehensive (if summary) approach makes the dynamics of intellectual property more clear than is possible in books giving specialized treatment to a single topic having more narrow relevance, such as U.S. corporate business strategy, or patent law. Beginners should thus be able to grasp the dynamics of intellectual property. More knowledgeable readers can gain new skills and knowledge about the global IP system and how to work within it, or change it.

Part one introduces fundamental concepts of intellectual property, and describes the dynamics by which it has shaped our world. Chapter 1 presents a social history of innovation and highlights the prominent role of intellectual property. Since the dawn of civilization, innovation has been winding through society in a cyclical fashion, from individuals through their communities and out to society at large. Creative individuals build on past knowledge, then share and develop their creative work with others in their community, until the innovative result of the collective effort can be adopted by larger society, thus enriching the pool of available knowledge for further creative effort.

The IP system affects these three stages of the innovation cycle, and serves as an engine driving the cycle forward. First, IP laws provide incentives that strengthen the individual's will to create. Second, they define exclusive rights that permit groups to share and invest in developing the creative works of individuals within their innovative community, and to control the dissemination of those works more broadly in society. Third, IP laws limit exclusive rights so that other creative individuals and communities can access the innovation, and the innovation cycle can go forward. Intellectual property thus captures and channels and shapes innovation, linking individual inspiration with collective labor and balancing the rights of creators against the rights of others.

Chapter 2 defines the several meanings of "intellectual property." It provides a history of the rise of the modern IP system from the dawn of history, 4,000 years ago, when the Egyptian scribe Irtisen wrote about trade secrets, to the Venetian invention of patent law five hundred years ago, to the recent global proliferation of IP laws, affecting human creativity around the world.

Chapter 3 summarizes the inherent tensions in intellectual property – between exclusion and access, private rights and the public domain, monopoly and competition, freedom and oppression, and the individual and society. Advocates and opponents have debated the pros and cons of the system through the centuries, while innovation itself puts the system out of balance so that it needs continuous readjustment. These political tensions and legal and business conflicts are a worthy subject of study, practice, and reform, in private corporations and public organizations, in rich and poor countries, and will likely continue to be important, forever.

Part Two introduces the basic elements of intellectual property in organizations. Chapter 4 introduces each of the four main types of intellectual property – trade secrets, patents, copyrights, and trademarks – followed by a summary of the legal basics for each, how it is obtained, and how exclusive rights empower the owner to prevent use of the innovation. This chapter uses the metaphor of an "innovation tree" in an "innovation forest" as a framework to help understand the innovation cycle, how intellectual property harnesses individual creative labor with available resources into specific bundles of rights, and how those rights can grow, flow, and eventually become accessible to the world. The creative act is like a seed using its internal energy to sprout in a forest, absorbing external resources (air, light, water, and minerals) to grow into a sapling, then a tree. While living, the tree enriches its surroundings, producing oxygen, giving fruit, shedding leaves, and eventually dying, returning to the soil and air to provide resources for new life. The external environment symbolizes the accessible domain of knowledge from which innovation arises. The green wood of a growing tree symbolizes IP rights. The inert old growth at the heart of the tree, the falling leaves and fruit, and the tree itself when it dies, symbolize how IP rights dissipate and ultimately become accessible to others. The innovation tree metaphor helps explain the different kinds of intellectual property and how they arise from and return to the accessible public domain. The chapter explains how groups of different rights can exist in one idea, and how these can be combined in an innovation forest.

Chapter 5 describes how intellectual property assets can flow among individuals and organizations, into a larger community, and out into society, in the form of permissions, from A to B to C to D, from creator to developer to producer to customer. Owners can enforce their own rights, but must beware of infringing the rights of others. These dynamics drive individual creativity, help organizations aggregate resources into IP assets, and expand access to innovations.

Chapter 6 presents the broad range of innovation communities around the world – private, public, and mixed – and for each, provides a description of how the innovation cycle works and how the fundamentals of intellectual property apply. Chapter 7 introduces the innovation chief as a person in each innovation community who pushes innovation forward, together with teams of people who can use IP management tools wisely to cultivate, preserve, and perfect rights in intellectual property, transfer rights successfully and ultimately help introduce innovations to society. Extending management theories about innovation, the innovation chief, working with an IP innovation manager, is described as the person who makes the decisions that lead these teams to effective (or incompetent) management of intellectual property in organizations.

Part Three, the longest section, turns to the practical steps that make up strategic management of intellectual property. Section A deals with planning. Chapter 8 shows how organizations can begin to take action, using strategic management of intellectual property to drive the innovation cycle forward and shape their environment, using practical legal and business strategies and tools. The chapter contrasts organizations that fail to take even the simplest steps to manage their IP assets from brilliant organizations. Essentially, strategic management means a process of first, understanding the organization's mission; second, assessing the internal resources and the external environment; third, developing a strategic plan by protecting internal rights while not infringing the rights of others; and finally, implementing that plan to help achieve the organization's goals.

Chapter 9 details the policy and practice tools and skills that can be used to implement an IP management strategy. Chapter 10 presents a menu of options from which organizations can choose. These are memorable strategies with colorful names like the burning stick, picket fence, patent jiu jitsu, and the cluster approach.

Section B deals with assessment. Chapter 11 describes how to assess internal resources and the external environment, including how to find the necessary information, primarily in terms of nonfinancial information. Chapter 12 focuses on financial valuation of IP rights. Examples are drawn from industry, the nonprofit sector, and developing countries.

Section C presents a systematic approach to implementing an IP management plan. Chapter 13 goes step-by-step through the decisions one should make to access innovations of others without infringing IP rights, using decision trees. Chapter 14 continues with a decision tree approach for protecting innovations with IP rights, and enforcing them. Chapter 15 surveys the many ways in which IP rights can be transferred to implement an IP management strategy.

Part Four illustrates the basic tools and practices with examples drawn from different organizations and situations. Chapter 16 describes the life sciences, communications, consumer products, and entertainment industries, and academia, comparing and contrasting the IP management strategies in each. This chapter shows people how to put intellectual property to work in their own organizations to achieve their goals, and how to analyze IP management in other organizations.

Chapter 17 compares national IP laws. Although there are many specific differences between them, the differences can be grouped into a few categories, and countries may be placed into several categories as well, making it easier for IP managers to adapt their practices to local requirements and international standards.

Chapter 18 provides a global view of the larger dynamics of intellectual property, and the tensions between different countries, regions, and industries. The dynamic concepts and strategies presented earlier in the book permit a practical new perspective on controversial topics like securitization of IP assets, balanced competition between branded and generic pharmaceutical companies around the world, marketing of national security technology, environmentally beneficial innovation, and the ironic alliances formed by those who favor and those who oppose biotechnology. This book's approach helps readers consider their own views of what are the good, the bad, and the ugly aspects of intellectual property, and what trends to expect in the future.

The final chapter, Chapter 19, revisits the themes of the innovation cycle and the innovation forest, and the tension and balance inherent in intellectual property. The chapter concludes with reflections on how these forces are tied not just to technological and cultural wealth but also to concepts of individual and collective freedom.

Hopefully the concepts and strategies in this book can help us understand how intellectual property drives the innovation cycle in our own lives, in our communities, and worldwide. With that knowledge, we can do a better job of managing intellectual property to put creativity to work, increasing freedom, joy, and the benefits of innovation throughout society.

PART ONE

INTELLECTUAL PROPERTY DYNAMICS IN SOCIETY

1   Intellectual Property and the Innovation Cycle

This first part of the book includes three chapters about intellectual property dynamics in society. Chapter 1 begins with a description of innovation as a force of creative destruction and then provides a brief history, asking the question of why people innovate. This chapter introduces the concept of the innovation cycle, with its three stages: individual creativity, social adoption, and access to knowledge. IP laws and practices affect each stage. First, IP laws provide incentives that strengthen the individual's will to create. Second, the exclusivity that defines intellectual property rights allows groups to share and invest in developing the creative works of individuals within their innovative communities, and to control the dissemination of those works more broadly in society. Third, the exclusivity of IP rights is limited, so that creative individuals and communities can access the innovations of others, and the innovation cycle can go forward. Intellectual property thus captures and channels and shapes innovation, ideally linking individual inspiration with collective labor and balancing the rights of creators against the rights of others. The chapter concludes by noting the dark side of innovation, and limits on the role of intellectual property

*   *   *   *   *   *

INNOVATION AND CREATIVE DESTRUCTION

Innovation is a powerful force of human nature. Innovation creates new businesses, cultural movements, and social institutions, and destroys, replaces, or leaves behind the old ones. Innovation feeds on the known and converts it into the new.

Innovation helps some individuals, companies, and nations win, while others lose. Roman roads, aqueducts, and military techniques conquered the ancient world. The telegraph and the railroad opened new regions and nations to commerce, as did the Internet. The computer age made one corporation – Microsoft – an economic force larger than many nations. But Microsoft may be only a memory in future decades. Innovation has shaped history over the millennia, and changes our world every day, bringing us new creations in fields such as pharmaceuticals, biotechnology, computer software, and the music and film industries. How we innovate today, and how well, shapes our future.

Half a century ago, Joseph Schumpeter developed a theory of dynamic competition in which innovation is a "perennial gale of creative destruction" that can open up new domestic and foreign markets, and revolutionize economic structures from within, "incessantly destroying the old one, incessantly creating a new one."[1] Schumpeter said that creative destruction is the "essential fact" about capitalism. Innovation, in this dynamic world view, is part of the destructive process, and, in a turn on Schumpter's phrase, can be referred to as a force of *destructive creativity*.

Innovation has become an ongoing concern for business managers, economists, and international policy makers. Intellectual property is one of the strongest of the tools available to stimulate and channel innovation, but the relationship of intellectual property and innovation is still poorly understood. This misunderstanding is not for lack of attention or controversy. There is more media coverage, increased emphasis in business management, and a broader and deeper international political debate about intellectual property than ever before. Controversy should come as no surprise, given the stakes, and the complexity of the task of harnessing something as paradoxical as creative destruction and the forces of destructive creativity.

What is surprising is how little has been said about the central role of intellectual property in channeling the dynamic processes of innovation. This is peculiar because the main justification for intellectual property is that it is a tool to promote innovation.

Intellectual property is a relatively new term that means different things to different people. Thousands of books and learned articles have been written about the specific legal, economic, political, and commercial details and complexities of intellectual property. This book takes a more interdisciplinary, dynamic approach by extracting fundamental concepts of intellectual property and proposing practical strategies by which these concepts can be applied in our changing world.

Lawyers, businesspeople, and our creative colleagues in science, engineering, and art can benefit from this big picture. Each of us, as individuals and as members of our communities, can learn how intellectual property shapes our world. With a heightened awareness of intellectual property basics, we can all deal with innovation more creatively and proactively. We can see how others use intellectual property as a tool to achieve their own ends, and we can do so, too.

A BRIEF HISTORY OF INNOVATION

Creativity and innovation are as old as humanity and are the most human of traits. From ancient to modern times, successful societies have been those that promote, reward, and capture individual creativity and innovation. History is written by the winners, and the individual, group, or country that innovates better than its neighbors tends to win – in business and in history. Those who fail to innovate, or to copy the innovators, are overwhelmed and replaced. Innovation holds a key to history. Modern nations will continue to compete for leadership in electronics, software, agriculture, medicine, and media. The future holds unimaginable developments in art, technology, philosophy, business models, and government institutions, and new leaders will inevitably emerge in these areas.

History can be seen as the endless story of individuals and groups creating new objects, techniques, machines, and institutions in their quest for subsistence,

---

[1] Joseph Schumpeter, *Capitalism, Socialism and Democracy* (Harper, 1975) [orig. pub. 1942], pp. 82–85.

commercial profit, victory in war, spiritual fulfillment through religion, and plea-sure through entertainment. Prehistoric people around the world worked clay into pottery, fibers into baskets and clothes, earth and wood into buildings, and ore into metal, and they identified which strains of grain grew best in particular soils. Imhotep invented the Egyptian pyramid, and the Egyptians developed beer and learned anatomy, but their innovations were limited, and they were overrun by the Nubians, then the Persians, and then by Alexander. The city of Athens in its Golden Age supported philosophical inquiry, art, and drama as part of its economic and military success but was conquered by the Romans. The Roman Empire expanded its domain with roads, aqueducts, and laws. Ancient Chinese inventors developed compasses and gunpowder more than 2,000 years ago, among other innovations. The silk and spice roads connected Europe and Asia and gave passing dominance to individual artisans and traders.

During ancient times, technical and cultural leadership moved from Africa (Egypt) to Europe (Greece and Rome) and then, during the Middle Ages, to Islamic societies and China. Europe has held a dominant technological position since the Renais-sance, and the United States expanded that dominance. Today, globalization has overcome geographic conditions as a force of creative destruction. As Tom Fried-man notes in his book *The World Is Flat*, the playing field is now much more even for countries such as India and China. The expansion of intellectual property laws around the world can be seen as further leveling the playing field, making the world more flat, but also tipping it in favor of those who know how to use intellectual property to their own advantage, to drive local innovation.

THE REASONS FOR INNOVATION

Why do people innovate? What causes creativity? What is it that causes some of us – as individuals, in groups and larger communities and nations – to innovate more, or less than others?

Some answers are suggested by economics, psychology, and biological necessity. According to economists and business management theory, people are motivated by self-interest in security, money, power, fame, and recognition – they innovate to contribute to their personal well-being. Related to self-interest is competitiveness – some people are creative because they want to do better than others. The converse is generosity. Many people create new things and ideas because they enjoy sharing them. Another motivation, observed even in children, is natural curiosity and the love of play and experimentation. This is a primary motivation for artists and sci-entists. Also, people are driven to solve problems or fill needs they have identified, just to survive or to finish a project that they started – necessity is the mother of invention.

Personally motivated creativity may not translate into broader social impact. There may be no social demand until long after an innovation is made. With modern prices so high, it is difficult to imagine that gasoline was originally discarded as a waste product of distilling nineteenth century lamp oil.[2] Many inventions are not seen to be socially significant for decades. Many artists are not widely recognized as great until after they die.

---

[2] Jared Diamond, *Guns, Germs, and Steel: The Fates of Human Societies* (W. W. Norton, 1997). p. 231.

Why have certain societies been more innovative than others over the long path of history? In his seminal book, *Guns, Germs, and Steel*, Jared Diamond considers and rejects the theory of racial or genetic superiority; and he also discards the "heroic theory" that innovation relies on the chance presence of rare geniuses. He asserts that the heroic theory of innovation is the ideal of patent law – that is, patent lawyers presume that a single individual or a discrete, small group is the "inventor" of a particular invention that "arises without any precursors, like Athene springing fully formed from the forehead of Zeus."[3] Diamond observes that to the contrary, inventions are usually the result of cumulative incremental improvements. For example, Watt is credited with inventing the steam engine in 1769, but forms of steam engines may be found at least 100 years earlier. The same is generally true of innovations culminating in Edison's light bulb and the Wright brothers' airplane. According to Diamond, if these individuals had not made their inventions, someone else would have.

In making his central argument that geography and biology decide the fate of history, Diamond downplays the role of individual creativity and patent incentives in driving innovation forward over the long term. Many people share a similar view, and it is worth examining more closely.

Diamond misses an important feature of innovation that is stimulated by intellectual property – the creative race itself. Competition drives many innovators. There are numerous examples of technical advances made almost simultaneously by two groups – those led by Bell and Gray with the telephone, Kilby and Noyce with the integrated circuit, Gould and Townes with the laser, Gallo and Montagnier with the first HIV/AIDS test kit, and Venter and Collins with the sequencing of the human genome. Competition drives many artists, too. It is narrow-minded or naïve to suggest, in hindsight, that there was no need to provide an incentive or reward in these close races on the theory that one or the other of these innovators would have reached the same result eventually. This is like watching one runner cross the finish line behind another and concluding that because they were both running that there was no need to organize a race. Without the race, neither would have run as fast, if they ran at all. The question is not just whether people will innovate as quickly but whether they will do innovative work at all. When there is a race, especially one with a prize, people join in, and it is natural for them to want to win, and that drives them to move quickly. Patents and other intellectual property help encourage innovation races.

Otherwise, Diamond is on solid footing when he describes how a society's success or failure is closely tied to its ability to adopt innovations – whether from within or from outsiders. Invention is only a small part of the larger process, whereby someone discovers a use for the invention, and it then diffuses outward where it is adopted in some societies, but not others.

One factor favoring some countries more than others is intellectual property law supporting innovation. Another is access to technical know-how. Social factors include individualism; risk-taking behavior; scientific outlooks; and religious and cultural tolerance. Also, prestige and compatibility with vested interests play a role – some societies reject innovation because it can be revolutionary and can overthrow

---

[3] *Id.* (Chapter 13, "Necessity's Mother"), p. 228.

the status of the powerful. Each society is more receptive to certain technologies and less receptive to others. For example, wireless mobile phone use leapfrogged over wired phone system development in developing countries that lacked the initial investment in wire lines found in North America and Europe.

Economic influences on innovation include availability of investment capital and lack of cheap labor. War, centralized government, climate, and abundance of resources can influence adoption of innovation. Ultimately, Diamond concludes that technology advances fastest in large, agriculturally productive regions that support large human populations, with many potential inventors and competing societies. Europe and China, bound together by geography, were able to innovate much more successfully than North and South America and Africa, which have many more natural barriers to diffusion of technology.

This quick overview is sufficient to show that innovation is a complex process. Intellectual property works within it to weave together individual acts and social movements. Innovation requires both individual creativity and broader social adoption, and societies that support both do the best. The evidence of creative competition, simultaneous inventions, and continued incremental improvements proves that all inventors – heroic or otherwise – are important, as are the incentives that support them. Curiosity draws individuals to be creative. We build on the work of others and see further than our predecessors because we "stand on the shoulders of giants" as Newton said. And then, because we may gain advantage by doing so, we race to finish our work and distribute it to society.

So innovation occurs at two levels. There is an initial, personal urge to create, and there is a subsequent social force that captures and expands the innovation over time so that it makes a difference in society.

As we will see, the intellectual property system is a central part of the process of innovation. The IP system drives individual creativity and adoption by society. The IP system also determines when and how an innovation becomes available for others to use by defining boundaries around what is accessible and what is not. Intellectual property rights help determine which innovations are widely available and which are closed off, separating innovation haves from have-nots.

THE INNOVATION CYCLE

Innovation is a cycle that revolves through history. The innovation cycle converts old knowledge into new, and links individuals with their broader society. Individuals engage in creative labor, building on the accessible pool of knowledge with their new ideas. These ideas are shared and developed collaboratively by a small group of people, often in a corporation or other organization. The work they develop is then distributed to the broader community and adopted by society, adding to the pool of accessible knowledge for others to use.

A traditional view of innovation has been of a straight line, an arc or arrow moving forward in time. In particular, the technology innovation cycle has been depicted as a linear process that occurs in private technology companies, in which a new idea (invention) is developed first into a commercial product (innovation), and then spreads within or across markets (diffusion). An electronics company develops a better display technology, adapts it to mobile phone screens, and puts them on the market. A pharmaceutical company discovers a new chemical compound, finds it to be effective, obtains regulatory approval, and sells it as a new drug.

This linear, assembly-line view of the technology innovation cycle has severe limitations. First, although it is helpful to distinguish three stages of innovation (from concept to commercial innovation, to broad availability), viewing the process as a straight line gives an incomplete picture. From where do new concepts come? Where do innovations go after they have spread throughout a market?

Second, although commercialization in a corporate setting is a central part of the process by which new ideas diffuse into society, there is also a role for public institutions and individuals. Third, innovation occurs much more broadly than in the technology sector alone. The characteristics of artistic and cultural innovation are often more fluid and collaborative than technology innovation, with its greater focus on solving problems. Fourth, the linear view focuses on a single isolated organization, rather than on groups of people and organizations working together, or at least learning from each other's work. Fifth, the linear model of technology innovation focuses primarily on major commercial innovations that become significant in the marketplace. In all sectors, creativity and diffusion of ideas into society seems to happen in a series of small steps of adapting, improving, and copying, by different people rather than in a monolithic act, a single trajectory of effort.

A better way to look at innovation is as a circular process, a true cycle that goes round and round.[4] The diffusion of ideas itself helps lead to new ideas, by expanding the public domain of knowledge for other people to build on. The process occurs in all settings, private and public, in nonprofit institutions and government agencies, and in technological and artistic and traditional communities in wealthy and developing countries as well. Individuals feed their ideas to groups, and these groups can then collaborate and compete as successful ideas become more broadly adopted. Collaborating or competing, these different groups expand and improve on ideas, adapting or copying them.

The innovation cycle involves creating new works from existing knowledge, sharing those works, and thereby establishing a new threshold for innovation, with IP rights applying selectively to some of those innovations. These concepts were described by Justice Kennedy of the U.S. Supreme Court in relation to patents, as follows:

> We build and create by bringing to the tangible and palpable reality around us new works based on instinct, simple logic, ordinary inferences, extraordinary ideas, and sometimes even genius. These advances, once part of our shared knowledge, define a new threshold from which innovation starts once more. And as progress beginning from higher levels of achievement is expected in the normal course, the results of ordinary innovation are not the subject of exclusive rights under the patent laws. Were it otherwise patents might stifle, rather than promote, the progress of useful arts.[5]

---

[4] Australia Academy of Technological Sciences and Engineering, *Australia Innovates*, "The innovation cycle," available at http://www.powerhousemuseum.com/australia_innovates/?behaviour = view_article &Section_id = 30. accessed January 4, 2007.

[5] *KSR International Co. v. Teleflex Inc.*, 127 S. Ct. 1727 (2007).

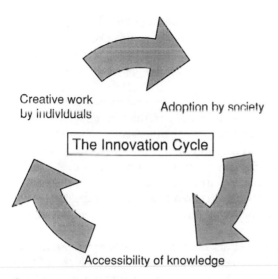

Creative work
by individuals

Adoption by society

The Innovation Cycle

Accessibility of knowledge

Figure 1.1. The innovation cycle. Creative people use available knowledge in their work, their new products are adopted in their community and broader society, and the innovations eventually add to the reservoir of accessible knowledge.

THE THREE STAGES OF THE INNOVATION CYCLE

Each stage of the innovation cycle is worth describing in more detail. (See Figure 1.1.) The first stage, *creative work*, occurs when an individual (or small group working together) comes up with a creative new idea, observation, technique, or work product. One force for individual creativity is human nature – our innate curiosity and our will to work to survive and use resources to improve our surroundings. As E. O. Wilson put it, a creative scientist "must be confident enough to steer for blue water, abandoning sight of land for a while," while an artist combines "exceptional knowledge, technical skill, originality, sensitivity to detail, ambition, boldness, and drive" and "an intuitive grasp of inborn human nature."[6] Nurturing, education, and training can also support creative behavior as opposed to rote repetition or slavish following of instructions. Ultimately, creative people are drawn to use and adapt as their own the great reservoir of available, accessible knowledge that is loosely referred to as the public domain, including the culture, art, science, technology, and collaborative networks that are accessible at any particular moment.

Even personal creative acts, without sharing, do not rise to the level of innovation, as we use the term here. Each of us is creative every day, in at least small ways. We may have creative ideas as we read, observe nature, or study other aspects of the public domain. We may solve scientific or commercial problems, or express ourselves artistically or socially. Such personal acts may give meaning to our own lives, and yet have no larger economic or historic significance. If we produce nothing, no innovation emerges. And if we produce something secretly, it does not feed into the

[6] Edward O. Wilson, *Consilience: The unity of knowledge* (Knopf, 1998), pp. 58, 213.

innovation cycle. Michelangelo's Sistine Chapel fresco, in public view for centuries, has had an enormous influence on art and religion, but it would have been irrelevant if it was painted secretly in a private barn and never viewed by anyone but the artist. Creativity that is not expressed and shared with others is lost at this first step and falls outside of the innovation cycle.

The second stage in the innovation cycle, *adoption by society*, or diffusion, occurs when individuals introduce their creative products into their immediate community, to be shared and developed in collaboration with others so that the innovations become available to society. Building a computer network for a business requires individual creativity. Combining computer networks into the Internet was an innovation. Dali's first painting of a melting pocketwatch was creative. The broader Surrealist movement was an innovation. Antoni Gaudi's architectural drawings alone would reach few people, but his dreamlike buildings, prominently displayed throughout Barcelona, influence many.

Brock and Freeze's 1969 paper about discovering *T. aquaticus* bacteria in the scalding hot springs of Yellowstone National Park was creative.[7] Explosive innovation followed in 1984 when Kary Mullis extracted a thermostable DNA polymerase enzyme from *T. aquaticus* to amplify DNA at high temperatures in what became known as the polymerase chain reaction, an invention that led to a patent that sold for $300 million in 1991, won Mullis a Nobel Prize, and unleashed gene sequencing.

Diffusion is a complex phenomenon. In addition to the creative, destructive force of innovation, economic forces of globalization can expand (or crush) certain technologies, businesses methods, and cultures and institutions around the world due to raw economic, political, or military force.

In the less fortunate parts of the world, the innovation cycle may be stuck at the first stage. A creative person living in a destitute community, plagued by hunger and poor health care, in a corrupt economy, or under the threat of violence from crime or war, faces great challenges in passing the fruits of creativity to others in the broader society.

Music provides an example of how the innovation cycle can run in poor countries. Vibrant local music scenes abound in poor countries in East Africa, the Caribbean, Asia, and Latin America, and modern electronics and Internet technology make it relatively easy for local artists to make and distribute innovative recordings, even if they do not receive much money for their effort. Local innovations in agriculture and health, on the other hand, are bound up in traditions and practices that are much more difficult to disseminate.

The third stage of the innovation cycle is *accessibility of knowledge*. Innovation requires interaction between creative individuals and their community. The innovation cycle moves forward when individuals promote their creative ideas and society adopts them. It stops when creative people lack access to information, when they do not share with their community, when innovations are lost, and when law and circumstances make innovations inaccessible.

[7] Kerry ten Kate, Laura Touche, and Amanda Collis, "Benefit-Sharing Case Study," Yellowstone National Park and the Diversa Corporation, Convention on Biological Diversity (1998), available at www.biodiv.org/doc/case-studies/abs/cs-abs-yellowstone.pdf, accessed December 31, 2006.

As an innovation is adopted more broadly in society, it becomes available to more and more people, either by purchase, license, or for free. Restrictions on distribution and control gradually weaken as intellectual property rights expire. A successful innovation moves out into society and eventually joins the reservoir of accessible knowledge. Publications, samples, products, and information become available for other creative people to use and improve on. When innovations successfully go around the innovation cycle, adding new knowledge to the accessible domain does not necessarily destroy anything. As the saying goes, a candle, like knowledge, does not diminish itself by lighting another.

But if an innovation fails, early or late, it may be neglected, fall into disuse, and even vanish from public availability. This exemplifies Schumpeter's concept of creative destruction. Products become obsolete and are no longer made, and their companies may vanish, along with all related knowledge. Old books can go out of print and become unavailable from a library. Traditional farmers and healers may create agricultural and medicinal knowledge in cultures where there is no written record or system of apprenticeship, so their knowledge dies out with each person's passing.

Innovation is not necessarily destructive. It can build on old knowledge, adding to it without taking away. A virtuous cycle results, one that is different from Schumpeter's paradox of creative destruction (or destructive creativity). We can refer to this nondestructive approach as "creative construction." Innovations that move into the third stage expand access to the great ocean of knowledge in the accessible domain. Creative people may then build on the innovation to begin the next revolution of the innovation cycle.

Without available knowledge, each subsequent wheel designer would be condemned to reinvent the wheel. With easily accessible knowledge about existing wheels, however, the designer can instead make an improved wheel. The innovation cycle is also driven by social forces encouraging adoption of a new idea or technology. As an innovation spreads from person to person, business to business, community to community, and nation to nation, ultimately the new knowledge, sooner or later, enters the accessible domain (and then the public domain, as discussed in Chapter 3).

Yesterday's innovation becomes part of today's accessible knowledge. Acetylsalicylic acid (Aspirin) and penicillin, Shakespeare's plays, and the incandescent light bulb are all available to anyone who wants them today because of creative effort long ago. Likewise, today's innovations – new painkillers, movies, and fluorescent bulbs – will become part of tomorrow's public domain. New drugs, better communications systems, and fuel efficient transportation will become available only through continued innovation. Unfortunately, some lost technology, lost cultures, and lost languages sink from view, deplete the reservoir of knowledge, and diminish humanity. And delays and limits in availability can lead to innovation gaps between wealthier communities who have ready access, and poorer communities, who have less and slower access to innovation.

A blockage can occur at each phase of the innovation cycle. The creative person may not have access to existing knowledge. A creative work may not become adopted by society. IP rights may preclude sufficiently broad accessibility. Any of these problems stop or slow the innovation cycle.

THE DARK SIDE OF INNOVATION

Innovation brings bad things with good. As the saying goes, the road to hell is paved with good intentions. An innovator trying to solve one problem may cause another. An innovation that provides benefits at the first stage of the innovation cycle may cause problems at the second stage as it becomes adopted more widely. Society then faces the challenge of solving these new problems. The solutions may start the innovation cycle anew. Otherwise society suffers.

Romans plumbed cities with lead pipes, improving hygiene but poisoning their citizens. Lead was used in modern times until copper pipe replaced it. Asbestos was used as fireproofing but turned out to cause lung disease, and so new fire retardants were developed. Freon coolant enabled the spread of refrigeration and air conditioning, improving food and comfort, but created a hole in the ozone layer. New refrigerants were invented.

Unregulated industrial pollution poisoned the air and water in the United States until the Clean Air Act and Clean Water Act and other laws began to limit the emissions from factories and power plants in the 1960s. New cleaner and more efficient manufacturing processes continue to be developed in response to environmental regulation. Similar problems and opportunities exist around the world.

Fireproof transformer oils based on polychlorinated biphenyls saved lives previously lost in electrical fires but caused long-term environmental damage. Replacements were found. DDT stopped malaria in many parts of the world, but by indiscriminately killing insects, it destroyed ecosystems. Many new pesticides have been developed (but none as powerful).

Fossil fuels have led to great convenience and freedom in transportation and supply of electrical power, but we have learned that the seemingly innocent carbon dioxide molecule is disrupting global climate in ways we are just beginning to understand. Nuclear power has the dark side of long-lasting toxic waste and nuclear proliferation. Nuclear bombs are the pinnacle of a history of innovation in lethal and disfiguring military technologies, justifiable if at all only for self-defense.

Innovation can be damaging politically too. Think of Hitler's best-selling book *Mein Kampf*, and video games being used by terrorist groups training young people how to carry out suicide attacks.

As these examples show, society must be cautious when adopting new technology. Innovation is not all good. On the flip side, of course not every innovation creates nightmarish problems. Agricultural biotechnology companies invented, developed, and put into production genetically modified plants and were met by deep public fear and concern of potential dangers. The precautionary principle was cited, saying that until we know a new technology is safe we should be cautious. The worst fears of environmental destruction due to agricultural biotechnology have not been realized, as the percentage of genetically engineered crops worldwide increases.

The latest fears surround nanotechnology, tiny particles of materials 100 nanometers or less in size, about half the size of the smallest bacteria. The chemical and physical properties of nanoscale materials are extraordinary and are very different than those of larger particles of the same things. Innovation in this area is intense, as is patenting, while governments, research institutions, and industry expand their investments around the world. There is much promise, but meanwhile virtually no regulation and few studies of the long-range impacts to health and the environment.

Ultimately, intellectual property law is not able to discriminate between helpful and harmful innovations. The IP system is focused on sorting out new from old, and exclusion from access. I have argued elsewhere[8] that it is not practical to reform the IP system to favor beneficial technologies and disfavor harmful ones. Other regulatory systems – environmental law and health regulation, subsidies and grants, for example – are structured to discriminate between beneficial and harmful technologies and innovations, permitting the former and blocking the latter. Meanwhile, such laws are not well-suited to promote innovation in beneficial innovation. In short, IP laws promote innovation, while other legal systems sort the good from the bad.

SUMMARY. Innovation drives history, paradoxically creating and destroying businesses, ways of life, and societies. Intellectual property shapes this dynamic competition, in a revolving innovation cycle in which creative ideas diffuse out to society, becoming accessible for others to build on, and supporting further creativity. Intellectual property laws and practices apply at each stage of the innovation cycle. The IP system regulates how creative people access existing knowledge. It stimulates creativity. It mediates between individual and society and has an impact on decisions about which fruits of creativity become widely available. Intellectual property issues greatly influence investment decisions. Through litigation and licensing, IP rights can determine which technologies and innovations succeed and which fail. Intellectual property laws influence when and how an innovation becomes accessible for others to use. Ultimately, the IP system affects which information society retains and which it loses. Unfortunately, intellectual property laws have little effect on avoiding harmful innovations. Intellectual property's dynamic role in defining the relationship between individuals and their communities is complex and diverse, but can be understood by most readers in general terms, and that is a central goal for this book.

[8] Michael Gollin. "Using Intellectual Property to Improve Environmental Protection." *Harvard Journal of Law and Technology* 4:193 (1991).

2 The Rise of the Intellectual Property System

This chapter begins by detailing the various definitions people use for intellectual property – from dictionaries, law, accounting, management, and scholars. The chapter continues by chronicling the rise of the global intellectual property system, from its roots in ancient times, through the Venetian innovation of patent law. The chapter finishes with a summary of the evolution of the modern international framework of intellectual property laws.

* * * * * *

DEFINING INTELLECTUAL PROPERTY

Before going further, we should clarify the definitions of intellectual property. People use the term "intellectual property" to refer to at least five different concepts, and this causes great confusion. By being aware of each definition, an informed reader can identify which meaning is intended in a given context. This is an important step toward intellectual property literacy in the global arena. Even people experienced with specific aspects of intellectual property may not be familiar with all the definitions. Being able to discriminate between them is a starting point for understanding the many conflicting views of the topic.

Dictionaries. Dictionaries define intellectual property essentially as something intangible, created by the use of mental ability, to which legal rights attach. The bundle of legal rights generally associated with ownership of property since Roman times includes the right to use a piece of property, to exclude others, and to benefit from, transfer, or destroy the property.[1] According to the Oxford English Dictionary, "intellectual property" first appeared in an early court opinion in the United States:

> [O]nly in this way can we protect intellectual property, the labors of the mind, productions and interests as much a man's own, and as much the fruit of his honest industry, as the wheat he cultivates, or the flocks he rears."[2]

In 1893, the term was used in the name of the United International Bureau for the Protection of Intellectual Property, the predecessor of the World Intellectual Property

---

[1] Adam Moore, *Intellectual Property and Information Control: Philosophic Foundations and Contemporary Issues* (Transaction Publishers 2004) pp. 14–15.
[2] *Davoll v. Brown*, 1 Woodbury & Minot 53, 57 (1st Cir, 1845) (upholding a patent on a cotton spinning machine).

Organization (WIPO). According to WIPO's Website, intellectual property now means "creations of the mind: inventions, literary and artistic works, and symbols, names, images, and designs used in commerce."[3]

Law. Practicing lawyers adopted the term "intellectual property" as a shorthand way to refer to a variety of separate legal doctrines which arose historically as (a) industrial property (patents, trade secrets, trademarks), and (b) literary property (copyright). The World Trade Organization's 1995 Agreement on Trade-Related Aspects of Intellectual Property Rights (TRIPS) sets minimum standards in all member countries for intellectual property protection, defined as copyright and related rights, trademarks, geographical indications, industrial designs, patents, integrated circuit layout designs, and protection of undisclosed information (trade secrets). See Appendix A. When I started practicing law in New York in the early 1980s, my law firm described its specialty as "Patent, Copyright, Trademark, and Unfair Competition Law." As we will see, some concepts become clear if we lump all these specialties together. However, as any well-informed professional knows, each type of intellectual property is unique, and in many circumstances the differences need to be detailed and addressed separately.

Accounting. Accountants view intellectual property as a form of intangible asset. In addition to intellectual property, intangible assets include goodwill, and reflect the fact that the market value of a firm is usually much more than the value of the "hard assets" such as cash, real estate, computer equipment, and so on.

Management. Business people consider intellectual property to be a management tool for converting human capital into value by defining and capturing new knowledge. For example, Patrick Sullivan uses the term "intellectual capital" to describe the human resources and intellectual assets of a firm.[4] Human resources are the creative people employed by the company, who have individual rights. Intellectual property is the legally protected form of intellectual assets, which belong to the company.

Scholars. Finally, philosophers, historians, and other scholars bring a broader set of ideas into their definition of intellectual property. To them, intellectual property refers to an ethical system that values all that is known. This includes individual creativity and socially adopted innovations as well as old and collective knowledge. For scholars, the term "intellectual property" may go beyond the legal definition to include everything in the public domain.

These definitions are so different that when a business person discusses intellectual property with a lawyer, or a lawyer discusses the topic with a scholar, they may completely misunderstand each other. Such discussions can resemble two people from different countries who try to make themselves understood by shouting and gestures when they don't share a common language. So, a first step to understanding intellectual property is to decide which definition is being used at any given time.

---

[3] http://www.wipo.int/about-ip/en/, accessed December 31, 2006.

[4] Patrick Sullivan, *Profiting from Intellectual Capital: Extracting Value from Innovation* (John Wiley & Sons 1998), pp. 5–9.

THE RISE OF INTELLECTUAL PROPERTY

Innovation is a doorway to success for individuals, corporations, public institutions, and communities around the world. And intellectual property – the system of rights, laws, and practices developed over millennia – provides a key to unlock innovation's door. In the remainder of this chapter, we touch on some highlights of the dynamics of intellectual property through history, including its origins and evolution into its modern form. We see that if intellectual property did not already exist, we would have to invent it.

Intellectual property is only one of several social forces that drive innovation, of course. The other drivers include the following:

(a) market forces including investor interest, market demand, entrepreneurial management skills, and the labor pool;

(b) geographical factors such as location and natural resources;

(c) laws regarding taxes, the environment, and product liability;

(d) government interventions such as educational standards, procurement practices, subsidies, and altering trade barriers; and

(e) governmental and philanthropic funding for research, cultural activities, and prizes and awards recognizing inventions.[5]

Intellectual property, as a system, stands apart from the other influences on innovation, making it a good subject for further consideration in its own right. First, intellectual property laws are specifically intended to promote innovation across society, as distinct from most of the innovation drivers listed above, which have other or narrower purposes. Intellectual property, by definition, relates to innovation. Second, the last decade has witnessed an ascendancy of intellectual property rights and issues in global trade and innovation policy, and so its political importance is rising. IP issues are in the news. Third, the rules and practices relating to intellectual property are so complex and so poorly understood that any effort to decode and understand them is worthwhile. Finally, there is no definitive history of intellectual property. To understand the future shape of intellectual property, and how to manage it today, we should be able to look back at the past with some confidence in our facts. Instead, it often seems we are left to work with snapshots, myths, and legends.

The accepted view in the 1980s, still believed by many practitioners today, was that the pillars of intellectual property derive from some kind of natural law, that they are inevitable and immutable. One day, sitting in the library of my law firm (the patent, copyright, trademark, and unfair competition boutique), I found the senior partner reading legal cases, and I jokingly told him, "I thought you knew the law already!" He replied, "Yes, I'm just checking to see if someone changed it." His humor reflected the assumption that the law was stable (and proper), and nothing major was likely to change.

The idea that intellectual property laws are inevitable and immutable is based on a mix of facts and faith that make it more a legend than truth. In the United States, the story goes something like this. The U.S. Constitution directs Congress "To promote the progress of science and useful arts, by securing for limited times to authors and

---

[5] Suzanne Scotchmer, *Innovation and Incentives* (MIT, 2004).

inventors the exclusive right to their respective writings and discoveries." (Article 1, section 8.) The framers of the Constitution derived this principle from English law and adopted it even before the Bill of Rights was adopted. Congress passed copyright and patent statutes to implement the Constitutional mandate, and Thomas Jefferson personally examined the first patent applications. The statutes have been amended from time to time primarily to make minor adjustments to judicial precedent and also to deal with new technology. U.S. Supreme Court decisions about patent and copyright dating back to the founding of the nation are still binding law applied by the courts today.

As the story goes, the U.S. system of patent and copyright law has the ideal balance set forth in the Constitution. Our trademark and trade secret laws are ideally suited to their purposes, too – preventing unfair competition and thereby upholding the fairness of our market system. Finally, because the current U.S. system is the right one, foreign intellectual property laws make sense only to the extent that they emulate ours.

In this rather chauvinistic view, the English came up with intellectual property, and the United States received it from them, along with our language. That is a traditional view of intellectual property, and it serves most U.S. practitioners well enough when dealing with individual assets – the day to day complexities of protecting and challenging patents, trademarks and copyrights, applying the law to the facts.

In about 1990, my eyes opened to some very different facts. As I researched the role of intellectual property in achieving social purposes like environmental technology innovation and conservation of biological diversity, I began to see the larger picture. IP laws are neither inevitable nor immutable. The roots of patent law grew long before the U.S. Constitution. The history of intellectual property in the United States has been extremely dynamic. Revisions to intellectual property laws over the years have been radical and fundamental and controversy has surrounded these changes all along. And similar forces are at work around the world. Each country has its own local reasons for its own intellectual property laws. It is therefore difficult to predict what intellectual property laws will look like in a decade, a generation, or a century, because that will depend on political, technological, cultural, and social forces that we can not predict.

This dynamic view of intellectual property took hold during negotiation and adoption of the 1992 Convention on Biological Diversity and the World Trade Organization's 1995 Agreement on Trade-Related Aspects of Intellectual Property Rights (TRIPS). A decade later, the dynamic world view of intellectual property is becoming dominant in publications written by lawyers, social scientists, economists, and business consultants. The new scholarship reaches farther back into historic precedent, deeper into economic and political analysis, across to business management case studies and lessons, and out into what we could call intellectual property studies, including jurisprudential, philosophical, literary, and cultural history.[6] The

---

[6] For a history of U.S. patent law, see Edward Waltersheid, "The Early Evolution of the United States Patent Law: Antecedents (Part 1)", *Journal of the Patent and Trademark Office Society* (JPTOS) 76:697 (1994), through Part 5 at JPTOS 78:615 (1996). A collection of some old and many newer essays about the history of patent, copyright, and trademark protection can be found in Robert P. Merges and Jane C. Ginsburg, *Foundations of Intellectual Property* (Foundation Press, 2004). John Barton published several articles in the early 1990s on intellectual property law reform as a consequence of technology change, including

increasingly intense examination of intellectual property is going on worldwide. For example, the Indian Institute of Technology in Kolkata opened the Rajiv Gandhi School of Intellectual Property Law in 2006, expecting to have 800 students enrolled by 2011.

As a result of so much attention, many new stories are being told about intellectual property and there is no one accepted history at this moment. The diversity of views about intellectual property and its roots helps to explain current controversies and uncertainties about the future of intellectual property.

THE ORIGINS OF INTELLECTUAL PROPERTY

As George Santayana said, "Those who cannot remember the past are condemned to repeat it." Knowing where intellectual property has come from may help us make better judgments about where it is going in the future, and what to do with it now. Therefore, although it is impossible to capture the full range of ideas about the evolution of intellectual property and its complex and controversial history, it is worthwhile to summarize some of the basic historical reference points. They suggest that there is a great deal of stability in intellectual property laws, but there is nothing inevitable about where we are today, and change can be expected to continue into the future.

In prehistoric times innovation was apparently slow – archeologists find that the same type of artifacts were used without much change over the course of millennia. Primitive social institutions such as authoritarian chiefs in those early times might have repressed innovation to maintain their authority. But the emergence of other social institutions and of writing brought with them history, and also different attitudes toward communication, knowledge, and innovation.

The roots of intellectual property may be found in the difficult skill of keeping a secret – choosing *not* to communicate information. The ancient Egyptians' respect for trade secrets is clear from Stele C-14 of Irtisen, a hieroglyphic tablet from 2000 BCE on display in the Louvre museum. (See Figure 2.1.)

According to a translation, Irtisen identifies himself as the chief scribe and artisan of Pharaoh Nebhepetra Mentuhotep of the eleventh Egyptian Dynasty, whom he praises. Irtisen then boasts of his extensive knowledge of hieroglyphics, offerings for festivals, magic, ink making, weights, construction, the force of the wings of ten birds, how to strike a prisoner, sculpture, and pigments. Irtisen vows that no one will know these secrets except for him, and his eldest son, permission having been given from

"Adapting the Intellectual Property System to New Technologies," in *Global Dimensions of Intellectual Property Rights in Science and Technology* (National Academy of Sciences, 1993); and "Intellectual Property Issues for the International Agricultural Research Centers, What Are the Options," (with W. Siebeck), *Issues in Agriculture*, 4, (1992). A collection of essays on international dimensions is in Keith Maskus and Jerome Reichman (eds.), *International Public Goods and Transfer of Technology Under a Globalized Intellectual Property Regime* (Cambridge, 2005). Business case studies are presented in Kevin Rivette and David Kline, *Rembrandts in the Attic: Unlocking the Hidden Value of Patents* (Harvard Business School 2000) and Julie Davis and Suzanne Harris *Edison in the Boardroom: How Leading Companies Realize Value from Their Intellectual Assets* (Wiley, 2001). An analysis of how the history of copyright could easily have led down different paths is in Brad Sherman and Lionel Bently, *The Making of Modern Intellectual Property Law* (Cambridge University Press, 1999).

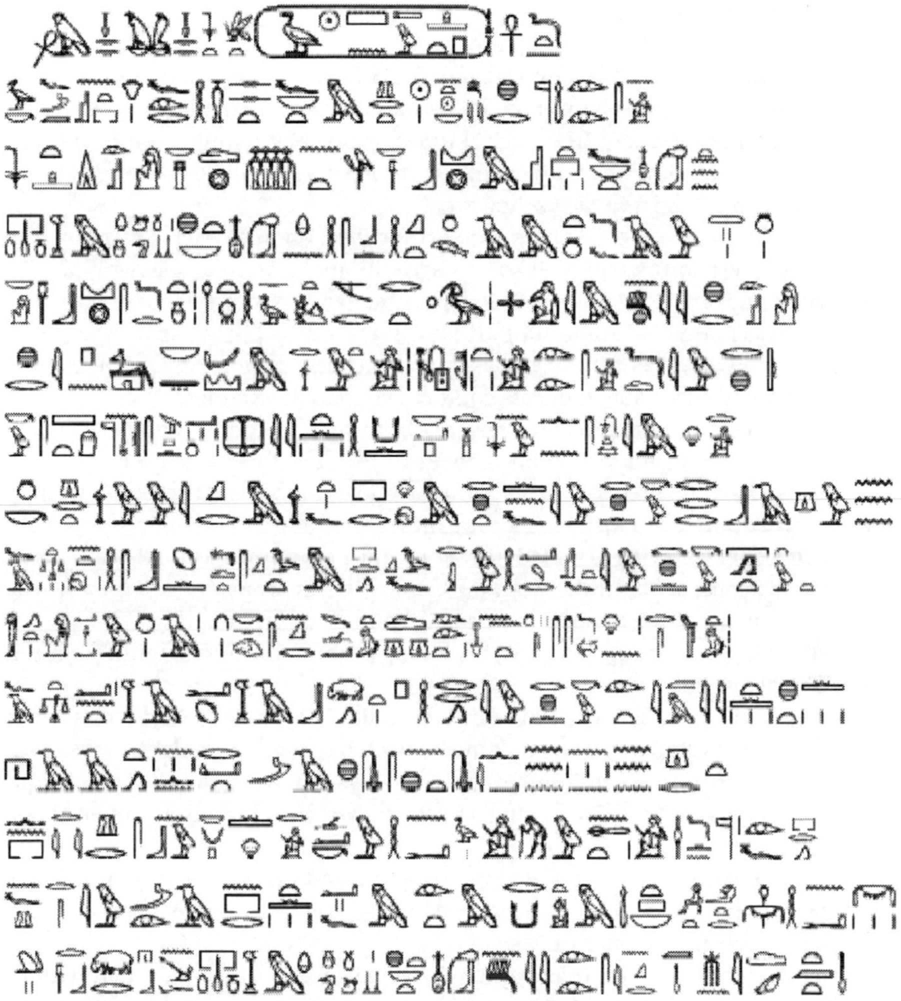

Figure 2.1. Hieroglyphic stele C-14 of Irtisen (on display at the Louvre). A 4,000-year-old employee confidentiality agreement with Pharaoh Mentuhotep, set in stone, defining the terms for dealing with secret information in a small group. (*Source:* www.iut.univ-paris8.fr/~rosmord/hieroglyphes/C14.gif.)

the divine Pharaoh (thus ensuring the son's inheritance of Irtisen's favored position).[7] Stele C-14, although it relates to a 4,000-year-old political and religious order, has the elements of a modern employee confidentiality agreement – the employee promises to keep the employer's secrets confidential within a limited group. (There, it was father and son.) Enforcement for breaking the promise of confidentiality would be

---

[7] Serge Rosmerduc, Hieroglyphic texts, www.iut.univ-paris8.fr/~rosmord/hieroglyphes/hieroglyphes. html (accessed January 28, 2007) and personal communication from Serge Rosmerduc.

different, of course – the modern employee might face a lawsuit and damages, while Irtisen more likely would have been executed.

Trademark concepts also date back to antiquity. Egyptians branded cattle, Chinese potters marked their porcelain, and Romans used logos and brand names for stores, lamps, and other products. In medieval times, guilds and manufacturers branded their products. Recognition of trademarks as enforceable intellectual property rights did not come until the mid-1800s, however.[8]

In ancient times there was little support for the notion of exclusive rights.[9] In ancient Greece about 2,000–2,500 years ago, the most popular playwrights, like Aeschylus and Sophocles, were awarded the Athenian prize for their best work. The ancient Greeks provided some support for innovation by paying researchers, and they attempted to preserve innovations by establishing universities and the Library of Alexandria, which made duplicate copies of all available scrolls.

Roman inventors could receive rewards from their emperor. Early systems of patronage and prizes flourished throughout history, but they were limited in their reach to the narrow interests of the patrons.[10] Government-sponsored innovation continues in the modern world in the form of research grants and public universities.

The concept of copying as theft dates back to the Roman poet Martial, who coined the term "plagiarism" from the word for kidnapping as an insult to someone who copied his verse.[11] Jewish law discouraged the theft of ideas and warned against falsely claiming authorship of a book, beginning in about the fifth to tenth centuries (about 1,000 to 1,500 years ago).[12]

In medieval times, 500 to 1,000 years ago, guilds, universities, and monasteries found ways to develop and transmit innovation. Craft guilds kept tight control over the transmission of knowledge in the apprentice system, while universities encouraged open access to ideas. The modern tension between exclusivity and open access systems can be traced to that time.

But systems for capturing and channeling innovation were haphazard, in the absence of public disclosure. The scrolls of Alexandria were lost in a fire, and so it went with much ancient knowledge.

Abraham Lincoln, in an 1858 speech delivered several times, said that writing, printing, the discovery of America, and the introduction of patent laws were the greatest inventions of history. Writing was "the great invention of the world . . . enabling us to converse with the dead, the absent, and the unborn," so that we could each learn and build on good ideas from others and hand our accumulated ideas down to our descendants. Printing expanded access to writing, thus emancipating people from a "slavery of the mind" so people could "get a habit of freedom of thought."[13] Printing led to the establishment of copyright laws, and patent laws with

[8] Sherman and Bently (1999), pp. 166–172.
[9] Pamela Long, "Invention, Authorship, 'Intellectual Property,' and the Origin of Patents: Notes Toward a Conceptual History." *Technology and Culture*, 32(4):846–884 (1991).
[10] Scotchmer (2004), pp. 5–8.
[11] Bruce Bugbee, "Genesis of American Patent and Copyright Law," in Merges and Ginsburg, *Foundations*, p. 269.
[12] Menachem Elon, ed., *The Principles of Jewish Law* (Keter Publishing House, 1975), pp. 344–345; and "Intellectual Property," http://en.wikipedia.org/wiki/Intellectual_property, accessed July 12, 2006.
[13] Abraham Lincoln, *Complete Works*, John Nicolay and John Hay, eds., (New York: Century, 1907), pp. 522–528.

them. Lincoln, who had obtained a patent on a system for bringing river boats over obstacles, concluded his remarks by praising the patent system. He said that before there were patent laws, any man could

> instantly use what another man had invented, so that the inventor had no special advantage from his invention. The patent system changed this, secured to the inventor for a limited time the exclusive use of his inventions, and thereby added the fuel of interest to the fire of genius in the discovery and production of new and useful things.[14]

THE VENETIAN INNOVATION

So where did the patent system come from? The core of most modern IP laws is a public grant of exclusive rights to reward favored citizens. This mechanism dates back to Roman times, when emperors rewarded their supporters with the right to sell specified products.

Renaissance rulers rewarded supporters with "patents," public documents evidencing exclusive rights, giving monopolies over particular land, goods, or services. In the fifteenth century, the city of Florence gave an award to a shipbuilder to induce him to make a ship by methods which he otherwise threatened to keep secret. Around the same time, the legislative council of Venice began awarding *privilegii* (privileges) to book printers, giving a temporary exclusive right to publish books in a particular language, or with a particular type.[15] Then came a remarkable innovation: the Venetian patent decree of 1474. (See Figure 2.2.)[16]

The Venetian patent decree is the first formal intellectual property law, and is strikingly similar to modern patent statutes. The dawn of our modern system of patents and copyrights can be seen in the research hall of the Venice City Archives, on Campo dei Frari. On long wooden tables in a hot hall under a high vaulted ceiling supported by Corinthian columns, researchers can look through sheets of old parchment, laced together in volumes dating to the fifteenth and sixteenth centuries. The Venetian patent decree is maintained there.

The Venetian patent decree recognized that ingenious Venetians and visitors would "exercise their minds," and invent and make things which would be useful to the state, so long as others could not imitate them and "take their honor." Venetians and visitors could disclose any new "ingenious device" to the city in a manner that can be used and practiced. Their names would be recorded, and copying without license would then be forbidden. Infringement would result in damages and the inventor would have the right to destroy the copies. The city retained the right to use inventive devices, but only if "exercised" by the inventor. (See Box 2.1.)

Apparently the statute had its intended effect, because hundreds of patents were granted in the subsequent years. Leonardo da Vinci, a prolific inventor living in

[14] Lincoln, *Complete Works*, p. 528.

[15] Pamela Long, "Invention, Authorship, 'Intellectual Property,' and the Origin of Patents." *Technology and Culture*, 32(4): 846–884 (1991).

[16] Long, 1991; Maximilian Frumkin, "The Origins of Patents." *Journal of the Patent Office Society* 27 (March 1945):1433–149, "Early History of Patents for Invention." *Transactions of the Newcomen Society* 26 (1947–49):47–56 and *Transactions of the Chartered Institute of Patent Agents* 66 (1947–48):20–60; Frank Prager, "The Early Growth and Influence of Intellectual Property." *Journal of the Patent Office Society* 34:106–40 (1952).

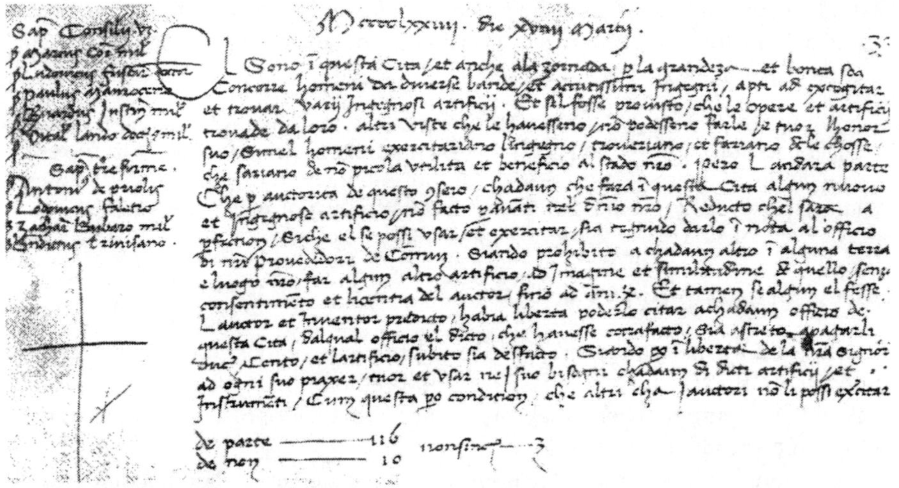

Figure 2.2. Venetian Patent Decree of 1474. The Venetians adopted the first known patent law, with many features of modern laws.

Northern Italy in the late 1400s, apparently did not pursue patent protection in Venice, but Galileo received a Venetian patent on a water pump a century later.[17] The idea of the patent system migrated throughout Europe along with Venetian commerce.[18] In England, excessive patronage by King James led Parliament to pass the Statute of Monopolies in 1623, banning all monopolies except "letters patent" limited to 14 years for "true and first" inventors.

In some respects the 1474 Venetian statute is more like modern patent laws than those that followed it. It includes some concepts that were not adopted in other countries for 400 years, like treating foreigners and citizens the same. The Venetian statute explicitly includes all the main components of modern patent law. The law –

(a) recognizes the public interest in innovation,
(b) recognizes the benefits of public disclosure,
(c) establishes the basic bargain of full disclosure by an inventor in exchange for exclusive rights for a limited period as an incentive for innovation and disclosure,
(d) does not discriminate between Venetians and foreign visitors,
(e) sets out an administrative process for obtaining a patent,
(f) provides for enforcement and damages,
(g) notes the possibility of patent licensing,
(h) establishes the principle of compulsory licensing whereby the state retains some freedom to use the invention for itself,

[17] Mario Biagioli, "Patent Republic: Representing Inventions, Constructing Rights and Authors," Goliath, Social Research (2006), available at http://goliath.ecnext.com/coms2/gi_0199-6605515/Patent-republic-representing-inventions-constructing.html, accessed August 16, 2007.
[18] Ikechi Mgbeoji, *Global Biopiracy: Patents, Plants and Indigenous Knowledge* (Cornell U, Press, 2006), pp. 27–28.

MCCCCLXXIIII the XVIIII of March

There are in this city, and because of its grandeur and virtue there come to us from other places, men of great genius, apt to invent and discover a variety of ingenious devices. And if it were provided that the works and devices discovered by such persons could not be imitated by others who may see them, stealing away the inventor's honor, such men would exercise their genius and invent and make devices of no small utility and benefit to our commonwealth. Therefore, it is decreed by the authority of this Council that any person in this city who invents any novel and ingenious device, not made previously in our dominion, as soon as it is reduced to perfection, so that it can be used and exercised, shall give notice to the office of our Provisioners of Common [guild office]. It being forbidden to all others in our land to make any other device which imitates and resembles the invention, without the consent and license of the author, for up to ten years. And, however, should anybody make it, the author and inventor will have the liberty to cite him before any office of this city, by which office the aforesaid who has infringed shall be forced to pay him the sum of one hundred ducats and the device immediately destroyed. Our government shall have the liberty, at its pleasure, to take and use for its needs any of such devices and instruments, but with this condition, that no others than the authors will be able to exercise them.

For: 116

Against: 10

Abstain: 3

Box 2.1. The Venetian Patent Decree of 1474.[19]

    (i) was established as a legislative act (the vote being 116 in favor, 10 against, and 3 abstentions), and

    (j) resulted in the issuance of patents.

The Venetian council members of 1474 deserve full credit as the inventors of the patent system. Like other innovators, the Venetian legislators took pieces of prior precedents and created something new. Following Lincoln's thinking, the 1474 Venetian patent statute may be the single most influential development in the history of intellectual property and innovation.

EVOLUTION OF THE MODERN INTELLECTUAL PROPERTY SYSTEM

During the Renaissance, systems of copyright for books and patents for inventions diffused throughout Europe and beyond, including at least England, France, and the

---

[19] Compiled from Prager 1952, p. 132; Ikechi Mgbeoji, *Global Biopiracy: Patents, Plants and Indigenous Knowledge* (UBC Vancouver, 2006), p. 16 and fn 46; and a facsimile of the original and a translation provided by Studio Torta, Milan. The translation cited by Mgbeoji suggests that the inventor could use the copied goods, but it appears instead that it is the city of Venice that was entitled to use the apparatus but only if it was produced by the author.

United States. The Industrial Revolution led to a continuous expansion of intellectual property laws, and many countries enacted patent and copyright legislation in the mid-1800s.

That was a time when the topic was important enough that, on the brink of a Civil War, when slavery and secession were the most important issues of the day, Lincoln took the time to speak out about innovation and intellectual property. Lincoln may have been influenced by the active debate about patent laws that occurred across Europe at that time. Between 1850 and 1875, the patent laws in England, France, Germany, Holland, and Sweden were subjected to an onslaught of criticism that undercut each of the four justifications for the patent system.[20] The same justifications are heard today:

(1) a natural property right in ideas gives rise to an inventor's right of exclusivity;
(2) inventions, as services useful to society, should be rewarded with a patent;
(3) patents provide incentives to invent, and promote desirable industrial progress; and
(4) exclusive patent rights induce inventors to publicly disclose their inventions, thus promoting progress.

The opponents of patents rebutted each justification on economic, philosophical, and practical grounds, leading to academic deadlock, but in each country, patent laws survived in a political climate of rising national protectionism. After the legislative success of the European patent laws in the 1870s, economists lost interest in opposing patents and were apparently silent until well into the twentieth century. So public concern about the role of intellectual property and its impact on innovation and freedom is nothing new, but it is episodic.

The burst of international activity in the late 1800s resulted in treaties that set standards for national legislation protecting intellectual property.

- In 1883, 11 nations established the Paris Convention to require member states to treat foreigners and citizens identically in patent and trademark law. As of 2006, the number of Paris Convention members had grown to 169 countries.
- The Berne Convention on copyrights, dating to 1886, had 162 member nations by 2006. It specifies how rights are obtained, defines the bundle of rights encompassed by a copyright, and describes fair use exceptions.
- The Madrid Protocol, an international trademark registration system, was adopted in 1989 as part of The Madrid Agreement dating back to 1891. It has 68 members, the United States having just joined in 2003. It provides for a single trademark application to result in registrations in multiple countries.
- The World Intellectual Property Organisation (WIPO) is the successor to the United International Bureaux for the Protection of Intellectual Property, established in 1893. It has a membership that had grown to 183 countries by 2006. WIPO administers the preceding treaties, the Patent Cooperation Treaty, and many others relating to intellectual property.

---

[20] Fritz Machlup and Edith Penrose, "The Patent Controversy in the Nineteenth Century." *Journal of Economic History* 10:1–29 (1950).

After World War II, there was a renewed international interest in strengthening intellectual property rights. There was much controversy and debate in the United States and European countries relating to national legislation as well.

- The International Union for the Protection of New Varieties of Plants (UPOV) was adopted in Paris in 1961 and was revised extensively in 1972, 1978, and 1991. It has 63 members. UPOV establishes an intellectual property right to protect new varieties of plants, with specific exceptions (in the different revisions) allowing breeders to use protected varieties in breeding newer varieties, and for farmers to save seed from year to year.
- Regional initiatives, such as the European Patent Convention, the African Regional Intellectual Property Organization (ARIPO), the African Intellectual Property Organization (OAPI) in Francophone Africa, and the Andean Pact in South America, play increasingly important roles in determining intellectual property rights in member states.
- The Patent Cooperation Treaty was concluded in 1970. Since then 132 nations have joined, about 50 of them in the last decade. It coordinates and streamlines international patent registration (prosecution) and is widely used.
- The Convention on Biological Diversity was adopted in 1993 and has 190 parties as of 2006. The CBD provides that nations have sovereign rights to their genetic resources, and establishes a system based on informed consent, whereby researchers can access the genetic resources in exchange for sharing any resulting benefits, such as information, inventions, and money.
- The World Trade Organization (WTO), which administers the 1995 Agreement on Trade-Related Aspects of Intellectual Property Rights (TRIPS) (Appendix A), had 149 members in 2006, up about 20 over the previous decade. The TRIPS agreement sets minimum standards for protection of trade secrets, patents, copyrights, and trademarks, and countries are subject to trade sanctions if they fail to comply.
- The International Treaty on Plant Genetic Resources for Food and Agriculture, administered by the Food and Agriculture Organization, was adopted in 2001 and has 103 signatories already. The ITPGR establishes a multilateral framework for conserving plant resources for the main food and forage crops, and provides international access in exchange for a share of resulting commercial benefits. It promotes the breeding of new varieties and the sharing of information. The treaty includes an open access provision – intellectual property rights can not be used to limit access to the conserved plant resources (12.3(a)) and innovations should be transferred to poorer countries on preferential terms, consistent with intellectual property rights 13.2(b)(iii).

The Bayh-Dole Act

Under the U.S. Bayh-Dole Act of 1980, universities receiving federal funds are able to pursue patent protection on resulting inventions, and encouraged to license those patents to corporations for development, with inventors retaining a share of any royalties. Prior to the Bayh-Dole Act, U.S. investment and leadership in research was on the decline. The U.S. government owned all patents deriving from federally funded research, but a miniscule percentage of these patents were ever licensed, much less commercialized. The Bayh-Dole Act established a partnership model, involving the nonprofit research institutions, the researchers, and the corporations which could invest the capital needed to develop the inventions into products and take them to market. The Bayh-Dole Act is a signature example of how to use the IP system to drive the innovation cycle, linking creative individual A with university B and corporate investor C, to reach the public D.

The bill's author, Senator Birch Bayh, explains that many people were skeptical of the bill because they believed the government should own the rights to inventions it pays for.[21] However, once Congress considered the evidence, the law passed overwhelmingly.

Since then, universities have become potent innovation engines, making good use of federal research funds. According to data from the Association of University Technology Managers, the number of invention disclosures increased from 250 in 1980 to more than 16,000 in 2004, about half of them resulting in patent applications. In 2004, nearly 5,000 licenses were executed. More than 4,000 companies were started with university support. Between 1998 and 2005, thousands of new products were introduced based on university research. These include many drugs, recombinant DNA technology, new crops, and even the original Internet search engine. The incentives to faculty make them eager advocates for their inventions, and the incentives to universities cause them to support the effort. There is no decrease in publication due to the desire to patent faculty inventions. The government retains the right to "march in" and take over an invention that is not being developed, but one measure of the success of this system is that it is rare to hear even suggestions of the need for government march in. Senator Bayh, now my law partner, proclaims that "we should be proud of this and bold in its defense," and warns us not to turn back the clock to promote government ownership of IP rights because that would undo all the good that has been done.

The Organization for Economic Co-operation and Development (OECD) has recognized the importance of promoting innovation at public research organizations, and several European and Asian countries have implemented their own versions of the Bayh-Dole Act. These measures rest on three pillars: reliance on market forces; strong protection of IP rights; and a commitment to public funding of education and research. Debates continue about how to join public and private innovation resources together, balancing such systems between exclusive rights and public access, to promote innovation without damaging economic distortions.[22] But the basic wisdom of the Bayh-Dole Act, like the patent system itself, has stood the test of time.

SUMMARY. The phrase "intellectual property" is used to mean different things by innovators, lawyers, business people, politicians, and scholars. The complex

---

[21] Birch Bayh, "Bayh-Dole: Don't Turn Back the Clock," *LES Nouvelles* (December 2006), available at http://www.venable.com/publications.cfm?action = view&publication_id = 1621&publication_type_id = 2, accessed August 14, 2007.

[22] "The Bayh-Dole Act at 25: A Survey of the Origins, Effects, and Prospects of the Bayh Dole Act," Bayh-Dole25, Inc., pp. 35–43, available at http://www.bayhdole25.org/resources, accessed January 13, 2007.

definition should come as no surprise because intellectual property's fundamental concepts go back to ancient times and to the Venetian innovation of patent law over half a millennium ago. The modern international framework of intellectual property treaties and laws has been put in place over the past century and a half, and the significance of IP laws and practices continues to grow and evolve around the world. In a sense, the rise of intellectual property shows that the modern IP system itself has undergone a process of creative destruction. It was assembled from pieces of prior laws. The roots of the modern legal rules are old, suggesting a high degree of stability and a broad recognition, in many cultures at many times, of the important role of intellectual property in fostering innovation. If an IP system did not already exist society would invent it. Indeed, IP laws are dynamic instruments and are continually being reformed. Chapter 3 outlines some forces driving that reform, and possible scenarios that lie ahead.

3 Keeping the System in Balance: Exclusion and Access

The chapter begins with an outline of the debate over the pros and cons of intellectual property laws. Eight arguments on each side are presented. Considering the points on both sides, we can see the need for IP laws to balance public access and private exclusivity. This leads to a critique of the term "public domain" and an effort to map a broader category of knowledge referred to as the accessible domain. Looking at IP rights in this way, we can find new ways to rebalance the international legal system. The tensions in the global IP system suggest such a rebalancing is underway. The chapter concludes by reviewing the possible future scenarios for IP laws, whether stronger, weaker, more uniform, or more diverse.

* * * * * *

INTELLECTUAL PROPERTY PRO AND CON

What is the modern rationale for protecting intellectual property? Intellectual property laws are intended to promote technical ingenuity and cultural creativity by granting private ownership rights. As the World Intellectual Property Organization states:

> Protection of intellectual property is not an end in itself: it is a means to encourage creative activity, industrialization, investment, and honest trade. All this is designed to contribute more safety and comfort, less poverty and more beauty, in the lives of men.[1]

But there is no consensus on whether intellectual property actually achieves these goals, and how strong the protections should be in any given situation. Ever-stronger intellectual property protection is surely not a panacea to promote technology progress and well-being in all countries and industries.[2] Rather, there is

---

[1] World Intellectual Property Organisation, *International Protection of Industrial Property* (1996), available at http://www.unicc.org/wipo/.

[2] Evenson, 'Survey of Empirical Studies', in Siebeck (ed.), *Strengthening Protection of Intellectual Property in Developing Countries: A Survey of the Literature*, World Bank Discussion Paper 112, (1990), pp 73–86; Frame, "National Commitment to Intellectual Property Protection: An Empirical Investigation."*Journal of Law and Technology* 2: 209 (1987).

ongoing debate among national and international government agencies, practicing attorneys, economists, trade associations for the pharmaceutical, agriculture, software, and entertainment industries, and public interest organizations, as to how intellectual property laws help or hurt a society in any particular situation. There are strong arguments on both sides, often based on economic or political faith or philosophy more than evidence.[3] The truth is surely somewhere in between – intellectual property creates winners and losers and on balance it helps in some situations, hurts in others. The one thing all sides can agree on is that intellectual property shapes society – whether for better or for worse.

It is simplistic to say that IP laws are "good" or "bad" in general, without reference to particular laws as applied in particular situations. A helpful approach is to review the arguments that people typically make supporting or opposing strong intellectual property rights.[4] There are eight points on each side and each may have relevance in a given country, for a given industry, or in a particular situation.[5] Principles of democracy and open debate say that we should consider the views on both sides. The Venetian legislative council, again, established a fine precedent, by voting on the 1474 patent statute, and although it was overwhelmingly approved, the decision was far from unanimous. Today, and into the future, we can expect debates and votes about IP laws. We should hope they remain open and substantive and lead to good results.

RATIONALE FOR INTELLECTUAL PROPERTY

The eight arguments for strong intellectual property rights may be referred to as theories of incentive, reward, labor, morality, public disclosure, technology transfer, technology development, and industrial policy. These interrelate and overlap, but those advocating strong intellectual property protection typically refer to the following goals.[6]

---

[3] Hughes, "The Philosophy of Intellectual Property." *Georgetown Law Journal* 77.287 (1988).

[4] Michael Gollin and Sarah Laird, "Global Policies, Local Actions: The Role of National Legislation in Sustainable Biodiversity Prospecting." *Boston U. Journal of Science and Technology Law* 2:16 (1996), para 38–44; Gollin, "Introduction," in D. Campbell (ed.), *International Protection of Intellectual Property Rights*, (FT Law & Tax, 1997); Gollin, "Using Intellectual Property to Improve Environmental Protection," *Harvard Journal of Law and Technology* 4:193, 199 (1991); Gollin, "An Intellectual Property Rights Framework for Biodiversity Prospecting," in Walter Reid et al. (eds.), *Biodiversity Prospecting: Using Genetic Resources for Sustainable Development* 159, 163 (1993).

[5] See Commission on Intellectual Property Rights, *Integrating Intellectual Property Rights and Development Policy* (CIPR, 2002), available at http://www.iprcommission.org/graphic/documents.htm, accessed July, 25, 2006 (CIPR Report); the statement of the Intellectual Property Owners Association available at www.ipo.org; Prima Braga, "The Developing Country Case For and Against Intellectual Property Protection," in Siebeck, (ed.), *Strengthening Protection of Intellectual Property in Developing Countries: A Survey of the Literature*, World Bank Discussion Paper 112, (1990), pp. 73–86; Scalise and Nugent, "International Intellectual Property Protections for Living Matter: Biotechnology, Multinational Conventions and the Exception for Agriculture," *Case Western Reserve Journal of International Law* 27:86–87 (1995).

[6] See, generally, Pauline Newman, "Speech to ABA-IPL Section," *Patent Trademark and Copyright Journal* 48:277 (BNA, 1994).

1. Provides incentives for people to be creative

The prospect of exclusivity secured by an intellectual property right is a potent motivator to encourage people to begin creative endeavors. Through its influence on such decisions, intellectual property holds a key to the innovation cycle. Society benefits through better, less expensive products and more artistic and cultural diversity. Economists refer to the lack of an exclusivity incentive as a market failure, a disincentive to invest significant effort in a new product that others could copy for free. Anecdotal evidence, including my own experience, shows that individuals and companies consider intellectual property carefully when deciding what to create or invent, and whether to further develop or invest in that work.

2. Rewards people after they are creative

Some people are creative without any incentive, either from curiosity or altruism. Even if no incentive is required to produce an innovation, providing a reward after the creative act encourages them and others to do more creative work in the future.

3. Gives people rights to the fruits of their creative labor

Aside from rewards, many people believe that laborers have claims to their work product, the "sweat of their brow." John Locke described the labor theory of property in chapter V of his *Second Treatise on Government* (1690):

> [E]very man has a "property" in his own "person:" This nobody has any right to but himself. The "labour" of his body, and the "work" of his hands, we may say, are properly his. Whatsoever, then, he removes out of the state that Nature hath provided and left it in, he hath mixed his labour with, and joined to it something that is his own, and thereby makes it his property.

The mind is part of the body, and labor of the mind belongs to the creator, to whom creative products should belong. This is a natural law argument for some form of intellectual property ownership for creative people. If their work went directly into the public domain, they would be left empty-handed, receiving neither reward nor recognition for their labor. IP rights give creators control, in the form of a choice of whether to exclude others or give them access.

4. Satisfies principles of moral or natural rights

Artists, inventors, and other creative people often feel an emotional sense of parenthood toward their work, a relationship that goes beyond tangible property rights or economics. Society can support this relationship by giving creators control over the use of their work and related intellectual property. For example, the U.S. Copyright Act prohibits the destruction or modification of works of visual art regardless of who owns the physical property. The Berne Convention on copyright goes further, giving all authors the right to claim authorship and to prevent distortion of their work. Debate on this topic erupted in the 1980s when Ted Turner acquired the

MGM library of classic black and white movies, and colorized them. The process was allowed in the United States but was barred under French law. These laws use IP rights to promote the third stage of the innovation cycle, maintaining access to important innovations and limiting the chance that they will be lost.

5. Promotes public disclosure of new information

Sharing of new information is enhanced if people are encouraged to disclose it and can do so on their own terms. For example, trade secret laws allow people to share information confidentially within their workplace. Patent laws require full disclosure about inventions in exchange for a patent. Copyright allows authors to choose how to publish their work, without fear of unauthorized copying. Without such laws, people would be reluctant to share their inventions – even with coworkers, much less with the wider public – and this would break the innovation cycle, as new information could not be adopted broadly by a community.

6. Facilitates transfer of innovation

By establishing assignable property rights, subject to recordation, intellectual property laws allow people to buy, sell, lease, or trade intangible property, or use it as collateral for loans, just as they would do with real or tangible property.[7] Intellectual property is something that can be traded, just like the goods that flowed along the ancient trade routes for silk and spice. The resulting market for innovation fits well in the capitalist model and lays the groundwork for an improved system with standardization, reliable enforcement, and shared risk and insurance. A strong system of intellectual property rights gives organizations some assurance that they can transfer innovations to other organizations on negotiated terms, and that the recipient will have to honor those terms. In particular, intellectual property creates a legal framework in which innovation-rich organizations can transfer innovation to developing countries without having their innovations stolen from them. If no protection is available, organizations have an incentive to keep their innovations secret.

7. Facilitates investment in innovation

Innovation is expensive. Development and dissemination of technology and other creative works – the second part of the innovation cycle – require substantial investments of effort and capital. Drug companies licensing a potential drug from a university can expect to invest hundreds of millions of dollars conducting clinical research, scaling up for manufacture, and other work necessary to bring a new drug to market. Intellectual property rights offer investors a way to obtain financial returns in the form of higher profits. Investors avoid investing in a technology that lacks exclusive rights because a competitor can always copy the product and sell it more cheaply

---

[7] Hernando de Soto, *The Mystery of Capital: Why Capitalism Triumphs in the West and Fails Everywhere Else* (2000); Donald Chisum and Michael Jacobs, *Understanding Intellectual Property Law* § 1(C) (Matthew Bender, 1992).

than the innovator. As with the act of creation itself, intellectual property rights provide an incentive for investment, and satisfy market principles that investors should be able to control what happens to their investments.

8. Implements industrial policy

National intellectual property laws can be used to drive the innovation cycle and influence its direction. By selectively establishing, strengthening, weakening, or eliminating intellectual property protection, a country can support or discourage particular industries and activities. Northern countries tend to support their innovative industries with strong intellectual property laws. Biotechnology and pharmaceutical companies are reluctant to invest in research in countries where patents and trade secrets cannot be enforced. Until it complied with the TRIPS Agreement, India supported its domestic generic pharmaceutical industry, which is expert at copying known drugs, by opposing stronger patent laws, but recently India strengthened its patent laws, thus promoting investment in a growing biotechnology industry. Developing countries have found that they can obtain other political advantages by strengthening their intellectual property laws as bargaining chips in exchange for improved trade relations with the United States.

CRITICISM OF INTELLECTUAL PROPERTY

Critics seek to restrict or even eliminate some types of intellectual property protection, using eight different arguments based on concerns about negative consequences. These arguments may be summarized as theories based on restricted access to technology, increased cost, monopolization, inappropriate investment incentives, competition, expense, institutional requirements, and ethics.[8]

1. Keeps innovations out of the public domain

Exclusivity is the primary characteristic of intellectual property, which precludes the public from having full access to an innovation. If exclusive rights are excessive (too long or too broad), they reduce access to innovation. Such over-protection may benefit the owner, but brings no larger advantage to society. Even though exclusive rights are crucial to provide the incentives, rewards, and other advantages outlined above, to ensure that innovation continues for the future, no one knows exactly the right balance.

Intellectual property creates tension between free access to today's medicines (or movies or mobile phones) and tomorrow's improvements. Reform of intellectual property laws over the centuries, decades, and years reflects the constant effort to rebalance intellectual property rights to deal with new technologies and the resulting economic realities such as the Internet and globalization.

---

[8] Hamilton, 'The TRIPS Agreement: Imperialistic, Outdated, and Overprotective,' in "Impact of the TRIPS Agreement on Specific Disciplines: Copyrightable Literary and Artistic Works." *Vanderbilt Journal of Transnational Law*, 29:613 (1996); Andrew Kimbrell, *The Human Body Shop* (1995).

2. Increases the cost of technology

An intellectual property owner's exclusive rights are typically used to charge a higher price than if there was competition.[9] An innovator's drugs cost more than a generic version.

As with the previous point, the increased cost to the consumer is an integral part of the way intellectual property rights serve as an instrument of incentive and reward for the innovator. Again, the costs may become excessive if IP rights are too strong. It is not possible to calculate precisely what the balance should be, because there are no adequate economic models, and IP laws apply to all kinds of innovations equally, without regard to the specific costs involved.

3. Creates monopolies

People say that intellectual property rights create monopolies around particular technologies, for particular companies, or for particular countries. Strictly speaking, owning a patent or copyright or portfolio of rights does not necessarily create the market control necessary for a monopoly. A patent on the antibiotic ciprofloxacin does not create a monopoly because other antibiotics that serve the same purpose are available as well. The underlying critique is that intellectual property portfolios, such as IBM's thousands of patents issued each year, leads to centralization of innovation and creativity in large corporations and a reduction in competition due to barriers to entry by other companies.

Antitrust laws can be used to keep IP rights from causing excessive concentrations of power in a monopoly. Not every limitation on competition, however, gives rise to an antitrust violation. Following Schumpeter's theory of dynamic innovation, a limited monopoly over a particular technology for a short time is not objectionable, if a competitor, through innovation, is able to destroy the old monopoly and replace it by a newer, better one.[10] Indeed, short-term limits on competition are necessary and therefore desirable in promoting innovation over the long run. Schumpeter's theory of dynamic competition has yet to be adopted by mainstream economics, which dwells on a static view of perfect market competition. In the static view, intellectual property creates monopolies which are offensive and undesirable.

For example, Nobel laureate Joseph Stiglitz wrote that intellectual property rights "enable one person or company to have exclusive control of the use of a particular piece of knowledge, thereby creating monopoly power. Monopolies distort the economy. Restricting the use of medical knowledge not only affects economic efficiency, but also life itself."[11] Such arguments can be simplistic and ignore intellectual property's dynamic role within the innovation cycle, balancing the actions of innovators and generic drug makers (see Chapter 18).

---

[9] Reichman, "Charting the Collapse of the Patent-copyright Dichotomy: Premises for a Restructured International Intellectual Property System," *Cardozo Arts and Entertainment Law Journal* 13:475 (1993).

[10] David Evans and Richard Schmallensee, "Some aspects of antitrust analysis in dynamically competitive industries," in Adam Jaffe, Josh Lerner and Scott Stern, (eds.), *Innovation Policy and the Economy, Vol. 2*, National Bureau of Economic Research (MIT Press, 2002).

[11] Joseph Stiglitz, "Scrooge and Intellectual Property Rights." *British Medical Journal*, 333:1279–1280 (2006).

4. Concentrates industry on what can be protected, not what's best

Intellectual property directs creative effort and investment toward innovations that can be protected by IP law, and away from knowledge that is in the public domain. Researchers and investors put more effort into developing and marketing drugs, crops, and technology that are subject to IP protection than comparable products with better performance characteristics, because of the prospect for higher economic return. Investor decisions about whether to invest in a startup company are based not only on the effectiveness of the technology, the skill of the management team, and the size of the market, but also on whether the IP protection is strong enough to warrant their investment. There is little or no incentive to protect knowledge in the public domain – for example, existing or traditional culture and agricultural practices, medicinal knowledge, and so on.

In a related concern, IP systems may lead researchers to concentrate only on profitable innovations. According to the Global Forum for Health Research, only about 10 percent of the US$106 billion spent on global health research goes to diseases causing 90 percent of the world's health problems, primarily diseases in developing countries.

5. Pushes people from cooperation into competition

At the individual level, intellectual property rights can promote commercialism as opposed to collaboration. For example, university technology transfer offices require researchers to use licenses and material transfer agreements to control and restrict interactions among academic researchers and corporate sponsors. Research is concealed until a patent application is filed. Corporations may deal sharply with competitors, trying to block or avoid each other's intellectual property.

On the other hand, as Robert Frost said, good fences can make good neighbors. Traditional economic theory generally favors competition. Also, careful intellectual property management schemes, such as the "copyleft" public license used, for example, by Wikipedia[12], can actually use intellectual property to promote collaboration and open sharing of information.

6. Is expensive to obtain and maintain

Although copyrights and trade secrets are relatively simple to protect, patents (and to some extent, trademarks) are expensive and complex to acquire. Therefore poor and unsophisticated individuals or organizations are at a disadvantage compared to multinational corporations and wealthy organizations.

To combat this unfairness, I founded the international nonprofit group Public Interest Intellectual Property Advisors (www.piipa.org), which provides access to intellectual property professionals who can provide assistance to needy organizations on a volunteer basis. Fair access to IP professional services helps lead to just results.

---

[12] http://en.wikipedia.org/wiki/Wikipedia:Copyrights

7. Requires elaborate national legal and regulatory institutions

To comply with the World Trade Organization's 1995 Agreement on Trade-Related Aspects of Intellectual Property Rights (TRIPS), many national legislatures have enacted new laws, and each country must fund a patent and trademark office and a court system able to handle intellectual property enforcement cases. These institutions require substantial commitments of national funds and expertise. Poorer countries required to comply with TRIPS need to divert scant resources to provide the elaborate governmental infrastructure that is required.

8. Conflicts with moral views opposing property rights

The French anarchist Pierre-Joseph Proudhon proclaimed: "Property is theft!" Some people now argue that intellectual property is theft.[13] This attitude is related to the collective on-line open access culture exemplified by Wikipedia and referred to as "digital Maoism."[14] There have been numerous challenges to patents on plants used in traditional farming or religious practices in India, South America, and elsewhere, on grounds that it is immoral to impose property rights on something that should remain freely available.[15] Patents on business method patents and surgical procedures have been opposed on the basis that these methods should remain free to use, not subject to exclusive rights of one owner.

Opposition has also been voiced against proprietary rights in genetic sequences, materials obtained from the human body. Andrew Kimbrell has argued in favor of a "gift principle" whereby components of the human body could only be transferred by gift, as is generally the case with blood and organ donations.[16] The notion that human body components should be treated as sacred, or at least that they should not be treated as property subject to market forces, appeals to many people on ethical grounds.

These eight arguments in favor and eight arguments opposed to intellectual property show the inherent duality and tension in the modern system. Many more illustrations are considered elsewhere in this book. Opponents of intellectual property like to say that a candle, like knowledge, is not diminished by lighting another candle, and hence the innovator loses nothing when someone copies their work. The counterargument is that this elegant image misses the point that someone first had to find the wax and the wick, and make and light that candle, and they should, in a free world with self-determination, be able to choose whether or not to use it to light other candles.

Intellectual property conceals many other examples of duality and conflict. Some of the tensions inherent in intellectual property systems are as follows: Old vs. new,

---

[13] John Naughton, "Intellectual Property Is Theft. Ideas Are for Sharing."*Observer*, February 9, 2003.

[14] Jaron Lanier, "Digital Maoism: The Hazards of the New Online Collectivism," *Edge* (May 30, 2006), available at http://www.edge.org/3rd_culture/lanier06/lanier06_index.html, accessed December 31, 2006; Stephen Johnson, "Digital Maoism," *New York Times* (December 10, 2006).

[15] CIPR Report; Center for International Environmental Law (2002). "Legal Elements of the 'Ayahuasca' Patent Case," available at http://www.ciel.org/Publications/ayahuascalegalelements.pdf, accessed December 31, 2006.

[16] Kimbrell, *The Human Body Shop* (Harper San Francisco 1995), p. 304.

rich vs. poor, creative vs. pirate, exclusive vs. accessible, public vs. private, closed vs. open, intangible vs. tangible, present vs. future, local vs. distant, freedom vs. slavery, us vs. them, north vs. south, capitalism vs. socialism, individuality vs. collectivism, ideas vs. expressions, man vs. nature, and intellectual vs. physical labor. This rich fabric of concepts can not be easily teased apart into individual threads.

Perhaps the most straightforward contrast is to imagine a world without intellectual property, and then one in which rights are excessively strong. In a world without intellectual property, or one where intellectual property rights are too weak, people would lack incentives and rewards for creativity, slowing down stage one of the innovation cycle. If people happened to create something new, they would be denied choice and control over what to do with it, and so they would be tempted to keep it completely secret, thus blocking stage two of the innovation cycle. If they did share the innovation with others, without secrecy, then it would be available for anyone to use, so there would be no incentive for others to invest substantial time or resources into developing and improving the innovation and disseminating it in society. This would also retard stage two of the innovation cycle. The innovation might diffuse by itself into social availability, making it to stage three of the innovation cycle, but instead it might just fade away and be lost, with no advocate pushing its adoption and use.

Garrett Hardin's 1968 essay, "The Tragedy of the Commons," argues that communities tend to overuse and degrade common property because no one has a reason to protect it.[17] If IP rights are too weak, and an innovation is available to all in the public domain, people would be free to exploit the innovation but would have little interest in promoting it. Relying solely on alternative incentives, like government prizes and purchases, would not work, because such decisions would be determined by a small committee of powerful insiders who predictably will play favorites or make mistakes about what innovations to reward – bigger mistakes, presumably, than the market makes with the intellectual property system.

At the other extreme, in a world with excessively strong or numerous intellectual property rights, individual creativity would be stifled by restrictions on access to information. A thicket of rights would preclude researchers from collaboration and improvement of existing technology, at risk of damages and injunction. Society would not benefit from innovations. This situation was critiqued by Michael Heller and Rebecca Eisenberg as the "tragedy of the anti-commons,"[18] with reference to "The Tragedy of the Commons." Perhaps the most widespread harm caused by excessive exclusivity would be a loss of competitiveness, caused by a tendency toward concentration of power in those who own IP, at the expense of those who do not, including consumers. But there is limited evidence for the tragedy of the anti-commons.[19] In a global context, developing countries argue that IP rights tend to concentrate in the wealthy countries at the expense of the poorer countries, who can't afford to support innovation or pay for its products. Monopolization and anti-competitive conduct would prevail.

---

[17] Garrett Hardin, "The Tragedy of the Commons." *Science* 162:1243–1248 (1968).

[18] Michael Heller and Rebecca Eisenberg, "Can Patents Deter Innovation? The Anticommons in Biomedical Research." *Science* 280: 5364 (1998).

[19] Ted Buckley, "The Myth of the Anticommons," Biotechnology Industry Organization (2007), available at http://www.bio.org/ip/domestic/TheMythoftheAnticommons.pdf, accessed August 15, 2007.

Balancing public access and private exclusivity

Public rights can limit private rights, just as private rights can limit the public, to provide a balance. In England, from the twelfth to the nineteenth centuries, controversy abounded as common lands were enclosed and made private. Now, anyone may walk the public footpaths, right through farmer's fields, backyards, and other private property. Landowners may fence their fields and yards for their own purposes, to keep livestock in and vehicles out, but they also provide some form of access for the public – stiles to climb over, unlocked gates that are easily opened and latched – so people can pass onto, across, and off the property. This is an example of how one community has balanced the private property right of exclusive control over land with the need for public access.

Likewise, the owner of a copyright in a book or computer software may stop people from copying the work, but people may still quote the work, use its ideas, and otherwise engage in fair use. A patent owner can not stop the public from learning from the published patent, or from acting outside the scope of the patent's claims. The rights of trademark and trade secret owners are limited, too. Like the farmers of England, the owner may wish for more exclusivity, and the public may want more access. Compromise permits these property owners to coexist with their neighbors in the broader community.

Balancing exclusion and access is one goal on which all should be able to agree. Balance as an ideal was stated in an intellectual property manifesto by the British Museum:

> Copyright law has traditionally sought to strike an appropriate balance, between the rights of creators to be recognised and rewarded for their work, and the public interest in ensuring access to information and ideas. Getting the balance right is intrinsic to a healthy creative economy and our education sector, for without reward there is nothing to be gained in innovation, and without access to the ideas that have come before, there is no inspiration for the future.[20]

Many countries are involved in an ongoing debate about how to refine their existing laws for patents, copyrights, trademarks, by clarifying legal standards, and how to improve the procedures for patent examination and enforcement. Ultimately, society can promote innovation and competition most effectively with an IP system that is in balance, with rights that are neither too strong nor too weak, and innovators who know how to use the system to meet their goals.

THE LIMITS OF THE PUBLIC DOMAIN

Intellectual property is often contrasted with its alter ego, the public domain. According to Wikipedia (which has a business model built around the concept of the public domain):

> The public domain comprises the body of knowledge and innovation (especially creative works such as writing, art, music, and inventions) in relation to which no person or other legal entity can establish or maintain proprietary interests within a particular

---

[20] "Intellectual Property: A Balance," The British Library Manifesto, www.bl.uk/news/pdf/ipmanifesto. pdf, accessed October 7, 2006.

legal jurisdiction. This body of information and creativity is considered to be part of a common cultural and intellectual heritage, which, in general, anyone may use or exploit, whether for commercial or non-commercial purposes.

In this view, the public domain is the absence of IP rights, and something protected by IP rights is not in the public domain. But, as with the concept of a yin–yang relationship, the dichotomy between private and public domains with respect to intellectual property is not so simple. Each includes part of the other.

Intellectual property affects the content of the public domain. The conventional view of intellectual property focuses on the private property domain that it defines, at the interface between the creative individual and society. It is important to consider also how intellectual property shapes the public domain as well. The innovation cycle can be seen as a flow of information from the public domain to an exclusive domain, to accessibility, and back into the public domain.

The collaboration, tension, and balance between access and exclusivity establish an underlying theme in this book. The dynamic relationship between intellectual property and the public domain can be framed in the following manner: Innovation is enhanced by access to knowledge. More access is better for innovation than less, and so building and maintaining the public domain is good for society at large. Intellectual property mechanisms compete with the public domain to the extent that innovators choose to wrap their innovations in intellectual property instead of putting them directly into the public domain at the time of inception. However, intellectual property ultimately, indirectly, enlarges the public domain over time because it stimulates new innovations, which can move eventually and step by step into the public domain.

So the concept of the public domain as a complete absence of intellectual property rights is fascinating, but I think it has little practical significance. It would be more helpful to say that there are many public domains, one for each type of intellectual property. Once we determine what intellectual property rights exist in an innovation, we can see in which domains there are no intellectual property rights. In many cases the existence of specific intellectual property rights does not interfere with access to existing innovation, and further creative growth. A published patent conveys information that can be used in non-infringing ways. A limited set of intellectual property rights can actually improve access to information, as with the open source/open knowledge licensing model, which uses copyright to force innovators to keep their work free and accessible, thus enhancing the flow of innovation in the innovation cycle.

Also, the dichotomy between the public domain and intellectual property is false and rests on a simplistic view of intellectual property as a binary, all or nothing system. That is, there are many intermediate levels of protection where the original innovators or successors have applied some form of intellectual property restriction somewhere, but members of the public may nonetheless access and use the work in practical ways that serve their own purposes, thus supporting the continuity of the innovation cycle.

Consumers have no particular interest in distinguishing between a generalized public domain and an intellectual property domain. A typical consumer has a simpler need – just acquiring a product for use, not further innovation. The consumer is concerned primarily with the quality of the product and the cost of acquiring it. Intellectual property rights are of only a secondary concern, in the sense that acquiring an infringing product may create a problem with the quality or cost. For example, as a Blackberry user in 2005 and 2006, I had very limited interest in the merits of the long-running dispute between Blackberry maker RIM and NTP, which asserted several patents relating to the Blackberry technology. I did not need to know anything about NTP's patents, what they covered, or if they were valid, what software Blackberry used, and whether it was protected by copyright. Nor were the financial details of the ultimate settlement important to me as a consumer (although they fascinate me as a professional). Rather, like millions of other users, I just wanted to know if there was going to be any inconvenient interruption to my service, or if the cost would rise.

Thus, we should not ask "Is this in the public domain?" because this question does not get to the ultimate goal – access to innovation. The key question an innovator should ask is the following: "Is there is any practical or legal obstacle to my use of this particular idea, technology, material, or cultural expression, and if so, how can I overcome that obstacle?"

In another example, a music consumer now has the choice of buying a CD, buying songs from an online vendor, copying a friend's CD, or downloading music from a free file-swapping service. Cost and convenience are the main factors here, although the aggressive enforcement and public awareness campaign by the Recording Industry Association of America has made the latter two options less desirable. By suing individual consumers, including teens, RIAA has demonstrated a very real threat of litigation to offset the ease of copying music. But the consumer's choice is a practical one, and as a general matter does not depend on whether a particular song is in the public domain or not.

With this practical view, the struggle for access to medicines for AIDS in poor countries can be seen as just that – a struggle for access. To needy patients, the question is only whether they can obtain the medicine. The complex global policy debate about whether patents on such medicines should or should not be allowed is less important, as is the issue of whether the medicine is protected by trade secrets, trademarks, or other rights.

For innovators and entrepreneurs seeking to protect their rights, again the distinction between IP rights and public domain is unhelpful. Innovators use exclusive rights to limit access, to gain control over their innovations in order to achieve their goals. The practical issue is not whether their innovations have zero or some IP rights, but whether they have IP rights that provide enough exclusivity for the innovator's purposes. A product that has insufficient IP rights to provide the desired degree of control is practically no different from a product that is in the public domain, with no rights attached at all. The music and movie industries have strong IP rights protecting their works, but they have difficulty preventing public access over the Internet and in pirated recordings. A product backed by weak trade secrets, sold with a weak trademark, is not in the public domain, but the IP protection may be so weak that it provides no exclusivity. At the other extreme, innovators must provide some access to their innovations or they will not be adopted. Most IP rights are not used to exclude the public completely, but rather to limit access in defined ways.

MAPPING THE ACCESSIBLE DOMAIN

So, the term "public domain" is impractical, misleading, and vague in that it does not distinguish between different categories of accessibility. Scholars and advocacy groups opposing stronger intellectual property rights have suggested alternate terminology, for example referring to an intellectual commons. Professors Dinwoodie and Dreyfuss note that the "public domain is more than a place where old intellectual property goes to die," and they coined a new and better term.

> What matters is whether the information a second comer needs is available for use – whether it is in a domain that might be called "the domain of accessible knowledge."[21]

Dinwoodie and Dreyfuss go on to suggest that we can map the domain of accessible knowledge, not only for copyrights, but for patents as well. This leads to an empirical task of measuring whether the recent increase in patenting activity reflects an enlargement of the domain of accessible knowledge due to robust innovation, or a shrinking, due to exceedingly lenient standards for patenting and excessive enforcement of exclusive rights under IP laws. To protect the domain of accessible knowledge, they consider taking affirmative action to protect access, by expanding fair use concepts in patent law, raising the obviousness standard for patentabilty, and narrowing the scope of patent claims, although such reforms may carry the cost of reducing incentives to invent.

A shorter way to refer to the key concept is "the accessible domain." The accessible domain echoes the older term (public domain) and properly emphasizes access as the counterbalance to the exclusive rights of intellectual property. (I enjoyed the irony in reserving the domain name "accessibledomain.com," thus removing it both from the public domain and the accessible domain.) The accessible domain is that which is available to innovators and consumers.

The accessible domain can be mapped into several parts. Specifically, we can discern a continuum of accessibility encompassing the public domain as currently understood, and various levels of IP protection. In order of openness, from most to least, we can characterize these parts as follows. (See Figure 3.1.)

1. Fully accessible, in the public domain, with no intellectual property rights

Information and materials are fully accessible by innovators, with unrestricted rights available without permission. Examples include government archives, most of the public GenBank database of genomic sequences (those that are not patented), Shakespeare's plays (older editions), and telephone directories. This category can be further divided into three subcategories.

---

[21] Graeme Dinwoodie and Rochelle Cooper Dreyfuss, "Patenting Science: Protecting the Domain of Accessible Knowledge," in Guibault and Hugenholtz (eds.), *The Future of The Public Domain in Intellectual Property* (Kluwer Law International, 2006), earlier version available at http://www.kentlaw.edu/depts/ipp/publications/PatentingScience2005.pdf, accessed January 6, 2007.

a. Information and materials for which no IP rights could ever be asserted

These would include materials as they exist in nature (physical materials like ore, unisolated biological materials like turf), and basic mathematic principles like numbers and multiplication.

b. Innovations for which the innovator could have obtained IP rights, but chose not to

An example is the U.S. government position that works authored by government employees are not subject to copyright.

c. Innovations which were once protected with IP rights that are now expired

Examples are older books and music whose copyright has expired, and inventions that were patented, if the patent is invalidated or expired. But often some IP rights remain, and such innovations fall into the fourth category, below. For example, Aspirin was a new drug in 1897, protected by Bayer's patents, trade secrets, and the "Aspirin" trademark. The original patents are long expired, the trade secrets have been reverse engineered, and the trademark was invalidated in the United States as part of World War I reparations from German companies. However, "Aspirin' is still a registered trademark in Germany and more than eighty other countries, so although it is quite broadly accessible we cannot quite say that Aspirin is entirely in the public domain.

2. Broadly accessible with minimal limitations

In this category, an innovator needs to obtain permission to enter or use the information, and to copy it, with a user fee, but there are no IP restrictions thereafter. Examples include most libraries, public collections in museums, university lectures, and many Internet websites.

3. Broadly accessible subject to agreed limitations

Here, in addition to access limitations, an innovator has to agree to use the materials only in certain ways. Most purchased goods fall in this category, the agreed limitation including the purchase price. For example, the end user license agreement for my computer software (free or purchased) permits me to use it, but not to modify it or reproduce it for others. A Wikipedia entry can be edited, but only if the modification is posted on Wikipedia. A botanical garden may give out specimens for academic purposes only, forbidding commercial use or patenting. A plant collector may be required to share any commercial benefits with the community from which the plant was obtained.

4. Accessible for limited purposes

This situation applies when a particular idea, product, material, an aspect of a product, or other subject matter is subject to at least one type of intellectual property in at least one country, which precludes public use in a certain way, but permits

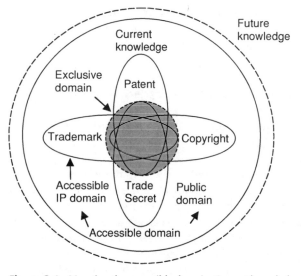

Figure 3.1. Mapping the accessible domain. Current knowledge (solid circle) includes an **exclusive domain** (inner shaded circle) where IP rights block access, and an **accessible domain** that includes everything else – the accessible IP domain where IP rights apply but access is available (outer portions of ovals for each IP type), and a public domain with no IP restrictions. The outer dashed circle represents future knowledge, not yet accessible or exclusive. Lost knowledge is not shown.

other types of access. For example, an innovator can not reproduce a published article subject to copyright, but can use the information freely. An innovator cannot practice a patented invention, but can read and copy the patent document, and design around the invention. A genetic assay may be patented in one country, but freely available for use in others.

5. Not accessible anywhere due to highly restrictive IP rights

In this situation, a thicket of intellectual property rights blocks almost any access to the relevant information absent permission from (or sale by) the innovator. Many private companies wrap their products in patents, copyright restrictions, trademarks, and layers of confidentiality including "black box" technology that prevents reverse engineering. Strategies for working through such thickets are provided in Part II.

The common understanding of the public domain is the first category. A common understanding of the intellectual property domain is this final category. We can gain a deeper understanding of intellectual property dynamics by rejecting the false dichotomy between the public domain and the exclusive intellectual property domain and considering also the intermediate levels of access.

The preceding categories all relate to current knowledge. If we add future knowledge (not yet accessible and not exclusive) and recognize lost knowledge, then we've mapped all knowledge, a lofty goal in itself. (See Figure 3.1.)

In this scheme, we can look at all current knowledge or any part of it as comprising an accessible domain and an inaccessible exclusive domain. IP rights span both.

Knowledge protected by IP rights may be accessible or not accessible. The accessible domain includes the public domain (as described in the first category above) and an accessible IP domain (described in the second through fourth categories above) in which there are some IP rights. Within the accessible IP domain, knowledge may be protected by one, two, three, or four of the basic types of IP rights (patents, copyrights, trade secrets, and trademarks). The degree of access depends on the strength of those IP rights and the licensing practices of their owner. Finally, the scope of the exclusive domain (the fifth category) is subject to the owner's decisions about whether to provide more access, and to legal reform to strengthen or weaken IP rights.

For innovators, depending on the task at hand, suitable access might be possible in any of the first four categories. For consumers seeking to acquire and use a product, suitable access may be possible in all five of the categories, although intellectual property rights may influence product costs in the fourth and fifth categories.

My corporate clients regularly come seeking an opinion on whether they have freedom to operate with respect to a particular project or product. Their concern is access. They do not much care if their competitor has one or one hundred patents in the general field, if none of them blocks the company's business path. If there is a single claim in a single patent that could block the company's path, they are concerned unless they can remove the obstacle by invalidating that claim, or obtaining a license, or modifying their approach.

Likewise, a key employee leaving one company and going to the next is not concerned with the broad issue of whether any of the knowledge learned in the first job is in the trade secret domain. The key issue is whether the employee can use (access) the relevant knowledge in the second job.

ACHIEVING BALANCE

By focusing on the issue of access, we can see more clearly how intellectual property serves as an instrument for balancing various interests. The public importance of this delicate balancing act was noted by the international Commission on Intellectual Property Rights.

> The crucial issue is to reconcile the public interest in accessing new knowledge and the products of new knowledge, with the public interest in stimulating invention and creation which produces the new knowledge and products on which material and cultural progress may depend.[22]

So the dichotomy of public domain vs. intellectual property can be redefined as a more subtle balancing of adequate access against the incentive of exclusivity. Each type of intellectual property balances different types of access and exclusivity.

- Copyright balances the free global flow of creative expression with incentive to express new ideas.
- Patent systems balance access to existing inventions with incentives to invent new ones.

[22] CIPR Report, p. 6.

- Trade secret law balances the benefits of sharing personal knowledge publicly with the possibility of keeping the secret safe within a limited group.
- Trademark systems balance the benefits of merchant creativity in marketing goods and services through commercial channels of trade with the consumer's need to know the source of goods.

Novel approaches to protecting genetic resources and traditional knowledge (under the Convention on Biological Diversity and the International Treaty on Plant Genetic Resources) also involve a balance. This balance is between open access to existing biological or cultural resources, on the one hand, and restricting access in exchange for benefit sharing as an incentive for conservation, on the other. An appropriate name for these rights is still lacking. They might be called "innovation resource rights," "accessible domain rights," or "custodial access rights," or (as Darrell Posey called them) "traditional resource rights."[23]

In 1992, I was invited to speak to the International Association for the Study of Common Property, and contemplating their uncommon name, I prepared a paper called "Carving Property Rights Out of the Public Domain to Conserve Biodiversity." My thesis was that the boundaries between the public domain and private property are determined by legal rules, which in turn derive from commercial practices, ethical standards, and principles of equity and justice. That is, as new practices and ethical standards evolve, the law evolves too, to reset the boundaries of the public domain.

My main focus was the Convention on Biological Diversity (CBD), signed that year, which established sovereign rights over biological resources, thereby removing biodiversity from the public domain. Intellectual property rights played a role in defining the new property rights in biodiversity. Specifically, the law protecting trade secrets could be used to protect the medicinal practices of a shaman, just as they are used to protect technology in a pharmaceutical company. Although the plant used by the shaman could not be patented and would remain in the public domain, purified drugs isolated from the plant and recombinant products made from the plant's genes could be patented. My conclusions then, still valid today, were that we should examine property rights in terms of what they leave in the public domain; that we should ensure that the sources of material and ideas for innovation are not constrained; and that the incentives for conserving our genetic heritage should be balanced with incentives for creating new and beneficial technologies.

Commercial and research practices and ethical standards have continued to evolve over the past 15 years, with the CBD, the TRIPS Agreement, the International Treaty on Plant Genetic Resources, and the open access movement. As a consequence, as predicted, we are witnessing a rebalancing of the legal framework to provide incentives not just for innovation, but also for conserving the raw materials of innovation in the accessible domain.

---

[23] Darrell Posey and Graham Dutfield, *Beyond Intellectual Property: Toward Traditional Resource Rights for Indigenous Peoples and Local Communities* (IDRC, 1996).

TENSIONS IN THE GLOBAL IP SYSTEM

Having briefly reviewed the social history of intellectual property, its varying assumptions, and its dualism with the public domain, we can now focus on some of the current controversies over intellectual property. Part III of this book deals with the practicalities of working within the existing framework of intellectual property laws, but those lessons can be of limited value absent a realization that the laws will likely continue to change over time. Here, we consider the tensions in developing countries, because their economic problems are so great and because they provide a perspective different from the received wisdom about intellectual property. Also, some of the same themes of excessive IP rights voiced in developing countries are being echoed in wealthy countries as well.

With the TRIPS Agreement, most of the countries in Asia, South America, and Africa have joined the intellectual property system established in Europe 500 years ago. This explains why some commentators consider all modern intellectual property regimes to be Eurocentric.[24] Prior innovation incentive systems based on secrecy and patronage, and communal traditional knowledge systems, have recently been replaced by the European system of patents, copyrights, trademarks, and trade secrets, and this can be a source of cultural tension.[25]

The intellectual property system formalized in the TRIPS Agreement has been enormously successful in the sense that it has been adopted universally. One reason for the broad adoption of intellectual property laws is that this was part of the bargain for becoming a member of the WTO. However, the strengthening of IP rights under TRIPS has been very controversial.

Some groups recognize that intellectual property systems helps drive the innovation cycle. The innovation cycle involves individual creative acts based on access to knowledge and materials, followed by adoption in society, and a return of knowledge and materials into the accessible domain. Specifically, patent rules dealing with inventive ideas, copyrights dealing with expression of ideas, trademarks addressing the marketing of innovative products, and trade secrets controlling the sharing of information in a small community all protect individual creative acts in all countries, and promote investment in the innovations so they may be adopted by society.

The biggest IP-related concern of the wealthy nations, particularly businesses in the United States, is enforcement. Many countries have enacted laws that, on their face, provide for adequate protection, but in practice, these laws are not enforced. China and Nigeria, among many other countries, are notorious for having thriving black markets of unauthorized copies of software, music, and movies. Likewise, file swapping and downloads from the Internet occur all over the world. The lost revenues for copyright owners are billions of dollars.

Developing countries have other concerns. One of the most comprehensive reports of how different intellectual property scenarios can impact developing countries was produced by the UK-funded Commission on Intellectual Property Rights

---

[24] Ikechi Mgbeoji, *Global Biopiracy: Patents, Plants and Indigenous Knowledge* (UBC Vancouver, 2006).
[25] CIPR report, chapter 4.

(CIPR) in 2002, "Integrating Intellectual Property Rights and Development Policy."[26] The CIPR, headed by Stanford law professor John Barton, rejected extremist positions on both sides that favor strengthening all IP rights for developing countries, or weakening them all. The CIPR instead reviewed the literature, interviewed industry and public groups in both wealthy and poor nations, and reached some original insights. The CIPR report tries to avoid myths and stereotypes and to focus on the lessons of available evidence. Because it was unprecedented and influential, it is worth reviewing the CIPR report's conclusions in some detail.

The CIPR report confirms that the increased duration, scope, enforceability, and territorial extent of patents and copyrights in the past generation has been unprecedented. However, objective studies of the benefits and costs of intellectual property are surprisingly inconclusive, especially in developing countries. The proper balance is not well understood. The private privileges conferred by intellectual property are not an end in themselves, but rather a means to promote the greater public good by fulfilling human economic and social rights.[27] Those ends are met by an optimal level of protection. Like taxation, the optimal level delivers desirable social results without undesirable economic effects. The optimal level of IP protection is a compromise between local social and economic interests, and the balance of costs and benefits will differ markedly in diverse circumstances.[28]

The CIPR report notes that the current debates about intellectual property are nothing new. Periods of great contentiousness about IP recur through modern history, and the CIPR report suggests we should welcome vigorous debate today. Prior to the 1883 Paris Convention, the United States and many other countries gave preferential treatment to their own domestic inventors and authors. Many countries have used weak patent laws for foreigners to protect local industry, including Switzerland in the 1800s. Until more recently Taiwan, Korea, and India denied patents on chemicals, drugs, and foods, thereby supporting local industries that reproduced these products cheaply. According to the CIPR report, developing countries should have a similar freedom to shape their IP laws to promote their social and economic interests, depending on their local circumstances. Thus, developing countries should consider limiting the reach of patent laws as much as possible, for example permitting researchers to use patented inventions in their research.[29]

The CIPR report rejected a "one size fits all" approach to IP laws, concluding that IP can benefit one group or country at the cost of another. The majority of the world's poor live in countries with some innovation infrastructure, including Brazil, India, China, Mexico, and South Africa, but many live in countries with very limited technical capacity. The private benefit granted to the IP holder is at the expense of the consumer, who may be in a rich or a poor country, and IP rights may also conflict with moral interests such as the right to life dependent on medicines and food. The cost of getting IP wrong in poor countries is even greater than in wealthy countries because they generally lack other systems to promote competition and stimulate

---

[26] CIPR Report. Available at http://www.iprcommission.org/graphic/documents.htm, accessed July 25, 2006.

[27] CIPR Report, p. 6.

[28] CIPR Report, p. 15.

[29] CIPR Report, p 50.

innovation. IP systems have high transaction costs beyond the ability of many poor countries to administer, even if they charge user fees.

The benefits of IP systems include economic productivity, and human rights, as under the Universal Declaration of Human Rights, which recognizes moral interests in scientific, artistic, and literary works. To be of benefit to poor countries, IP systems should contribute to sustainable development by stimulating local innovation, and making more technology and cultural innovation available locally at competitive prices.[30] Developing countries have weaker environments for innovation than wealthier countries, based on the nature of local businesses and markets, and government capacity to coordinate innovation policy. Intellectual property systems may not be sufficient to promote innovation without local scientific and technological capacity, education, and financial resources.

In agriculture, public research funding exceeds private funding and is more evenly divided between rich and poor countries. Plant variety protection can serve as a marketing tool, like trademarks, for larger producers in developing countries. Agricultural biotechnology innovation occurs predominantly in developed countries. Developing countries may choose to deny utility patents on plants and microorganisms, instead using an alternate system like UPOV plant variety protection with breeders' rights and farmers' rights.[31]

For the chemical and pharmaceutical industries, and in the more advanced developing countries, the benefits of strong IP systems seem to outweigh the costs, but in the less developed countries, there are advantages in permitting local copying.[32] The CIPR report suggests that IP rights are irrelevant for drugs to treat diseases peculiar to poor countries (malaria, tuberculosis, Chagas disease, and so on). Without a functioning market for those drugs in rich or poor countries, the exclusive rights provided by intellectual property have essentially no value. This problem may be addressed in part by public measures such as increased research funding and government promises to purchase new drugs at certain prices if they meet certain standards. For diseases that exist in both rich and poor countries (such as AIDS, cancer, diabetes), access and pricing depend on the existence of patents not in those countries but in the exporting countries.[33] More advanced developing countries may be able to make generic versions of drugs domestically, using compulsory licensing laws. The CIPR report concluded that compulsory licensing proceedings, by which a local manufacturer can produce patented drugs without permission from the patent owner, would be no help to the poorest countries because they lack the capacity to make their own drugs and must import them.

The World Health Organization (WHO) arranged for a followup report focused on health. The 2006 report of the Commission on Intellectual Property Rights, Innovation and Public Health (CIPIH), "Public Health, Innovation and Intellectual Property Rights," like the CIPR report before it, concluded that the market for diagnostics, vaccines, and medicines in developing countries is small and uncertain, so the incentive

---

[30] CIPR Report, p. 8
[31] CIPR Report, pp. 60–66.
[32] CIPR Report, pp. 20–24.
[33] CIPR Report, p. 36.

effect of intellectual property rights is limited or nonexistent. The CIPIH report generally supported the role of intellectual property systems in promoting innovation, but suggested additional measures would be required to stimulate research and provide access to drugs for developing countries, such as more partnerships and funding; and a more active coordinating role by the WHO.

FROM THE PAST TO THE FUTURE

The general trend over the past decades has been to expand protection several ways, including the scope of subject matter covered, the duration of exclusive rights, and the countries in which the rights are available. Innovations that have become subject to protection in many countries include engineered microorganisms, plants, animals, isolated genes, software, and business methods, as well as traditional knowledge. However, disparities remain with regard to protections available for each of these types of innovation.

Just as IP laws drive innovation, technology innovation changes IP laws and practices. The proliferation of reproduction technology in the hands of consumers has led to reform of copyright law and marketing practices for music, film, and other arts. Commerce on the Internet has led to copyright reform and new trademark doctrines relating to domain names, hyperlinks, and so on. The rise of distributed computing on the Internet has forced courts to confront the issue of extraterritorial enforcement of patents – whether a patent can be infringed in any one country, if the computing steps take place in several different countries.

Although there are many initiatives for greater harmonization, there are also strong local interests in many countries favoring unique domestic variations, such as the United States' "first to invent" patent system, which stands apart from other countries that give patents to the first to file an application. Groups from outside the formerly insular intellectual property community have become actively involved, including international trade practitioners, as in the TRIPS Agreement; environmentalists, as in the Convention on Biological Diversity; and advocates for indigenous groups. In particular, the idea of protecting traditional knowledge set forth in the Convention on Biological Diversity has led to new measures to collect and use traditional knowledge in India, Peru, and elsewhere and has led WIPO to expand its work exploring novel forms of intellectual property protection for traditional knowledge.

Also, there has been a growing recognition that limited access to medicines in developing countries is due in part to poor distribution channels, availability of health clinics, and patient ability to pay, and these problems go beyond IP rights. That is, IP rights are not a sole cause of limited access, and they cannot immediately solve the problem either, so other solutions are required.

Intellectual property protection remains at a global crossroads, with four possible outcomes, and it is difficult to predict where it will go.[34] The first scenario is

---

[34] Michael Gollin, "Introduction," in D. Campbell (ed.), *International Protection of Intellectual Property Rights*, (FT Law & Tax, 1997). See also "Scenarios for the Future: How Might IP Regimes Evolve by 2025? What Global Legitimacy Might Such Regimes Have?" (European Patent Office 2007) (possible future IP regimes are defined according to the four "drivers" of the market ("Market Rules"), geopolitics ("Whose Game"), society ("Trees of Knowledge") and technology ("Blue Skies").

preservation of the status quo, with minimal changes to the scope of protection available, beyond the gradual expansion of rights as countries come into compliance with TRIPS.

The second option is a broad expansion of protection of all types of intellectual property around the world. The United States extended the term of copyrights in 1998. Expansion of IP rights, including enforcement, remains a foreign policy goal of the U.S. government and global industry in implementing TRIPS and other bilateral and multilateral agreements.

The third option is a rollback or reduction of protection in certain areas. Some developing countries have extended their time for complying with TRIPS, others are pushing to expand compulsory licensing for national health reasons, and the research community advocates exempting scientific research from patent infringement. Some countries, notably those rich in biodiversity, are adding restrictions on patents by requiring the applicant to identify the source of any genetic material or traditional knowledge used in the invention.

The fourth option, only an idea a decade ago, is to find new ways in which intellectual property can promote social goals consistent with a population's need for health, free trade, and sustainable development. This is the most promising road. As scholars and activists work on the complex issues, new ideas are evolving and may help improve the workings of the innovation cycle and the intellectual property laws of the future.

Open source licensing, and the open access movement it spawned, are only a few years old, and the impacts of this strategy are yet to be fully understood. Public-private partnerships for providing medicines to developing countries have also pioneered new licensing arrangements. Anil Gupta's Honeybee initiative in India (see p. 98) has created a precedent for expanding the impact of innovation involving traditional knowledge. Expansion of intellectual property management skills will help organizations use intellectual property rights to pursue their goals, whether for profit or for the broader public interest. Intellectual property management has become a course topic in business schools, and a consulting community has grown to provide these services to corporations. The non-profit organization Public Interest Intellectual Property Advisors designed ways to deliver the relevant intellectual property services to developing countries and public organizations at affordable cost.

The accessible domain is crucial to innovation as the source of future ingenuity, and therefore one desirable goal is to enlarge the accessible domain, by ensuring that innovations join the reservoir of knowledge in the accessible domain, and that they are not lost or destroyed. One criticism of IP laws is that they keep knowledge out of the accessible domain, but one can also argue that exclusivity increases access to innovation. That is, IP rights can expand the accessible domain. Patent publication makes knowledge of the inventions available to others, even though they may not use the invention immediately, ensuring that the information will not be lost as trade secrets. Also, upon patent expiration, limitations on use of the invention do end. Intellectual property stimulates innovation, so that in the long run more is known and accessible than if there was no intellectual property, and less innovation.

If we view innovation as a force of creative destruction, we may well fear that innovations will destroy old knowledge. Can we envision a system of creative construction, instead? Can IP rights counteract the destructive tendency, by creating incentives to conserve knowledge for the future? Intellectual property rights do not apply well to conserving accessible knowledge and materials, especially old knowledge and knowledge that is held collectively by more than one individual or a small group. Perhaps other cultures can contribute additional ideas on how best to preserve the libraries, universities, museums, gene banks, databases, archives, landraces of plants used and saved by farmers, and other traditional practices, which together embody the repository of the accumulated wisdom of the ages.

Looking at the history and tensions in the modern system of IP rights, here are a few predictions about larger trends and practical implications of international intellectual property protection. These are revisited in Chapter 18.

- International exchange and transfer of technology and culture will continue to increase.
- Levels of innovation among nations will increase but remain divergent.
- Innovators will continue seeking new ways to use intellectual property rights to secure competitive advantages in a global economy.
- IP rights will continue to be reformed, whether strengthened or weakened.
- The international system of IP rights will continue to expand and be harmonized in some regards, through regional and international organizations like the WIPO and the WTO.
- National practices under IP laws will continue to vary dramatically.
- New rights, for example, for traditional knowledge, will be crafted.
- Theorists and policymakers concerned with the social and economic aspects of intellectual property protection will promote these changes in pursuit of a healthy balance.
- IP managers in organizations will try to find strategies for protection that will last and be enforceable for decades, despite such uncertainty.

One overarching lesson from studying the rise of IP is that IP laws are crude tools for coping with a very complicated world of innovation and the dynamics of the innovation cycle. The optimal level of IP rights needed to balance social and economic interests is hard to find. The difficulty is compounded by the desire to have an IP system balance private and public interests, current and future interests, and local and foreign interests. This may be impossible to do in any precise fashion. Try as we might to keep the system in balance, we may just have to tolerate a certain amount of "wobble" in which some interests are not optimally balanced.

Imbalances in the system are no reason to toss it out. Some people favor a full open access economy in certain areas, like medicine, in which researchers accept public support of their innovation in exchange for a promise not to assert IP rights. They suggest that grants, prizes, and awards would provide the necessary incentives. That is a simplistic view. Whoever makes the decisions on what to fund could stifle innovation. Also, once research under a grant is complete, or a prize is won, the innovation cycle does not stop, but keeps turning with new improvements, and broader adoption into society. The Ansari X Prize gave US$10M to Bert Rutan's company, Scaled Composites, for its successful flight of SpaceShipOne, but that was only the beginning of the development process for a private space ship, so the prize is no substitute for patent protection. Likewise, the contestants for the Archon X Prize for Genomics are seeking IP rights for the genome sequencing methods and equipment they invent in seeking a US$10M prize for being the first to sequence 100 human genomes in 10 days.

I don't see how society can advance without a balanced system of IP rights to channel innovation. Despite its crudeness, the IP system is driven by individual decisions and because of that it may be better tuned to local needs and interests than other approaches, such as a pure system of government initiated grants or prizes awarded by a particular organization.

The ideal of individual choice echoes Adam Smith's concept of the invisible hand of the market in his 1776 book on free markets, *The Wealth of Nations*. Individuals and creative organizations decide what is important to them, produce innovations, and then decide independently whether to share the innovation or protect it with IP. These decisions express individual freedoms, and serve as invisible hands turning the innovation cycle.

SUMMARY. Proponents of robust intellectual property laws assert eight arguments that revolve around promoting innovation and the rights of innovators. Opponents also raise eight arguments. They criticize IP laws as leading to excessive privatization of creative activity, and limited access. These groups are concerned with exclusion and access, private rights and the public domain, monopoly and competition, freedom and oppression, and individual and society. Their differences conceal a shared view that IP laws are worthy of attention because they shape society in many important ways. One way to resolve the tension and ongoing debate through the centuries is to consider the IP system not as inherently good, or bad, or an end in itself, but rather as a means to balance public access and private exclusivity. Balance might be found using the concept of the accessible domain, which is broader than the "public domain," and includes innovations that are protected by IP rights, but nonetheless available for use on reasonable terms. Balance is elusive, and innovation itself puts the system out of balance so that it needs continuous readjustment. Modern tensions in the global IP system suggest such a rebalancing is underway. The possible future scenarios for IP laws remain uncertain, and include stronger, weaker, more uniform, or more diverse systems. Ultimately, in a balanced system, innovators have sufficient exclusivity to achieve their goals, while people wanting to use innovative information, material, or products have sufficient access to reach their own goals. Exclusivity and access are part of a dynamic system of creativity in which organizations and communities must constantly struggle and change, or fade away. Hence this topic will continue to be important far into the future. The creative tension sustained by the IP system requires study, practice, and continued reform, in schools, in private corporations and public organizations, in legislatures, in rich and poor countries. The next part of the book introduces concepts that are helpful in such endeavors.

PART TWO

BASICS OF MANAGING INTELLECTUAL PROPERTY IN ORGANIZATIONS

4 The Innovation Tree: Intellectual Property Rights and How They Grow

This second part of the book provides the basic concepts necessary to understand intellectual property dynamics and to manage intellectual property in organizations. This chapter introduces the innovation tree as a metaphor for intellectual property. Like seeds grow to saplings in a forest, ideas sprout and grow and mature in society. Old knowledge leads to growth of new ideas that can then be protected with IP rights. In time the new becomes old, and broadly accessible. The boundaries between protected and accessible knowledge are defined by laws which continue to change over time and differ from country to country. The next section is a guide to the different types of intellectual property — trade secrets, patents, copyright, trademarks, and other related rights — each of which has a different scope of protectable subject matter, scope of rights, rules for government registration (or not), duration, and legal basis. Each type of IP right interacts with others, and one type may convert to another. IP rights can be grouped into bundles, like groves of trees, and managed that way.

* * * * * *

THE FOREST FOR THE TREES

The expression "He can't see the forest for the trees" refers to someone who is mired in details and therefore misses the context, the overall situation, the big picture. Unfortunately, the complexities of intellectual property draw us deep into the trees, so it becomes hard to see the shape of the larger forest, the dynamics of the IP system. In this book, we try to understand both the trees and the forest of intellectual property.

We have looked at how the modern intellectual property system arose to help support and channel innovation, balancing exclusion and access, as the innovation cycle revolves through history. IP systems operate by giving innovators exclusive rights that are limited so as to permit others to access the innovation. It is inevitable that there should be tension between exclusivity and access, and social debate about how to keep the IP system in balance. We leave that debate now, and turn to a dynamic conceptual framework for IP rights. Several fundamental features of intellectual property become clear at this level of detail, including the distinguishing characteristics of the different types of IP rights, and some general principles of how these rights can be obtained, transferred, and enforced.

THE INNOVATION TREE AS METAPHOR FOR INTELLECTUAL PROPERTY

The dynamics of the innovation cycle, and intellectual property's role within it, can be understood by analogy to the life cycle of a tree growing in a forest – an "innovation tree." The creative act is like a seed using its internal energy to sprout in a forest, and then absorbing external resources – air and light through its leaves and water and minerals through its roots – to grow into a sapling, then a tree. While living, the tree enriches its surroundings, producing oxygen, sugar, limbs, leaves, flowers, and fruit. The woody core is built from past years' growth. This year's growing green wood will become next year's core wood. Likewise, this year's leaves and fruits fall to the ground and become part of the nutrient cycle for the tree and forest, and perhaps seeds for new trees. Eventually the tree dies, topples, and the wood decays, returning to the soil and air to provide resources for new life to complete the tree's life cycle.

In this model, the innovation cycle is like the life cycle of a tree. The knowledge and resources that flow into creative human endeavors, giving rise to innovation, are like the air, earth, light, and water that flow into a tree and make it grow. Innovative ideas, susceptible to IP protection, are like the new growth – the green wood enveloping the tree beneath the bark, the growing leaves and ripening fruit. The ideas can flow from the innovator to other people, from A to B to C to D, and eventually join the accessible domain. Ideas are like the fruit, leaves, and sap that come from a tree and enrich the forest and its inhabitants, and eventually the old growth of the tree itself when it dies and supports new life. The fallen leaves and fruit, and the tree trunk when it dies, symbolize how IP rights dissipate and ultimately become accessible to others.

The innovation tree serves as a metaphorical entry point to explain the different kinds of intellectual property and how they arise from and return to the accessible public domain. Each type of intellectual property right – trade secrets, patents, copyrights, and trade secrets – can be distinguished from the other, like different types of trees. Each has different legal basics and dynamics, and different ways it can be protected, converted, transferred, aggregated in an organization, and passed on in the process of social adoption of the innovation, until it becomes accessible, to complete the innovation cycle. Groups of different rights can exist in one idea, and can be combined in an innovation forest.

Most people, around the world,can grasp this "natural" metaphor at a subliminal level because it suggests that all the parts of the IP system are mutually interdependent in ways not easily perceived. The innovation tree as metaphor is not precisely accurate of course, but it does complement the typical "mechanistic" view of intellectual property, where each part performs a specific rationally predetermined function. Things are not that simple, but they are simple enough to be understood.

THE OLD AND THE NEW

Intellectual property rights attach only to innovations, not to that which came before. A new idea is like a sprouting seed. As the tree grows, new wood turns to old. Likewise, yesterday's innovations become part of the accessible domain.

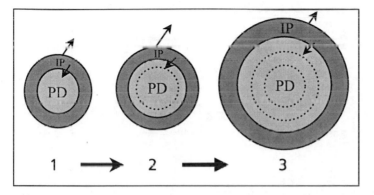

Figure 4.1. Cross-sections of a growing innovation tree. As the tree grows outward (arrows in 1 and 2), the proprietary domain of intellectual property (IP) expands, and so does the accessible or public domain (PD), as IP converts to PD (trees 2 and 3), with past expansion shown by dashed lines.

If you imagine a growing innovation tree in cross section, you see that as the tree grows outward year by year, the outer ring (new ideas, knowledge, creative works, and technology) expands. (See Figure 4.1.) This is the proprietary domain subject to intellectual property. As time passes, or in the absence of legal protection, new ideas move from the intellectual property domain to become part of the accessible domain (or public domain) at the core of the innovation tree, like the growth rings of a tree that become visible when it is cut down. The creators of new information, art, or technology may choose to move the new knowledge quickly into the public domain by disclosure, or may passively fail to take steps to protect it. Or the creator may decide to protect the innovations with IP rights for a period of time, until the IP rights lapse and the innovation becomes accessible. So, eventually, the public domain expands outward, along with the IP domain. The accessible domain grows along with the IP domain.

As we know, the trunk of a tree is mostly built of old wood, which gives the tree its strength, girth, and height. The living tissue of a tree is in the outer growth ring – the cambium – where new growth occurs. If the outer ring is cut through or stripped, the tree dies. Also, if the woody core of the tree is destroyed by rot or insects, the tree will fall and die. Thus, the tree requires both the old and the new. Likewise, a healthy society needs to stimulate the new growth of the intellectual property domain, while conserving and expanding the old knowledge of the public domain. Creativity feeds from available resources and is supported by the body of available knowledge. The IP domain builds on the accessible/public domain.

DIFFERENCES FROM COUNTRY TO COUNTRY

Intellectual property remains a creature of national law, although it is increasingly subject to treaties. The national laws of many countries that are members of the World Trade Organization are undergoing great change as they implement the Trade Related Aspects of Intellectual Property (TRIPS) Agreement. Intellectual property is

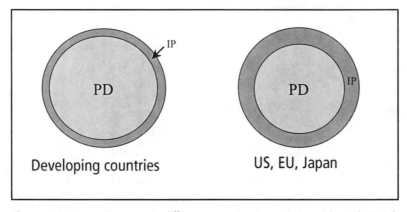

Figure 4.2. Innovation trees in different countries. In countries with weak IP rights, there is a relatively small IP domain, while in developed countries with stronger laws, the IP domain is bigger.

receiving greater protection, and entities which misappropriate or infringe others' intellectual property face increasing liability.

The relative extent of the intellectual property domain and the public domain differs from country to country. In developing countries with a history of weaker intellectual property laws, the IP domain is relatively small and the public domain is relatively large. In the United States, Europe, and Japan, which have longstanding IP systems, the IP domain is larger and the public domain is relatively smaller. This simplified concept is illustrated in Figure 4.2 by comparing innovation trees for two countries.

As we saw with Figure 4.1, the relationship between the intellectual property domain and the public domain changes over time. The TRIPS agreement required stronger IP laws in developing countries beginning in 2000 (and 2005 in the least developed countries). As a result, the IP domain has begun to grow larger relative to the public domain in those countries.

A GUIDE TO TYPES OF INTELLECTUAL PROPERTY RIGHTS

All trees have common features, but each species – maples, oaks, pines, and sycamores – has unique and distinctive characteristics. A field guide can help to identify a tree in a forest. The same is true for the four basic types of intellectual property – trade secrets, patents, copyrights, and trademarks. There are common features, but each has its own rules and standards, and the differences can be readily learned so each can be identified.

Although the rules applicable to each type of intellectual property vary somewhat from country to country, the fundamentals are established based on the international standards set forth in the TRIPS Agreement.[1] The following summary is based on these general principles, with some examples from the United States.

---

[1] The TRIPS Agreement (Trade-Related Aspects of Intellectual Property Rights) is Annex 1C of the Marrakesh Agreement Establishing the World Trade Organization, signed in Marrakesh, Morocco, on April 15, 1994. (See Appendix A.)

Table 4.1. Trade secret basics

TRADE SECRETS	
PROTECTABLE SUBJECT MATTER	Information that has commercial value and is not generally known or readily accessible in a trade, for which there is evidence of efforts to protect secrecy (product formulas, chemical compounds, blueprints, dimensions, tolerances, customer lists, suppliers, financial information, etc.)
GOVERNMENT REGISTRATION	Generally none available or required
SCOPE OF RIGHTS	Prevent disclosure or acquisition by dishonest means, or use of the secret information without permission
DURATION	As long as information remains secret (potentially forever)
LEGAL BASIS	National laws consistent with TRIPS Section 8, Article 39 (see Appendix A) In the US, protected by common law, state statutes, principles of express or implied contracts, federal and state law of unfair competition, and federal criminal statutes

Trade secret essentials

Trade secrecy is the oldest and original form of intellectual property, dating back at least 4000 years, when Irtisen the scribe promised to keep Pharaoh's secrets, in hieroglyphics on Stele C-14. (See Figure 2.1.) We may easily imagine that prehistoric humans shared information with their own clan, but kept information secret from rivals – the location of good hunting grounds, or their own stores of grain. Any child knows the importance of keeping a secret – and how hard that is. As the saying goes, I can keep a secret, but the friends I tell it to can't.

In intellectual property law, a trade secret is any information used in the operation of a business that is sufficiently valuable and secret to give an actual or potential economic advantage over others. Examples include customer lists, financial information, and secret formulas like the legendary recipe for Coca Cola. The owner must take measures to keep the information secret, such as by having confidentiality agreements, but no government documentation of trade secrets is generally available. (See Table 4.1.)

Trade secrets are generally protected by "self-help" measures. There is no government registration process available or required. Owners protect trade secrets by affirmative acts such as locked file cabinets and confidentiality agreements. Trade secrets have no international boundaries. The courts in most countries will enforce trade secret infringement claims against people who improperly take trade secrets or break their agreement in that country. Criminal sanctions may apply. In civil actions, the legal theory used in enforcement is generally breach of contract or tort, although some countries have criminal penalties as well.

There are three general situations in which a violation of trade secrets occurs. One occurs if someone misappropriates a trade secret by stealing a document or obtaining the information by other dishonest means. The second occurs when the owner discloses the information in exchange for a promise to keep it confidential,

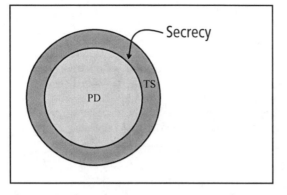

Figure 4.3. The trade secret tree. New secret information arises in the IP domain as a trade secret (TS), but moves into the public domain once secrecy is lost.

and the recipient of the information breaks that promise. In these situations, the trade secret owner can go to court and seek an injunction against disclosure or use of the trade secret, and payment of damages incurred by the victim of the loss of secrets. The third violation can arise when information is disclosed confidentially to government agencies, such as with patent applications (prepublication), applications for permission to market drugs or agricultural products that require extensive disclosures of technical data, or confidential disclosures made in court cases. Government employees are prohibited from disclosing such trade secrets outside the narrow confines of the particular proceeding.

Although trade secrets extend internationally, they may only be enforced in the courts of individual countries. The accused party may assert that the owner did not safeguard the information as secret, or that it was in fact not secret. Unfortunately for the trade secret owner, once the secret has been disclosed, "the cat is out of the bag" and a court injunction has little meaning.

The name "trade secret" itself reminds us that protected information has to have value in a particular trade, and it needs to be secret. The boundary between the domain of trade secrets and the public domain is the concept of "secrecy." (See Figure 4.3.) Any information that is already publicly known is in the public domain (with respect to trade secrets.)

Any new idea that occurs to a person, if it has value, and is not previously known, can be considered to be a trade secret from its inception. For example, individuals may come up with valuable information such as ideas, processes, formulas, lists, or designs. Then, instead of publishing that information, they conceal it, keep it secret. As long as the efforts to keep the information secret are successful, the information is intellectual property, in the proprietary domain. In theory a trade secret could last forever. But if the information is made public by its creators, intentionally or inadvertently, it loses its status as a trade secret and converts and becomes part of the public domain with respect to trade secrets.

Trade secret information enters the accessible public domain (with respect to trade secrets) if the information is published in paper or electronic form, discussed openly, or made widely known in the workplace. Trade secret information can also enter the public domain if someone other than the creator discloses it–whether the information originated with the creator and was told to someone else who then improperly made it public, or was separately and independently created and published by someone else. Trade secrets can be protected internationally but generally, once published anywhere, they are gone everywhere.

Even after loss of trade secret rights, however, other proprietary rights might remain, such as copyright or patent rights. For example, when a journalist comes up with a news story "scoop," the information remains a trade secret until the journalist publishes the story in a newspaper – or someone else does. After publication, the story is still protected by copyright but the information itself becomes part of the public domain (with respect to trade secrecy).

In another example, researchers in the public Human Genome Project and private Celera Genomics each determined the sequence of sections of the human genome, leading to a draft sequence in 2000, and project completion by both in 2003. The genetic data was secret until published. Public researchers published their DNA sequence information in the free GenBank database almost immediately, transferring the information into the public domain. Private researchers at Celera also published the sequence information they found, but only after a period during which confidential access was provided to commercial subscribers, and only after Celera filed patent applications on the separate, isolated, genetic sequences, with annotations about the proteins encoded by those genes. Upon publication, the information entered the public domain with respect to trade secrecy. However, the DNA sequences stayed in the proprietary domain with respect to patent rights.

Patent essentials

Inventions, including improvements to existing technology, can be patented if they are useful, new, and not obvious (having an inventive step). Patentable inventions include processes and products such as compositions, and devices. The most significant type of patent is a *utility patent*, as shown in Table 4.2.

Patent rights exist only in the form of "letters patent," a public document issued by a national government. The process for obtaining a patent (known as patent prosecution) involves preparing a detailed application describing the invention and how to make and use it, and claiming its inventive features, then filing the application in the patent office of a particular country. The applicant may also file the same application in other countries to gain international protection. There is no international patent.

After filing an application, patent rights are preserved, and the invention is considered to be "patent pending" until the patent issues, or is abandoned. The patent office examines the application and if it meets the statutory requirements, issues a patent in that country. If the claimed invention is not sufficiently distinct from prior publications, or is poorly described, the application is rejected and the applicant can then amend the claims. After patent issuance, the patent owner must pay periodic maintenance fees in each country, or the patent will lapse there. In some countries, other parties can file opposition actions in the patent office, challenging the validity

Table 4.2. Patent basics

PATENTS

PROTECTABLE SUBJECT MATTER	Useful, new, and nonobvious processes and products (machines, articles of manufacture, and compositions of matter, e.g., chemical compound)
GOVERNMENT REGISTRATION	Patent application disclosing the invention, filed by the inventor in each country's patent agency (e.g., U.S. Patent and Trademark Office), examined, and issued as a patent
SCOPE OF RIGHTS	Exclude others from making, using, selling, offering to sell, or importing the patented invention, as defined in claims issued in a particular country
DURATION	From issuance of the patent to 20 years from filing of the patent application
LEGAL BASIS	National laws consistent with TRIPS Section 5, Articles 27–34 (see Appendix A) In the United States., federal legislation codified in Title 35 of the U.S. Code, and interpreted in regulations and judicial decisions

of a newly allowed patent. Patents expire, generally, 20 years from the earliest filing date of the application.

An invention can be protected as a trade secret until the patent application is published or the information is otherwise disclosed. Publication of the patent application generally occurs 18 months from the application filing date. At that point, the patented invention enters the public domain with respect to trade secrets, although patent rights are preserved.

Inventors can lose patent rights through self-inflicted damage if they disclose or publish the invention or sell inventive products *before* they file a patent application. Prior publication commits the subject matter to the public domain with respect to patents, in most countries. In the United States, Canada, and Australia, there is a one year grace period before publication would bar the patent. Prior publications by other people (referred to as prior art) are also considered by patent examiners in determining whether the invention claimed in a patent application is new and nonobvious.

A patent gives the owner the right to exclude others from making, using, selling, offering for sale, or importing the invention as set forth in the claims of the patent. Such acts constitute patent infringement. For process patents, the exclusive rights extend to products made by the process. A patent owner may file a lawsuit against an infringer, and the court may issue an injunction prohibiting the accused party from infringing the claims. The court may also award damages, including a reasonable royalty or the patent owner's lost profits. Punitive damages are sometimes available against willful infringers.

Accused infringers generally assert that their conduct does not fall within the scope described in the claims of the patent. Also, accused infringers try to assert that the patent is invalid and that it was a mistake for the patent office to issue the patent.

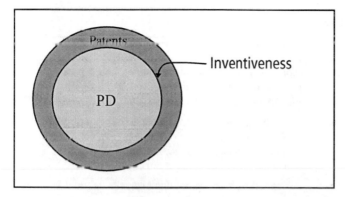

Figure 4.4. The patent tree. New inventions can be patented if they differ from what is already in the public domain, but they fall into the public domain after patent expiration.

A common misconception is that a patent is a permit that gives the patent owner the right to make the invention. A patent provides only a right to exclude others from the scope defined in a claim. For example, if you patent "a chair having legs," and I later invent "a chair having legs with wheels on them," I can obtain a patent on the wheeled chair, but I can not make it without infringing your patent on the chair having legs. My patent would be no defense to an infringement action.

The boundary between the patent domain and the nonpatent domain can be summarized as "inventiveness." If there is no invention, there is no right to a patent and even a creative new discovery remains in the public domain as to patents. Then, too, as the innovation cycle rolls forward, patents lapse and expire, and the invention moves from the patent domain into the public domain. (See Figure 4.4.)

In addition to utility patents, there are several related legal rights. For example, patents on industrial designs, or design patents, apply to new, original, ornamental designs for articles of manufacture. Design patents last for at least 10 years from patent issuance (14 years in the United States). TRIPS Section 4, Articles 25–26 (see Appendix A).

The TRIPS Agreement does not specify what kind of protection is required for plants and microorganisms. In the United States, new varieties of asexually repro-ducible plants (like tubers) can be protected with plant patents, which last for 20 years. Sexually reproduced plants (like grains) are protected with plant variety cer-tificates issued by the Department of Agriculture. Plants may also be protected by utility patents. In many countries plants are protected under the provisions of the International Union for the Protection of New Varieties of Plants (UPOV). Unlike util-ity patents, protection under UPOV can allow breeders to use the protected variety for breeding purposes, and farmers to save and plant the seeds from year to year.

Copyright essentials

Copyright is the proprietary intellectual property domain of ideas expressed in a tangible medium. A copyright protects original works of authorship such as literary, dramatic, musical, artistic, and certain other intellectual works. (See Table 4.3.)

Table 4.3. Copyright basics

COPYRIGHT

PROTECTABLE SUBJECT MATTER	Works of authorship, including writings, books, papers, photographs, music, art, movies, recording, software, and the like, reduced to a tangible medium of expression
GOVERNMENT REGISTRATION	Generally not required once a work is fixed in a tangible medium of expression Judicial enforcement generally requires a copyright notice, and in the U.S., registration at the Copyright Office
SCOPE OF RIGHTS	Prevent others from reproducing or distributing copies; preparing derivative works; performing or displaying the work publicly; and transmitting sound recordings
DURATION	At least 50 years from publication (under TRIPS Agreement) In US, for new works, life of author plus 70 years or 95 years from first publication for works made for hire
LEGAL BASIS	National laws consistent with TRIPS Part II, Section 7, Articles 9–14 (see Appendix A), and the Berne Convention In the U.S., federal legislation codified in Title 17 of the U.S. Code, and interpreted in regulations and judicial decisions

Copyright attaches to a work upon publication, without need for notice or registration. Publication automatically puts a work of authorship into the copyright domain, internationally. However, certain formalities may be required before copyrights can be enforced. These include providing notice (most easily given with the conventional © symbol, author, and year of publication), and, in the United States, registering the work in the copyright office.

A work can remain in the copyright domain for a very long time, typically for 50 or 95 years, after which it becomes part of the public domain. Alternatively the author may, by dedication to the public, allow the publication to become part of the public domain upon publication. For example, the United States government takes no copyright interest in any of its publications. Alternatively, many copyright owners issue a blanket license to users permitting them to use the work freely without fee. Although copyright still remains with the author or publisher, most people think of such blanket licenses as putting the publication into the public domain with respect to copyrights. As discussed below, the concept of public domain is unhelpful here, the more significant issue being whether other people can access the work to meet their needs.

A copyright gives the owner the right to prevent others from reproducing or distributing copies of the work; preparing derivative works; performing or displaying the work publicly; and making digital transmissions of sound recordings. Although copyright is international in scope, the right of enforcement is limited to the courts of individual countries. The owner may file a lawsuit in a particular country and seek an injunction against reproducing or distributing copies, and damages. Damages may include a reasonable royalty, lost profits, and damages set by statute. A

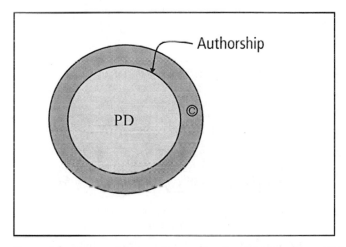

Figure 4.5. The copyright tree. New works of authorship, when published, go into the copyright domain (©), and move into the public domain upon expiration, or by dedication.

defendant may argue that the accused work is different than the copyrighted work or may argue that the copyrighted work is mere data or otherwise not entitled to protection by copyright.

The boundary between the domain of copyright and the noncopyright domain may be simplified to the concept of "authorship," as shown in Figure 4.5. Newly authored works are copyrightable. Mere data, and old works, are not.

As a practical matter, no intellectual property right is air tight. Copyright is particularly leaky. Enforcement is very difficult because of the huge number of copyright works, and the ease with which they may be reproduced. With photocopiers, audiotape recorders, videotape recorders, and now DVD and CD duping with computers, the sure rewards of authorship may be limited to the point of first sale. As the saying goes, for some countries, only one legitimate copy of a computer program is sold there. All the rest are duplicated without permission.

The possibility of arrest and criminal prosecution for copyright violations presumably deters some illegal copying, but copyright owners often compete with piracy by self-help measures. For example, they provide licensed copies of superior quality (books being nicer than photocopied packets), or package their work with additional attractive materials (CD cover art and lyric booklets), or use electronic means of thwarting the copying, effective with most casual copiers but not with skilled "hackers" common in many countries.

Trademark essentials

Trademarks are words, symbols, colors, phrases, designs or combinations of these which identify the source of goods or services, and distinguish the goods and services of one seller from those sold by other sources. A good old example is the brand burnt by a cowboy into the haunch of a heifer to mark the cattle from a particular ranch. (See Table 4.4.)

Table 4.4. Trademark basics

TRADEMARKS

PROTECTABLE SUBJECT MATTER	Words, personal names, letters, numerals, figurative elements, and combinations of colors, symbols, or other devices used to distinguish goods or services Includes service marks, certification marks, and collective membership marks
GOVERNMENT REGISTRATION	Trademark application depicting the mark and the goods or services is filed in each country's trademark agency (e.g., U.S. Patent and Trademark Office), examined, and registered as a trademark In the United States, no registration needed for common law rights based on using a trademark
SCOPE OF RIGHTS	Exclude others from using the mark to cause a likelihood of confusion to the consumer (e.g., counterfeiting) For famous trademarks, prevent others from commercially "diluting" the mark
DURATION	Generally 10 years from registration, renewable indefinitely for additional 10 year terms, as long as mark is used properly and not abandoned
LEGAL BASIS	National laws consistent with TRIPS Part II, Sections 15–21 (see Appendix A) In the United States, federal legislation codified in Title 15 of the U.S. Code, and interpreted in regulations and judicial decisions, and state laws

A person or organization typically obtains rights to a trademark by registering the trademark under the trademark laws of an individual country. The applicant identifies the trademark with a drawing, and specifies the goods or services with which it is associated (e.g., Coca-Cola for carbonated soft drinks). If there is no confusingly similar mark, the registration is granted in that country. In most countries, the first to file an application is generally entitled to a trademark. This often leads multinational businesses to race to file trademark applications in many different countries. In the United States, first use of a trademark in commerce also provides some legal rights, and in the absence of registrations, trademark rights are allocated based on first use in each geographic locality.

The value of a trademark is grounded in its distinctiveness – the capability of the public to rely on the trademark to identify goods or services as being provided by a particular source and to distinguish those goods and services from those provided by other sources. A trademark conveys an expectation of a certain quality (or lack thereof) of the goods or services produced by that source. Almost anything distinctive can serve as a trademark, including distinctive colors, smells, and sounds, and even the shape of a product or packaging can be protected as "trade dress." Trademarks are characterized, in order of distinctiveness from most to none, as inherently distinctive or fanciful ("Kodak"), arbitrary ("Apple" for computers), suggestive ("Grameen," meaning rural, for banking services for poor villagers in Bangladesh), descriptive ("Daily News" for newspapers), or generic names that can not serve as a trademark ("Bread" for bread).

A trademark registration lasts 10 years but can be renewed, in theory, forever. Some brands are over a century old, but few are much older than that (including for example Cambridge University). Many formerly great trademarks have lapsed for nonuse as names change and companies go out of business (like Pan American Airways and Studebaker cars). This reflects the continuous process of innovation and creative destruction. Indeed the PanAm trademark has been revived by a small local airline.

A trademark owner may enforce exclusive rights by filing a lawsuit in a particular country to prevent someone else from using a similar mark with similar products. The main issue is whether there is a likelihood of confusion to the consumer in that country. Counterfeiting is the simplest case – same mark, same product, as with fake "Rolex" watches sold on many street corners – and criminal prosecution may be possible. In civil litigation, punitive damages can be awarded for counterfeiting. In many cases, the marks and goods are somewhat different, and the cases turn on whether consumers would likely be confused as to the source of the product. Civil remedies include injunction, seizure, and damages (royalties or lost profits). A defendant generally argues that the marks and goods are not similar, and that the mark is weak.

There are several pitfalls that can cause a trademark owner to lose exclusive rights. These include selling or licensing a "naked" trademark without the associated goodwill, or licensing without monitoring the quality of the licensee's trademarked goods. Rights can also be lost by failing to stop others from using the trademark. Finally, exclusivity can be lost if a formerly strong trademark comes to represent the generic form of the product or service – if the trademark no longer distinguishes the specific goods or services from those of others. This is a risk for the most innovative products. For example, if a trademark such as Xerox becomes the common identifying name for the trademarked product (copiers), the mark becomes generic rather than an identification of the trademark owner's particular photocopiers. If this happened, Xerox would no longer distinguish its own copiers, and anyone could sell "Xerox" machines. This is the fate that befell "cellophane," "escalator," and many other former trademarks.

Owners of famous marks can prevent others from commercially "diluting" the mark by using it on other goods, even if there is no immediate confusion. For example, use of "Toyota" as the name of a breakfast cereal might be prevented under this theory, even though no one would be confused into thinking that the auto manufacturer had manufactured the food.

The boundary between the trademark domain and the nontrademark domain with respect can be represented by the notion of "distinctiveness." (See Figure 4.6.)

For example, an innovator selects a new word or design that is distinctive when used in marketing the innovator's goods or services (for sale or otherwise), and this symbol serves as a trademark for the goods or services with which it is associated, in the trademark domain. If the word or design is not distinctive, it remains in the public domain, available for use by any one. A trademark generally remains accessible

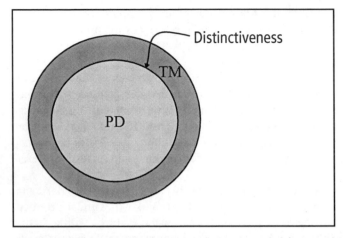

Figure 4.6. The trademark tree. A new distinctive symbol for a product expands the trademark domain (TM), but remains in the public domain for other purposes, and moves into the public domain if it no longer distinguishes the product's source.

for other people to use. (A trademark on "Apple" for computers or records does not prevent us from using the word for a fruit.) Eventually a trademark may lose exclusivity and move into the public domain. Nothing lasts forever.

Related intellectual property rights

There are numerous other legal rights established under the TRIPS Agreement and various national laws, but for purposes of this book, we shall relate each of them to the main four types of intellectual property. If trade secrets, patents, copyrights, and trademarks can each be thought of as a type of innovation tree, these rights might be referred to as shrubs.

Domain names. Domain names are conceptually closely related to trademarks. Since they burst on the scene in the 1980s these assets have become extremely valuable and are intermingled with brand names. Imagine the value of www.google.com. Domain names may give rise to trademark rights, but because there is no connection between a domain name and a particular good or service, they are distinct from trademark rights. Many different organizations around the world can use the same trademark in different countries and on different goods, but there is only one "dot com" domain for that name. Also, a domain name need not serve as a trademark. The source of protection, the right to exclude, and the duration of domain names differ from trademarks. Domain names must be reserved with one of the domain name registries, and are paid for on an annual basis. Very similar domain names may coexist.

Geographical indications. Protection of geographical indications is established under the TRIPS Agreement and many national laws. These rights are also related to trademarks. They restrict use of terms such as Champagne and Tequila, goods that have a specific geographical origin and have certain qualities associated with that place. A geographical indication is usually the name of the place of origin of the goods. For example, agricultural products often have qualities that derive from local factors, such as climate and soil. There has been an effort in recent years to extend this type of protection to Basmati rice and other developing country agricultural products.

Databases. Databases are not subject to copyright protection if they consist merely of data, without meeting the legal standards for originality required for copyright protection. Quasi-copyright concepts apply, however, because databases can require extensive investment of time and effort to compile and maintain, and be very valuable when used in a computer readable form, individually or on the Internet. The European Union's Database Directive (1998) calls for laws preventing unauthorized copying of substantial portions of a database for 15 years after the database was produced. International treaty negotiations continue, as do legislative discussions in the U.S. Congress. The full range of intellectual property arguments (pro and con) are being brought to bear on the topic. A necessary feature of database protection is that it is limited to a proprietary compilation of data, not the original sources of data, which remain accessible to anyone else.

Biological materials. Plant variety protection was mentioned in connection with patents, above. Biological materials themselves (microorganisms, plants, and animals, and parts of them) are of course tangible things, not intellectual, and originate in nature, not invention. Nonetheless, the legal rights that attach to biological materials have certain similarities to intellectual property. Obtaining access to biological materials may be analogous to accessing trade secret information. Genetic materials can be readily reproduced, without change, like copyright works. And biological materials can be extracted, modified, and used, like inventions. Like intellectual property rights, biological materials can be transferred by agreement. The 1992 Convention on Biological Diversity (CBD) set out some general principles for obtaining and transferring biological materials, and has been implemented in various national laws.

Employee rights. People are the source of all intellectual property, and therefore they have certain intellectual property rights that they can retain or transfer to an employer. In most countries employees are entitled to bring with them into their employment whatever generalized knowledge and training they have learned, and they are entitled to take those skills with them when they leave. Thus we continue to enjoy the legacy of the abolition of slavery. U.S. law distinguishes between the employee's general skills and the employer's specific trade secrets, which belong to the employer. Employees may also have certain rights to their own inventions. European patent law requires that the inventor be given notice if her employer files a patent application. In the United States, patent applications must be filed in the name of the inventor, which provides similar protection to employees. In many countries, employees have the right to be recognized as authors of copyright material, but generally that right is transferred to the employer.

Traditional knowledge. Traditional or indigenous knowledge refers to the cultural heritage that identifies many communities, generally passed down through generations, orally. It may include music, folklore, stories, religious practices, legal systems, and medicinal and agricultural practices. Globalization is overwhelming many traditional communities, wiping out their language, knowledge, and practices. This topic is undergoing extremely intense scrutiny by scholars and advocates for developing countries. The CBD, in Article 8(j), recognized traditional knowledge as a quasi-IP right, stating that members should "respect, preserve and maintain knowledge, innovations, and practices of indigenous and local communities embodying traditional lifestyles relevant to the conservation and sustainable use of biological diversity" and should promote use, subject to approval of the traditional knowledge holders and sharing of any resulting benefits. WIPO formed a standing committee on Genetic Resources, Traditional Knowledge, and Folklore to explore ways to apply principles of intellectual property to traditional knowledge. India and other countries are establishing national systems to register and reward traditional knowledge, but the task is extremely difficult for many reasons. Traditional knowledge is not well documented. It may be collective, not individual. It may be old, not new. The social and moral value of traditional knowledge seems to far exceed its economic value in financial terms.

Although the process is far from complete, the effort to apply intellectual property rights to traditional knowledge teaches us much about the fundamental concepts and dynamics of the IP system, including how the innovation cycle revolves in very different global communities, the difficulty in defining a boundary between the public accessible domain and an exclusive proprietary domain, the inherent controversy between access and exclusivity, and the continuous process by which social debate changes intellectual property law, which in turn shapes society. In time, we can hope for legal systems to evolve that may help protect traditional knowledge so as to provide incentives to conserve it, and to develop and renew it in living traditions.

INTERACTIONS BETWEEN DIFFERENT TYPES OF INTELLECTUAL PROPERTY

We have highlighted some essential characteristics of the four basic types of intellectual property – trade secret, patent, copyright, and trademark – by looking at isolated cross sections of innovation trees. This simplified analysis is a necessary step to understanding intellectual property because each separate type of intellectual property asset is distinct, and gives the owner distinct legal rights. For example, a patent gives the right to prohibit others from using the invention. A trademark gives the right to identify goods or services using that trademark and to exclude others from using it.

However, by looking at IP rights in isolation, and the innovation tree in cross-section, we omit much of the dynamic complexity of intellectual property – the fruits and leaves and larger growth process that makes up the innovation cycle. Usually, different forms of intellectual property rights exist concurrently in a particular innovation. For example, several different intellectual property rights coexist in the Georgetown University logo on the school's website. The logo itself serves as a trademark for educational services. The graphic image and colors might also be subject to copyright. The HTML code that resides on the webpage is copyrightable computer code. The computer network serving the website contains numerous patented components. And so on.

Indeed, most innovations implicate several different types of intellectual property protection. It is therefore a mistake to look at any one type of intellectual property right at a time, in isolation. Databases with limited access are covered by trade secrecy, and may be subject to copyright protection if they include original text, or the way they are arrayed is in itself original, and the data structure may even be patented, as with certain gene chip arrays used in genomics laboratories. Genetic sequences can be patented if their utility is known, and can be kept secret in the meantime. Biological materials including plant varieties can be kept as closely held trade secrets, or patented. Computer programs are subject to copyright, the general methods they employ can be patented, and the source code can be kept as a trade secret. All these innovations can have trademarks associated with them. As we will see below, all these rights can be transferred to someone else by assignment or license.

An invention may lead to trade secret rights as well as the right to obtain a patent in the invention. A technical manual may be subject to trade secret rights and also copyright. A substance may be patented and the product may be marketed under a strong trademark.

Fictional characters in a movie or comic book present another combination of rights. A Superman comic is of course protected by copyright, and the artwork cannot be copied. But the Superman character himself is a registered trademark of DC Comics, and any use of the character or the "S" logo (as in the Superman movies) requires a license of trademark rights from the owner. Mickey Mouse's image is owned by the Disney Co., which, in addition to managing its vast copyright collection, has mastered the business of merchandising the trademark rights in its characters from all of its movies in all sorts of products from stuffed animals to school supplies.

So, just as several different kinds of trees can grow together in the same forest, the act of creation gives rise to the possibility of several types of intellectual property protection, and gives the creator a choice as to which ones to pursue. That decision strongly influences the future path for the creative product, and whether it becomes widely adopted in commerce and the broader society.

Conversion from one type of intellectual property to another

Intellectual property rights are dynamic and can be converted from one form to another. An innovator's new idea originates as a secret. If published, the trade secret is lost and copyright is created. (See Figure 4.7.) The copyright would simply protect the specific text of the article from being copied. The public would have the right to use the information in the article, to create or use the process or device described there, and to write their own articles about the process or device, without violating the copyright owner's rights.

Similarly, if the innovator includes the information in a patent application, which is then published, the trade secret as such enters the public domain. However, if and when the patent is issued, the patent rights will vest in the patent proprietary domain. For example, for a new antiviral AIDS drug developed in a pharmaceutical company laboratory, the drug may be patented while information about its chemical structure and synthesis are no longer trade secrets, having been published. In practice,

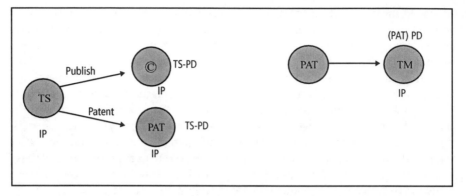

Figure 4.7. Conversion between types of IP rights. An innovation that begins as a trade secret can be converted to a copyright by publication, or to a patent, with loss of trade secret rights. A patent can be leveraged to expand trademark rights that survive after patent expiration. The proprietary domain is shown in the circles, with the accessible public domain outside.

innovations are complex and some aspects may be published, some patented, and others kept as trade secrets.

Another example of conversion between types of IP rights is the use of a patent as leverage to expand trademark rights that survive after patent expiration. For example, the popular artificial sweetener aspartame was discovered accidentally in the 1960s and a patent on a process for making it issued in the 1980s to G. D. Searle & Co., which gained approval for its use from the U.S. Food and Drug Administration in 1985. Searle built up its market and its trademark under the "Nutrasweet" brand. Monsanto acquired Searle and spun out the aspartame business into the Nutrasweet Company to strengthen the trademark. When the patent expired in 1992, "Nutrasweet" remained the dominant brand of aspartame, even though competitors became free to manufacture the product under other names, such as "Equal."

The compatibility of copyright, trade secrecy, patents, and trademark is outlined in Table 4.5. This shows how different activities convert the various forms of IP rights one to another.

Upon creation, a valuable idea can automatically be considered a trade secret but lacks protection as to other proprietary rights. Referring to the innovation cycle, if the creator does not share the idea, then it can never be widely adopted in the community, and can never enter the broadest sphere of the public domain where others can access and benefit from the information. The first step on the path from creation to adopted innovation occurs when the creator discloses the idea with someone else. If this is done confidentially, trade secret rights remain. If the creator decides to tell the idea to someone else, without any restriction, the idea moves fully into the public domain.

If the creator publishes the idea, for example in an article or book, or on a blog website, copyright attaches to the publication (but not the idea). Publication can also occur as part of the patenting process, and trademark rights might attach to a publication as well. Upon publication, no trade secrets remain.

Table 4.5. Matrix of conversion and compatibility of various types of IP

Valuable idea	Copyright	Trade secret	Patent	Trademark
Create	−	+	−	−
Disclose	−	?	?	−
Publish	+	−	?	?
Patent	?	−	+	?
Use as trademark	?	?	?	+

IP rights that necessarily arise at each stage are shown as "+," those that may be obtained are shown as "?," and those that can not be obtained are shown as "−".

If the idea leads to a commercial product or service, the innovator will likely protect the associated trademark. Trademarks can exist whether or not the underlying product is secret, or protected by copyright or patent. It is possible to have copyright in a product or its packaging, and although the trademark itself, by definition, can not be secret, one can maintain the trade secrets in a commercial product if it can not be easily reverse-engineered. For example, the components of a formulation may be listed in the ingredients, but the process for combining them may be secret. Trademark rights are also compatible with patented products.

AN INNOVATION FOREST

A single innovation tree is a limited metaphor for intellectual property's passage through the innovation cycle. The life and death of one tree is a linear process – sprouting, growing, maturing, and dying. When many different trees grow together and interact with each other in a forest, the cycle of life is much more apparent. At any time, new trees are sprouting from the soil, young saplings are growing in the understory, and the oldest trees form the forest canopy and contribute the greatest number of seeds. Finally, dead standing and fallen trees create habitat for wildlife and food for the insects, bacteria, and fungi that return the tree slowly to the soil.

The image of an innovation forest is meant to convey the diversity of ideas and intellectual property, and the longer term cycles of innovation. (See Figure 4.8.) Many ideas can exist together, and several IP rights may coexist in each.

The identification of a new gene may spawn a trade secret and rights in the biological material, suggested in the first column of Figure 4.8. Older ideas may have one, a few, or all types of IP rights associated with them. Idea 1 may be a new antiretroviral drug, with a trade secret, a patent, a copyright (covering the publications and packaging relating to the drug), and a trademark (for the brand name), as well as other rights related to biological materials used in producing the drug, all of which are symbolized in the second column. In short, there can be a full portfolio of intellectual property rights associated with idea 1.

Similarly, idea 5 may have a full portfolio of intellectual property rights, but idea 2 may have no copyright associated with it (no publications), idea 3 may have no rights other than the main four, and idea 4 may have no patents. To complete the

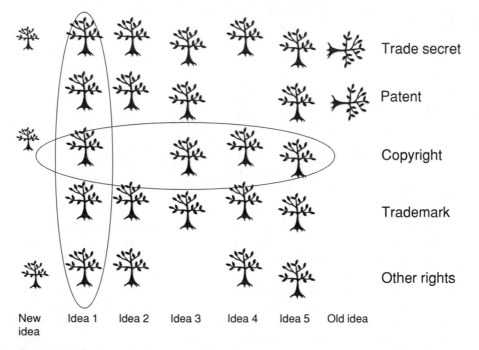

                                                              Trade secret

                                                              Patent

                                                              Copyright

                                                              Trademark

                                                              Other rights

New   Idea 1   Idea 2   Idea 3   Idea 4   Idea 5   Old idea
idea

Figure 4.8. The innovation forest. New ideas give rise to young innovation trees of the various IP types, which mature, become old, and die, joining the public domain, as other ideas join them. Two IP portfolios are shown; one covers all aspects of idea 1, the other includes just copyrights from ideas 1–5.

picture, IP rights expire in old ideas, metaphorically represented by dead and fallen innovation trees, shown on the right of Figure 4.8.

A different type of IP portfolio can be defined. Here, one person holds one type of IP right in a range of ideas, for example copyright, as shown by the horizontal oval in Figure 4.8. This is the situation, for example, with a publisher who holds copyright to a series of books and journal articles on a wide range of topics, but has no other rights to the information in them, or any patentable inventions or trademarks that apply to the products discussed there.

The important features of an innovation forest are a variety of ideas in various stages of development, covered by appropriate types of intellectual property. The IP rights can be aggregated into useful end products suitable for adoption in the broader community. How they can be transferred and used is the topic of Chapter 5.

SUMMARY. The innovation cycle is dynamic, like the cycle of life in a forest – creative people use existing knowledge to come up with new ideas and works, which then mature and grow and are adopted in society, or die and decay, and can be used by others as the cycle revolves. New ideas can be protected with IP rights, and as they become old, they become increasingly accessible. The boundaries between protected and accessible knowledge are defined by laws which change over time and still differ some from country to country despite harmonization and a trend toward stronger rights under the TRIPS agreement. Some essentials for each type of intellectual property are outlined in this chapter, with details revisited later. Each IP type has a different scope of protectable subject matter, scope of rights, rules for government registration (or not), and duration, as outlined in this chapter. **Trade secrecy** has roots as old as Egyptian Pharaohs' scribes, and covers valuable information not generally known in a trade. National trade secret laws prohibit people from stealing or disclosing trade secrets. Rights arise from self-help secrecy measures, and can theoretically last forever, but usually dissipate after several years when the information loses value or becomes publicly known, and therefore accessible. **Patents** date back more than 500 years. Governments grant patents based on a detailed description of an invention, which is published and therefore available for others to read. But the patent gives the right to exclude others from making, using, or selling the patented invention during its 20-year term, after which the invention enters the public domain. Old knowledge is not legally patentable, and in principle remains available for anyone to use, although the patenting process is imperfect and patents are sometimes granted for old ideas. **Copyright** law also has ancient roots, and applies to a wide range of authored works upon publication. Copyright lasts at least 50 years and up to 95 years in the United States. Copyright notices and registration are required to perfect rights in some countries. Copyright works are accessible but only through authorized distribution channels – a copyright owner can prevent copying, distribution, or adaptation of the work. **Trademarks** are protected words and symbols that distinguish and identify the commercial source of goods and services. Trademarks must be registered in each country for rights to apply, although rights arise in some countries based on use. A registration provides the basis for excluding others from using confusingly similar symbols on similar goods or services. Registrations expire but are renewable indefinitely. Other **quasi-intellectual property rights** apply to domain names, geographical indications, databases, biological materials, employee rights, and traditional knowledge. Each has its own balance of exclusivity and accessibility. As with the trees in a forest, these many types of rights interact with each other and can be converted from one to the other, as when a trade secret is disclosed in a patent application or a copyright publication. Innovation, as part of life, is a messy process, but we can begin to manage it by learning to categorize the individual ideas, both new and old, the types of IP protection that apply to them, and how these innovations and IP rights relate to one another in the products and works flowing from creative people out into society.

5 The ABCDs of Intellectual Property: Flow and Infringement of Rights

This chapter gives a broad conceptual overview of the transfer of intellectual property from A to B to C to D, and how it relates to the innovation cycle. The summary includes the types of rights that can flow, how they can be transferred in whole, or in part, and the nature of joint works and collaborations. Transfer of IP rights provides users of innovations with sufficient permission for their activities. Infringement can be understood as an absence of such permissions. Liability for infringement can flow in a similar fashion to the flow of IP rights. The topics of this chapter are revisited in Chapters 14 and 15.

* * * * * *

In a broad sense, laws in most countries treat the various types of intellectual property rights like any other type of property – land, buildings, lumber, crops, electronics, cars, money, or stock certificates. That is, people can buy or sell intellectual property, use it, profit from it, and exclude others from using it. However, the transfer and flow of intellectual property has its own general rules, and each particular intellectual property "tree" has its peculiarities.

The transfer of ideas from creator to developer to consumer is a complex process that is crucial to how the innovation cycle operates. The channels of distribution for the rights may be commercial markets, or noncommercial channels such as educational, academic, or governmental agencies. The decisions made by the creator and each of the people and organizations downstream influence whether the idea is broadly disseminated, narrowly adopted in a particular community, or not adopted at all, becoming lost to society. Intellectual property management plays an important role in this process.

The availability of IP can influence the strategic decision of what ideas to invest in. And, certainly, once the decision is made about which ideas to pursue, intellectual property management becomes central to the tactical implementation of that strategy.

The transfer of intellectual property rights is very similar to the transfer of tangible, physical property. Rights may be transferred by sale, by gift, by license, by court order, or by operation of law. Generally, the owner of intellectual property rights can transfer some or all of those rights. Some rights may be withheld or reserved, and not transferred. For example, most consumer software copyright licenses give the user the right to use the software, but not to make copies for other users.

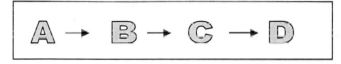

Figure 5.1. The ABCDs of IP transfer. Rights flow from creator A to subsequent recipients of the rights and of products that embody them, such as employer B, licensee C, and customer D.

We refer to the "ABCDs" of transferring intellectual property, a general model that can be used to decode even the most complex intellectual property transaction. (See Figure 5.1.)

Intellectual property transfer agreements are limited to the parties involved. In the A → B → C → D (or ABCD) model, the arrows show that there is some type of relationship between each of the parties. A strikes a deal with B, B has a deal with C, and C has a relationship with D.

For example, employee A takes a photograph, and transfers rights to her employer B, who licenses the rights to publisher C to use on the cover of the magazine, which is sold to consumers D. Or inventor A obtains a European patent on a new pump, A sells all the rights in the patent to investor B, via a complete assignment. A has no exclusive right to the machine after the assignment. Investor B then grants company C an exclusive license to use the pump for five years. Investor B retains the right to use the pump after five years. The license that B granted to C permits C to sell the pumps to consumer D.

Even clicking "I accept" on a software license agreement downloaded from the Internet establishes a relationship between the software licensor and the end user licensee. But generally A has no relationship with C, B has no direct connection with D, and D has no connection with A. Therefore, how can A control what C does? And what kind of responsibility does A have to C or D? According to the doctrine of "privity," only the parties to a contract are bound by it. More distant third parties have no direct relationship and their rights and obligations are limited.

In contrast, intellectual property rights generally apply to everybody in those countries in which rights exist, and do not depend on a contract. You would violate copyright law if you copied this book, whether or not you agree directly with me that you will not copy it.

WHAT CAN FLOW?

The ABCD model could generally apply to anything in commerce, of course, including food, shelter, clothes, and stock certificates, which can be transferred from A to B to C to D. Here, we focus on transfer of the fruits of the innovation tree. This includes anything that results from human creative effort, typically the different intellectual property "trees" and "shrubs" described in Chapter 4. The unifying concept is that the recipient gains access to the fruits of the innovation tree from the person holding it, and could not otherwise have access. Here are some examples:

- Intellectual property rights (patents, trade secrets, trademarks, copyrights)
- Information including text, data, and software
- Electronic equipment
- Biological material
- Chemical reagents
- Music, videos, and artworks
- Employee rights on joining and leaving an employer.

Dell sells computer equipment bundled with licenses to patents and software. Sigma–Aldrich sells proprietary chemical reagents and biological materials to industry and academic researchers, with associated licenses. Hospital patients sign informed consent forms allowing cell samples to be used by researchers. A farmer sells a rice plant to a breeder who will use it to try to improve disease resistance. A musician goes into a recording company studio, and plays into a microphone to make a recording, which can then be sold onward to consumers. All these transfers are premised on the choice of the owner, and in principle any of them may choose not to transfer their rights.

Basic deal terms

More details about the transfer of intellectual property are provided in Chapter 15. For now, we can identify some basic concepts in the flow of IP rights. First, IP deals relate only to the domain of intellectual property. Information in the public domain, for which no exclusive rights are involved, can flow without the need for any transfer agreement. You can't give what you don't have. If you don't have IP rights, you don't have the right to exclude others. The rest of the world is free to operate in that domain without permission.

Second, intellectual property rights are usually transferred individually. Even in a blanket license of all IP rights – patent, trademark, trade secret, and copyright – each one has separate scope and should be considered separately. Third, the scope of any license can be determined using a "who, what, when, where, and why" type of journalistic approach:

- Who are the parties?
- What types of IP rights will be licensed, in what countries, for what fields of use?
- When is the license effective, what is its term and how can it be terminated?
- Where – what is the geographic field of the license, and where will performance take place?
- Why – what is the goal and purpose of the deal?

In negotiating an intellectual property license, as with any other transaction, it is important to remember the elements of the deal. Even though the technology may be complex and the legal definitions difficult to grasp, transactions for intellectual property are fundamentally the same kind of deal-making people have always done for as long as there has been human society. The most basic terms of a deal are the same for intellectual property as they are for a fruit seller in the markets of ancient Athens, the silk seller in Bangkok, or the computer dealer in lower

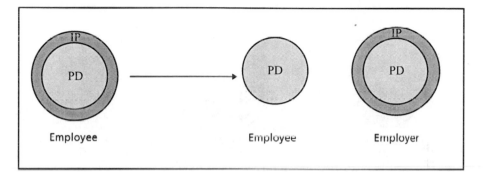

Figure 5.2. Full transfer of IP rights. An employee has IP rights and transfers them to the employer so that the employer has all rights and the employee has none, although both may still use what is in the public domain (PD).

Manhattan – the parties exchange something of value (consideration) and agree to be bound by the terms of the deal (mutual assent). If so, there is a binding contract that can be enforced in court. Of course the rules differ from country to country and there are many more exceptions than would fit in this book.

As a general rule, as long as both parties commit to provide each other with consideration, there will be a binding contract that would be enforceable in court.

Full or partial transfer

Creator A may transfer to B all or only some of the IP rights in a particular innovation. For example, employee A may assign all trade secrets, patents, and copyrights to the employer. These rights are transferred absolutely and entirely (by assignment). See Figure 5.2. In this case, the employee ends up with no intellectual property rights, and the employer obtains all of them. The employee and the employer both have access to matter in the public domain because it is unrestricted.

Alternatively, rights can be transferred in pieces so that creator A divides out and transfers to B one portion of A's rights, but keeps the rest of those rights. See Figure 5.3. For example, A could retain title to the IP right and give B a license for a limited field of use or geographical scope. Person A could license use of a chemical for agricultural but not pharmaceutical uses. Author A may give an exclusive license for a Spanish language book to be distributed in Mexico, but not other countries.

Joint works and collaboration

The fruits of invention often come from the creative work of several individuals working together. Because of the joint effort, the individual rights flow together into a single intellectual property asset. The collaborators can then become joint owners of the intellectual property by virtue of their joint creative endeavor. See Figure 5.4. For example, for most Beatles songs, Paul McCartney wrote the music and John Lennon wrote the lyrics, and the band performed them together. Likewise, biotechnology inventions are usually made by several employees of a corporation or research

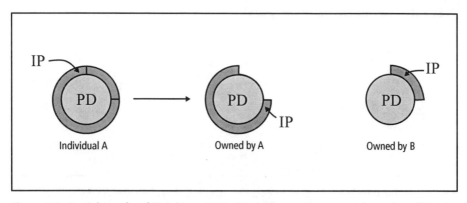

Figure 5.3. Partial transfer of IP rights. Individual A divides out the upper right section of IP rights and transfers it to person B, who owns that portion, while A owns the remainder.

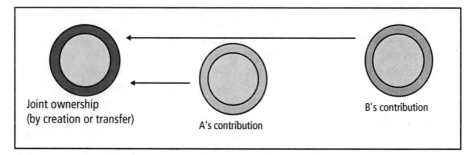

Figure 5.4. Joint works. Creators A and B both contribute to a joint work, depicted as two light outer rings representing IP rights flowing into one darker ring, either by joint creation, or by transfer.

institution, working together. A Peruvian collective of Alpaca growers developed ALPACAMARK as a trademark to identify their fabric products and received assistance from PIIPA.

With joint ownership, each individual generally has separate and equal rights to use, modify, sell, or license the work. What a joint owner lacks is full exclusivity and the right to grant exclusive licenses or assign full title. That is, joint owner A generally cannot stop joint owner B from practicing an invention or performing a copyrighted song, or licensing rights to a competitor of owner A. Such exclusive rights may only be granted with the agreement of both joint owners. The principles are generally similar to joint ownership of real estate by a husband and wife, or joint ownership of the shares of a privately held corporation. Depending on the specific asset and the country, each joint owner may have certain obligations to the others, analogously to shareholders in a corporation.

Collaborators may each contribute a different type of intellectual property to a broader technology or other innovation. For example, person A may make a patentable invention that speeds the passage of DNA through a sequencing machine, person B may author copyrightable software that permits the machine to track the DNA, person C may come up with a new trademark, and person D may put together a

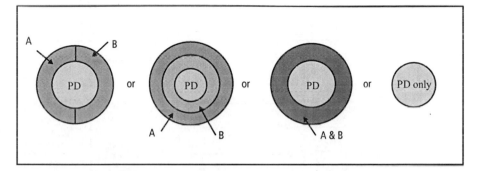

Figure 5.5. Allocations of rights by two parties. A and B can each own specific shares of IP rights they created or obtained (first image), B can own earlier rights and A later rights (second image), A and B can be joint owners of completely commingled rights (third image), or both can donate their rights to the public domain (fourth image).

trade secret business plan on how to commercialize the sequencer. These four individuals may have an agreement for them to jointly own all the combined intellectual property rights, together, or each may own his or her own rights.

In the most common case of joint ownership, both creators transfer their rights to a third party, often their employer, or sometimes a separate entity set up to aggregate the intellectual assets of participants. Lennon and McCartney did not hold their copyrights jointly, but transferred them to a partnership entity set up by the Beatles, and later to Apple Records.

There are several different ways to allocate rights in joint works. In one, A and B share the same intellectual property divided up into discrete and separate parts, for example by geographic area or technical field of use. (See Figure 5.5.)

Second, A and B can share separate types of intellectual property, or intellectual property in different overlapping technology (such as two components of one device). For example, with respect to a website, aspects are in the public domain, for example, the linkage to the Internet. Other aspects remain in A's intellectual property domain. Examples are design features, software scripts, trademarks, the domain name, photographs, and patented methods such as Amazon.com's "one click shopping." The creations of B might be separately protected, such as the software platform on which the website is based, a database linked to the site, and copyright in certain text and images posted by the service provider. Because these two individuals work separately, without collaborating, they each have their own sphere of intellectual property, and there is no overlap between them. Both can work in their own IP domain, but not in the other's.

In a third way to allocate rights, A and B can have pure joint ownership with IP rights completely commingled. Fourth, A and B may both dedicate their work to the public domain, so neither holds any IP rights.

Transfers between collaborators

When working with collaborators, it is important to choose which arrangement is best, and to plan the relationship so that intellectual property is allocated to the

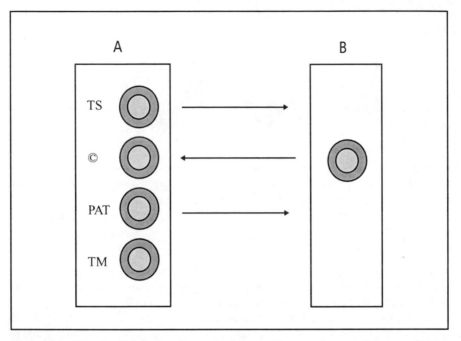

Figure 5.6. Allocating IP rights in software development. Company A owns a full range of IP rights in a program, and licenses trade secrets and patents to consultant B so that B may write a new program, the copyright for which is transferred back to A.

proper person. The different components of intellectual property may be packaged and transferred or exchanged, together or separately. By way of illustration, collaborative development of a software program for genomic analysis may involve trade secret, copyright, patent, and trademark rights. Each of these rights can be transferred (licensed or assigned) individually or together. In one scenario, party A has trade secrets regarding genetic data of cancer patients to be embedded in the computer program; a patent on the underlying method; copyrighted source code; and a trademark for the program. (See Figure 5.6.) Party B is a consultant with software programming skills. Party A pays B to write a new program to help find cancer drugs, and gives B a license to use the trade secrets and the patent for programming purposes, but not to use the trademark or existing copyrighted material. Party B agrees to give a cross license or assignment back to A covering B's copyright in the new program.

In this example it clearly makes sense for party B to author the program and to transfer the copyright to party A. It is often a much trickier problem when establishing a collaboration to allocate the rights to future intellectual property. This is difficult because at the time of entering into the collaboration it may not yet be clear who will do what work, what intellectual property will be created, if any, and who will actually succeed in being the creator. Nevertheless, good strategies are available by which each party may retain control over that which is most important to its future activities. This will be covered in more detail in Chapter 15.

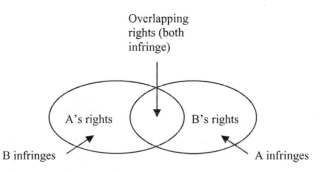

Figure 5.7. Blocking rights. Two parties can infringe each other's IP rights, and if their rights overlap, both infringe each other's rights in the area of overlap.

Infringement: Basic dynamics

To understand the basic dynamics of infringement, it is helpful to consider the distinctions between the IP domain and the accessible domain. No one infringes any rights with activities that fall completely in the public domain, or otherwise in the accessible domain. Infringement occurs when party A undertakes an unlicensed activity that falls within an intellectual property domain owned by party B. Likewise, party B infringes by acting without permission within the boundaries of party A's rights.

A critical issue in evaluating infringement is the exact boundary of the intellectual property domain. This is a simple concept to master, but in practice, the boundary defining the scope of intellectual property rights can be very difficult to define. Indeed, much IP lawyering and management work is devoted to researching and analyzing where such boundaries exist, and possibly negotiating or litigating over disagreements to resolve the issue.

If the rights of party A and party B overlap, then each would be infringing the other's rights by undertaking activities in the other's IP domain, and this would include the overlapping zone. (See Figure 5.7.) One who holds IP rights merely has the right to exclude others, not permission to practice the protected innovation. In the area of overlap, each party holds blocking rights. Both parties would need to obtain permission from each other (via a cross-license) to undertake any activities in the overlapping area without infringement.

Blocking rights are pervasive in biotechnology. For example, a particular genetically modified plant ready for agricultural use might include several different sections of DNA, each patented separately by different corporations or research institutions. Another example is found in the pharmaceutical industry, where one company owns a patent on a particular drug, another company owns a patent on a method for using that drug for a specific disease, and a third company holds a patent on a delivery system that provides the best clinical results. For example, party A holds rights to drug delivery patches that attach to the skin and administer whatever drug is in the patch. Party B holds rights to a particular drug. Neither A nor B could produce A's patch with B's drug without permission from the other.

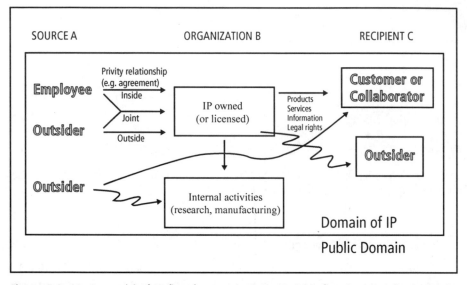

Figure 5.8. Master model of IP flow for organizations. IP rights flow into an organization by agreements with its employees and outsiders (solely or jointly), and can be used for internal activities, or transferred out to customers or collaborators; activities by outsiders that infringe the organization's IP rights are subject to enforcement action by the organization (right, wavy line), and unpermitted activities that infringe the IP rights of outsiders are subject to claims against the organization (left lower wavy line) or its customers (central wavy lines).

INFRINGEMENT – THE MASTER MODEL

At its simplest, IP management takes place at the level of an individual organization. Here, we consider the flow of intellectual property in to and out from a single organization. The basic principles are the same in corporate and public organizations, and in wealthy and poor nations. Creative activity produces intellectual property rights, and those rights can be transferred to organizations, or abandoned, in whole or in part, as reflected in the simple ABCD model for the flow of IP rights.

IP rights can affect an organization in two ways. First, the organization must actively protect its own rights by enforcing them against infringers. Second, the organization must gain access to the rights of others without exposing itself to infringement liability. This management rule may be summarized as PROTECT and ACCESS. Following is a general overview of the flow of IP rights and its relationship to protecting and accessing those rights. More details are provided in Part III of this book.

Consider organization "B", our client. (See Figure 5.8.) Assume that the source of rights "A" is a creative individual employee working for the organization, or an outsider (a vendor, contractor, or other organization), or both working jointly, in collaboration. IP rights may be transferred from A to B (solely from inside or outside of the organization, or jointly) in any appropriate manner such as by purchase, grant, license, or implied rights. Organization "B" thereby aggregates the rights of its employees and collaborators.

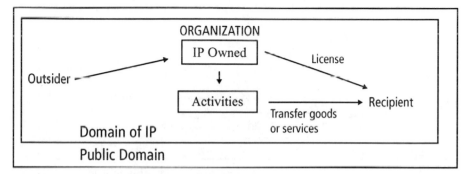

Figure 5.9. Noninfringing path. An organization acquires IP rights from an outsider, and licenses them to recipients, or uses them in its own activities and then transfers goods or services to recipients; because these activities are permitted, there is no infringement of the outsider's rights.

Once it gains access to the IP rights by acquiring them, organization B may freely use them in its internal activities, such as research, manufacturing, and sales. Also, organization B can pass its IP rights on to recipient C (a customer or collaborator) giving C access, as needed. For example, organization B can transfer IP rights by direct sale of any products or services that embody the rights (such as a bottle of medicine, a potted plant, or a book), or by formal licenses and assignments of legal rights. Whatever the way, organization B acquires intellectual property rights and then either uses them internally or transfers them out. We can refer to these as essential IP rights, sometimes referred to as core assets. In contrast, nonessential IP rights are those that are acquired, but neither used nor transferred.

As noted, infringement liability arises from activities that fall within the scope of an IP asset only if those activities are not licensed or otherwise permitted. An IP owner cannot enforce its rights against those who have permission.

So, IP rights can flow along a noninfringing path (by agreement) or an infringing path (without agreement). In the noninfringing path, an outsider gives permission to the central organization through some kind of transfer of IP rights. (See Figure 5.9.) The organization then acts within the scope of its rights, and provides the necessary rights to its customers and collaborators. For example, an inventor may assign an organization a patent for a drug for human use. The organization produces the vaccine, and sells it to pharmacies. **Privity** (a legal term for the relationship between two contracting parties) exists in all of these inputs and outputs because there is some kind of agreement or relationship between A and B, and between B and C. There is a clean transfer of rights into and out of the organization, and no infringement.

In the infringing path, there is no permission, no flow of rights. What flows is liability for infringement. (See Figure 5.10.) Infringement arises when there is no contract, or when there is a contract, but the recipient of rights breaches it. An organization that undertakes activities that infringe the IP rights of outsiders without permission becomes subject to enforcement claims. The outsider A can file an infringement claim (Claim 1) against the organization B.

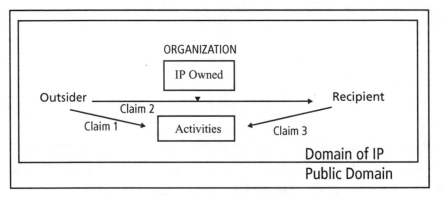

Figure 5.10. Infringing path. An organization that acts without acquiring IP rights from an outsider infringes (claim 1), and its customers may also be infringing (claim 2), with a right of contribution or indemnity against the organization (claim 3) for selling infringing goods.

Infringement also occurs where an organization sells its products to a customer, and they fall within the scope of an outsider's IP rights, but there is no license or other permission from the outsider. See Figure 5.10. Here, the outsider can make an infringement claim (Claim 2) against the customer. Depending on the type of IP right, even an innocent infringer may be liable. In the drug seller-pharmacy example used above, the pharmacies might be sued for infringement, and they could then seek indemnity from the manufacturer. Under intellectual property law, like commercial law in most countries, contracts may provide an indemnity or warranty or guarantee whereby the provider promises the recipient that the products or services do not infringe any intellectual property rights of third parties. In that situation, the recipient can come back and make a claim against the client organization (Claim 3). If there is an indemnity, the client organization would need to reimburse the recipient for any infringement damages. The manufacturer and the customer are both exposed to infringement liability. It is generally the supplier's responsibility to makes sure that its products do not infringe anyone else's rights. This is consistent with the general rule that products sold in commerce should not be defective.

Infringement is a two-way street. Each actor must be concerned both about infringing other people's rights, and about other people infringing the actor's own intellectual property. Organizations must take steps both to protect their own rights and to respect the rights of others.

IP AS A MOTOR FOR THE INNOVATION CYCLE

So we can see that the IP system can drive the innovation cycle like a motor, alternating dynamically between exclusivity and access. First, IP rights affect what information creative people can access, and provide incentives for creative work- Second, IP rights define how their creative ideas can be protected. Then IP rights shape the behavior of entrepreneurs and channel new ideas as they flow from the creator and combine with other entrepreneurial efforts in the process of introducing

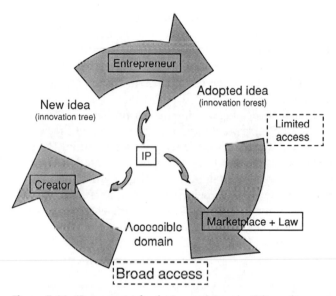

Figure 5.11. IP as a motor for the innovation cycle. IP laws give creators tools for controlling new ideas, give entrepreneurs incentives to invest in innovations, and establish marketplace rules that define the terms of public access to the innovation; if the system is in balance, IP is a dynamo, but if it is out of balance, the innovation cycle may be blocked.

an innovation into broader use in society. Owners of IP rights can use them to control who has access and who is excluded from the innovation. Finally, the innovation becomes part of the accessible domain, sooner or later, and more or less, depending on the specific IP rights. Access increases, while exclusivity diminishes as the IP rights expire. With the next improvement, the cycle starts again. (See Figure 5.11.)

SUMMARY. The flow of IP rights can be understood as the granting of permissions, with liability for IP infringement resulting from a lack of permissions. IP rights flow from creators, among individuals and organizations, into a larger community, and out into society – like goods – from A to B to C to D. Owners can choose to enforce their rights by excluding others, or grant permission. No permissions are required for public domain knowledge. The basic deal terms used in transferring IP rights are comparable to those in any market or any commercial contract between a buyer and seller. Rights can be transferred together or separately. Collaborators and joint owners can each transfer their overlapping rights and this is easier when the rights have been clearly allocated between them. Users of innovations must beware of infringing the IP rights of others, generally gaining permission for their activities by acquiring IP rights from owners, as when a tenant obtains a lease from the landlord. Infringement can be understood as an absence of permissions. Liability for infringement can flow in a similar fashion to the flow of IP rights, as seen in a master model of IP flow among organizations. An organization acquires the IP rights necessary to carry out its functions, and passes those rights on to its customers or other downstream constituents. The organization has a legal claim against someone who uses a protected innovation without permission, and also faces its own legal liability if it (or its customers) infringe on third party rights. These dynamics frame individual creativity and lead organizations to aggregate resources into IP assets. The dynamic between permission and infringement, between access and exclusion, creates a motor force helping to drive the innovation cycle.

One of the most important skills in dealing with intellectual property, both in organizations and in larger communities, is an ability to condense complex technical, legal, commercial, and global circumstances into a simple plan of action. The concept of the innovation cycle, the innovation forest metaphor, and the ABCD model together provide a useful framework for explaining how IP rights grow, how they are owned and protected, and how they flow, as owners use them to control who has access and who is excluded from the innovation. The following chapters describe the broader social framework in which these dynamics play out. The topics of this chapter will be revisited in Chapters 14 and 15.

6 The Role of Communities in Innovation

Innovation occurs globally in different types of communities. This chapter outlines their unique characteristics. Private innovation communities tend to be profit-driven and include individuals or small groups working together, small localized businesses, and large diversified corporations having many divisions. Public innovation communities have nonfinancial missions. Universities and public research institutions are devoted to innovation, while political parties and religious groups innovate and use intellectual property to lesser extents. Mixed communities include both private and public activity, such as regional innovation communities in various parts of the world, including developing countries, public–private partnerships, multinational research consortia, global innovation initiatives, and ad hoc arrangements such as open innovation communities. Together all these groups may be described as part of a global innovation community.

* * * * * *

INNOVATION MADE IN COMMUNITIES

Your computer, cell phone, sneakers, medicines, and book collection are all products of the innovation cycle. In each case, individuals working creatively used available knowledge and resources to come up with a new product, which became popular through wide adoption in society, and become available around the world for others to use.

For an idea to become a full-fledged innovation, something that is widely available in society, it must pass from person to person, either by transfer of intellectual property rights, or by publication or collaboration. Most products include the creative ideas of many people, combined and transferred. As John Donne said, "no man is an island," and the same is true for an idea. Innovation requires numerous people working together, combining their ideas, and passing them on to others. We can refer to a group of people working together in the creative process as an innovation community.

All of us, in our interactions with others, can learn something new, and can bring this new awareness to our own work. I have represented creative individuals on their own, in private companies ranging in size from small startup companies to multinational publicly traded corporations, and in public interest research institutions, large universities, and national and international biotechnology research agencies, in Asia, Africa, the Middle East, Europe, and North and South America. In all these experiences I have seen how creative scientists, engineers, authors, and artists use the reservoir of knowledge and resources available to them, create a new product, and spread their creation to their community and out to the broader society. They take ideas from their predecessors, give their ideas to others, and collaborate with many more. Most of these creative people struggle, many fail, while others succeed in making their creative labors accessible to the wider world. Some make vast profits for themselves or their colleagues or shareholders. Some serve the broader public interest.

There are common threads linking these different people. All have a drive to innovate. All are concerned about intellectual property. In each case, intellectual property helps define a community out of individuals, and plays a role in driving innovation.

In principle, every community can be an innovation community. In every home, village, neighborhood, and workplace, around the world, there are people trying to work, solve problems, make things, improve their lives, protect themselves, or find artistic or spiritual fulfillment. These creative people tap into the available, accessible domain of knowledge, overcome obstacles, and make new creations and inventions. Some of them find the resources to put their ideas to work in their communities, and some of their achievements go on to broad adoption. Others fade away and are lost.

This is not to deny that there are radical differences between leading innovation communities (such as those at Apple Computers, Genentech, or the University of California), and struggling communities (such as a farming village in civil war-torn Ivory Coast or a local health clinic in Belize). Some communities have more resources at their disposal, in terms of money, materials, education, information, a legal system that can enforce rights, and security from crime or war. But each type of community has its own creative groups and individuals within it, its own ideas, and its own intellectual property system (whatever it may be). Each can advance through the innovation cycle, and can grow its own portfolio of intellectual property rights.

There are several kinds of innovation communities. Private communities include individuals and small groups, small innovative businesses, and large corporations. Public communities include universities and public research institutions. Mixed communities include different regions within countries, developing countries, public private partnerships, multinational research consortia, and global initiatives. Open, collaborative communities provide a new approach to innovation. We now consider each community.

PRIVATE COMMUNITIES

Individuals and small groups

The simplest starting place is individuals and small groups. They may be farmers, craftspeople, independent inventors, artists, or authors. These innovators may seem to be heroic individuals, but even creative individuals work in a broader community.

I first met management professor Anil Gupta just after he established a volunteer program in Western India called the Honeybee Network back in 1990. Dr. Gupta and various volunteers walk from village to village, collecting innovative ideas from local farmers and craftspeople and publishing them in their newsletter. Now, with some 50,000 of these grassroots innovations, the project has been taken up by the Indian National Innovation Foundation, which is working to find investment and markets for the best ideas, and to protect appropriate innovations with patents or other forms of intellectual property. Some of the leading innovations include a coconut tree climber, threshers, sprayers, and a lotion for treating psoriasis. This work disproves the view that traditional knowledge is just a static archive of information. It demonstrates the dynamics of creativity in individuals living in traditional communities and the importance of national systems for protecting local innovations.[1]

In Bangladesh, local organizations developed a process they call an "innovation tree," helping farmers in traditional agricultural communities solve problems such as how to dry rice in the rainy season. A facilitator helps different families track and link various ideas and devices, tracing the linkages between the ideas, thereby stimulating diffusion and adoption of the most acceptable ideas and devices (e.g., drying rice on tables).[2] Creative individuals in the community share their ideas openly with the rest of the community, allowing the ideas to move directly into broader use, without asserting individual property rights. Such sharing is voluntary. Others presumably keep their ideas secret.

In the United States, independent inventors (those who have not assigned their rights) are given special treatment at the Patent and Trademark Office, and they wield important political clout. About 25 percent of U.S. patent applications filed by U.S. citizens come from independent inventors. In developing countries the percentages may be much higher, for example, 66 percent in Brazil, and from 25 to 50 percent in European countries.[3] These creative people stem from a long line of predecessors, all the way back to the "ingenious" people who could obtain patents for their inventions in Venice in 1474 when the first patent law went into effect. Many of the inventions patented by individual inventors today are mere novelties, gizmos, or gimmicks (such as U.S. patent 5971829, a "Motorized ice cream cone," for turning ice cream against an outstretched tongue). But others become enormously important and successful. Examples of successful inventors who remained independent include Gordon Gould, an inventor of lasers, Robert Kearns, who patented intermittent windshield wiper circuits, and Jerome Lemelson, whose patents on machine vision (bar codes) have yielded hundreds of millions of dollars in licenses and damages based on the broad use of that technology by manufacturers and retailers. Such individuals tend to be iconoclastic, and they can be a thorn in the side of corporations.

---

[1] "Calling Innovation Insurgents: Efforts on to Transform 50,000 Grassroots Ideas into Applications," *Sunday Times of India*, New Delhi, February 19, 2006, available at http://www.sristi.org/anilg/. See *Honeybee* magazine at http://www.sristi.org/honeybee.html.

[2] Paul Van Mele and A. K. M. Zakaria, "The Innovation Tree: A New PRA Tool to Reveal the Innovation Adoption and Diffusion Process," *Participatory Learning and Action*, PLA Notes 45, 2002, available at http://www.iied.org/NR/agbioliv/pla_notes/documents/plan_04511.pdf.

[3] WIPO/IFIA/BUE/00/11, "How Can Patent Offices Encourage Inventive and Innovative Activities?" WIPO IFIA International Symposium, www.wipo.int/edocs/mdocs/innovation/en/wipo_ifia_bue_00/wipo_ifia_bue_00_11.doc, accessed January 4, 2007. Farag Moussa, "The Role of Innovation," International Federation of Inventors' Associations (IFIA, 2001), www.invention-ifia.ch/role_of_innovation.htm, accessed January 4, 2007.

Independent innovators may try to commercialize their innovations by themselves, or by licensing to others. Unfortunately, most independent inventors fail to achieve any financial success, and indeed many of them spend too much money on marketing campaigns and other development schemes that are doomed to failure because the invention prototypes are not ready for broad marketing, or the marketing services are inadequate.

The most successful independent inventors are those who move on, building a business around their ideas with a larger community of people who develop the ideas, identify and solve problems, and scale up the enterprise into a larger volume product or service, and then adapt the product or service into new versions or situations. Building a business is in its purest sense the process of bringing people together with the resources necessary to produce a product. The biggest modern pharmaceutical company was founded by Charles Pfizer and his partner in 1849, when they invented, then borrowed money to produce, a better-tasting medicine to treat people who had intestinal worms. The same business model includes some of the most important innovators of the past century in electronics and entertainment: Thomas Edison, Walt Disney, Bill Gates, and Steve Jobs.

Similar innovation cycles occur every day on a much smaller scale. This book is an example. It began with my own experiences and those of clients and colleagues, and ideas from hundreds and thousands of others who have studied innovation and intellectual property issues, which I have collected, examined, and organized in my own way. I am linked to prior authors by reading their work, giving credit where credit is due, without infringing their own copyrights. Colleagues and family read and commented on portions of the book and shared their ideas with me. My publisher had a team of people who reviewed, edited, printed, and marketed the book in exchange for a license of exclusive rights under my copyright. The book itself is distributed to the public by the publisher, book stores, and electronic retailers, and finds its way to readers in hardback, paperback, or electronic form. Even though I am an individual author, this book was completed in an innovation community that includes those whose work I drew upon, those who provided comments, the publisher, distributors, and readers.

Small innovative businesses

The innovation community of a small business is, by definition, small, and therefore relatively focused. Small businesses generally rely on investment capital and lack revenues sufficient to cover expenses. Typically, a new or emerging company has a leader and a small team of people focused on a single product or service. Indeed, a principal reason people start a new business is because they have come up with a new idea for a product, or service, or business model. The small business clients I know have three priorities: to establish a corporate structure, confirm the arrangements for financial support, and align the intellectual property rights with the company's business plan. As a general rule, once the business plan for a small business is completed, it is relatively straightforward to formulate a strategy for its intellectual property management, for capturing the relevant intellectual property rights and avoiding infringing the rights of others.

Successful small businesses tend to have a limited number of people in their focused innovative community, resulting in a narrow cluster of innovations. If each invention, trademark, artwork, or computer program is a single innovation tree, a large corporation's innovations are an innovation forest, and we can refer to the portfolio of a small business as a grove. Managing a grove is in principle simpler than managing a larger forest. However, small businesses face complexities due to the lack of specialized expertise inherent in a small organization, and the urgent need to maintain funding in the absence of sufficient market revenues. Making innovations and protecting them with IP rights on a shoestring is a major challenge for small businesses.

Large corporations

Large corporations differ from small corporations in that they tend to have broad interests in more than one product or service. Consequently, the innovation community in a corporation like Apple or Pfizer includes thousands of people engaged in a broad and diverse set of activities, in distant locations around the world. Such a complex community gives rise to a very large and complex innovation forest.

The ten corporations receiving the most patents in the United States in recent years have consistently been large companies, including electronics companies with more than 1,000 new patents each, and chemical and pharmaceutical companies with about 500 patents each. Worldwide numbers are consistent. These numbers are orders of magnitude higher than the portfolios grown in small businesses and give some sense of the complexity of innovation in these companies.

One of the leaders, IBM, views the world as having private and open innovation communities. Chairman Sam Palmisano was quoted as saying:

> I believe we need a new path forward, an approach that offers a balance of these two extremes. We must protect the interests of individuals and companies that create truly new, novel, and useful inventions. But at the same time, we need to protect the interests of innovative communities, creative ecosystems – groups that are not incorporated or chartered but that nonetheless are engaged in genuine – and genuinely important – innovation. We need expanded notions of ownership, for a postindustrial world.[4]

In my experience in representing corporate clients, and in the case studies prepared by students in my intellectual property management classes, I have seen a direct correlation between the size of a corporation and its success at creating and managing itself as an innovation community. This impression is consistent with the reports of management experts such as Peter Drucker, Clayton Christenson, and others. That is, no small company will succeed at growing, and no large company will succeed over time, unless it constantly innovates in its products, methods, and business management models. Otherwise a corporation quickly becomes a victim of creative destruction – destroyed by another more innovative company's creativity. As a result of this imperative for corporate innovation, a huge body of literature and expertise has blossomed in recent years, attempting to teach corporations how

---

[4] Thomas Friedman, *The World Is Flat*, p. 254.

to organize themselves so that their employees have access to relevant information from inside and outside the company, engage in creative problem solving, and capture their innovations as institutional assets.

Part III of this book provides details about intellectual property management strategies for large corporations, among others. For now, the point is that corporations are large and complex innovation communities and produce correspondingly vast and dense innovation forests, and there are many approaches to managing them. Even choosing the right governance structure is a challenge. A multinational corporation may struggle between centralizing management of its intellectual property at its headquarters, and decentralizing so that each operation can manage its own IP locally, in different countries, under local conditions. It may debate whether to hire in-house IP lawyers, or to outsource the IP legal work.

Universities

Much of the innovation in the world is conducted by people working in public organizations. Broadly, these include government and nongovernmental organizations such as universities and research institutions. Both types of organizations share certain characteristics.

Although the definition of a university is a degree-granting higher educational institution, universities are generally dedicated not just to teaching, but also to research and public service. Institutions of this kind were established in the ancient world in China, India, and Egypt, and Wikipedia reports that about 40 universities have been in continuous operation for more than 500 years. Indeed, universities can outlast the nations in which they were founded, and some would say their purposes are more important to humanity. Peter Drucker observed that profit-oriented businesses can learn valuable lessons about organizational innovation from universities as they have evolved over the centuries.[5]

A university's mission is public service through teaching and research. Princeton University's motto is "Princeton in the Nation's Service and in the Service of All Nations," and its intellectual property policy calls for "the sustained production, preservation, and dissemination of knowledge." This is not necessarily inconsistent with receiving payments – students pay hefty tuition fees. The University of California ties its research and education mission to public service, stating that it "disseminates research results and translates scientific discoveries into practical knowledge and technological innovations that benefit California and the nation," and also makes available its various libraries and museums. Cambridge University's mission is "to contribute to society through the pursuit of education, learning, and research at the highest international levels of excellence." The three goals of research, teaching, and public service are echoed everywhere else around the world, for example at Makerere University in Uganda, the University of Capetown in South Africa, and Chiang Mai University in Thailand.

Both the faculty and research staff at universities are actively engaged in the innovation cycle. They study the known, create new courses, publications, and scientific projects, and disseminate knowledge into their communities by teaching

---

[5] Peter Drucker, *Innovation and Entrepreneurship*, pp. 23–24.

students, publishing, maintaining libraries, and making inventions. They thereby add to the collective knowledge of humanity, and correct mistakes from the past. Universities are quintessential innovation communities, and grow thriving innovation forests as the innovation cycle turns.

Two general characteristics of university innovation are notable. First, faculty members are usually entitled to own copyright in their books, journal articles, and software. Although these are generally written for peer respect and prestige rather than money, some works can be quite valuable. Second, more recently, faculty must assign patentable inventions over to their university. The latter policy stems from the U.S. Bayh-Dole Act of 1980, which handed over title for federally funded inventions from the government to universities.

Nonprofit research institutions

There are many research institutions around the world which differ from universities primarily in that they do not grant educational degrees. These research institutions include government agencies and nongovernmental research institutions. Their missions are generally to conduct research and advance human knowledge in certain fields, and then make the results publicly available. Some of the research institutions I have worked with include the U.S. National Institutes of Health, the Smithsonian Institution, the Food and Agriculture Organization in Rome, Bioversity International (formerly IPGRI), the International Livestock Research Institute in Kenya, the Institute for Genomics Research, and the J. Craig Venter Institute. These public and private organizations conduct scientific research in the fields of health, agriculture, biodiversity, and genomics.

Research institutions often conduct active scientific laboratory research and produce technical innovations as a result, though they also conduct policy research as well, and sometimes engage in advocacy for particular positions in national and international forums, and in this respect they overlap with the broader community of nonprofit organizations (NGOs) around the world. For example, the J. Craig Venter Institute engaged in a policy study of the risks and benefits of making synthetic genomes before making them.

Public museums, botanical gardens, and zoos are repositories of artistic, cultural, and scientific samples. Plant germplasm collections are maintained by many national agencies and international agricultural research centers. Libraries and government archives hold the world's collections of publications and original documents. These institutions are typically government run or publicly funded and although their primary purpose is conservation, they also support communities of scholars who analyze the collections and distribute the fruits of their research by publication and display. The gravest concern to such organizations is that they will lose access to new acquisitions, or that restrictions will be placed on their ability to publish their results. These concerns are apparent in their current efforts to digitize their collections with photographs and databases available to everybody.[6]

---

[6] For example, the Smithsonian Institute National Museum of Natural History established a Collections-based Information and Databases Policy, available at http://www.mnh.si.edu/rc/db/collection_db_policy1.html.

The mission for members of research organizations is to conduct research and make it accessible to all. With no revenue stream from tuition, the funding for research institutions comes primarily from government grants and private philanthropic contributions, which leads us to expect that the fruits of the research should benefit the public. This is in marked contrast to the corporate goal of benefiting shareholders, which leads to focusing as far as possible only on research and innovation promising profit in the near future. A commonplace distinction is that research institutions and universities more often engage in "basic" research, while private corporations engage in "applied" research with a more immediate prospect of profitability. Yet, although the missions of research institutions and universities differ radically from those of private corporations, many of the same principles apply. Both institutions are organized for innovation, and produce much intellectual property.

Scientific research generates trade secrets, copyrightable and patentable information, and trademarks for the organizational identity as a crucial tool for obtaining funding and disseminating knowledge. Even nontechnical research can generate substantial intellectual property, in the form of websites, publications, and organizational identities and logos. These assets need to be managed like other institutional resources.

There are many NGOs for whom research is a secondary part of their mission. For example, Public Interest Intellectual Property Advisors (PIIPA) is an innovative organization that makes matches between a network of volunteer intellectual property professionals around the world and developing country organizations seeking their assistance. Although its primary mission is providing access to professional services, PIIPA also conducts surveys and produces publications and training materials to help spread its knowledge into the broader global community.

Nonprofit innovation communities are more focused on disseminating knowledge than profiting from it. Nonetheless, IP rights drive and shape innovation in such organizations.

Political parties

In a democracy, political parties innovate every election cycle, using new technology and new media to convey political messages to potential voters. The parties distinguish themselves from each other and compete aggressively, trying to protect their advantages while accessing those of the other party. These political activities are influenced by intellectual property, strange as it may seem.

Trade secrecy applies in political campaigns. Some candidates ask volunteers to sign nondisclosure agreements regarding fundraising lists, voter phone lists, precinct mapping software, and campaign planning documents.

Trademark theories can also apply in electoral politics. For example, in the 2006 Maryland Senate race, fliers asking people to vote for Republican candidate Michael Steele raised questions because the fliers were titled "Democratic Sample Ballot" and included pictures of prominent Democratic politicians who had, contrary to the implication of the fliers, endorsed the opponent Ben Cardin. Senator Cardin, once elected, called for an investigation of whether campaign laws were broken,[7] raising the question of whether such literature would also infringe trademark rights of the political party or the individuals whose pictures were shown incorrectly as endorsing the candidate – just as with the endorsement of a famous athlete or other celebrity. In this theory, voters, like consumers, should be able to distinguish the source of the political information they receive, and political parties should be able to protect their identities and political positions.

Religions

The principles of the innovation cycle apply to every creative community, even religions. Around the world, the great and minor religions, the living and dead ones, have produced a vast domain of accessible knowledge. In modern congregations, the established liturgies are updated by religious leaders who sift through sacred texts and teachings, and apply their own creative insights. Today's religious services are based on yesterday's, with modern adaptations. Tomorrow's religious services will arise from the creative spirituality of today's religious innovators. Small religious innovations can be adopted more widely in the community, until they become broadly accepted.

Occasionally, people experience revelations that lead them to break with past religious beliefs and to create new pathways for spiritual pursuits and new guidelines for behavior. Like other innovators, their creative spirituality may be adopted more broadly, or may fade away. Schism can be understood as the process that occurs when a religious innovator radically changes the beliefs, the liturgy, the text, or other basics of the religion, and the new practices deviate so far from the accepted principles of the original group that they separate into different congregations and are considered to be different denominations, sects, or religions.

Generally, religious organizations have a mission of spreading their message broadly, without restriction. Thus, secrecy is exceptional, and open access to religious ideas is the norm. However, the fundamental principles of IP management do apply to religions, in particular trademark and copyright principles.

Established religions, denominations, and congregations are known by their chosen names and symbols, which serve, one might say, as trademarks. These names serve to identify the particular religious group and distinguish it from other religions. This helps the public understand what to expect if they go into a Catholic church, a Jewish temple, a Moslem mosque, a Buddhist shrine, or a Hindu temple. Conceptually (but not spiritually!), this is like the predictability of McDonalds, Starbucks, or other chain restaurants around the world. Adherents of a particular religion know what to expect if they attend services at another congregation of the same religion in a foreign city or country (aside from language differences). If congregations have religious practices that differ, in different places, or because of schism or changes over time, there may be a dispute about who may use the original name of the religion.

---

[7] "Cardin Asks Gonzales to Investigate GOP Election Fliers," the *Examiner*, January 18, 2007, www.examiner.com/a-516327~Cardin_asks_Gonzales_to_investigate_GOP_election_fliers.html, accessed January 28, 2007.

Those who follow the old approach may try to block the innovators from doing so, forcing them to change the name of their group.

Members of a religion often choose to conduct commerce with others having the same faith, and there are many organizations and publications associated with the various religions that use their names. The U.S. trademark registry includes about 160 entries using the term "Catholic," about 200 using "Jewish," about 60 using "Islamic," about 150 using "Buddhist," about 40 using "Hindu," and so on, including various denominations (79 Lutheran, 106 Baptist).

Copyright applies to religious artwork and to essays, adaptations and translations of religious texts. Before printing led to the establishment of copyright, Jewish law established certain rights for authors and publishers of religious texts. In 2006, the new Pope, Benedict XVI, asserted copyright over papal works published by the Vatican press, and sought 15 percent royalties from a publisher that reproduced his first encyclical in its entirety. In response to broad media criticism, the Vatican said that its purpose was to assure the integrity of the texts, rather than to make money, and noted that journalists remained free to quote Vatican texts without payment. Essentially, the Vatican used copyright law to limit access to its publications, to help control the Pope's message. The Vatican's actions are not much different from those of, say, a university press or environmental group, using copyright principles to help disseminate its messages in the manner it chooses.

Religious morality has limited relevance in IP law. I once helped representatives of indigenous groups challenge a U.S. plant patent for an ostensibly new, distinct variety of *Banisteriopsis caapi*, known in the Amazon as "ayahuasca," or "yage." The plant is considered sacred and is used in religious and healing ceremonies.[8] The challenge was based on patent law (prior art showing that the patented variety was not new or distinct, but was rather the wild uncultivated type) and moral grounds. The USPTO proceeded on the patent law grounds, but said it had no basis for considering the moral/religious arguments.

MIXED COMMUNITIES

Regional innovation communities

Michael Porter of the Harvard Business School is well-known for his work on the competitive advantages of countries and regions, and the role of local clusters of companies and public institutions. These include innovation-driven technology clusters, such as Silicon Valley, "DNA Alley" in Maryland, Silicon Fen in Cambridge UK, and Bangalore, India, in which an entrepreneurial community of investors and managers create and grow companies around local research institutions. Very different examples are the gambling and entertainment industry in Las Vegas, Nevada,

---

[8] Center for International Environmental Law, "The Ayahuasca Patent Case," www.ciel.org/Biodiversity/ayahuascapatentcase.html, accessed January 28, 2007; Stephen Hansen and Justin VanFleet, *Traditional Knowledge and Intellectual Property: A Handbook on Issues and Options for Traditional Knowledge Holders in Protecting their Intellectual Property and Maintaining Biological Diversity* (American Association for the Advancement of Science, 2003), p. 14, available at http://shr.aaas.org/tek/handbook/handbook.pdf, accessed January 28, 2007.

and the film industries in Hollywood and Bollywood. An accumulation of knowhow and resources in one region, coupled with a comfortable standard of living, leads to a competitive advantage, so that a successful cluster tends to grow larger and stay where it is. These regions compete for funding and provide various economic incentives and benefits to innovators who locate there.

Many economists study patenting activity in different countries and regions as measures of innovative activity. Counting patents is easy and can yield surprising results. For example, more than 20 percent of patent applications filed by U.S. inventors are filed by Californians, more than the next four states (New York, Texas, Massachusetts, and Michigan) combined. Such data shows that Californians are very inventive, though it does not by itself provide information about the nature of the innovation community there.

Individual countries, like organizations, can be seen as innovation communities promoting their own interests in the world. IP policy can help them do so. Such countries optimize their IP systems and management approaches to promote competitive advantages with other countries. They try to buy low, sell high. Technology-wealthy countries aggressively seek to convince other countries to strengthen their IP laws. Technology importing countries resist strengthening laws in a way that might hinder their importation of technology. Comparing nations to private organizations is complex and beyond the scope of the book, but a few points are worth noting here. Nations, unlike corporations, have the authority to legislate and enforce laws about innovation, including IP laws. They are bound by international treaties in ways that private parties can avoid. They generally reserve to themselves the right to use as they wish the innovations otherwise protected by IP rights. Meanwhile, their ability to acquire, protect, and enforce rights is more limited than private parties. And of course their efforts are subject to the changing winds of politics.

Innovation in developing countries

People in developing countries must overcome obstacles quite different from those in Europe or North America or Japan. They face intermittent power outages, limited access to the Internet, difficulty transporting materials, and disease. But even though it is more difficult in some places than others, creative activity, adoption of new ideas, and wide access to better products can occur anywhere in the world. And intellectual property generally plays a role.

In 1999, I visited WARDA, the African Rice Center in Ivory Coast[9] to help them conduct an intellectual property evaluation. At the time the country, though poor, was a success story in West Africa, as were the center's researchers. Led by Dr. Monty Jones from neighboring Sierra Leone, they had succeeded in using modern breeding techniques and the center's collection of rice plants, along with those from institutes in the Philippines and Nigeria, to produce a line of rice plants that local farmers could

---

[9] Officially known as the West African Rice Development Agency (WARDA), one of the sixteen agricultural research centers of the Consultative Group on International Agricultural Research (CGIAR), funded by the World Bank, national governments, and philanthropies such as the Rockefeller Foundation. www.warda.org.

grow without much water, fertilizer, or pesticide. These lines were called NERICA for "New Rice for Africa," a name the institute protects as a trademark. The center has released several varieties which are in increasingly broad use in Africa. Dr. Jones expected no personal financial profit but received the $250,000 World Food Prize for his work, and has used his reputation to promote expanded plantings for NERICA seed. WARDA chose to publish its results, and did not obtain plant breeder's rights or patent protection for NERICA rice. With this trademark-protected yet open access model, WARDA has been able to conduct its research over the years with collaborators from many countries, maintaining confidentiality where appropriate, managing the biological materials involved, and using trademark principles to help disseminate the new rice seeds because farmers could trust the source.

The obstacles to innovation in developing countries were made clear to me at dinner one night during my visit to WARDA when one of Jones' colleagues, Dr. Robert Guei, had to excuse himself because he was suffering from malaria. The disease was so commonplace in Ivory Coast that he had come to work that day anyway. The disease burden, however, was nothing compared to the civil war that broke out in 2002 and again in 2004, leading to the death of at least one scientist and forcing the entire center's operation to move to Benin.

Trademark rights are particularly important in supporting innovation in developing countries. An East African lawyer told me about the problem of a regional vegetable oil producer known for its fine quality and distinctive cans. A competitor was trying to pass off lower quality oil as the quality product, putting its inferior oil into used cans from the higher quality producer, and selling them to grocery stores at a reduced price. Here was a clear example of a developing-country business – with an incentive to invest in innovation to produce better quality goods – being undercut by another company that was misappropriating its goodwill and misleading the public.

Some countries remain impoverished due to their authoritarian governments. Visiting a research institution in the Middle East, I was warned about pervasive government surveillance at the institution, which made it more difficult to maintain trade secrets. The practice at this institution was to hold conversations about sensitive topics while walking outdoors, to avoid electronic eavesdropping. Governmental invasions of personal privacy can restrict the freedom of expression that is necessary to build an innovative community.

Vast disparities of wealth and technology also characterize some developing countries. The Indian agricultural research center ICRISAT breeds improved chickpeas, pearl millet, and sorghum, and grows them in its beautiful experimental fields outside of Hyderabad, using modern farming equipment. In stark contrast, on the other side of the boundary fence, I saw a barefoot farmer in a loincloth turning the same soil with an ox and a wooden plough. The physical distance was small but the technological gap was huge.

Developing countries may also have a cultural preference for traditional practices rather than modern technology – largely due to access and availability. In Belize, the late Don Elijio Panti was a well-known practitioner of traditional Mayan medicine. Rosita Arvigo worked with him for a decade as an apprentice to learn what he knew and document it, and also established a 5,000-acre medicinal plant reserve in the mountainous jungle. That knowledge has thus been preserved and developed into local educational programs, books (copyrighted), and commercial products (trademarked) and prepared by a collective of traditional healers. Arvigo's Ixchel Farms has become a tourist destination. The well-educated minister of health in Belize told me his view that if traditional medicines are not harmful, people should be encouraged to use them even if there is no evidence that they are effective. Indeed, he had recently obtained some traditional Belizean medicine for his grandmother to help with her diabetes.

Innovation in developing countries often involves collaboration with wealthier organizations. The International Livestock Research Institute in Nairobi, Kenya has worked closely with the Institute for Genomic Research in Maryland and others to produce vaccines against the parasite that causes East Coast Fever and plagues the livestock of Masai herders in East Africa. The team used state of the art genomic sequencing, bioinformatics, and molecular biology to identify proteins to use in the vaccine, which will be developed into a commercial vaccine and adapted for use in local herds. Patent protection for the innovation is important to the collaboration.

Such innovation communities often lack access to trained IP professionals who can provide sound advice and assistance in dealing with IP issues. Such expertise is rare in many countries, and expensive. The 2006 PIIPA Survey by Public Interest Intellectual Property Advisors showed that innovation communities in developing countries on every continent want help with all types of IP issues, especially trademarks and patents, in protecting their rights and challenging the rights of others, and in drafting legislation to establish IP legal frameworks consistent with international law and local needs.

Strengthening innovation is one way to alleviate poverty and improve the standard of living. Innovation communities in developing countries need help to accomplish that goal. Providing funding, technical collaboration, and expertise in IP management will help these communities move forward.

MULTINATIONAL RESEARCH CONSORTIA

Some research projects are so large that they involve many different universities, research institutions, and in some cases private corporations as well. Such international consortia usually focus on complicated scientific problems that are vastly expensive to investigate. Examples include huge particle accelerators constructed to study subatomic physics, and the Human Genome Project established to identify the entire sequence order of the DNA base pairs in the human genome. The East Coast Fever vaccine project mentioned above is a smaller project, but still cost about US$20 million. These international innovation communities are diffuse and overlapping, with innovators coming from many different organizations, each with their own goals, policies, and practices. Management of intellectual property in a research consortium presents special problems; it can be extremely challenging to merely conclude the necessary inter-institutional agreements.

As related in James Shreeve's book, *The Genome War*,[10] it can be even more challenging for a consortium to operate in the face of corporate competition. The Human Genome Project (HGP) was a research consortium initially funded by the U.S.

---

[10] James Shreeve, *The Genome War: How Craig Venter Tried to Capture the Code of Life and Save the World* (Knopf, 2004).

Congress in 1990. In 1998, the HGP was expected to complete its map of the human genome sequence by 2005 at a cost of $3 billion, under the leadership of Frances Collins. Craig Venter, then head of Celera Genomics, brazenly promised that his corporation would complete the job by 2001 at a fraction of the cost, using private funds instead of tax dollars. The HGP public consortium used a slow, thorough, and expensive technique, and was committed to put all genomic data immediately into a public database, not to retain any patent rights in the information. In contrast, Celera's business model was to use high-power computing technology to move quickly and inexpensively, to hold back certain information for a limited period, to sell early-access subscriptions to pharmaceutical and other large research corporations, and to obtain patents on certain DNA sequences as they were identified. The resulting rivalry created a race in the international research community, and challenged both the public genome project's fundamental assumptions and those of Celera. But by June 2000, forced into a reluctant collaboration, Venter and Collins stood with President Bill Clinton at the White House and announced the simultaneous publication of the first complete draft of the human genome, years ahead of schedule, and at a huge saving to the tax-paying public. Since then, Celera stopped its sequencing operation, Venter donated his wealth to the public research institution he founded to pursue his own genomics priorities, and the public genome consortium has finished its original task ahead of schedule and under budget.[11]

The Global Health Program of the Bill and Melinda Gates Foundation established a new model of nonprofit venture capital. This program strives to improve health in developing countries by making new vaccines, diagnostics, and drugs available to poor people there who suffer from diseases such as malaria, tuberculosis, and HIV/AIDS. The Gates Foundation grants about US$1.5 billion annually to consortia of public institutions and private companies. Some grantees are "product development partnerships," nonprofit pharmaceutical companies that team with private enterprise to conduct research and develop, manufacture, and distribute new medicines. Given the divergent goals of the participants in such consortia, it can be difficult for them to agree on consistent policies for IP management, including sharing of data, materials, and patent rights. The magnitude of the grants – $100 million, $500 million, and more – has led to increasingly sophisticated arrangements to overcome differences between grantees, and to stimulate invention and delivery of the medicines to poor patients. For example, private partners may be allowed to own IP rights and to control access to medicines in wealthier countries, but they must give preferential pricing in the target countries, and cannot use IP rights to block access there.

The Gates Foundation model forces health advocacy groups and nonprofit research institutions to learn new commercial approaches to health product development, including a focus on products instead of basic research. The new approaches require careful due diligence and close monitoring of highly structured multisite research plans while protecting IP rights. Meanwhile, the private profit-making

---

[11] See http://www.ornl.gov/sci/techresources/Human_Genome/home.shtml, accessed December 21, 2006.

corporate participants learn to build the public interest into their innovation plans, letting some rights go in order to obtain valuable rights in other areas.

Ultimately, the public can benefit tremendously from competition and collaboration between public consortia and private companies. Each type of innovation community brings its own strengths and weaknesses, which can complement each other. Private companies do not invest in innovation unless they expect a financial return. Public organizations have limited funds to invest, and limited skills in turning innovative ideas into products that can be distributed throughout society. Putting the two together overcomes these limitations, creating synergy, but this requires careful and sophisticated IP management.

GLOBAL INITIATIVES

Moving beyond specific consortia, there are also loosely linked groups of public and private organizations which increasingly coordinate their efforts for particular purposes, outside of but in conjunction with the United Nations and its related international organizations. Billions of dollars are being spent, for example, on medicines for diseases in developing countries. This includes the World Health Organization and the Global Fund to Fight AIDS, Tuberculosis, and Malaria. These groups, by acting in a concerted fashion, can set broad standards of conduct that reach beyond the individual projects they fund, and they have more flexibility than UN-related international organizations might have.

The World Health Organization is exploring ways in which national governments can stimulate innovation to cure diseases that are endemic in poor countries. Pharmaceutical companies are generally opposed to any plan that would call for weakening their intellectual property rights. However, there is an increasing recognition that the private incentives provided by intellectual property work to stimulate innovation in medicine only if there are remunerative markets for these new medicines, and that such markets are generally lacking for many diseases such as malaria and tuberculosis.[12] Given the gravity of the problems and the lack of success in existing innovation communities (universities and private corporations), we are likely to see new global initiatives take shape in coming years in order to tackle these massive health problems.

For example, in 2006, Indonesia threatened to boycott the WHO's longstanding vaccine development program, in which countries freely provide samples of influenza virus. Indonesia wanted a guarantee that it would receive adequate supplies of avian flu vaccine when it was developed. This led to an international effort to find ways to reassure Indonesia and other countries threatened by avian flu that they would have access to the new vaccines.

The Internet itself can be viewed as a global innovation community. Domain names illustrate this point. The Internet Corporation for Assigned Names and Numbers (ICANN) is a nonprofit organization that coordinates the assignment of domain

---

[12] See "Public Health Innovation and Intellectual Property Rights," Report of the Commission on Intellectual Property Rights, Innovation, and Public Health, available at http://www.who.int/intellectualproperty/en/.

names, Internet protocol addresses, and other essential parts of the Internet's computer infrastructure, with input from technical, business, academic, and noncommercial communities. The World Intellectual Property Organization (WIPO) established an inexpensive arbitration system in the 1990s to resolve any disputes that arise over the right to use a particular domain name. Otherwise, the parties have to proceed in court under a theory of trademark infringement. The WIPO procedure has been extremely productive – the 25,000th case was handled in 2006.

Global initiatives supporting innovation blend international law and agreements with good practices involving intellectual property ownership, compulsory licensing, patent pools, standardized licensing arrangements with set royalties, and alternate forms of dispute resolution.

OPEN INNOVATION COMMUNITIES

The newest – and in some ways quirkiest – model is one we can refer to as an open innovation community (otherwise known as an open access, or open source community). The initial example was open source software, exemplified by the Linux operating system for personal computers. In 1998, software programmers came up with a new approach for distributing their software to the broader community. Until that time, typical copyright licenses such as those used by Microsoft, gave the end user only the right to run the program on a computer, which makes a copy of the object code (the code used by the computer). In this approach, the source code (program lines that can be read by a person) is kept secret. This way, only the original innovator can control and modify the program.

In the new open source model, the user is given access not only to the object code, but the source code as well, and no fee is charged. This permits a user who has the necessary talent to modify the program as desired, to correct bugs, or to add new features. An innovative user is required to keep access to the modified source code open and unlimited, and to make that code available on the same terms as the original program, for free. At each link in this innovation chain, programmers are not permitted to privatize any part of the source code – not the original source code nor the changes they made – by asserting copyright beyond the terms of the original license. Any privatization breaches the open source license and exposes the violator to damages for copyright infringement.

Thus, through a copyright licensing scheme, a chain of open access is maintained, from programmer A to programmer B to programmer C to end user D. In contrast, if the original Linux programmer had put source code straight into the public domain with no copyright restrictions, any user could have modified the program and then kept it secret, or charged a fee for access to the modified program.

This brilliant licensing strategy is one of the most innovative ideas ever in intellectual property. It has already spawned rethinking in many innovation communities. A prominent example is Wikipedia, www.wikipedia.org. Operated by a nonprofit service organization, the Wikipedia website is written and edited by users, pursuant to a "copyleft" license analogous to the open source license described above. Anyone is free to add content or to correct, delete, or modify entries made by someone else, and over time a self-correcting and ever-expanding database collects the knowledge of everyone interested in any particular topic. Thus, the open knowledge model creates a virtual innovation community consisting of a self-selected group of people who are interested in any particular topic. This "open" model is less profitable for creators than a closed private model, but it is more diverse and vigorous in the innovation it stimulates.

The open access concept has been expanded to cover media content, where user communities create, post, share, and revise their own work. The revenues in this system are being derived through advertising by the hosts whose trademarks, copyright, and subscriber lists led to sale prices of $580 million for MySpace, for example, and $1.65 billion for YouTube, despite the possibility of substantial liability for copyright infringement due to unauthorized files on these sites. As *Time* magazine said in naming "You" as 2006 person of the year:

> "We're looking at an explosion of productivity and innovation, and it's just getting started, as millions of minds that would otherwise have drowned in obscurity get backhauled into the global intellectual economy."

New models based on open access communities of collaborators are springing up all over, and in some surprising situations. For example, the U.S. Patent and Trademark Office began a pilot program for "open peer review," an open online system to help patent examiners examine patent applications. Members of the public will be able to post prior publications they believe are relevant to a patent application, helping the examiner determine whether to allow a patent. Many patent attorneys thought the proposal was far-fetched, but IBM, General Electric, Microsoft, and others quickly signed up for the trial.

The J. Craig Venter Institute and the University of California, San Diego are building an open scientific database for bioinformatic analysis of the genetic sequence of bacteria collected from oceans around the world. The new system, called CAMERA, uses a "lambda rail" (a super high speed link) to move huge amounts of data around the Internet.

Open communities are a new paradigm for collaborative innovation. Many people confuse open innovation communities with the public domain. On the contrary, open access communities are built on complex IP foundations that raise issues both in establishing and operating an open community. The contracts that set the ground rules for these networks may not be effective in some countries, and commingling of information from open sources with private, proprietary information leads to conflicts that have yet to be resolved. Free open software may not remain free. For example, one company may take a section of open source code, put it in a new proprietary program, and sell it for a fee, even though this breaches the open source agreements and infringes copyright. In a country with strong copyright enforcement provisions, like the UK, the open source licensor (Linux or otherwise) could actually preclude sale of the proprietary new program. In a country such as China, however, it would be difficult to enforce the copyright to force free sharing of the new program. On the other hand, widespread infringement of the new program in China might in effect achieve a similar result as that sought by the open source license.

SUMMARY. This chapter describes the many types of innovation communities around the world, private, public, and mixed, that together form a global innovation community. The fundamental principles of the innovation cycle and intellectual property apply to each community, differently. Private organizations innovate for profit, and use IP rights in that endeavor, whether the innovators are individuals, small groups, local businesses, or multinational corporations with many divisions. Public organizations have missions other than returning profit to shareholders, and their use of IP rights should be tailored to their missions. Universities and public research institutions are devoted to innovation. Community groups including political parties and religious groups innovate to lesser extents, but IP rights affect their missions as well. Mixed communities link private and public activity, as in regional innovation hot spots in various parts of the world (including developing countries), public-private drug development partnerships, multinational research consortia, global innovation initiatives, and ad hoc arrangements such as the open source movement and the open innovation communities it has spawned. IP rights increasingly define the structure of such mixed public-private communities. In all innovation communities, the creative efforts of individuals are shared and combined within a group defined by common goals or interests. Innovation communities produce communal ideas and IP assets to be used to help in the work of the community. Chapter 7 describes the role of leadership in that process.

7 The Innovation Chief

This chapter introduces the innovation chiefs found in different organizations. IP management requires leadership by someone who manages IP to further the organization's goals, and teamwork between creative, entrepreneurial, and legal talent. Successful innovation chiefs bring much benefit to their organizations. Drucker and others have given useful advice about managing innovation but not about managing intellectual property. Studies of intellectual asset management are also limited, focusing on corporations. IP management is also important outside of corporations. These insights lay the groundwork for Part Three.

* * * * * *

TYPES OF INNOVATION CHIEFS

Ideas, like money, do not actually grow on trees. Rather, ideas are innately human, and it is people who plant the seeds of innovation and cultivate them into an innovation forest. I remember the oldest partner in my first law firm describing the patent lawyer's job as planting acorns (filing patent applications for the client's inventions) and growing them into mighty oaks (litigating to enforce the resulting patent). His analysis was accurate from the narrow perspective of a law firm, but a quarter century later, I see a much broader human role in using intellectual property to grow the mighty oaks of innovation.

Intellectual property helps organize innovation communities of people whose new ideas can grow and flow to meet their needs. For most innovation communities, there is at least one person who makes decisions about intellectual property – an innovation chief, IP chief, or IP manager. This chapter explores the crucial decisions that such chiefs – innovators, entrepreneurs, and managers, in small or big organizations – must make, and the means they have for carrying out those decisions.

An innovation chief may either be a creator of new ideas, an entrepreneur, or a manager who helps ideas flow. In a corporate hierarchy, the innovation chief may be a manager or a director, and likely holds the title of chief "X" officer (CXO), such as chief executive officer (CEO), chief operating officer (COO), chief financial officer (CFO), chief legal officer (General Counsel), chief marketing officer (CMO), chief science officer (CSO), chief technology officer (CTO), chief information officer (CIO), chief business development officer, or increasingly, chief intellectual property officer or chief innovation officer. In a nonprofit organization, the innovation chief may be an executive director or a chancellor. In a government agency, the chief may be a minister of science, health, or agriculture, or department head. I have worked with all these types of innovation chiefs.

Depending on the structure of the organization or community, the chief's authority can be that of a dictator, a leader selected by the community, or a facilitator of a consensus-driven group. Independent innovators who group other people around themselves become innovation chiefs. In an indigenous community guarding its traditions, the innovation chief may be a shaman or a tribal chief – a classic chief. In some settings there is no innovation chief, and we will consider the consequences of this nonmanagement approach.

There are no set rules about who should be in charge of innovation and intellectual property. But in each innovation community, somebody, by plan or default, takes on the necessary functions.

THE IMPORTANCE OF LEADERSHIP

There are three reasons to focus on the innovation chief. First, focusing on an innovation chief brings us back to the real world from the abstractions about exclusivity and access used earlier – the innovation cycle, innovation tree, and innovation forest. Discussions about intellectual property and innovation too often descend into mechanical recitations about legal doctrines, economic models, corporate case studies, historic records, policy positions, and administrative practices. Important as such analyses are, they can leave out the human dimension of the innovation cycle, the ghost in the machine – who does what, why, and how?

Second, the concept of a chief implicitly includes the team of people working with him or her. No chief is an island. Managing intellectual property requires a team of people with legal, business, and technical expertise.

Third, the concept of an innovation chief highlights the significance of decision making in intellectual property management. Innovation begins with human creative activity, but managing intellectual property involves strategic action – obtaining the right information and making decisions based on it. The innovation chief, or an IP manager working under the chief's direction, is the person who makes the key decisions about using IP rights, to help new ideas grow and flow from A to B to C to D, and out into society.

By focusing on the individuals who make the innovation cycle revolve, we can more readily answer the main questions any chief or manager must address:

- What should we do?
- When should we do it?
- How do we do it?
- Why is it important?
- Who will work on the team?

These questions are addressed in the remaining chapters of this book.

Finally, the innovation chief is one of the central characters in the human story behind every innovation, whether in technology or art or business. These stories go something like this: The protagonist, a person who is creative in technology, science, art, or business, is motivated to do something new. After early trial and error efforts, this innovation chief has a first success and makes an initial decision regarding intellectual property protection. The early success opens up funding opportunities, leading to improvements and variations. The innovation chief enjoys expanding recognition, and the new product is gradually adopted in society. The creative person increasingly influences other innovators and builds an innovation community by exercising control over the intellectual property created. Obstacles appear at every step, including conceptual, financial, and technical problems, as well as direct competition. Here the stories diverge. For every story with a happy ending there are many more that end in failure, with the idea fading away or taken up by someone else. There are tales of interpersonal conflict, intrigue, and greedy and generous behavior.

Steve Jobs's career is an innovation story, from his early days in 1976 starting up Apple Computers, where he decided to keep exclusive rights to the Apple software and hardware rather than licensing them out broadly like PC manufacturers and Microsoft, to his departure for NeXT computers where he led the design of computer workstations and software, which found its way into Apple equipment when Apple acquired NeXT. Jobs cofounded Pixar Studios, which created movie hits beginning with *Toy Story* and was sold to Disney, making Jobs Disney's biggest shareholder. Jobs also created a new business model upon his return to Apple, with the iPod and iTunes service selling copyrighted songs over the Internet. Jobs has led a series of innovation cycles, involving patents, copyrights, trade secrets, and trademarks on hardware, software, movies, and music, consciously balancing exclusive control over technology and media with broad consumer access.

The innovation chief may not be the most creative individual, but instead an entrepreneur who brings creative people together and helps them bring their ideas to life, by investing, developing the ideas further, making deals with others in the community, and putting the ideas to work in the larger community. Entrepreneurial innovation chiefs are not necessarily creative themselves, but they enable creative people to bring their ideas out into social acceptance. University of California, San Francisco biochemist Herbert Boyer pioneered genetic engineering with Stanley Cohen. Silicon Valley venture capitalist Robert Swanson joined with Boyer to form Genentech in 1976, and helped lead the company in developing the world's first recombinant DNA product, insulin, followed by growth hormone, t-PA anticoagulant, and other products of biotechnology.

Corporate chiefs are usually business people, not necessarily innovators, who must rely on innovative leaders in positions of authority in their organizations. Ranbaxy, the largest Indian pharmaceutical company, is privately held and currently led by Malvinder Singh, son of the founder, who is trained in business. Ranbaxy also has an IP director, Vijaya Raghavan. Ranbaxy competes aggressively in the $100 billion global market for generic drugs. Its IP strategy has involved manufacturing in countries with weaker patent protection (Nigeria, Malaysia, Vietnam), and challenging patents in developed countries, most recently Pfizer's U.S., U.K., and Austrian patents on its blockbuster drug Lipitor. But with India's patent laws strengthened in 2005 to permit pharmaceutical patents in compliance with the TRIPS Agreement, Ranbaxy, like its Indian competitors, has invested heavily in innovation, including research on new drugs, with 1,100 researchers and active patent filings.

So the central characters in any innovation story are the creative people and the entrepreneurs who bring the ideas forward into society. The innovation chief may be the early creator of the entrepreneur or someone else to whom the role was delegated.

In innovation stories, like any other, there may be struggles for control between the various people involved, between the original creator and the entrepreneur, or between the entrepreneur and the innovation chief. For example, *The Genome War* describes how Craig Venter, as leader of Celera Genomics, was focused on a trade secret model in 2000, giving paying subscribers first access to the DNA sequences of the fruit fly *Drosophila melanogaster* and the human genome, and then making the data public thereafter. Tony White, head of parent company Applera wanted to maximize IP protection, and so corporate patent counsel filed patent applications on a rush basis each week before the sequence data could be loaded onto publicly available databases.

An effective chief brings good results for the organization. IBM sets the record for obtaining vast numbers of patents (more than 40,000 active patents worldwide, and the most U.S. patents issued annually), and licensing them effectively to generate huge amounts of money for the company ($1.2 billion in 2004, 15 percent of its total income). IBM's patenting and licensing campaign is credited with bringing the company out of its poor performance in the early 1990s. Offsetting its strong exclusive position, IBM has pledged not to assert 500 of its patents against the open source community and to provide a blanket license of patents for selected healthcare and education open source programs.

The University of California system is the leading group of research institutions involved with patenting and licensing intellectual property, and in 2004 reportedly handled 1,196 invention disclosures, filed 515 patent applications, entered into 273 new licenses, spent almost $19 million in legal fees, and received almost $75 million in license income. The UC system has instituted dozens of intellectual property policies on everything from patents to copyrights and data rights, balancing exclusivity with access to achieve the university's public mission. Being a university system, there are numerous IP Chiefs at each campus interpreting these policies. Because of UC's aggressive intellectual property management – its faculty are among the most successful in having their creative ideas find ways to enter the marketplace where they can, in principle, become available to everyone in California, the United States, and the world. Because of the way the IP chiefs at UC use intellectual property, the faculty are not sequestered in ivory towers but instead are linked tightly with the broader community.

Nathan Myhrvold left his position as Microsoft's chief technology officer to start Intellectual Ventures, a company that has acquired thousands of patents, creating a portfolio that can be used to generate revenue by licensing or by suing infringers. The investors include his former employer and many other major technology companies. Myhrvold refers to the business as invention capital, a natural outgrowth of venture capital. Myhrvold, a physicist, is active in innovating and generating and managing IP rights, and is active both as an innovation chief and an IP manager.

An innovation chief who makes bad decisions about IP rights may do great damage, wasting valuable assets and leading the organization into a potentially ruinous posture, and alienating customers. Many loyal users of the Blackberry personal digital assistant, sold by Research in Motion (RIM), were dismayed by the company's apparent game of "chicken" with patent owner NTP. RIM was held liable for patent infringement and was ordered to pay NTP $54 million dollars in 2003. Instead of resolving the dispute at that time with no disruption in the market, RIM fought hard to avoid the judgment – appealing the trial court decision to the US Federal Circuit Court of Appeals, lining up political allies, and filing requests to reexamine the patents in the U.S. Patent and Trademark Office. RIM achieved mixed results in this later stage of the dispute, and spent substantial funds preparing a noninfringing program that reportedly was inferior, all of which were ultimately a wasted effort, because RIM started losing customers to competing personal digital assistants and ended up settling for over $600 million.

Twenty years ago, Eastman Kodak had an even worse result when it was found liable for infringing Polaroid's instant film patents. Kodak was forced to pay Polaroid almost $1 billion and also to stop making the cameras and buy back all the existing cameras in the market. This caused great losses for the company and its shareholders and Rochester, New York, its home town. Although Kodak's decision to sell its instant film camera may have been reasonable at the time it was made, a better decision by its leaders might have avoided such catastrophic results.

THE INNOVATION TEAM

An innovation chief's primary responsibilities are to set strategy and to deploy the talents of employees and consultants to implement the strategic plan. Some people may try to go it alone. They would do better to involve others with the specialized knowledge and skills necessary to achieve their innovation goals.

In some instances, strategies are set by an individual working alone, and decision-making and implementation are do-it-yourself projects. The United States is home to thousands of independent inventors who write and pursue their own patents and try to develop commercial products on their own. More and more authors self-publish books using print-on-demand services. Individual artists and craftspeople protect the copyrights and trademarks for their own products, sold in galleries and markets and on the Internet. Musicians increasingly record and distribute their own songs, and protect their own copyright.

But these individuals do well to bring together a team of collaborators and consultants with the necessary creative, legal, and business talent to develop ideas into products and services that can be pushed out into the broader community. Even the most creative and talented solo entrepreneurs with endless enthusiasm will fail to have their work product adopted broadly unless they are able to bring other people into the project. Therefore, although the following material will be helpful to do-it-yourselfers, it is mainly addressed to organizations, in which a larger team is involved.

The team of players involved in forming and implementing an IP management strategy can be quite large. Generally, expertise in creativity (technology or art), law, and business is required. There are countless people who are experts in one of these areas, and some who are competent in two of the three – a scientist who has gone into business development and licensing, for example, or a marketing executive who has learned the legal basics for managing a trademark portfolio, or a patent attorney with an advanced technical degree. However, I have never met anyone who is an expert in all three areas–creativity (technology or art), (2) intellectual property law, and (3) business. It seems that good intellectual property management requires a team of at least two or three people, and often many more. One of them, by rank or circumstance, usually becomes the innovation chief.

Depending on the size of the organization, the complexity of the innovation, and the market potential, people with any or all of the following skills may be involved. Each group has to deal with its own particular types of complex issues.

- **Creative**. Creatively talented people generate the new ideas that keep the innovation cycle moving. In a technical organization such as a pharmaceutical company, the creative talent may be found in the research and development (R&D) group. Engineers and scientists engage in basic research and product development, and operate in a situation of high technical complexity. In a software or telecommunications company, the information technology and data management staff operates with high information intensity. In an artistic organization, such as a music or graphic arts company, the artistic people work with high aesthetic sophistication. Other less creative employees may have tacit knowledge that is very useful in developing ideas further. The creative group uses its talents to conceive the new ideas that are the building blocks of intellectual property, ideas that can grow into socially accessible innovations. They understand the innovation and its relation to the state of the art. The innovation chief is often in the creative group.

- **Legal**. Legal professionals are able to analyze, protect, and give advice on how to avoid intellectual property infringement. These professionals include lawyers, patent attorneys, and paralegal professionals, such as patent agents and licensing specialists. The legal group deals with high legal complexity. Some organizations have no legal staff in house, relying entirely on outside law firms and consultants. Others have internal legal departments capable of handling all routine matters, going to outside counsel only for help with unusual situations, to conduct litigation and document intricate transactions. Most organizations have a hybrid approach, with some work carried out in-house, and some outside. An effective legal team is necessary for analyzing internal and external information, proposing alternative courses of action, and implementing any management plan within the necessities and procedures of established law. The innovation chief may come from the legal group, but more often these people serve as IP managers, working with an innovation chief to design strategy and then implement it.

- **Business**. Operations managers also play a key role in forming and implementing intellectual property strategies. In a corporate setting, marketing staff are often the best source of information about the desirability of new product and service features, based on their knowledge of market demand. They also generally keep informed about the features of competitive products. Business development managers arrange relationships with collaborators, including vendors, competitors, and customers. They often have a keen appreciation of opportunities for innovation and for transferring technology and associated IP rights into or out of the organization. Similarly, merger and acquisition teams need to evaluate opportunities objectively to determine how intellectual property issues may influence the deal. Finally, financial leaders are responsible for setting budgets for IP activities, including protecting rights, obtaining licenses from others, or litigating to enforce against infringement. The cost and accounting methods for IP assets need to be consistent with the accounting practices of the company. A business-oriented innovation chief needs substantial input from IP managers and creative talent to be able to make wise decisions about IP practices.

- **Senior management.** Last but not least, the internal human resources include other senior executives beyond those described above, who can obtain the necessary information, retain it in a central location for ease of reference, bring together the necessary people and make the necessary decisions, locate the necessary funding, coordinate an IP management plan, and then follow through to make sure it is implemented. Unfortunately, senior managers in some organizations are not proactive and knowledgeable, and may make unwise decisions about intellectual property or otherwise thwart good work by staff – investing unnecessarily to protect worthless projects, failing to take measures necessary to protect valuable projects, or structuring unworkable relationships with collaborators.

As commerce becomes more global, organizations increasingly operate internationally. This adds a further level of complexity because most intellectual property assets are determined on a country-by-country basis, and so a network of professionals familiar with the legal and commercial situation in each country is required. Most organizations, other than the largest multinational corporations, do not have internal staff based in all significant countries, and so they need to work with outside consultants around the world. For example, my law firm has relationships with other firms in every country, firms that can file patent and trademark applications in their countries for our clients, and who reciprocate by having us file patent and trademark applications in the United States for their clients.

Today, companies have more choices than ever in structuring their intellectual property management teams. One traditional approach has been to have in-house staff conduct searches and write patent and trademark applications, prepare licenses, and provide opinions about third party rights, and to use outside lawyers only for litigation. A second strategy is to minimize in-house legal activities, focusing on creativity and business management while outsourcing all IP work to outside lawyers and professionals, who conduct searches, write patent and trademark applications, and negotiate licenses, as well as handling litigation. Outsourcing may be done through a law firm, a creative talent agency, or a consulting firm.

Some major companies in the United States and Europe are experimenting with a third approach, outsourcing to service providers abroad, particularly in India. However, there are many concerns surrounding international outsourcing of intellectual property and innovation. These include technology export restrictions, quality oversight, and concerns for piracy of intellectual property. Thus, most organizations prefer to deal directly with a primary outside consultant in their own country. In the United States, domestic U.S. law firms are still the preferred providers.

Business consultants and IP advisors are becoming increasingly sophisticated worldwide, resulting in increased competition for their services. This phenomenon suggests a new approach for assembling a team to handle IP management issues: a globalized virtual IP services industry network. Globalization generally has increased the sophistication of the business community. In India, for example, the newly strengthened patent laws have driven innovations at drug companies, and the burgeoning software industry there is linked to strengthening copyright enforcement. Consequently, business leaders, lawyers, patent agents, and other consultants are also becoming increasingly knowledgeable about IP management practices. At the very least, heightened interest in IP will mean fiercer competition for traditional service providers such as patent law firms. The importance of teamwork is growing in light of current trends in the industry, as in-house attorneys, outside attorneys, and other services providers must work together seamlessly to capture ideas and put them to work as innovative products and services available worldwide. If the migration of legal and IP management services to foreign countries expands, it will change the dominant role of patent and trademark attorneys in the United States, Europe, and Japan. There may be a shift to international services that manage a disaggregated virtual network of IP service providers in many countries.

Public Interest Intellectual Property Advisors (PIIPA) is an example of a nonprofit organization that serves groups in developing countries that need help with IP matters. PIIPA helps those groups identify their needs, and matches them with patent attorneys and other IP professionals around the world who have volunteered to represent them pro bono, as a public service. PIIPA is in the vanguard of new models for representation in international IP matters.

DRUCKER'S VIEWS ON MANAGING INNOVATION

What is the nature of innovative activity within organizations? What management experts say about innovation is a good starting place, although they have little to say specifically about intellectual property. Understanding the sources and processes of innovation, and the management issues confronted by an innovation chief leads in turn to understanding how innovation becomes intellectual property.

Innovation, as Schumpeter said, is a process of creative destruction. Peter Drucker, himself a leading management expert, was one of the first people to extend Schumpeter's historical concept of creative destruction into the pragmatic world of entrepreneurial business management. Drucker recognized seven "sources" of entrepreneurial innovation – circumstances that lead people to be creative.[1] The most reliable circumstances that provide an occasion for innovation are internal, and should be apparent to attentive managers:

- Unexpected success, failures, or events
- An incongruity between assumptions and actual events
- A need to change a process
- A changed industry or market structure.

Other circumstances that can lead to innovation are external:

---

[1] Peter Drucker; *Innovation and Entrepreneurship: Practice and Principles* (HarperBusiness, 1985).

- Demographic changes
- Changes in attitudes
- New knowledge (scientific and social).

The seventh category, new knowledge, is what most people think of when they consider what leads to major breakthrough innovations. Drucker concluded, however, that the other six situations are much more reliable in leading people to create new products and businesses. Indeed, Drucker believed that the least valuable source of innovation is "bright ideas" that result from spontaneous rather than concerted creativity. In many cases, management enthusiasm for a spontaneous bright idea far outweighs its actual value to an organization.

Drucker's advice is as follows:

- Analyze all the opportunities and sources of innovation.
- Pay attention to perceptions as well as concepts.
- Keep the innovative product simple and focused.
- Find ways to be a market leader.
- Identify risks and learn how to avoid them.[2]

Drucker said that knowledge-based innovation is the least reliable and is "temperamental, capricious, and hard to manage."[3] For one thing, there are long lead times between creation of new knowledge and its development and adoption in the market. Paul Ehrlich's theory of antibiotics preceded the first sulfa drugs by 25 years. Penicillin was discovered in the 1920s but not used until World War II. The Diesel engine was invented in 1897 but not commercialized until 1935. Leonardo da Vinci kept detailed records of countless brilliant ideas that were so far ahead of his time that they were not viable as innovations.

Also, knowledge-based innovation may require the convergence of several different kinds of knowledge.[4] For example, the early development of computers involved convergence of a technical invention (the audion tube), a mathematical theory (the binary theorem), the logic of the punchcard, and the concept of programming. Mass circulation newspapers came out of telegraphy, high speed printing presses, and the business model of mass advertising. Finally, knowledge-based innovation requires clear strategic focus to find a marketable product, and sustained entrepreneurial management.

Because of the long lead time required and the need for convergence of several ideas with a receptive market, knowledge-based innovation follows a pattern of long term effort and investment, followed by a brief explosive window of opportunity when the pieces come together.[5] A shakeout follows with unpredictable results. Because of this boom and bust dynamic, unpredictability, and high risk, Drucker compared "bright idea" innovation to gambling in Las Vegas and advised most companies to look elsewhere for steady, systematic sources of innovation.

---

[2] Id. at 134–138
[3] Id. at p. 107.
[4] Id. at p. 111.
[5] Id. at pp. 120–129.

Drucker's advice is practical. Analyze opportunities. Observe carefully. Focus on doing one thing. Start small. Aim for leadership. Don't be too clever. Innovate for the present, not the future. Edison waited to work on light bulbs until knowledge from other inventors was sufficiently advanced for him to finish the job. Successful innovators, according to Drucker, are conservative, focused on opportunity, not risk.

To capture innovation, Drucker recommended policies and practices that separate new ventures from old as separate businesses with different policies, and separate management teams, performance measures, and compensation structures. He identified four strategies for innovation: "Fustest with the mostest" means getting into a market first and overwhelmingly, as with Federal Express overnight delivery services. "Creative imitation" requires finding substitutes for a successful product, such as the marketing of Tylenol brand of acetaminophen as a replacement for aspirin. "Entrepreneurial judo" means finding a niche that is not being well-served. Finally, an "ecological niche" is a toll-gate technology necessary in a particular industry, a specialty skill for a specialty market.

Surprisingly, Drucker neglects intellectual property management, although it is crucial to each of the strategies he mentions. Being first is no help if the second comer can copy and compete on price. Imitating the leader or entrepreneurial judo will not work if the business leader has IP protection. If an ecological niche is profitable, then IP rights can be used to keep competition away. Intellectual property can protect all of the types of innovation he identified, whether arising from internal observation or external forces. Drucker's advice about how to manage innovation is much more useful when coupled with means for managing intellectual property to channel and control innovation for profit, or human betterment, or technological change, as laid out in the following chapters.

Drucker said that innovation should extend throughout society, in public service organizations like universities and in governments as well as corporations. To avoid violent revolutions, he recommended an entrepreneurial society in which innovation is normal, steady, and continuous.[6] The fresh ideas of today become tomorrow's afflictions. Innovation is the path to self-renewal. Government planning has a very limited role to play, because innovation as Drucker describes it is decentralized, autonomous, and microeconomic, based on specific opportunities, throughout the economy.

Drucker's vision of a society with steady innovative progress – what we may call "creative construction" – is more appealing than the disturbing prospect of creative destruction. Intellectual property policy can help create such an entrepreneurial society, one where individuals are motivated to find new solutions, to be creative, or to invest in the innovations of others. Improved intellectual property management can capture routine, steady innovative activity as assets to be invested into new ventures which successfully compete with their predecessors and replace them.

OTHER VIEWS ON CORPORATE INNOVATION MANAGEMENT

Other experts have added their own views about managing corporate innovation. Davila distinguished between technical innovations, and business innovations

---

[6] Id. at p. 254.

affecting how products are produced and marketed. He gave the following advice for utilizing both kinds.[7]

- Involve strong leadership.
- Integrate innovation into regular operations – use resources, competencies and experience from different parts of the organization and from outside organizations.
- Coordinate and synchronize activities to move abstract ideas to products.
- Establish solid internal and external collaborations.
- Do not relinquish control over the technologies or the business model.
- Align the innovation to the company business.
- Manage the tension between the creative act and how its value is captured.
- Neutralize opposition within the organization.
- Organize networks based on technology or business platforms.
- Use proper measures and incentives so as not to promote too much or the wrong innovation.

Davila also failed to recognize the role of intellectual property management. IP management can be a tool of strong leaders. IP strategies can help synchronize and coordinate activities and effort. IP assets can form the basis of collaborative networks fusing people and knowledge both inside and outside the organization. IP management can diffuse the tension between individuals and the organization. Management practices can protect IP assets (creative ideas that have been thought or invented, and expressed, and treated in such a way as to be recognized under law as providing exclusive rights), and can find ways to access innovations of others without violating their IP rights. IP management can also involve measuring and rewarding innovation, as many companies with inventorship incentive programs have learned.

Clayton Christenson is known for his series of books, *The Innovator's Dilemma*, *The Innovator's Solution*, and *Seeing What's Next*. Christenson has tried to develop a coherent theory of management consistent with the concept of creative destruction. Christenson's view is as follows.

- Existing companies have advantages over new entrants in making incremental innovations. But new entrants have advantages with disruptive innovations that reshape or create new markets.
- Innovation can relate to a company's resources (people, technology, products, equipment, information, cash, brands, and distribution channels), business processes for turning resources into a product or service; or values.
- Organizations should control and integrate any activity within the value chain that drives performance that matters most to customers, but they can outsource other activities.

Christenson's work is helpful in understanding the dynamics of explosive innovation and incremental innovation in various settings. Although he underplays intellectual property as a tool for controlling and taking advantage of innovation, his analysis is helpful to an innovation chief setting a strategy for IP management.

---

[7] Tony Davila, Marc Epstein, and Robert Shelton, *Making Innovation Work: How to Manage It, Measure It, and Profit from It* (Wharton School Publishing, 2005), pp. 13–26.

Michael Porter is known for his cluster theory of competition. Clusters are localized groups of interconnected companies with a particular specialty. Examples abound for technology companies: electronics in Silicon Valley, California; software in Bangalore, India; and biotechnology in Montgomery County, Maryland outside of Washington, DC. The clustering and networking of companies can promote innovation by establishing a larger community that supports new ideas, shared ideas, and the broad adoption of both. Intellectual property can support successful technology clusters by regulating the sharing of ideas, and providing a framework for licensing and collaboration, providing a basis for pricing for investments and acquisitions, and regulating the mobility of creative people from company to company.

INTELLECTUAL ASSET MANAGEMENT IN CORPORATIONS

In the last decade, innovation chiefs at major corporations and other consultants have published their thoughts about how corporations can best manage intellectual property and broader categories of intangible assets. Most of their work focuses on corporations in the United States and other wealthy countries, not on nonprofit organizations and poorer countries. But the growing literature includes some very useful approaches, the basis for much of what is summarized in subsequent chapters in Part Three.

Patrick Sullivan and executives from major companies shared their experiences in *Profiting from Intellectual Capital.*[8] There are many features common to the management approaches described by Stephen Fox of Hewlett-Packard, Joseph Daniele of Xerox, Gordon Petrash and Sam Khoury of Dow Chemical Company, Leif Edvinsson of Skandia, and others. Managing intellectual property is central to what these authors call intellectual capital management (ICM) or intellectual asset management (IAM). They referred to a hierarchy of corporate capital that distinguishes intellectual capital from physical and financial capital. Intellectual capital, in turn, includes human resources (the skills and know-how of workers) plus intellectual assets. Intellectual assets comprise all the knowledge and learning within the company, whether legally protected as intellectual property, or not. For example, relationships with customers and collaborators are intellectual assets but not intellectual property assets. In this scheme, companies extract value by having the human resources create new ideas, which become intellectual assets, and then those ideas may be protected as intellectual property.

So the person leading the effort (an innovation chief) ascertains the company's goals, brings together a skilled management team, and catalogues and classifies the IP portfolio. The innovation chief puts in place policies to coordinate the process by which employees document their good ideas, so that they can be screened for protection as intellectual property. The chief measures the value of the various intellectual assets relative to the corporation's priorities, and measures corporate performance in terms of IP value. Decisions are made on a regular, routine basis. The chief also assesses the activities of competitors and takes appropriate steps, such as collaboration, licensing, or enforcement. All the relevant information is made available

---

[8] Patrick Sullivan, ed., *Profiting from Intellectual Capital: Extracting Value from Innovation* (Wiley, 1998).

either in a central location, or as a network of information captured at the level of individual corporate divisions.

In this book, we also focus on management of intellectual property, broadly defined to include patents, copyrights, trademarks, and trade secrets. Because technical know-how and relationships can be protected as trade secrets, and managing trade secrets requires certain human resources practices, the distinction between IP management and intellectual asset management as defined above is largely a semantic one. That is, the lessons of intellectual asset management can be applied quite well to the task of IP management as defined here.

Two important lessons can be derived from this discussion. Do not let the complexity of intellectual property stop you from being strategic. Understand your goals, learn the facts, make a plan, and try to implement it.

The literature on IP management has continued to grow, much of it concentrating on particular assessment tools, much if it anecdotal about the practices at various companies. Here, we go further, in an effort to place intellectual property management in the context of innovation in a global society, including not just technology companies but creative and nonprofit organizations around the world. Drucker reminds us to view the mission of an innovative organization not only as an instrument to extract profit, but as a participant in the larger goals of society. Taking that perspective, we will see how organizations can balance exclusivity and access to innovations to meet their needs while ultimately bringing benefits to society.

MANAGING INNOVATION OUTSIDE OF BUSINESSES

Entrepreneurship and innovation can be practiced in the largest corporations.[9] Further, innovation is important to small businesses, universities, and government agencies, and is the primary task for artists and research institutions.

In a corporate setting it is easier to manage methodical innovation than to coordinate unique creative ideas that are not subject to repetition, development, or management. But intellectual property management is helpful both with routine innovations and with sudden or more chaotic creative acts. IP management includes useful tools for engineering geniuses as well as creative people whose muses lead them to express themselves in music, paintings, sculptures, poetry, or scientific ideas, all of these unique and essentially unmanageable otherwise. An artist, through copyright, can prevent other people from making unauthorized copies of the works and can control the types of reproduction of the work (as prints, photos, posters, or coffee mug decorations). A university biochemist can use a patent to convince a corporate sponsor to invest in a new drug, especially to invest in the enormously expensive process of clinical trials.

Intellectual property management can be very important to noncorporate communities. Public Intellectual Property Resource for Agriculture (PIPRA) is an organization whose mission is to bundle agricultural technology from universities and

---

[9] Vijay Sathe, *Corporate entrepreneurship: Top managers and new business creation* (Cambridge 2003); Richard Koch, *FT guide to strategy: How to create and deliver a winning strategy*, 3rd ed. (FT Prentice Hall, 2005).

corporations for use in developing countries. A key issue in that work is to map out any relevant patents and other intellectual property rights, and to find ways to put those technologies to use growing crops in developing countries, for possible export to the United States or Europe, without creating liability for intellectual property infringement.

The Brazilian government has aggressively managed local pharmaceutical innovations to make HIV/AIDS medicines available locally at low prices. On several occasions, when the Health Ministry believed that a multinational company was not supplying a key medicine at a low enough price, the agency threatened to use its compulsory licensing authority to permit a local manufacturer to produce the drug at a much lower price. Drug manufacturers Abbott, Gilead, and others have relented, and agreed to provide the drugs, for example, at half the price originally demanded. This can be seen as intellectual property management in a nonentrepreneurial setting. Although some would argue that Brazil's tactics amount to extortion, others observe that governments award patents to provide public benefits through exclusive rights, which need to be balanced against the public benefit of providing its population with access to medicines. So an agency can be expected to exercise its legal authority, in this case using compulsory licensing as a way to extract price concessions. That is part of the fundamental balance between exclusivity and access.

SUMMARY. An innovation chief may be an entrepreneur, chief officer of a corporation, or an executive or administrator of a nonprofit group or government agency. Leadership implies human interaction and teamwork in a concerted endeavor, such as found in news stories about intellectual property. The chief or someone on the team manages IP to further the organization's goals through interaction between creative, entrepreneurial/business, and legal staff. Successful leaders and teams use IP management tools to cultivate, preserve, and perfect IP rights, transfer them successfully, and ultimately introduce innovations to society. An unsuccessful leader squanders resources and creates risk and liability. Management consultants are focusing increasingly on global innovation leadership, but not enough on intellectual property. Drucker suggests that the most valuable source of innovation is close observation of the ongoing work of an organization rather than spontaneous bright ideas. Davila, Christenson, and Porter add their approaches for managing innovation, none of which deal with IP management. Sullivan and other proponents of intellectual asset management focus on corporate models, without tying IP management to the broader range of innovation communities. Successful IP management involves finding the right balance of exclusivity and access in any given situation. In short, an innovation chief is the leader of an innovation community or an IP manager within that community who knows how to use various strategies to pursue the organization's objectives, working within the international system of IP laws – a system whose purpose is for individuals and organizations to help society by helping themselves. That completes the framework of Part Two, involving growth of IP rights, flow and infringement, innovation communities, and leadership. The specific strategies and steps leaders and managers can take to improve IP management in their organizations are presented and discussed next, in Part Three.

STEPS TO STRATEGIC MANAGEMENT OF INTELLECTUAL PROPERTY

8 Becoming Strategic

This third part of the book is organized around the steps of strategic management of intellectual property, and the first section deals with the first step – planning. Chapter 8 describes a hierarchy of IP management beginning with the lowest level, nonmanagement, to defensive, cost control, profit center, integrated, and visionary levels. To move up this scale, an IP manager should form a strategy, define goals, assess internal human resources and intellectual property resources, study the environment, develop a management plan, and implement it. These are the basics for becoming strategic.

* * * * * *

To succeed, innovators, business and public managers, academics, and politicians shaping intellectual property policy must all know the basics of IP management and be aware of how IP law affects them in their day to day decisions and practices. These basics can be readily understood without any specialized training in law, business, economics, or science.

LEVELS OF IP MANAGEMENT

Intellectual property can be managed well or poorly. People who lack basic literacy about the differences between the four types of intellectual property – how they grow and how they flow – cannot make wise decisions about using intellectual property to channel innovation. Also, people who are literate in one area (such as patent litigation) but know nothing about another area (such as trademark prosecution) are unable to see the forest for the trees and will have difficulty linking decisions in one area to overall organizational goals. At the other extreme, someone with a basic understanding of the concepts and dynamics of the main types of intellectual property, and how it grows and flows, is well-positioned to make important decisions that will benefit an organization. An IP manager who gains experience beyond the basic skills can come up with increasingly sophisticated and effective approaches.

IP management skills are hierarchical. At the lowest level is an organization lacking any intellectual property competence at all. At the highest level is a visionary organization with a skilled innovative chief and IP managers who can integrate the organization's goals with its innovation potential, and even use intellectual property and innovation to shape the society within which the organization prospers.

A useful hierarchy for conceiving intellectual property management has six levels, from least to most effective. Each organization, for-profit or nonprofit, in wealthy or poor countries, fits into one of these categories. As one moves from lower to higher levels in this hierarchy, fewer and fewer organizations qualify. Each level is discussed in turn below.[1]

Level zero – Nonstrategy
Level one – Defensive
Level two – Cost control
Level three – Profit center
Level four – Integrated
Level five – Visionary

Level zero – Nonstrategy

Many organizations, particularly smaller ones and nonprofits, have no concerted intellectual property strategy or policy in place. Unfortunately for them, inaction leads to what is, in effect, a default policy with potentially destructive consequences. Without an IP strategy, an organization misses opportunities to build its assets, has no control over competitors' activities, and can incur catastrophic liability for infringement of others' rights.

Why would an organization lack any coherent IP strategy? The first explanation is ignorance – some people have not yet recognized the rising significance of intellectual property, so they may be ignorant of the advantages to their organization of methodical actions to maximize control, protect assets, and minimize liabilities. A second explanation is inertia. If no strategy has yet been put in place, there will never be one until somebody takes the initiative and begins the process of assessing internal resources and the competitive environment, comes up with an appropriate plan, and finds the resources to implement it.

Third, managers may believe that intellectual property is too costly to protect and analyze; and they may simply be unable or unwilling to invest the necessary money. Fourth, they may conceive themselves to be in a low risk or low yield situation especially if they have no creative personnel and no research group, or if they are in a nonprofit public institution. They may be in a country without a strong system of IP laws so that the risk of IP infringement and opportunities for licensing are minimal. Fifth, some organizations are philosophically or politically opposed to the idea of intellectual property and may choose to ignore it.

Finally, the organization may lack a staff sufficiently skilled to take on the tasks recommended in this section, and may not know where to find such people, either to hire them or bring them on as consultants. For whatever the reason, nonstrategy is the worst alternative for most organizations.

---

[1] Levels 1 to 5 were first outlined by Julie Davis and Suzanne Harris in *Edison in the Boardroom: How Leading Companies Realize Value from Their Intellectual Assets* (Wiley, 2001). They referred to an IP Value Hierarchy, in the form of a pyramid, with level one at the bottom and level five at the apex. That model reflects the view that most organizations are managed at a very low level, with very few organizations operating at the visionary level. I have found many organizations that have not even achieved Davis' Level One defensive approach, so I added the Level Zero organization. Also, because Davis and Harris focused on U.S. corporations, I have adapted the original categories to deal with nonprofits and foreign organizations as well.

To have no strategy at all has consequences. (See Appendix B.[2]) One is that staff and consultants are unable to contribute to the strength of the organization's intellectual property position. Depending on the country, the organization may derive some common-law rights from its employees by operation of law, but these are limited and largely unpredictable. A second consequence is that competitors can free ride on the organization's innovation. Competitors and others can use the organization's intellectual property in research, development, and marketing of products and services, with no payment or recognition. Third, a zero-level organization cannot limit risks to third parties. Few insurance policies are written for intellectual property infringement, so most organizations are vulnerable. In short, a zero-level organization neither protects its own assets, nor respects the rights of others. These failures by management may be so severe as to constitute a breach of the officers' duty to shareholders not to waste corporate assets.

On the other hand, a zero-level organization does save short-term costs and the effort involved in reporting, tracking, and protecting trade secrets, inventions, copyright works, and trademarks. Although some organizations may wish to contribute intellectual property assets to the public domain, with a non-policy there is no control over this process. They would be better advised to consciously and methodically adopt an open access intellectual property management plan.

A zero-level organization may also violate contractual commitments to protect the secrets of collaborators, vendors, and former employers of its staff. In particular, confidential information that may be lost includes: (1) technical information such as formulas, processes, and specifications; and (2) business information such as customer lists, supplier lists, pricing information, salaries, and benefit packages for employees. All of this trade secret information may enter the public domain. Employees can leave, taking confidential information with them and using it to compete. A zero-level organization may also unwittingly violate growing systems of privacy laws that mandate secrecy about users and customers.

A zero-level organization holds very limited rights to its own documentation, software, and graphic designs as these appear in reports, packaging, and web pages. If prepared by consultants, these consultants own the copyrights in the absence of written agreements. The value of copyrights can also be lost due to nonmarking of works, and nonregistration. A zero-level organization is also likely to violate software user licenses.

Without a confidentiality or invention disclosure program, there is no process leading toward patent protection. The rights of an inventor's employer vary from country to country and from state to state. In the United States, in general, the employer's rights are limited to a license, without the right to exclude others. Employees have certain other rights as well in different jurisdictions. Without a patent portfolio, competitors may copy and practice inventions freely. If a zero-level

---

[2] Appendix B contains a tongue-in-cheek EMPLOYEE INTELLECTUAL PROPERTY NON-POLICY, the implied rules a company has in place by default in the absence of any other IP management policy. The Non-Policy is written as if the company had affirmatively decided to accept only the minimum duties imposed by law, without any of the typical obligations companies impose on employees by agreement. The Non-Policy may inspire people in level zero organizations to begin managing their organization's intellectual property.

organization infringes someone else's patent, there can be enormous damages, and if the infringement occurs in the United States and is willful (knowing), damages can be tripled. Without a patent portfolio, there can be no bargaining chips or leverage for counterclaims. The company loses the opportunity for patent licensing revenue. There may also be violations of, federal rules which – in the United States – require that recipients of federal research grants (primarily universities and research institutions) disclose information about any inventions.

With respect to trademarks, zero-level organizations may find that their consultants own the rights to logos and marketing materials, and that foreign distributors or collaborators own the organization's trademarks. Similar or identical domain names may confuse Internet users. Finally, an organization that fails to clear use of its own trademarks may carelessly use trademarks belonging to others, and may end up having to change the trademarks and pay damages after expending vast resources to establish goodwill toward the trademarked products.

In short, there are few circumstances where a rational IP manager would affirmatively choose the zero-level strategy. Unfortunately, many organizations choose it by default. They are on a road to failure.

Level one – Defensive

The goals of an organization at a defensive level of IP management are to build a portfolio of patents and other IP assets, to protect the core business, and to maintain freedom to operate. The practices used in such organizations include taking stock of internal assets (including inventions, software, trade secrets, and licenses), protecting inventions with invention disclosure programs, enforcing rights where necessary, and checking new products for potential patent and trademark infringement.

Many creative organizations locate themselves in this category, which avoids the worst problems with zero level management. In technology companies, the most important product innovations are likely to be protected with patents. With the arts, suitable copyright notices, licenses, and registrations are employed routinely. Defensive organizations take some of the obvious steps to protect their innovation assets and avoid mistakes leading to liability or disruption. There is a continuum of management skills in level one.

Level two – Cost control

A level-two organization does what the level one organization does, but also takes steps to prioritize its IP protection. It establishes a cross-functional IP committee and establishes clear criteria for deciding what to protect, utilizing estimates of market value to distinguish its core assets from its noncore assets. Valuation includes past, present and expected future value. This allows the organization to focus its resources on the IP assets with the strongest relation to its core business activities. Weak assets that are not essential to the organization's mission are weeded out. Benchmarks can be established based on comparison with competitors' IP activities.

By maintaining a comprehensive overview, the organization can overcome inertia that may favor protection even for unimportant assets (perhaps due to emotional attachments that inventors and proponents may have for pet projects). Such cost control approaches are useful to emerging companies with substantial IP portfolios, where expenses can become a major limitation.

Level three – Profit center

A level three organization goes beyond the cost control model, and learns how to extract value directly from its IP portfolio quickly and inexpensively, selling off noncore IP assets that may have some value to others. The IP management team is more aggressive, focusing on finding possible infringers, commencing enforcement proceedings, negotiating licenses, and reviewing royalty payments as appropriate. They are proactive in business development, looking for licensing opportunities. They also conduct careful due diligence in transactions, and consider unconventional ways to generate revenue, by offering donations to nonprofits and worthy causes, for example, the which may yield tax savings and a public relations boost.

Management in a level three organization may be centralized, as with a level two company. Alternatively, some organizations, including multisubsidiary companies and multicampus university systems, may have a decentralized operation where the separate offices each have some discretion in looking for and following up on their competition.

Many universities and research institutions reach level three by focusing on licensing. The best managed corporations, particularly in the life sciences, are actively involved in business development and collaboration, and this gives them a tendency to be aware of opportunities for outlicensing. It remains, however, that most organizations approach licensing in a reactive, not a comprehensive fashion, and so never move to a level three status.

Level four – Integrated

In a level four organization, there is a thorough integration of IP strategy with corporate or organizational strategies. IP management is integrated beyond its own department, out across the entire organization. The way the management team is structured may be centralized or decentralized, but either way is consistently based on the strategic plan.

The best run organizations maintain this level. Much of this book is intended to help an IP manager achieve the integrated level.

Level five –Visionary

At the highest possible level, the organization looks carefully into the future to discern likely trends in intellectual property law and practice, and uses that prognosis to shape its strategy. Visionary organizations go so far as to create new rules, and in effect try to change the future to meet their ends. They use sophisticated tools to measure performance, and to revise strategies.

Google is an example of a company that has changed the paradigm for sharing information and is changing the structure of copyright law with its actions. Its efforts to bring all information into a readily searchable format online have spawned litigation and controversy about whether or not Google infringes the copyrights of others.[3] For example: A Google search may respond to a search request for one company by displaying a competitor's advertisement – this led the Geico insurance company to file a trademark infringement suit. Google News uses headlines downloaded from news services, and Agence France Presse sued Google for copyright infringement, leading to a settlement. Google Books is scanning all the books in major libraries, declaring that publishers who do not want to participate may opt out, but publishers have nevertheless sued for copyright infringement. Google acquired the YouTube video service, which contains many unauthorized copies of music and videos, so even more infringement actions are likely. Because its services are so popular and widely used, and Google is so big and powerful, Google has already reshaped expectations about access to information, and is likely to prevail in many of its efforts to expand access, for its own commercial gain.

Intellectual Ventures has based its "invention capital" business model on the successful patent licensing businesses of IBM and others who receive substantial portions of their income in royalty payments rather than product sales. Intellectual Ventures has acquired more than 1,000 patents in all technology sectors, and is actively promoting inventions in-house, with the goal of generating revenue without selling any product other than intellectual property. IV's business model is challenged by a global political environment that is hostile to patents on medicines, biotechnology, and software. In the United States, there are legislative proposals to limit the rights of patent "trolls" who collect royalties without selling products. The U.S. Supreme Court decisions in *MercExchange*[4] and *Medimmune*[5] have made it harder to get injunctions blocking competitors from using patented technology, and easier to challenge patents. Founder Nathan Myhrvold has kept active politically, intervening in Supreme Court arguments and testifying in Congress to overcome the antipathy toward his business model and to avoid legislation that would undercut the value of 's portfolio. Visionary companies do not just work within the intellectual property system. They reshape it to help them meet their goals.

Numerous groups including industry trade associations, nongovernmental organizations, and governmental agencies are involved in advocating for stronger or weaker IP rights, for legislative reform, and for international measures of different kinds. Advocacy groups for developing countries seek to reform international and national laws to benefit their own constituents. These groups do not readily fit into one of the other levels (except to the extent that they protect their own assets). But because their purpose is to identify trends and influence the IP systems of the future, it is appropriate to include them among the level five visionaries.

WHAT IS STRATEGIC MANAGEMENT OF INTELLECTUAL PROPERTY?

We have seen that different organizations manage intellectual property in different ways, from a negligent to a visionary approach. What can an IP manager do to move an organization to an appropriate level in the pyramid of effective IP management?

---

[3] Jeffrey Toobin, "Google's Moon Shot: The Quest for the Universal Library," *New Yorker* (February 2, 2007).

[4] *eBay Inc. v. MercExchange, L.L.C.*, 127 S.Ct. 1837 (No. 05-130) (2006).

[5] *MedImmune, Inc. v. Genentech, Inc.*, 127 S.Ct. 764 (No. 05-608) (January 9, 2007).

The best approach – being strategic – can be surprisingly simple and yet people rarely follow it. Intellectual property seems inherently elusive and complex, with its legal, technical, and business implications, and its rules change constantly. Yet the good news is that there is a basic approach that can readily be followed in any organization dealing with innovation, and there are criteria by which people in the organization can judge how well they are doing with the management task. Likewise, people outside the management team of an organization can learn how to analyze the level of care given to managing intellectual property. With that perspective, investors, collaborators, employees, and policy makers in national or international settings can make intelligent decisions about the organization, its likelihood of success, and ways to improve its situation.

Strategy, whether in a military or commercial context, refers to the process of establishing priorities and deploying resources to achieve them. Strategy can be understood as a process that bridges the gap from ends to means. It requires establishing strategic objectives, deploying resources, making tactical decisions, and implementing or executing them.[6]

In this book, the strategic management of intellectual property means the art of using intellectual property tools systematically over time to help an organization meet its goals, whatever they may be. With good strategic management, an organization can increase its assets, reduce its liabilities, and exert control over its environment. Corporations can improve their competitive position and increase the return to shareholders. Nonprofit organizations can improve their "social return on investment," delivering services more effectively, and so can government agencies. Strategic management is also relevant to the work of policy makers, who seek to stimulate innovation in public and private institutions to benefit society as a whole.

Strategic management takes place when a leader sets **simple, long-term consistent goals** based on an **objective appraisal of available resources** and a profound **understanding of the competitive environment**, and then follows up with effective **implementation**.[7] Reduced to the simplest terms, to be expanded below, strategic management involves only two tasks, repeated as necessary:

(1) Form a strategy for managing intellectual property.
(2) Implement it.

Although these tasks can become extremely complex, they sound simple, and can be relatively simple to do. But many organizations get it wrong because they act without planning. Done right, strategic management can have powerful results.

For example, a client CEO once contacted me for help with his start up company, which had recently acquired a software-based technology for which a provisional patent application had been filed. This CEO wanted to sell the technology to a larger company at some later time, but he first wanted to assemble a strong intellectual property portfolio. He had a simple plan – to improve the patent application and to find out if there were any other patents that might block commercial exploitation

---

[6] Fred Nickols, "Strategy Definitions and Meanings," available at http://home.att.net/~discon/strategy_definitions.pdf, accessed December 27, 2006.

[7] Robert Grant, *Contemporary Strategy Analysis* (1998).

of the software system. We looked more broadly at the company's needs, decided to take initial steps to protect all types of intellectual property simultaneously, and then went forward rapidly to implement the plan. Over the course of about two months we prepared confidentiality agreements to keep trade secrets from becoming public, we filed an expanded patent application to capture aspects of the invention lacking in the earlier application, and we conducted a search to identify and distinguish similar patents held by competitors. When we researched the company's trademark, we found it already in use by someone else and rejected it, rejected several more proposed by the CEO, but finally confirmed that yet another trademark he selected was available. We filed trademark applications for that, arranged to change the corporate name to match the trademark, and reserved domain names. We confirmed there were no copyright restrictions on the software, and we took steps to register copyright in the program. We prepared a license agreement to protect the trade secrets and define rights during a complex field test by a government agency. By completing these tasks in a concerted fashion, the company was able to assemble a strong IP portfolio, providing the assurance required to grow further or to sell the business profitably.

This series of actions illustrates how an IP manager carries out an intellectual property strategy. First, the CEO committed to improving the intellectual property posture of the company. Second, he identified people to handle the task (including me and my colleagues), delegated work, and established a budget. He set an overall goal for the organization, and then, based on analysis of internal assets and external obstacles, came up with a plan for protecting the fledgling technology. Together, we took steps to implement the plan. He committed to correcting past problems. He brought together the professional team and the financial resources to accomplish his goals. He protected his company's assets and avoided the catastrophic loss and liability that might have arisen from use of an infringing trademark, misuse of someone else's trade secrets, infringing on patent claims, or copying someone else's copyright work.

Intellectual property professionals take great pride in such projects. Unfortunately, many organizations fail to perform the necessary steps, and they suffer as a result. For example, I have worked with innovative organizations that spend significant effort analyzing corporate strategy, but do not even try to come up with a strategy to protect their intellectual property. Other organizations develop an IP management plan, but don't implement it systematically. Yet others may have a good plan for a small task (for example, protecting a new electronic widget) but no comprehensive plan (covering the organization's overall innovative activities and all IP assets).

A surprising number of organizations operate nonstrategically, reactively, with employees left to cope with intellectual property issues only on a case-by-case basis as problems arise. They are in the position of airline passengers who hear their pilot announce that he has bad news and good news: "The bad news is that our navigation equipment has malfunctioned, so we have no idea where we are or where we're going. The good news is that the engines are running fine, so we'll get there very quickly."

An organization that makes decisions about intellectual property without a strategic plan is like a pilot flying blind. Fortunately, organizations with the least strategic approach to intellectual property – those at levels zero or one – can make the biggest improvements most quickly. They have the most to gain.

FORM A STRATEGY

First, forming a strategy requires the following:

- Define the organization's overall goals.
- Assess internal resources objectively.
- Evaluate the competitive market thoroughly.
- Form a simple, long-range IP management plan consistent with resources, competition, and goals.

Any plan should be subject to adjustment and improvement as circumstances change.[8] So an IP manager should periodically review the IP management plan and modify it as needed, especially as the skill levels of those involved at the organization improve.

Define goals

Everybody involved in managing an organization should know the general goals of the organization, what it seeks to do and what it does not, often defined in its mission statement. For a money-making corporation, the mission statement explains how the company makes its money. For a nonprofit organization, the mission statement explains what public purpose the organization serves, and how. Within large organizations, managers of each subdivision should know their own specific goals and be able to express them clearly. In multinational corporations, the subdivision may be an entire business unit. Within state university systems, each campus may have somewhat different goals.

Apple Computer's mission statement is "Apple will be a leader in providing simple, powerful, high-quality information products and services for people who learn, communicate, and create." This mission holds true across the range of Apple products including computers, the iPod, iTunes, and iPhone. Mission statements and organizational goals are intended to be broad and inspiring, and may not be very useful in defining what an organization should and should not be doing. But they are the logical place to start. For organizations whose management has not prepared a clear mission statement, the IP manager should try to craft one anyway. The IP manager may takes an official or unofficial organizational statement and translate it into a specific set of goals and a plan for managing the organization's intellectual property.

By expressing at least a general goal, and formulating at least a tentative plan, the IP manager can avoid making ad hoc decisions in a reactive manner, managing an "adhocracy" that leads to overspending on some assets and underprotection for others, increased stress and cost, and less time and financial resources available for other purposes.

---

[8] Richard Koch, *FT Guide to Strategy* (2005).

The goals need to be readily communicated, understood, and remembered by the many people who coordinate their efforts. If they are too complicated, they cannot be communicated clearly, and as in the children's game of telephone, the message will change with each retelling.

The common goal of any IP manager is to increase control over both internal innovation and the outside community, to protect internal assets and accessing external IP rights. The resulting control may be used to increase profit (for corporations) or social impact (for nonprofit organizations). Put in accounting terms, the goals are to maximize assets, and minimize liabilities. Organizations can maximize IP assets by converting human capital into IP rights protected by laws, converting IP rights into profit, and avoiding their loss. They can minimize IP liabilities by enlisting employees' help in avoiding exposure by infringement.

What does an IP manager do to increase control? The IP manager can apply general goal to particular circumstances. Some actions carried out with IP assets include:

- Sell a product or service at a premium by blocking price competition.
- Create a product or service with extra value due to innovative internal methods and technologies (such as the pioneering Internet marketplaces created by Amazon, eBay, and Google).
- License rights to a competitor to increase capacity, settle a dispute, or profit without further effort.
- License to someone in an alternate sector where the innovator does not compete – universities and nonprofit research institutions do not compete with the companies that they license.
- Sell the IP rights.
- Give the rights away (as with Merck's donation of ivermectin to treat river blindness in Africa).[9]
- Control the actions of downstream users (as with the open access licensing model used by Linux, Wikipedia, and others).
- Use the IP as a defensive bargaining chip in the event an outsiders accuses the owner of infringement.

The goals should be directed to long-term as well as short-term results. Many organizations do not manage their IP strategically but rather reactively. If a product is about to go on the market, they file a rush patent application. If a competitor is using a similar trademark, they send off a cease-and-desist letter. If a key employee leaves the company, they worry about how to stop loss of corporate secrets. Their common outlook – a perspective of the next task or of only the next year – is much too short. A more useful horizon is three to five years, maybe as long as ten years for a long-lived innovation. The long view provides the innovation chief, the IP manager, and those who work for them with guidance for many individual day to day decisions, even about details such as where to file trademark or patent applications, whether to keep an application pending by paying the costs to maintain them, what terms

---

[9] Kimberly Collins, "Profitable Gifts: A History of the Merck Mectizan Donation Program and Its Implications for International Health" in *Perspectives in Biology and Medicine*, 47(1):100–109 (2004).

to put into a license agreement, and so on. A longer view promotes consistency, but can still be changed as necessary.

IP management goals must also be internally consistent. For example, it could be inconsistent for a company to amass an expensive portfolio of software patents while pursuing an open source software copyright licensing model – gaining the right to exclude users is not worthwhile if they will be permitted free access without restrictions. Or if there is a marketing drive to expand into Asian markets with new products, it is important to ensure that there is sufficient IP protection in those markets. If there are no plans to expand in Latin America, then it is less important to pursue protection there, since there is no immediate expansion potential.

Assess human resources

In forming a strategy, the IP manager must make an objective appraisal of the internal innovation resources of the organization or community. Human resources are first and most important – the talents of people available to the organization, including employees and consultants, the creative, legal, and business talents of employees working inside the organization or retained as outside consultants. By identifying these people, the IP manager can determine the magnitude of the organizational challenge and the human resources available.

The IP manager should have a clear sense of who generates creative ideas in the organization. Different kinds of innovative organizations have different creative people. In a technology company, the creative people are generally engineers, scientists, or designers. In the entertainment industry, they are writers, artists, and musicians. In financial services, they may be economists. In addition to those whose job is to be creative, other employees may contribute ideas. They, too, can be an innovative force.

The IP manager should also know where to find good legal advice, and how to implement decisions involving intellectual property. Generally, legal expertise is provided by an in-house legal department and by outside lawyers and professional consultants. A patent-rich organization may have in-house patent attorneys and agents. A trademark-rich company typically has trademark attorneys and paralegals. An organization with extensive business relationships may have a licensing specialist in-house. All of them supplement with outside expertise, especially for litigation and other situations requiring special skills.

Business talents may be found throughout organizations. However, few business managers understand intellectual property or are experienced with managing it. And they may be scattered around an organization. It can be helpful for an IP manager to identify members of the business staff who have relevant skills in dealing with intellectual property, whatever their job description, so that they may be involved in further planning and implementation.

Innovative organizations operate increasingly in an international environment. So their legal and business teams must know or learn how to assess IP-related information and laws around the world, to make decisions that will work globally, and to implement plans in many countries at once. This too requires networks of internal employees and external consultants.

Once the creative, legal, and business teams have been identified, they can be brought together to compile information, make decisions, and take action. The next step they should take, under the IP manager's leadership, is assessing the organization's IP portfolio.

Assess intellectual property resources

The second internal resource that the IP manager needs to assess is the existing portfolio of IP assets that have been developed or acquired in the past. This involves identifying all relevant types of intellectual property (patents, trade secrets, copyright, trademarks, and any other rights). Most organizations maintain lists of their patents and applications, trademark registrations, copyright registrations, and licenses. If not, the IP manager must begin by creating the IP portfolio list. If there is an existing IP portfolio list, it may not have been prepared to document available resources as a strategic tool. Instead, it may have been assembled for a tactical purpose – to obtain financing, to sell or license a product line, or to inform accounting reports. Such listings tend to be incomplete and out of date. The IP manager should take steps to update and expand whatever the available listings.

In addition to the basic listing of assets, a corporation's accountants may be able to provide information used in evaluating the corporation's goodwill according to current accounting standards.[10] Much of the value of goodwill can be attributed to the brands and trademarks of the organization, as well as other intellectual property. But accounting records serve financial purposes, and are not well adapted to the needs of IP management. Many of the organization's IP assets – for example, business plans, customer lists, supplier information, and financial data – may be ignored or glossed over by accountants, but they nonetheless require specific attention by an IP manager.

For listing and valuing the most important IP assets, more detailed analysis may be appropriate. One approach used with patents, pioneered by Kevin Rivette, is to prepare a topographical map showing the relationships between clusters of patents and their relevance to particular technologies. For important decisions about the most important assets, such as whether to enforce them against an infringer, or how to build or expand rights around a particular technology, the IP manager can assess the strength of the intellectual property in three dimensions.

- Legal scope: What is the scope of exclusive rights in the covered subject matter? What activities and products do they cover? How easily can they be enforced? What weaknesses or exceptions are there in exclusivity?
- Duration: How long will the right last? When does it expire?
- Geographical range: In what countries are the rights valid? In what regions of those countries?

A three-dimensional assessment is shown in Figure 8.1.

These three dimensions of value provide a well-rounded understanding of the relative value of different IP rights and portfolios. Valuation of IP assets is considered

---

[10] Baruch Lev, *Intangibles: Management, Measurement, and Reporting* (Brookings Institution Press, 2001).

Figure 8.1. IP strength in three dimensions. An IP right or portfolio can be visualized in terms of its legal scope, geographical range, and duration; a famous trademark may have moderate scope, international range, and unlimited duration, while a trade secret in a product about to be marketed may have narrow scope, local value, and short duration, and a patent in several countries may have strong legal scope, moderate geographical range, and a duration of 20 years.

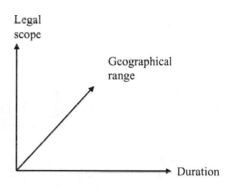

separately in Chapter 12. Here, it suffices to note that the ideal situation is to have a valuable IP asset, with strong legal scope, enforceable in many countries, with a long time left until the IP right expires.

Specific situations fall short of this ideal. IBM's portfolio of 40,000 patents could be separated into various subgroups with different strengths and weaknesses, and each assessed in this manner. A famous trademark like Coca-Cola may have moderate legal scope (preventing use of the name on competing soft drinks, but not their sale), global range, and unlimited duration. Trade secrets relating to the timing, pricing, and features of a new product may have narrow legal scope (the marketing details for the product), local value in the countries where it will be marketed, and short duration ending when the product is launched. A patent on a laboratory instrument may have strong legal scope for that device, moderate geographical range (if filed only in the United States, Europe, and Japan), and a duration of 20 years.

Assess intellectual property practices

Third, the IP manager needs to consider the established practices and policies already in place at the organization affecting intellectual property. The IP manager should determine whether the organization has established practices dealing with confidentiality, disclosure of inventions, gaining approval for use of outsiders' technology, and transferring legal rights. If not, part of the IP strategy will be to implement or improve such practices.

Because organizational practices and relationships are not readily protected as forms of intellectual property, some people refer to them as intellectual assets. This is reasonable, because such practices and relationships do not necessarily share a fundamental characteristic of intellectual property – the right to exclude others. However, some aspects of these practices and relationships are protected by trade secrets and these would be considered to be intellectual property. So, though the practices and relationships of an organization may be considered intellectual assets, aspects of them may also be intellectual property.

Internal relationships and practices determine what individual employees and consultants can accomplish. Relationships and practices can be very helpful if they support innovation and the wise use of the intellectual property system. If they inhibit collaboration and disclosure and effective decision making, organizational practices can create a challenge to the IP manager.

Other resources

Finally, there are other physical and financial resources that the IP manager needs to consider. These include inventories of supplies and finished products, equipment, buildings, and of course money available to invest in intellectual property. These resources are relevant not only to intellectual property management, but rather may be important throughout the organization. These resources are more tangible than the other categories described above, and most organizations know how to track and manage them following established practices.

Study the competitive environment

The IP manager must identify any intellectual property rights that interfere with the organization's access to information or materials, or markets. Generally it is best to learn in advance about any obstacle that might restrict the organization's freedom to operate – its ability to take action that would otherwise be desirable. Any obstacles then have to be evaluated and dealt with.

In assessing any IP rights that turn up as potential obstacles, as with the assessment of internal resources, the IP manager needs to consider their strength in several dimensions. Is the IP right broad enough to encompass the intended activity? Will it expire soon enough to stop being an obstacle in the near future? Is it applicable in the relevant countries? How valuable is the right to the owner, and is there an opportunity to acquire a license? There are many issues that go into assessing the IP rights of others, and there is a straightforward decision tree analysis that IP managers can follow to achieve maximum available freedom to operate (as discussed below in Chapters 11 and 13).

Researching the IP portfolios of competitors also serves a broader goal of competitive intelligence, beyond simply assuring freedom to operate. That is, any activity taken to protect IP gives a strong measure of what innovations the organization considers most important, and is reflected in the public record built from the patents, copyrights, and trademarks.

Another reason an IP manager should carefully assess the IP of competitors is for benchmarking – to compare the relative efforts of the organizations in protecting their IP. For example, as a student reported in his term paper, one of the brewing companies has a vast trademark portfolio, but relatively few patents. Other smaller brewers have much larger portfolios of patents on brewing methods, bottling, and other aspects of the complex task of converting barley, hops, water, and yeast into the beverage that we can hoist to our lips and enjoy. With such information, a company may choose to increase its patenting activity, to ensure that it will never be put at a competitive disadvantage by other brewers.

Develop an IP management plan

With all the basic information outlined above (about the overall organizational mission, the internal resources, and the competitive environment), the IP manager needs to put together a management plan. Ultimately, there are only two possible purposes for such a plan:

(1) to **protect** the organization's own IP assets, and
(2) to **access** innovations of others without violating their IP rights.

The IP manager should be aware which type of activity is called for at any given time. The difference between protecting rights and accessing the innovations of others without infringing their rights can be very tricky conceptually. Many people have difficulty with the principle that most intellectual property rights are exclusive but not permissive. That is, it is often possible to obtain an intellectual property right to exclude someone else, without being free to carry out the activity yourself due to exclusive rights of someone else.

For example, if there is an existing patented product, and an inventor obtains a patent on an improvement – such as a new method of using the product – the later patent does not give the right to use the original product without permission from the first patent holder. The prior patent may be relevant to patentability of the new improvement (protecting intellectual property), but it is separately relevant to freedom to operate (accessing innovations of others). With regard to copyright, an author who samples and uses parts of existing works to produce a new work can protect it by copyright, but depending on the scope and nature of the use of the prior work, the author may need permission from the original authors to distribute the new derivative work.

Therefore, it is usually necessary to run through key IP management issues twice – once with regard to protecting innovations with IP rights, and again to deal with accessing the innovations of others without violating their IP rights. Even for experienced professionals, it can be cognitively difficult to analyze both issues – protecting and respecting IP rights – simultaneously. When coming up with an IP management plan, the IP manager will generally need to treat both activities – protecting rights and freedom to operate – separately.

To protect assets, the IP manager uses intellectual property to further build the organization's own intellectual property portfolio – to grow its own innovation forest. To protect assets, the IP manager must find the right combination of the following activities, consistent with budget and need:

(1) preserving,
(2) perfecting,
(3) transferring, and
(4) enforcing IP rights.

In order to respect the IP rights of others, the IP manager must analyze the competitive environment and map out the IP rights of others – in other words, explore their innovation forest. The IP manager must then find a noninfringing path to achieve the organization's goals and a plan for action.

IMPLEMENT THE PLAN

The IP manager, having developed a long range, simple, consistent plan for managing IP, attuned to the organization's goals, resources, and environment, must then take steps to implement the strategy. Implementing a strategy involves taking the necessary steps, measuring performance at each stage, and following up as necessary. Implementing a plan across an organization involves causing a group of people to take concerted action within their field of expertise. Again, this is more difficult than it sounds. Protecting intellectual property, or working through a thicket of rights belonging to others, may be difficult and expensive, and may take a long time to accomplish. For example, a pharmaceutical company may include in its plan the decision "expand patent protection for new uses, variants, and formulations of anticancer drug X." The necessary action may include months of analysis and drafting to complete new patent applications, and then years of effort at prosecuting the patents in various national patent offices.

A software company may put into its action plan a commitment to reduce copyright infringement. The action required may lead to a massive global program to identify infringers, strengthen copyright protection for the software, identify test case defendants, and commence litigation in key locations while promoting marketing channels that make it easier for people to obtain licensed copies of the software.

In short, the IP manager is the person responsible for managing a particular section of an innovation forest, and to manage it strategically. This involves three tasks:

• Assessing: and identifying the organization's goals, reviewing the available internal innovation assets, and mapping the surrounding environment defined by other people's rights.
• Being decisive, selecting a simple long-range strategic plan for achieving the organization's goals, protecting and using internal assets and constantly re-assessing the environment.
• Implementing the plan with active steps, employing resources in specific situations to put the strategy into practice, measuring results, and adjusting the strategy over time.

SUMMARY. A hierarchy of IP management begins with level zero, with no management at all. The first level of management is defensive. A second level involves cost control. The third level turns IP management into a profit center. A fourth level integrates IP management into the core activities of the organization, and a fifth, visionary level, changes laws and practices to help achieve organizational goals. Strategic management is the process whereby a leader finds and achieves the right level on this scale. Strategic management refers to a process of first, understanding the organization's mission; second, assessing the internal resources and the external environment; third, developing a strategic plan by protecting internal rights while not infringing the rights of others; and finally, implementing that plan to help achieve the organization's goals. A strategic IP manager forms a strategy, defines a goal, assesses human resources and intellectual property resources, develops a management plan, and then implements it systematically over time. Organizations use strategic management of intellectual property to drive the innovation cycle forward and shape their environment, using practical legal and business strategies and tools. The rest of this section describes the process of planning, assessment, and implementation.

9 Strategy Tools: Policies and Practices for Managing Intellectual Property

IP managers perform their jobs by establishing certain policies and practices, grouped here into six categories. An overarching **policy on managing IP** sets the basic guidelines for an organization, and links the other categories together. **Personnel practices** ensure that rights flow properly from employees. Good IP **portfolio management** increases assets and avoids liabilities to outsiders. Sound practices for **procurement** (supply chain management) help aggregate IP rights in the organization and avoid liability to suppliers. Effective **partnering practices** avoid loss of rights, and help promote development of good ideas. **Policing** activities help maintain control over innovations, and if necessary lead to enforcement actions. These "Six Ps" provide a basis for managing costs, and for continuous reassessment, and are the foundation for good IP management in all organizations.

* * * * * *

Like crafts and farming, intellectual property management relies on certain tools and practices to shape starting materials into desired end products. This chapter introduces the basic management tools and practices that an innovation chief and IP manager can use to drive the innovation cycle.

THE SIX Ps: POLICIES AND PRACTICES

Managing intellectual property in an organization regulates all three steps of the innovation cycle: the individual's creative act in conceiving a new idea; the organization's development, adoption, and marketing of that new idea; and the flow of the innovation into the accessible domain. By managing intellectual property, an organization can take an individual's new idea and cultivate and grow it into legally recognized rights shared by increasingly broader groups of people, first inside and then outside the organization, and can regulate the passage of the innovation from the IP domain to the accessible domain.

In a typical scenario, an employee conceives of a way to improve the performance of the employer's commercial product, so that it can be used in new markets. The IP manager helps protect the improvement as a secret and then as a patented invention, and helps select a strong trademark, and eventually licenses the rights to others for use in different products. How does an IP manager manage this process?

Organizations generally coordinate the activities of staff through official policies and practices, as well as custom and "culture." Policies and practices are typically communicated among staff with documents such as manuals, memos, checklists, and forms; and in person, via lectures, training sessions, mentoring, and while performing individual projects as the need arises. The same is true for IP management. There are several practices and procedures that organizations can establish and communicate to staff, with documents and in person, to cultivate intellectual property and drive the innovation cycle. They fall into six categories we can refer to as the "Six Ps." They are:

- Policy for IP management
- Personnel practices
- Portfolio management practices
- Procurement practices
- Partnering practices
- Policing activities.

The Six Ps denote the principal tools available to an IP manager. Imagine two organizations, one strong in IP management, and the other weak. The well managed organization has each of the six policies and practices in place, while the poorly managed organization is weak in one or more of them.

The Six Ps are a logical way to identify and group important tasks. By focusing on the Six Ps, an IP manager can understand available choices and can communicate and implement chosen strategies. These practices and procedures can ensure that the organization is using its assets wisely, and can locate and correct any weaknesses.

Guidelines are described for each of the six.

Policy for IP management

An IP manager should begin by putting into place a general plan or policy statement about how the organization manages its intellectual property. Organizations that manage IP at more advanced levels summarize their current policies in an IP management policy document. A typical IP policy states some variation of the following basic principles.

Intellectual property management is important to the organization. We make strategic decisions about the importance of protecting IP assets and accessing innovations of others, and we plan actions and budget accordingly. We carry out these plans according to policies and practices regarding personnel, IP portfolio management, procurement, partnering, and policing IP rights.

The organization will protect its own IP assets. We preserve, perfect, transfer, and enforce intellectual property rights in a methodical way, to maximize assets, in conformity with the organization's goals.

The organization will respect the IP rights of others. We take reasonable steps to learn about the rights of others, and to make sure not to infringe, to minimize losses.

The organization has a confidentiality program. We inform staff of their obligations toward trade secrets; we control access to premises, confidential documents, and electronic files; we include appropriate confidentiality provisions in employment agreements, consulting agreements, and partnering agreements.

The organization has a copyright program. We put copyright notices on all publications, packaging, and website pages, and we register significant works. We require work-for-hire and/or assignment agreements from our consultants and contractors. We license rights as appropriate, for example, with click-through user agreements.

The organization has a patenting program. Employees submit invention disclosures to IP managers, who review the invention disclosures, file timely applications on important advances to obtain diverse coverage, and file foreign applications on the most important applications. We maintain or drop applications depending on their value to the organization, and we enforce patents as appropriate. With significant projects, we obtain clearance opinions, and license rights from others if necessary.

The organization has a trademark program. We clear new product/service marks before putting them into use, and we register significant marks. We mark products and marketing materials consistently, and we follow the rules when licensing others to use our marks or when obtaining a license to use someone else's mark.

This policy differs radically from that of the level zero organization described in Chapter 8 and in Appendix B.

When would the leaders of an organization adopt or amend such a general policy on IP management? When would they wish to consult that policy for guidance? Most organizations adopt a general policy or plan on IP management either because they recognize its advantages or because they are asked to do so by investors, insurers, or collaborators. Many other triggering events can also remind an IP manager to review the existing IP management policy and to follow or update it. They include:

- Buying, selling, or starting a business
- Developing or improving a new product or service
- Selecting a new name or logo, preparing new product literature, or launching a new website or marketing campaign
- Creating original art, crafts, or software
- Bringing on a key employee or consultant for design, research, or development work
- Providing business or technical information to investors, suppliers, customers.

By stating a general policy for IP management, a leader can communicate within the organization (or a broader or narrower innovation community) the most crucial practices, and can help people follow them. As noted, the main IP management practices relate to personnel, portfolio management, procurement, partnering, and policing. A general policy helps the organization put the right staff in place, collect the right information, make the right decisions in timely fashion, and ultimately protect and respect IP rights consistent with the organization's goals.

In forming a strategy for managing IP in any given context, a good place to start is to review the organization's general policies As we have seen in connection with zero-level organizations, if an organization has no comprehensive policy for managing IP, establishing one should be a high priority. If there are sound policies in place already, then this minimal prerequisite may be satisfied. Nevertheless, it is important to revisit the general IP management policy from time to time to see if it needs to be changed.

Personnel practices

The general goal of IP management is to maintain control over the innovation cycle, to help the organization serve its constituency, for example by increasing profit (for corporations) or impact (for nonprofits). The most obvious way to exert such control is to coordinate the efforts of everyone within the innovation community – typically, the employed staff of a corporate organization.

Employees are central to IP management. They are the biggest source of intellectual property flowing into (and out of) innovative organizations. Their conduct is also the biggest cause of IP liability.

The distinction between employees and outsiders extends to IP rights as well, and an organization is defined in large part by the distinctions between internal and external IP rights. Organizations should protect their internal rights and pay attention to external rights, to find ways to access external innovations in an appropriate fashion.

Personnel practices deal with both internal and external rights. The desired result of good personnel practices is that the flow of IP into the organization is maximized, the flow out is minimized, and infringing activity is avoided. Personnel practices like those that managers use to coordinate staff behavior can serve also to convert the ideas and creative work of staff into IP assets belonging to the organization. The organization can use such practices to shape itself and its environment, by limiting needless access to innovative work and thereby avoiding loss of IP, yet assuring that creative staff have whatever they need. Good personnel practices also help employees take responsibility for identifying risk and avoiding liabilities that arise from infringing the rights of others.

The best place to state personnel practices consistent with good IP management guidelines is in an employment contract. Although the rules differ from jurisdiction to jurisdiction, generally some combination of the following clauses are found in most modern employment relations. First, restrictive covenants limit the employee's freedom to take certain actions that would undercut good IP management. One important clause obliges the employee to assign any inventions to the employer. Perhaps the most common restrictive covenant for intellectual property is a promise to keep secrets – to maintain the confidentiality of confidential information during and after employment. Related covenants include a promise not to work for a competitor for some set time after employment ends, and a promise not to solicit other employees to leave the old employer to come work for the new employer.

Such post-employment covenants can help protect the old employer's trade secrets, but they are difficult to enforce, and may not be binding in some jurisdictions. For example, some software programmers left one of my clients in India and went to work for a direct competitor, reportedly taking a secret copy of the program with them. We notified the competitor that the programmers had contractual obligations not to use any confidential materials learned in their past employment, under an international form of employment agreement used by that company. We sent copies of the employment contracts signed by the employees to prove our point. The competitor responded that the employees had not taken and were not using any of my client's confidential information. We decided not to start an enforcement lawsuit in India, with uncertain results, but took some comfort that the competitor would behave properly after being put on notice of a possible infringement. Copyright protections were also in place.

Personnel practices affect intellectual property rights at each stage of the employment relationship. When recruiting a new employee, the new employer should be careful to respect the rights of the former employer by not interfering with the prospective employee's contractual relationship with the former employer. New employees want to use all the skills and experience they gained in past positions, and there is a natural tendency for new employers to ask new employees to describe projects they worked on at their former employer's. However, such disclosures can violate confidentiality obligations to the former employer, and the new employer may be liable for resulting damage. Also, any inventions reported by the new employee shortly after arrival may actually be subject to an obligation to assign them to the former employer. The recruiting employer should therefore take affirmative steps to advise new employees not to use any secrets or inventions belonging to former employers.

During the course of employment, there is an ongoing need for employees to protect intellectual property, to avoid loss of trade secrets, and for many, to create new confidential information. Employees should be shown how to secure confidential information, and prevent misappropriation of trade secrets by others.

As for copyright, the employer is generally deemed to be the author of any work created by its employees in the scope of their work (but not in their spare time), so there may be no need for the employee to assign specific rights in the copyright. In a looser employment relationship, part time or with consultants, it is crucial to have an explicit written agreement (at least in the United States) that the work will be considered a work made for hire, with a fall-back agreement to assign copyrights to the employer. In many situations, the employee may retain ownership of works of authorship.

The terms of employment of college faculty, for example, typically treat them as authors and allow them to retain copyright of their own publications. A professor with a successful text book may earn more in royalties than in salary. This is distinct from a typical university patent policy, where faculty members are obliged to assign inventions to the university. Faculty may, however, still receive substantial royalties even after assigning their patent rights. (I find it ironic that in corporations, which are profit-oriented, inventors rarely get any share of their inventions' profit, whereas in universities, which are nonprofit, faculty do receive a share.)

If their agreement requires it, employees must learn to follow the employer's invention disclosure program. Typically, an employee who makes an invention in the course of employment is required to disclose the invention and to assign patent rights to the employer. On the other hand, absent a very strong clause in an employment contract, an employee has no obligation to assign an invention that the employee made completely independently, that is, not on company time, without using employer funds, equipment, or facilities, and without using any confidential information of the employer. If the employee used any of these resources, the employer may have some rights to the invention.

For example, Steven Jobs and Steven Wozniak were working for the Atari game company when they built their first personal computer using Atari components, in Jobs's parents' garage. They asked their manager if Atari had any interest in the device, and were told they were free to develop it on their own. That led to the independent formation of Apple Computer, Inc. in 1976, which worked out well for Jobs and Wozniak, but not so well for Atari.

At the end of the employment relationship, either because the employee quits or is fired, it is important to have a termination process to maximize protection of intellectual property. Typically, this involves an exit interview in which a manager reminds the employee of the obligations to maintain confidentiality and to assign inventions, and asks the employee if there are any trade secrets, copyright works, or inventions that should be given or reported to the employer. All confidential materials, including physical samples, models, laboratory notebooks, and computer files, need to be returned.

Also, some employment agreements include a clause providing that a patent application filed shortly after departure (e.g., 6 months) will be presumed to have been invented at the prior employer, so they would be assigned to the former employer, not the new one. The departing employee needs to be reminded of any such post-employment obligations. If a key employee departs and goes to a competitor, the former employer may want to monitor any patent filings and commercial activities for some time to be sure that no infringement occurs.

Some of the highest profile trade secret theft cases arise from termination of employment. For example, in 1993, General Motors' high profile purchasing executive Lopez de Arriortua went to work for rival Volkswagen in Germany. He allegedly took with him thousands of pages of confidential documents relating to GM's procurement practices. In 1997, after a protracted lawsuit, Volkswagen agreed to pay $100 million to GM. De Arriortua claimed defamation, but faced criminal charges for industrial espionage in Germany, which he was able to defeat, and in the United States as well, which he was able to avoid only by fighting extradition from Spain, his home country. This sad story serves as a cautionary tale for employers and employees to be careful about trade secrets on leaving employment, particularly when going to a competitor.

In summary, employment practices are a crucial starting point for any organization seeking to protect its intellectual property rights. The innovation chief or IP manager has to deal with different concerns when hiring staff, supervising them, and managing their transition when they leave. Personnel practices should be reviewed when establishing or improving an IP management plan, or when forming a new IP management strategy.

Portfolio management

By establishing good personnel practices, an organization optimizes the influx of intellectual assets from staff. The next logical step is to protect those assets as intellectual property, and build up a portfolio. As summarized in the guidelines set forth in the general policy for IP management described above, the components of portfolio management are a confidentiality program, a copyright program, a patenting program, and a trademark program. In each program, the organization needs to take steps to protect its own rights, and follow up to police its IP assets, by diligent licensing and enforcement activities. The way in which these programs are deployed depends on the strategy selected for each particular organization. (See Chapters 13 and 14.)

There are fundamental differences between the rules and procedures for protecting and policing trade secrets, patents, copyrights, and trademarks. Nonetheless, there are some similar elements for each, worth mentioning here.

First, in each case the IP management process begins with someone coming up with a new idea and communicating it to the IP manager. In a well-run organization, there is a clear channel for communicating new ideas to those responsible for evaluating and then protecting valuable innovations. For example, many organizations have regular meetings to review new developments. The IP manager or representatives can participate in such meetings, gaining familiarity with the tempo and types of innovation at the organization. Consider a product recall due to manufacturing defects. In solving its technical problems, the manufacturer likely comes up with combinations of new secrets, patentable inventions, copyrightable software, and new brands for the next generation of improved products, trying to leave the bad reputation of the old product behind. Competitors may go through the same process to avoid the defect. The engineering team reports any innovations, through the research department, to the IP management team.

The second common element for all types of IP rights is the need for affirmative steps to protect the innovation as intellectual property. Different kinds of action are required for each type of IP, but no IP right can be protected passively.

The third element in protecting IP rights is that they require special care in monitoring and evaluating them. (See Chapters 11 and 12.) An organization cannot reasonably protect and police its IP rights without knowing what they are. A crucial aspect of IP management, therefore, is assessment of the overall intellectual property portfolio. Specifically, portfolio management practices include how to monitor it, evaluate it qualitatively, and place economic valuations on it as well. This is a crucial activity for an IP manager, and one requiring a high degree of expertise, at least for complex portfolios.

In essence, there are three approaches typically used to evaluate IP. The first is to list all registered assets. The second is to determine whether appropriate IP management practices are in place, in particular for unregistered assets such as trade secrets. The third is to focus on a particular product and characterize all of the IP rights that exist or could be brought to bear on it. Portfolio assessment is important at all stages, from strategy formation, to implementation in various contexts. In each approach, it is desirable to categorize each asset by its value to the core of the organization's business, or its value as a peripheral asset.

In sum, portfolio management involves carrying out the general IP management policy, protecting the various types of IP rights, evaluating them, and policing them (a separate issue to be discussed below). The details differ widely by industry practice and by the particular strategies employed in different organizations.

Procurement practice

According to the A → B → C → D model, all intellectual property flows into an organization either from insiders (employees and consultants) or outsiders (including suppliers and competitors). (See Figure 5.8.) Here, procurement is meant to include all flow of information and materials from outsiders into any one organization. Some people refer to this process as supply chain management.

What can be procured by an innovative person or organization? The list is long and broad. It includes information (including text, data, and graphic content, and process technology), computer software, and also tangible things like mechanical and electrical equipment, chemical reagents, and biological materials. Legal rights can also be acquired, including patents, trade secrets, trademarks, copyrights, and contract rights associated with intellectual property (such as licenses and an employee's obligation to assign innovations to the employer). This includes computer hardware and software, "dryware" in the form of information, and "wetware" (a jesting term for biological materials).

Procurement creates two risks. First, an organization that acquires "hot" goods that infringe an IP right may also acquire an infringement lawsuit. Second, an organization that provides infringing goods and services to its customers may need to indemnify those customers, who will feel cheated if they are sued, and will seek reimbursement. If the organization acquires clean title to all its inputs, then it can use the material and information within the organization, and can provide them to customers as goods and services without infringement. If clean title comes in, clean title goes out.

The basic thrust of good procurement practice is to ensure freedom to operate. There are three ways to ensure this. One is if the innovation is not protected by IP rights at all – if they are completely in the public domain. Another way is to own the asset. An organization has no exposure to infringement actions regarding its own IP assets, or those it co-owns with others.

A third way to assure clean title is to obtain a license. A license is permission to use the innovation in certain stated ways, in exchange for consideration. At its essence, a license is an agreement by the IP owner not to exercise its exclusive rights. A good license permits the organization to carry out whatever acts it plans, and to transfer to customers whatever is intended.

For example, consider a vaccine company's purchase of equipment to set up a new gene sequencing center for determining the genetic sequence of bird flu virus samples. The gene sequencing center's shopping list includes microbiological culture equipment for handling the samples and processing them to grow in bacterial host cells (microbial samples, Petri dishes, test tubes, and incubators), biochemical equipment for separating out and amplifying the DNA (fluid handling systems, thermal cyclers), analytical instruments for reading the DNA sequence (optical scanners), and computer hardware and software for interpreting the data and assembling the sequence from many bits and pieces. Much of this equipment can be purchased outright, and the sale agreement would typically include an assignment of the physical device itself, with an implied license to use any patents held by the device's manufacturer, to the extent necessary to use it. As to the software, the vaccine company would need to check the user agreement to make sure it includes the right to carry out the company's intended screening activities, and that there are no restrictions, say, to academic research only. The software license also needs to cover a sufficient number of computer users. For the biological materials, the company needs to be sure that adequate consents have been obtained, and that genetic analysis and use of the data is permitted. Finally, if the company needs genetic data available on public databases, to compare to the newly screened data, it can access most such data without restrictions. From the company's point of view, then, the procurement succeeded in providing freedom to operate, through assignment of rights and purchase of equipment, by actual and implied licenses, and by use of public domain materials.

If freedom to operate can not be achieved, then the IP manager must make a series of decisions about how to obtain access to the desired information, materials, or technology. For example, if a genetic sequencing center is not able to buy an important patented instrument at a reasonable price (or at all), then the organization must choose whether to use an alternative instrument, to challenge the patent, or to find another line of work altogether.

Sometimes, despite the IP manager's best efforts, through negligence or as a result of a calculated risk, an outsider asserts that the organization is liable for infringing IP rights. The claim may come in the form of a letter or a lawsuit asserting misappropriation of trade secrets or infringement of patent, copyright, or trademark rights. Procurement practices are implicated in this situation, because the organization may choose to negotiate an agreement with the outsider who is asserting IP rights, or it may choose to stop using the accused product or method and find an alternative, as with a new procurement. Alternatively, if the legal grounds are strong, the organization may seek to defend itself and deny the accusation.

Good procurement practices hold the key to obtaining access to the fruits of innovation by others. When an IP manager wants to obtain and use information, medicine, or other materials or technology, the concern is generally whether access can be had on reasonable terms, and if so, how to arrange it.

This is usually a practical, not a political or philosophical issue. Should I buy a computer, chemical or biological reagents, a copy of a book, or a new cell phone? Should I download software, a book, or a song, and agree to the user license? How much will it cost? In these situations and others, the primary concern is accessibility, not whether the information or materials are protected by intellectual property or are in the public domain. There are various pathways whereby an IP manager can find a way to obtain access, even when obstructed by intellectual property rights. (See Chapter 13). Of course, access may be impossible in some circumstances, or very expensive. Those with more experience in managing IP are better able to figure out how to acquire protected intellectual property, and people who do not know how are at a disadvantage.

There are many voices today proclaiming that the IP rights of one group or another are too strong. Manufacturers complain about patent "trolls," small companies that acquire patents so they can license them and sue manufacturers who do not obtain a license, but never plan to sell a product themselves. Economists and industry experts worry about a thicket of patents obstructing progress in agricultural biotechnology. Public health advocates argue that patents block access to affordable medicines in poor countries. Scholars, policy advocates, and government officials in developing countries complain that private IP rights in the form of copyright and patents are too strong and that the public domain should be larger.

To some extent, these criticisms could be blunted by a broad improvement in procurement practices, such that those who need the fruits of innovation can find a way to acquire them. The key question, both for practical purposes and from a policy perspective, is not whether intellectual property rights cover a particular innovation, but whether society – individuals, companies, customers, universities, and other members of the public – can find meaningful access to the innovation. Good procurement practices often provide practical solutions in specific situations that mitigate more general and theoretical concerns about excessive IP rights.

Good procurement practices also keep an organization out of trouble with outsiders' IP rights. Skilled practitioners can find ways to gain legitimate access to most creative assets, including technology, though the paths may be complicated and expensive.

Partnering practices

"Partnering" is used here not in the legal sense of forming a partnership entity, but more loosely, to refer to established relationships with outside organizations with respect to their intellectual property rights, other than straightforward procurement relationships with suppliers. Partnering relationships involve other entities in the organization's environment, including collaborators, customers, users, or clients who receive products, services, information, or rights. The relationship is usually based on some kind of license, joint venture, franchise, inter-institutional research agreement, or the like. If the organization has a negotiated relationship with a supplier that is more specific than an arms-length arrangement, that could be considered as a partnering relationship, too. The partner can be a licensor who gives intellectual property rights in exchange for royalty payment or other consideration. The outsider can be an intellectual property licensee. The outsider can be a customer – it is popular to think of customers as a sort of partner of an organization.

In all partnering relationships, both parties need to consider and agree on certain fundamentals. Although more details about the deals that lead to partnering and licensing agreements are provided in Chapter 15, the main concerns can be summarized here as:

- Who owns IP rights existing at the outset?
- What existing IP rights will each party share, and what rights are being retained?
- What becomes of new IP rights (patentable inventions, secrets, trademarks, and copyrights) that are created in the partnership?

In many innovative sectors, sellers partner with their customers. In these situations a service contract is just as important as the original equipment purchase. For example, when a hospital buys a Magnetic Resonance Imaging (MRI) machine, it also needs a long-term service contract with the manufacturer to train staff and maintain and upgrade the equipment. The MRI machine's manufacturer can limit the intellectual property rights given to the hospital, including limited licenses and assurances of confidentiality, for example, to avoid loss of trade secrets to a potential competitor. And by having a closer relationship than an arms-length purchase and sale contract, the manufacturer, through its representative, is also able to learn directly from the hospital staff what works well and what needs improvement. This feedback can be used directly in making the next generation of improvements. The servicing seller retains IP rights, may gain new IP rights, and earns extra revenue, a triple win.

In another example, when businesses or government agencies install the open source Linux operating system on their computer networks, they do not have to pay for the software, but they do generally enter into a partnering relationship with a distributor like Red Hat, which installs the software in a useful package and customizes or upgrades it. Linux is a trademark of Linus Torvalds in the United States, and distributors generally need to obtain a license from the Linux Mark Institute to offer the program to customers. Through copyright and trademark, Linux retains some control over the open source model it promotes, while the distributor, by providing services, gains new insights and IP rights through the service contract.

Although subsidiaries, parent organizations, and other affiliates are not necessarily considered outsiders, it can be useful to think of them that way in making IP management decisions. For example, one might presume that all affiliates share their intellectual property without the need for written agreements, but there is no universal rule to that affect. Affiliates may hold an implicit license to use all of the intellectual property of parents, subsidiaries, and sister organizations, or they may not. Parent companies generally hold implicit trademark licenses to the trademarks of their subsidiaries, and vice versa, without a written agreement, but affiliates may not be entitled to use each other's trademarks without a written agreement. If one corporate entity owns a patent, that entity must generally be party to a lawsuit to enforce the patent, and if another affiliate owns a copyright, it too must generally be a party.

Therefore, it can be convenient and advantageous in larger organizations for all IP rights to be held in a single entity. That entity can then give a blanket license to its affiliates to use all of the organization's intellectual property. Moreover, multinational corporations sometimes choose to establish an IP holding company in a country with low tax rates. In this scheme, the holding company licenses the IP rights to its affiliates in higher tax countries, and they pay licensing fees from the high tax to the low tax location. Tax laws may require that the holding company actively manage the IP portfolio, so that it is not just a shell with a post office box, or the arrangement might be considered a sham, a tax evasion scheme that is disallowed. These tax rules vary depending on the jurisdiction.

A franchise is another type of partnering relationship. A franchisee obtains a license to the franchisor's trademarks, copyrights, and trade secrets. For example, an entrepreneur who wants to run a fast food restaurant may choose to start her own restaurant business from scratch, or may instead obtain a franchise license from McDonald's, Pizza Hut, or another franchisor. (Starbucks generally does not have individual franchises for its coffee shops – it owns most of its stores, but does license regional rights to business partners outside the United States.) A McDonald's franchise would include the right to use the name and double arches trademarks, the copyrighted packaging and advertising materials, and the brand's trade secrets – ingredients, cooking times, and the intricate details of how to move customers quickly through their fast food purchasing experience. Interestingly, the features of the fast-food dining experience that are covered by IP rights are those that lead to speed and convenience, at the expense of the personal creative touches of individually owned restaurants.

Corporations often form strategic alliances or joint ventures with each other to achieve a result neither could accomplish on its own. For example, a drug company with a new drug that cannot be taken in tablet form may collaborate with a company that has developed a nasal spray delivery system. Microsoft and Apple, generally rivals, cooperated to adapt the MS Office suite (with Word, Excel, and PowerPoint) for use in Apple computers.

Partnerships are also common during early stage research, for example in biotechnology and nanotechnology. In the United States, under the Bayh-Dole Act of 1980, when research organizations receive federal funding, they own the resulting inventions, and are required to license them to corporate partners for commercial development. Preference is given to domestic small businesses.

Scientific research contracts often involve collaboration between several nonprofit entities, generally universities or other nonprofit or government research institutions. The prevalence of such collaborations can be explained by the fact that research projects are generally directed to cutting edge technical problems, so it makes sense to bring together the leaders in the field, who tend to work in different organizations. The scope and terms of such nonprofit collaboration are usually outlined in the grant documents, but there is often a need for an inter-institutional agreement that defines who will own and control the IP that is likely to arise from the research.

Policing

An organization should have an active policing program to make sure that competitors are notified of IP rights, to monitor the marketplace for infringements, and to confront competitors who do infringe. Policing requires a two way information flow – providing notice to the market, and learning information from it.

Passive approaches tend to be ineffective. True, an IP portfolio has some inherent value as a passive deterrent. Competitors may become aware of an organization's IP rights and avoid infringing them, so the organization maintains its exclusive position without lifting a finger. However, if competitors are not aware of relevant IP rights, the likelihood of infringement increases. Also, if competitors do learn about the IP rights but do not take the organization seriously, they may ignore them. Most organizations therefore provide notice of their IP rights, including confidentiality notices, patent marking, the ® symbols for registered trademarks, and the © symbol for copyrights (the symbols shown on this book's cover). Websites, marketing literature, licenses, and other documents should identify IP assets. An organization should also make sure that its intention to enforce its rights is well known, in commercial literature, press releases, agreements, and so on. A particularly effective way to convince a large group of competitors that the organization is serious about enforcing its rights is to file an infringement lawsuit against one of them.

Active monitoring is also wise. If a competitor or licensee infringes IP rights, it may be a long time until the owner discovers the infringement, and the damage may already be done. Or the owner may never become aware of the infringement. But if an organization is proactive, it will police its rights by collecting information about what competitors are doing, and consider carefully any activities that may imply an infringement. If suspicions arise, then the next step is to conduct factual research, such as interviewing witnesses and reverse engineering the suspected products. If there is evidence of infringement, then the infringer should be confronted. An IP asset is essentially irrelevant if it is never asserted when there is an infringer.

Rights may actually be lost if the owner sleeps on them. A trade secret may be lost by failure to enforce the right against someone who has misappropriated those secrets. A patent claim may be barred after a period of years of inaction under the doctrine of laches or the statutes of limitation that require a lawsuit to be filed promptly after learning of an infringement. A licensed trademark may be ruled invalid if licensees routinely violate the terms of the license.

The highest profile act in policing IP rights is a confrontation between the accuser and the accused. This can take many forms, but generally begins with a letter from the IP owner advising the suspected infringer of the IP rights in question, summarizing the evidence of infringement, laying out the damage to the owner, and asking for a response. The desired response may be to provide more information about the suspected activity, to enter into licensing negotiations, to cease the infringing activities, or to pay damages for past actions. Depending on the facts, the psychology, and relative strengths of the parties, these exchanges can go on for months or even years. They may end in stalemate, with one party backing down, or in a lawsuit.

A lawsuit to enforce an IP right can be a drastic and expensive step, both in terms of staff time and money. Many times a negotiated settlement is preferable, but sometimes there is no alternative to a lawsuit. A series of questions that should be asked and decisions that should be made before commencing a legal action are presented in Chapter 14, but for present purposes, in summary, an organization should have in place a policing program which provides adequate notice of IP rights, monitors activity in the marketplace, and confronts suspected infringers in a methodical fashion.

COST MANAGEMENT ISSUES

The cost of protecting IP assets can be very high. Strategic management through use of the Six Ps can reduce these costs and make sure that money is spent wisely.

For example, a good reason why it is less expensive to acquire patents on some inventions than on others is because there is less to describe in these patents. This is analogous to building a house. If you need a one room addition on your house, you might get several different bids that might range by 20 percent. If you were going to build a three room addition, the cost would be substantially more than even the highest bid for the smaller addition.

One way to economize on IP management costs is to decide what to protect and what not to protect. If the organization pursues patents and trademarks that bring no value to the company, or expands them beyond their reasonable scope without a strategic focus on their value to the organization, then whatever the cost it will be as needless as building the three room addition when only one room is required.

Another way to control costs is by managing people wisely. A good IP manager is one who assembles a team with an optimal combination of literacy and expertise in law, creativity (in the science or arts), and business, and then divides the work among them in a thoughtful way. For example with patents, it is best to have the inventors do as much of the work as possible (drafting, analyzing prior publications, and focusing on the novel aspects of the invention), instead of patent attorneys, who – whether in-house or outside – work at a much more expensive rate. The most efficient approach is to let the patent attorneys concentrate on writing the legal claims and on expanding the patent disclosure. With trademarks, the marketing department can identify potential marks, do some prescreening, and bring ideas to trademark counsel when they are already well-advanced. With copyright, proper use of notices and (in the United States) registrations can be done in-house, with some training and after a template has been designed by counsel.

Internal cross-training is advisable. For example, a scientist can learn how to read patent claims, a lawyer can learn the financial demands of the company, and a business person can learn how the invention is technically distinct from the prior art. Ideally, there should be some sort of an intellectual property committee that gets together to review all patent management decisions, on a monthly or quarterly basis.

As for staffing legal functions, hiring outside patent counsel can be an expensive approach, but it has the great advantage of flexibility and access to special expertise. Hiring in-house counsel may be more or less expensive than outside counsel over the long-term, but generally will be less expensive if there is routine legal work that needs to be done over a long period. A bad scenario is to have an outside counsel with no internal IP manager and nobody coordinating or supervising IP activities in-house.

The options differ from organization to organization, from small nonprofits and start up companies with no lawyers to companies with one or two patent profession-als in-house, all the way up to multinational companies that have over a hundred patent, trademark, and licensing attorneys in-house. In any case, the objective is to have the right mix of people, with clear responsibilities and division of labor.

A well-managed organization is best qualified to implement a strategic plan and enjoy the benefits of its innovations. Indeed, good IP management is one measure of how well-managed an organization is overall. As outside counsel, I find that it is most efficient to take instruction from, and work with, a central contact person or group that handles all internal communications at an organization. With other clients, I have to collect all the information by interfacing with two, three, four, or five different people in different parts of the organization, which can be time-consuming and difficult to manage. It is hard to do a good job with IP management in a poorly managed organization. It is, of course, much easier to work with a well-managed organization.

Ultimately, to make strategic management work, there must be leadership from one or more chief officers, and budgetary guidelines. The chief executive needs to give overall guidance, and the chief legal, research, technology, artistic, marketing, business development, financial, and/or operations officers need to be involved. In nonprofit universities and research institutions, there is generally a centralized system with an intellectual property or technology transfer office that handles all decisions about what to file, how to license, how much money to spend, and so on. Larger corporations may have a chief intellectual property counsel, a chief research officer, or some other IP manager who coordinates everything, or there may be a decentralized system where each division has some authority to make its own decisions about what to protect and enforce, with limited guidance from headquarters, within a general budget. Each approach has its own advantages and disadvantages.

STRATEGIC REASSESSMENT

One aspect of strategic management is measuring success – it is important to know if the process is going well. This requires re-evaluation, and that means that the outline of strategy formation, assessment, and implementation, is actually a recursive process, that it feeds back on itself. It is hard to measure exactly what companies are getting out of the process of protecting their IP, but the outcomes can be reasonably evaluated financially and otherwise.

Financial portfolio valuation analyzes how much money the portfolio is worth. This can be measured by the standard approaches (described in more detail in Chapter 12) by cost, income, or market approaches. All these measures are flawed. Reasonable people may disagree widely on the value of a patent or portfolio, and trying to put a dollar figure on one remains a mystery. To assign actual numbers is a business exercise that requires much accounting and sophisticated business projections. Nonetheless, if an organization is consistent about its valuation process it can track progress over time, and if it uses measures that other companies use, it can benchmark its performance against competitors.

Noneconomic evaluation involves questions that are more readily answered, such as: How many patents have been issued? How many other patents cite to the organization's patents? In what countries are there counterpart patents? How many years of life do they have left? It also includes qualitative questions, such as how strong or weak are they? Similar questions can be asked about trademarks and for the more valuable copyrights. As noted, the nonfinancial value of an IP asset can be described in three dimensions, lifespan, geographical scope, and strength of exclusive rights. (See Figure 8.1.) This approach gives a qualitative sense of the three-dimensional strengths of a particular IP asset or portfolio, and whether it is growing over time.

A strategic plan should be simple and long term, so that it can be implemented consistently over time. The hardest part of the process is juggling so many questions at the same time, including technical, legal, and business issues. For example, with patents, it is hard enough just to figure out what the differences are between the prior art and what is patentable, but one must go the extra step to figure out what aspects of the invention are most valuable, and how important its various aspects are to the organization. These answers need to be meshed with information about other rights. Finally, legal standards for protection are constantly changing, and differ from country to country.

A decision maker needs to stay focused, to do all of those things at the same time. This is why it is so important to be able to articulate a simple plan. Otherwise, while trying to implement the plan, most people will get lost in the details, and a coherent policy will never emerge.

SUMMARY. There are six categories of policy and practice tools and skills that IP managers can use to select and implement an IP management strategy. *A general policy on managing IP* sets the basic guidelines for an organization – protecting internal IP rights and avoiding infringement of external rights. *Personnel practices* ensure that rights flow properly from employees and that employees do not create liability to others when they arrive at the organization or while they work there, and when they leave. Good IP *portfolio management* requires identifying, tracking, and deciding whether and how to protect new ideas with one or more kinds of IP rights, and to maintain an inventory so as to increase assets. *Procurement practices* help ensure a clean flow of IP rights into the organization so it may aggregate what is required for freedom to operate – the ability to act without liability (or with manageable risk) to suppliers and customers. *Partnering practices* define close working relationships with collaborators and customers so as to avoid loss of rights, and maximize the benefits of developing good new ideas. *Policing* activities help maintain control over innovations, through monitoring, notice, and if necessary, enforcement actions. These "Six Ps" require some effort to adopt and follow, but they also help manage costs, support continuous reassessment, and are the foundation for good IP management in all organizations.

10 A Menu of Strategy Options

This chapter presents a wide range of general and specific IP management strategies and plans. After describing goals applicable to most organizations, the chapter identifies IP strategies that apply to more than one type of IP asset, identified as follows: switching from a do-nothing to a do-something organization, minimalist, budget, burning stick, suit of armor and shield, IP thicket, IP forest, citadel, bargaining chips, mutual assured destruction, sword vs. shield, and "the first one's free." There are many patent-specific strategies, including fences, supermonopoly, transition from patents to trademarks, and several patent jiu-jitsu tactics – invent around, anti-invent around, the new submarine, staying out of treble trouble, and counterattack. Trade secrets require eternal vigilance. Trademark strategies include branding, move quickly and hold on, and trademark clusters. Finally, copyright strategies include getting it in writing, and open source arrangements.

* * * * * *

When an organization sets out to choose an IP management strategy, what are the options? This chapter presents some basic strategies for an IP manager to consider. In keeping with the thrust of this book, we look for fundamental concepts and practical strategies that hold true for corporations in all industrial sectors and nonprofit organizations, and those that apply in developing countries as well as in the wealthier nations. The most appropriate strategy depends on the organization's mission, its resources, and its competitive and market environment. An IP manager can choose a plan from this list and then customize it to the specific circumstances.

GENERAL GOALS FOR IP MANAGEMENT

The goals of intellectual property management are narrower than the broad social goals of IP. If the larger dynamics of the innovation cycle are part of macroeconomics, IP management in organizations is more a part of microeconomics.

Societies have ambitious expectations for IP: expanding access to the fruits of creativity by stimulating creative work, helping innovations spread from person to person, promoting public disclosure, establishing investment vehicles, providing a framework for fair competition, and satisfying principles of morality and justice. These social goals are met by subtle balancing between access to innovation and limitations on that access. If the limitations are too strong due to excessive exclusivity, the social goals are not met, and instead, problems arise.

Organizations, unlike societies at large, are less concerned with striking balances between access and exclusivity. Their goals are more selfish. Even nonprofit or public organizations focus on their own missions and needs. Generally speaking, organizations can use exclusivity to control and limit use of their innovations while nevertheless accessing the knowledge and innovations of others. A basic rule of commerce is "buy low, sell high." This adage can be adapted to IP in a slightly more complex way:

Obtain open access to innovation from others, but limit their ability to obtain access from you.

IP management has its limits, but it can be a powerful tool to help organizations achieve their goals. Here is a list of general goals for IP management, to be combined and adapted depending on circumstances.

- Increase enterprise assets
- Attract capital
- Protect investment
- Obtain a short-term competitive advantage
- Maintain long-term competitive advantage
- Improve marketing
- Avoid liability
- Manage relationships with personnel
- Ensure access to technology, materials, software, and data
- Strengthen relationships with suppliers
- Coordinate relationships with partners
- Protect relationships with customers and protect them from IP challenges to products and services provided (with resulting liability for indemnification)
- Control the use of innovation
- Facilitate dissemination of knowledge
- Facilitate dissemination of products
- Build goodwill.

Many of these goals apply in for-profit and nonprofit organizations alike. For-profit companies tend to be more focused on the first three goals (increasing assets, attracting capital, protecting investments). Nonprofits tend to focus more on the last three goals (dissemination of knowledge and products and increase goodwill). The other goals are relevant to all organizations and apply generally in all countries, though the steps to achieve such goals differ widely.

GENERALIZED IP STRATEGIES

Individual organizations and their leaders can select, combine, and adapt the general goals summarized above, when coming up with strategies for handling IP. There are an infinite variety of strategies, but here we identify the common characteristics of some of the more common approaches.

To be successful, a strategy must be simple to grasp, memorable, and easily communicated to others. Simplicity is especially important because IP rights are so abstract, and managing them is complex. Real world analogies and colorful names help make the ideas memorable. Vivid names can serve as shorthand so all the people involved in a task can share the same vision of what they are trying to accomplish, and to coordinate their actions.

The first group of strategies described below can be used with more than one IP type. The next section describes strategies that are specific to one or another IP type. There is some overlap between these strategies, and the distinctions are not complete. Any specific strategy an organization selects may fit into several of the categories listed below. But there is something here for everyone.

Switching from a do-nothing to a do-something organization

In Chapter 8, we encountered the lowest level of IP management, level zero, where there is no IP manager and the organization does nothing to protect its IP or to respect anyone else's. Although few leaders would consciously choose this approach, many do so by inaction.

If leaders of a do-nothing, zero-level organization recognize the problems created by doing nothing, they also face the problem of how to change direction. Their goal is to do something – almost anything – to begin managing their IP. The first step is for some one executive to take responsibility for IP management, to assemble a team within the organization, to retain outside counsel and consultants, and to establish a budget. The second step is to decide on a strategy, to inventory assets, to analyze the environment, and to come up with a plan. The third step is implementation, through new personnel and portfolio procurement, and through partnering practices. Do-nothing organizations typically create legal problems, and in switching to a do-something approach, the IP manager must find a way to correct them. For example, a do-nothing organization is likely to have been infringing others' IP rights. To correct this, the organization may need to obtain a license from the IP owner, paying a reasonable amount for past as well as future use of the IP. Alternatively, the organization can change its operations to avoid increasing its liability going forward. If there is any liability from the past, a prudent company might establish a reserve fund to pay for it.

An officer of a stock brokerage company once contacted me to report he had learned that for years his company had been copying training manuals from a broker training company, without permission. There was no proper defense. So when the copyright owner filed a complaint asserting copyright, the brokerage company set aside enough money to pay a reasonable fee per book to compensate for past misuse. Ultimately, the officer convinced the copyright owner to apply those funds toward purchasing a large number of books for future training programs, and the lawsuit was dismissed. This settlement resolved both past and future problems economically, within the infringer's budget.

Converting a do-nothing into a do-something organization is not an easy task, and doesn't always work out so well. It can take a long time, require new staffing, and cost substantial amounts of money. But the rewards generally exceed the costs.

Minimalist

A minimalist strategy is one step more active than a do-nothing approach, but not much. It is appropriate to an organization somewhere between level zero and level one. A minimalist IP manager recognizes that by doing nothing to manage the IP, the organization loses assets and faces liability to others. But instead of establishing a comprehensive response, the chief reacts only to the highest risks. Generally, minimalist management is opportunistic and reactive. If an employee brings up a possible invention, the minimalist company may file a patent application for it, without planning what to do with the patent, without even appointing a management team to deal with it. A minimalist organization does not investigate IP rights belonging to others. If a competitor notifies the organization that it is infringing rights, the IP manager will investigate and respond either by refuting the charges, seeking a settlement, or changing practices. This is a purely defensive posture. Such organizations keep a low profile with their IP and we do not hear about them, except when their strategy fails and they end up paying a substantial amount in damages or settlement.

Tight budget

In many organizations, the IP manager decides to undertake a higher level of activity than a minimalist, but on a tight budget. This is a variant of the level one approach of the five levels described in Chapter 8. The tight budget philosophy for protecting rights is to preserve the greatest scope of protection for the longest period of time at minimum cost. Cost plays a role in every decision about what patent applications to file, whether to hire outside counsel, when to search outsiders' rights, what terms to get or give in licensing, and whether to pursue litigation. A manager pursuing a tight budget strategy frowns on spending the money and effort necessary to register trademarks and copyright, because rights can arise without registration. Patent prosecution is done in as economical a way as possible, and if the perceived value of a patent application goes down, then foreign and U.S. maintenance fees are not paid and applications and patents are pruned out of the portfolio.

As to respecting the rights of others, a tight budget strategy avoids spending money to research outsiders' rights. However, if a patent, copyright, trade secret, or trademark is asserted against the budget-minded company, the typical approach is cautious, and may lead to changing a process or a product to avoid liability rather than facing litigation, which can be fantastically expensive.

Cash poor companies usually follow the tight budget approach. For example, a high technology start-up company may recognize the need for IP protection, but be short of cash while seeking financing. IP prosecution may be a significant proportion of the expenses of such companies, and therefore it is logical to keep IP costs down. Larger corporations and nonprofit organizations also face cash shortfalls sometimes, when financial circumstances take a downturn. Such companies may need to shift to a budget approach, shrinking their IP budget to remain at the same percentage of total expenses as when the overall company budget was much higher. But ultimately, even cash-rich organizations should budget carefully for IP management.

Burning stick

The law of the jungle is eat or be eaten. A lone person sits in the jungle at night, afraid of the wild beasts that lay waiting and ready to attack and gobble him up. Since time immemorial, our ancestors learned that the best solution in this situation is to build a fire. The fire itself will scare off most of the animals. If any beasts come too close, our protagonist picks up a burning stick and jabs it menacingly at the animal until it decides to back off.

In the burning stick strategy, the protagonist is an innovative individual, a small start up company or nonprofit organization with a new product or creative idea. These people have good reason to feel alone in the jungle of competition. The more successful they become, the greater the likelihood that their efforts will attract the attention of a big competitor with superior market share, or a low cost competitor with lower costs of production, who can then destroy our protagonist's business.

To carry out the burning stick strategy, the first requirement is to build a campfire to scare off the wild animals. In this strategy, the fire does not have to be big, but should include strong IP rights on the key assets. Trade secrets are maintained. Any inventions are patent pending. Copyright notices are used, and important copyrights are registered. Trademarks are pending or registered. Second, our protagonist gives notice that key IP assets are protected. Trade secrets are withheld unless there is a nondisclosure agreement. Patent pending notices are used along with copyright and trademark notices on all relevant literature, websites, and packaging. Finally, the protagonist pays close attention to competitors and asserts rights vigorously if any of them seems to come close. No information is provided without a nondisclosure agreement. Website downloads require the user to complete a registration form.

If any possible patent, copyright, or trademark infringement is detected, a letter is sent promptly to advise the competitor of the protagonist's rights. Such letters often discourage competitors from continuing infringing acts by warning them of the dangers, even if the warning has limited impact given the small company's limited resources. If a competitor is not scared off by the burning stick of asserted rights and keeps closing in, the protagonist may be unable to follow through on the threat by filing a lawsuit, because of the high cost of litigation and the small size of the IP portfolio being defended.

Nevertheless, this strategy is more than a bluff, because there are substantive rights to back up the assertive actions. It works well against many competitors. However, it requires a high degree of vigilance, and ultimately if the IP rights are not strong enough, and if the big competitor is aggressive enough, the small portfolio jungle beast may pounce anyway, and take market share, erode prices, or weaken the organization's good will.

Suit of armor and shield

The suit of armor strategy adds defense (avoid infringing rights) to the offense (protect rights) approach of the burning stick strategy. Here, the metaphor is a warrior wearing a suit of armor and carrying a shield for protection when walking out into the world. If someone attacks, with burning sticks or other weapons, the shield deflects the blows and the armor protects the wearer, helping provide a strong defense. Without armor, mortal injury could occur.

For an organization practicing the suit of armor strategy, an attack can come in the form of an infringement law suit. The resulting injury could be a court injunction blocking the organization from its line of work, and a potentially crippling damages award.

To guard against such an attack and to minimize injury, an organization can dress itself in defensive armor. The first step is to avoid IP conflicts where possible and prepare for them when necessary, by identifying major risks of infringement liability (as discussed in more detail in Chapter 11). The second step is to reduce those risks. One way to reduce the risk is to study the threatening patent, copyright, or trademark, and assemble the evidence and arguments necessary to conclude that there is freedom to operate because that particular IP right is invalid or is not infringed.

A second way to reduce risk is to shift activities to avoid likely exposure to infringement liability. Just prior to paying the patent owner NTP more than $600 million to settle its patent claims, Blackberry maker Research In Motion was preparing to roll out a new software system that was clearly outside the contested patent claims. This would have cost RIM millions and might have annoyed their customers, but it gave RIM a fallback position immune from attackers, encouraging negotiation toward a settlement. Having alternatives available provides strong protection from attack.

A suit of armor and a shield are of limited use if unaccompanied by weapons. Here, the weapons are a strong portfolio of secrets, patents, copyrights, and trademarks that cover important aspects of the business environment. If a challenger in the same industry attacks, there is a good possibility that the challenger may be doing something that infringes the rights of the protagonist organization. If claims are asserted by the challenger, the protagonist can counterclaim using his own rights.

A third way to avoid risks is to prepare in advance for litigation. This requires having an idea of the costs of defending lawsuits based on trade secrets, patents, copyrights, and trademarks, setting aside a "war chest" if need be to finance the lawsuit, and maintaining relationships with IP counsel who can move quickly to shield the company from harm. Indeed, good counsel can be the best shield and armor a company can have.

Finally, if the opponent's strength is overwhelming, the protagonist may decide to obtain a license from the IP right owner. But being ready for battle, with armor and shield, places a warrior in the best position to negotiate a peaceful outcome.

IP thickets

An innovation thicket grows where there is a collection of innovation trees and smaller growths – trade secrets, patents, copyrights, and trademarks, covering a particular idea or innovation or product, along with domain names, and so on.

To create an IP thicket, an innovator grows as many different types of IP rights as possible around a particular product or method, creating a thicket that is hard for competitors to penetrate. Because this approach may be expensive, it is usually reserved for extremely valuable innovations that may be the subject of fierce competition.

For example, the Coca-Cola Company has created a thicket of rights around its most valuable brands. It owns trademark registrations for COCA-COLA and

COKE, the wasp-waist Coca-Cola bottle, the red-ball graphic, and many domain names, including coca-cola.com, .org, .net, .biz, .info, and .ca. It also owns coke.com, coke.org, and others.

Pharmaceutical companies typically create a patent thicket around their important drug products. When a pharmaceutical company discovers a promising new drug, it generally tries to grow a patent thicket, seeking patent protection on a wide range of chemical variants and analogs, methods of synthesizing the drug, chemical intermediates in the synthesis, different crystal forms, different finished dosage forms, and various methods of use.

And pharmaceutical companies continue to grow thickets at the end of a patent term, too. Most pharmaceutical companies seek to expand their patent protection for a commercially successful drug by developing and patenting variations. According to a survey,[1] between 2004 and 2006, to protect themselves from generic competition for their drugs when the original patents expired, 82 percent of pharmaceutical companies sought to bring out new formulations, 55 percent produced a next-generation product, 55 percent found new disease indications for their drugs, and 3 percent produced combination drugs. Each of these strategies was built on a cluster of patents. New formulations, including salts and different crystal forms, methods for treating new diseases against which the drug is active, new dosage forms (sprays or patches instead of intravenous or tablet forms), and combinations of different drugs are all independently patentable.

Some commentators use the term "patent thicket" more broadly than to refer to a group of patents held by one owner. Here, the term refers to an array of patents owned by different companies that cover a particular technology area and block innovation by outsiders. For example, in agricultural biotechnology, new varieties of corn, soybeans, cotton, and other crops often include numerous genetic markers and traits to improve growth, flavor, nutritional value, pest resistance, and herbicide resistance. It can be very difficult or impossible for a breeder to get permission from all the different right holders to develop a new crop including these markers and traits.

IP forest

Growing an innovation forest can be a conscious strategy for an organization. If a thicket is a small group of IP rights, like patents on different characteristics and uses of a particular drug, an IP forest is a broader portfolio of IP rights on different innovations. In this strategy, a whole line of products is blanketed with all available types of protection, from all sides, making copying of any kind too risky.

A drug company may use IP rights to protect every aspect of its technology, for all its products, including research methods, supply and distribution channels, and marketing. An electronics company may protect each product, component, software, shipping system, and financial model. A consumer product company protects its

[1] Cutting Edge Information, *Combating Generics: Pharmaceutical Brand Defense for 2007 Executive Summary* 12 (2006), http://www.cuttingedgeinfo.com/pharmagenerics/PH76_Download.asp#body, accessed October 1, 2006.

various brands, its products, its endorsements, and its customer base. Where an IP thicket makes it hard for a competitor to acquire market share for a particular product, an IP forest keeps competitors from challenging the overall business of the owner of an IP forest.

The number two company in the athletic footwear market, Reebok, obtained about 150 U.S. patents in a single 10-year period, many of which were design patents. They also had about 100 trademarks (registrations and applications) in the United States, and a similar number of copyright registrations on commercials. The company has reasonably well integrated IP portfolios, but this coverage would probably not be considered dense enough to be called an IP forest. In contrast, the number one company, Nike, has grown a forest around its products. Nike has obtained ten times as many patents in the past decade as Reebok (about 1,500), and about 350 trademarks. It is a challenge for Reebok to even begin to approach the areas protected by Nike's IP forest.

The Aleppo Citadel

Aleppo, Syria, is home not only to the modern International Center for Agricultural Research in the Dry Areas (ICARDA, one of the CGIAR centers), but also to a much older structure, the Aleppo Citadel, a World Heritage Site. Built on a hill settled by the Hittites, by the thirteenth century, the Citadel had become a formidable fortress. To enter, an invader would have to descend into a deep moat, pass through arrows shot by guards in towers placed in the moat, climb up to an enormous gate, break down an iron door, charge down a short hall, turn 90 degrees, break down another door, and continue down that hall, changing directions and facing defenders at each turn. Above, defenders could drop stones and pour boiling liquids on the invaders. If the invaders managed to pass through the halls and climb into the throne room, the sultan could escape out into the moat through a secret passageway, and the gates could be dropped to hold the invaders in.

The Aleppo Citadel, like the Tower of London and other castles, provides an architectural guide for a layered intellectual property defense system. There are outer forms of protection like a moat, broad, but not so strong. There are several fall back positions, and special measures to protect the organization's crown jewels.

Most well-constructed patents follow this model. The broadest claims cover many infringing acts though they are easily invalidated by an accused infringer. The narrower claims cover a smaller scope, but are harder to invalidate. To give a simplistic example, a broad patent claim referring to "a seat" may attempt to cover many types of stools, chairs, and benches. Because it is broad, it may cover prior seats, and be found invalid. A narrow claim to a seat having five rolling legs attached at a 45-degree angle would cover only one specific type of office chair, but be less likely to be found invalid.

Bargaining chips

The principal reason for obtaining patents and trademarks is to restrict the actions of others in the marketplace. However, they can also serve as bargaining chips to protect freedom of action for their owner. This is one reason organizations obtain and maintain patents and trademarks on technology that may not be very important to the company itself. If a competitor asserts intellectual property rights against the organization, then the IP assets can be used in a counter-attack, and be used as bargaining chips to barter with the competitor, leading to a cross-license.

For example, in 1999 Dell computers and IBM announced a $16 billion technology cross-licensing and supply deal. IBM holds many thousands of patents in the computer field, particularly on hardware components. Dell holds many patents on its methods of taking custom orders for computers, assembling them, and delivering them, all without an inventory or "bricks and mortar" store. Dell agreed to purchase components from IBM, and IBM was in turn licensed to use Dell design technology in its own computers. If either Dell or IBM had held weak patent rights, there would have been a strong incentive for the party with the dominant patent portfolio to use it to attack the other one. For example, Dell could have bought lower priced components from an IBM competitor, or IBM could have competed with Dell by using a similar approach for the custom design and sale of IBM computers.

Another example arises if an organization selects a trademark without an adequate search, or expands into a new region and then discovers that there is another company using a similar mark in a certain geographic area (say, France). Bargaining chips can be obtained by filing new trademark applications in many other areas (say, other European countries). After several years, when those new trademark applications mature, there will be a good basis for settlement between the parties, providing for coexistence in both France and the other European countries.

Sword vs. shield

As noted, intellectual property rights can serve as a sword to strike competitors and stop them from infringing. The threat of a sword can be used to bring peace in the form of a license agreement. Likewise, as with the bargaining chip strategy, IP rights can serve as a shield to block against an attack from someone else.

The best shield may be good intelligence in the form of a careful "freedom to operate" analysis. An organization should periodically review what other companies' patents and other rights exist that might limit its activities. If any conflicting rights are found in such a review, or if any rights are asserted by their owners, then those rights should be studied carefully until a path is found to avoid them without facing a destructive attack.

Mutual assured destruction

This is a counterpart to the bargaining chip strategy. Here, each company holds rights over the other. Instead of settling with cross-licenses, the companies decide to litigate to the bitter end. This can cause serious financial hardship to both companies. Because it is generally more difficult to avoid infringing a patent than a copyright or trademark, most of these situations involve patent infringements. The patent lawsuits may resolve in a judgment blocking one company from the field, or the dispute may be settled.

Patent trolls

Established companies fret loudly about so-called patent "trolls." These patent holding companies have no activities except to acquire patents and enforce them against wealthy companies with substantial market activity. From the perspective of active companies with products to sell, patent trolls are immoral, because they produce no useful products, but also troubling because they are immune to negotiation with the bargaining chips of the active companies. There is no possibility of a counter-suit, and only one side (the active company) faces destruction. This was the dynamic for Research in Motion, which faced an injunction putting all Blackberry handheld devices out of operation, while the plaintiff, NTP, had only to maintain enough cash to pay its patent attorneys. Inventors and investors look more favorably at such patent aggregators. Viewed from a societal perspective, a more neutral, less derogatory term than troll is "patent entrepreneur," because such companies help direct value toward strong patents, giving inventors a greater incentive to innovate. These companies serve as brokers so inventors can invent, sell to the entrepreneur, and return to inventing without bothering to market or exploit the invention.

The first one's free

Many organizations have found that giving away IP rights is sufficient to meet their needs. Authors using Creative Commons copyright licenses allow others to copy their works with only a few limitations, such as a requirement for attribution, a restriction to noncommercial reproduction, or a prohibition against making derivative works based on the work in question. Adobe gives away its Acrobat Reader software for free to users, but sells that software to content producers. The same is true for Internet Explorer. Flooding the market with a product without IP restrictions can help establish the technology as a standard and allow the inventor to reap its rewards later. Antitrust concerns may apply in these situations.

PATENT STRATEGIES

Patents are generally the most valuable IP assets, and the most difficult to obtain. It is no surprise that there are many strategies for dealing with patents.

Fences, mazes, walls, and gates

Newcomers to patent strategy may appreciate the metaphor of IP homesteading as a guide for long-term planning. First the homesteader clears one patch of pasture and fences it in. Then he clears some more trees to make a new pasture and extends the fence to cover that – and so on, as the homestead grows. As the innovation cycle moves around, an innovator makes orderly progress from basic research toward a first product, then into improvements and new products. At each stage, the innovator takes time to fence in the innovations with intellectual property rights, including patent applications, copyrights, trademarks, and trade secrets.

Another way to describe that strategy is as follows. Dominate the technology with a broad pioneer patent, putting eggs initially in one basket. Then, protect improvements inside and outside the scope of the dominant patent with follow up patents, to put more eggs into more baskets.

Jackson Knight describes several patent strategies with analogies to building fences.[2] A pioneering invention may lead to a single patent with broad claims, like fencing in a large pasture. A risk to the owner is that individual claims made by the patent may be invalidated, leaving sections of the field open to competition. A bigger risk is that the entire patent may be invalidated. Another metaphor for this approach is a "beachhead," where an inventor jumps onto the beach of an uncharted island and plants a flag there, claiming the entire land as his own, but awaiting challenge by later claimants arriving on the island.

An alternative to having one broad, pioneering patent is to have several narrower patents fencing off the field into smaller sections. A series of narrow patents leaves gaps, but creates a maze through which a competitor must pass at his own risk. The maze approach, with many narrow patents, is more typical of IP practices in Japan than in the United States or Europe.

Building a patent cluster around a new technology area is sometimes referred to as a blanket, or flood strategy. A team methodically researches an entire technology area surrounding a research goal, and then files a set of medium-scope patents covering each facet of the technology. The blanketing team can obtain exclusivity, and because the published patent applications become prior art against others, the team can prevent themselves from being cut out of the technology by others' patents.

For example, a medical device manufacturer may discover that a particular polymer coating provides desirable characteristics for an insertable device – making it visible in medical imaging equipment, or slippery, or carrying a drug that stops infections. Instead of patenting just one particular combination, the company tries to blanket the technology by describing all conceivable polymer combinations, and all conceivable such devices. Just describing the combinations may not be enough. Because patent claims can only be allowed if the invention is adequately described, it may be necessary to make many samples and demonstrate that the invention works with a reasonable number of variants.

Blanketing can also be used by a second-comer. It often happens that one company is the first to file a patent application for a valuable invention, such as a new electronic component or new chemical compound. If that company does not blanket the technology, a competitor with sufficient resources can then blanket every conceivable variation, such as related electronic components and their software, or chemical variants defining a larger family around the previously patented compound.

Stephen Glazier (an early patent strategist) refers to this approach as a "toll gate."[3] The second company can block the competitor from using its dominant patent with a simultaneous flood or blanket of narrow patents, without giving warning. This can force the pioneer to license the dominant patent in exchange for a cross license to get through the toll gate, or can force some kind of joint venture or collaboration. This is a good strategy but it requires a substantial investment of resources, and is

[2] H. Jackson Knight, *Patent Strategy for Researchers and Research Managers* (Wiley, 1996)
[3] Stephen Glazier, *Patent Strategies for Business* (Law & Business Institute, 1997).

difficult to accomplish because of the general patent law rule that one example (the first patent) bars patenting of the entire family to which that example belongs.

A wall (or hurdle) strategy relies on steady investment in research and periodic inventions. The inventor files a first patent or group of patents on the first embodiments of the technology. By the time the patent applications are published, and competitors begin to figure out how to get around them, the strategist has already made new inventions and filed a new wall, or hurdle, of patents, which can then delay and complicate the efforts of any competitor. This strategy can be maintained indefinitely. The wall strategy is especially effective when the direction of research is apparent, for example with the constant drive for faster computer processors and larger memory capacity, better sound quality on cell phones, or less expensive DNA sequencing.

A refinement of the hurdle strategy may be referred to as a patent trap. Toyota's hybrid car technology provides an example. Toyota licensed its hybrid technology to Ford, which used it in some trucks, and also established a collaboration with First Auto Works to make hybrid cars in China. But, apparently, Toyota licensed only its previous generation technology, while Toyota prepared to roll out its new generation of hybrid technology, presumably protected behind a new wall of patents.

Supermonopoly

An ideal situation for a patent owner occurs when there is an external imperative to use the patented technology. Then, competitors are obliged to use the patented invention or to stay out of the market. The patent owner holds extraordinary leverage in such a situation. For example, many environmental regulations require companies to use the best available technology to reduce smokestack emissions or clean up polluted groundwater. Such regulations drive the innovation cycle in environmental technology. When an innovator develops a new environmental technology, the market must rapidly adopt it, abandoning the older technology. If the innovator obtains a patent on the scrubber or cleanup technology, then other companies that need the technology have no choice but to buy it or license it from the innovator.

Union Oil Company of California (Unocal) achieved a supermonopoly in the 1990s when a California environmental agency decided to require use of a low emissions gasoline that was patented by Unocal. Unocal obtained patents on that formulation but did not tell the agency or a private standard-setting group. Unocal then filed suit to enforce its patents against other gasoline refineries. This led to antitrust charges against Unocal in 2003. The supermonopoly ended when Chevron acquired Unocal in 2005, and the U.S. Federal Trade Commission required them to agree not to enforce the patents as a condition to the merger.

Another type of supermonopoly can occur when companies privately agree on an industry-wide technology standard. Rambus, a computer memory maker, participated in an industry committee called JEDEC that set standards for memory chips. As it turned out, the standards called for using technology patented by Rambus, giving Rambus a supermonopoly. Rambus failed to disclose that its patents covered the technology, and so Rambus's supermonopoly was challenged as deceptive and a violation of antitrust laws. But the committee's rules did not require members to disclose their patents, and the antitrust challenge initially failed. However, on appeal, the FTC concluded in 2006 that Rambus had engaged in deceptive conduct, concealing its patents to distort the standard-setting process and obtain a monopoly. Remedies for such abuse can include a forced license or an order preventing enforcement of the patents. Similar anticompetitive laws are in place in many countries, and serve to limit the exclusive rights of IP owners.

Transition from patents to trademarks

Trade secrets and trademarks can last forever, and a copyright term is so long (at least 50 years worldwide, and at least 95 years in the United States) that it might as well last forever. Patents, however, are relatively short-lived – 20 years from their earliest filing date. For most companies, it may be a rare patent that becomes important in protecting market share, and no company will want to give up that commercial advantage when the patent expires. Many strategies have been developed to maintain advantage.

When patents for blockbuster antihistamine Claritin expired, owner Schering-Plough switched the drug from a prescription to an over-the-counter remedy and boosted advertising dramatically, so that consumers would choose it based on its brand name, instead of its generic name loratidine. G. D. Searle, the inventors of the artificial sweetener aspartame, named the company that owned the patents The Nutrasweet Company, building on public recognition of the sweetener's trademark.

The Delta faucet company invented the famous goose neck, single-handled hot and cold water mixing faucet. When the patents expired in the 1980s, Delta invested heavily in protecting the goose neck shape as a trademark, so competitors had to use differently shaped handles.

There are limits to this approach. Traffix Devices held a patent on a highway sign mounted on springs so it bent over in high wind instead of tipping over. After the patent expired, Traffix tried to prevent competitors from using the same spring design, arguing that the shape was protected by trademark law. The U.S. Supreme Court held in 2001 that the shape could not serve as a trademark. A significant reason was that the spring design had been patented, so the shape was functional.

Patent jiu-jitsu

In jiu-jitsu, the "gentle art" of self-defense, a series of quick hand and foot strikes, throws, and joint locks are used to repel and neutralize an attacker. Some patent strategies likewise rely on skill, agility, good timing, and leverage.

Stephen Glazier collected many of these approaches in his seminal 1997 book.[4] Individually, each might be characterized as tactical rather than strategic. But it is strategic if an organization decides to learn a jiu-jitsu approach to patenting, to become a "black belt" able to make any one of these moves as the situation requires.

Invent around. This book generally treats protecting an innovation as a separate act from avoiding violation of the IP rights of others. The patenting process is as follows: do some research, make an invention, describe it, and patent it. Avoiding patents is a different process: design a product, review existing patents, and

---

[4] *Patent Startegies for Business.*

if need be "design around", the other patents – modify the product so it does not infringe.

An integrated approach can be referred to as an "invent around." To invent around a patent, the innovator finds a valuable patented product, studies the patent for weaknesses, and then finds a way to avoid the patent while inventing a new patentable variation. This involves a sophisticated understanding of patent law, but can sometimes be easier than it sounds. A product or method does not infringe a patent claim unless each and every feature recited in the claim is present in the accused product or method. Therefore, all that is necessary to avoid infringement is to remove or change one element recited in each of the claims. For example, if the patent claim requires two separate parts, the design around becomes an integrated, unitary device. If the patent claims a medical formulation with 10–50 percent hydroxymethylcellulose, the competitor may avoid the patent by eliminating the hydroxymethylcellulose.

In these examples, if the unitary design or the hydroxymethylcellulose-free formulation is patentable, then the innovator kills two birds with one stone. By going through the design around exercise to avoid the patent, the innovator simultaneously may make a patentable invention, completing the "invent around" process. This is tricky, because the patentability of the alternative design depends not just on the particular claim, but on what the rest of the patent says, and the legal standards for infringement and for invention are different. Like jiu-jitsu, following this approach requires extensive training and practice.

Anti-invent around. There is a good defense against every attack, and a good attack to evade every defense. The "anti-invent around" approach is a defense against the invent around approach. The inventor and patent attorney test the claims in their own applications for weaknesses. They imagine that they are the competitor, finding a way to eliminate or change an element of each patent claim. Then they broaden or revise the claim to make it harder to avoid. Some people would consider this to be just good patent practice, not a strategy. But it can be pursued quite aggressively. Each time claims are amended they should be tested this way. And even after a patent issues in the United States, if a competitor finds a way to avoid a patent claim, in some circumstances the owner may be able to resubmit the patent to the Patent and Trademark Office, change the claim, and reissue the patent with claims that would now be infringed.

New submarine. In most of the world, patents have been published 18 months after filing, and have a term extending 20 years from *filing*. In the United States before 1995, patents had a term of 17 years from the date of *issuance* regardless of when the application was filed, and they were not published before they issued. Gordon Gould filed a patent on lasers in 1959, but it did not issue until 18 years later in 1977, when the world was filled with lasers. The patent term extended to 1994. In the so-called laser patent wars that went on from 1977 until the 1990s, Gould and his company were able to obtain royalties far in excess of what the independent inventors (and Nobel laureates) Townes and Schawlow earned, and much more than if his patent had issued in a timely fashion in the 1960s.

Gould's delays were not intentional. However, clever patent attorneys exploited the "17 years from issuance" rule by "submarining" patents – keeping a patent application secret and pending for years (or decades) and then finally having it issue, or surface and fire torpedoes, after other companies already commercialized the technology. The late Jerome Lemelson obtained more than 600 patents, many of them submarines, and collected over $1B in royalties. In one case, he filed an application on "machine vision" in 1954, and refiled it about 19 times, with new information, with patents issuing as late as 1994 (39 years later) eventually covering bar code technology. One defendant, Symbol Technologies, finally convinced the Court of Appeals for the Federal Circuit that Lemelson's delays were inequitable, and the patents became unenforceable.[5]

Since 1995, US applications have been treated like those in other countries. They are published 18 months from filing and have a term of 20 years from filing. One reason for this change was to block the strategy of Jerome Lemelson. Under the new law, competitors learn what patents are pending and may feel confident that the term cannot be extended by delay.

However, a new variant form of submarining has developed in the US. Here, even after a patent application is allowed and issues as a patent, applicants can dive down, refiling the application as a continuation, maintaining flexibility so they can amend the claims to improve their position against an infringer. The claims can be narrowed to avoid prior art to make them valid, and they can be broadened to capture competitor conduct that might have fallen outside the scope of the claims that originally issued. A new patent can then surface and put the owner in a stronger position than the original patent.

The U.S. Patent and Trademark Office announced new rules in 2007 that limit the number of continuation applications that may be filed. This might limit the new submarine strategy. But applicants can find ways to avoid the new limits.

Some people feel that these tactics go beyond fair play and are a form of "gaming the system." But that is the way legal systems work. Rules are set, people find ways to work within them and use them to advantage, and if there are unintended consequences, the rules can be changed.

Staying out of treble trouble. Patent owners can threaten accused infringers in the United States not just with damages and an injunction, but also with treble damages and attorneys' fees if the infringement was willful. Interpreting patents requires a high degree of expertise, and courts have ruled that a company can avoid a finding of willfulness if it first obtains a thorough analysis from competent counsel. Therefore, the best insurance available to a company aware of a problematic patent is to obtain a "freedom to operate" (FTO) opinion from patent counsel before commercializing a product that might infringe a pre-existing patent. With an FTO opinion the worst case scenario is that the company will have to pay damages, but they will not be trebled. If counsel concludes there *is* a risk of infringement, then the company should design around to avoid the patent – avoiding liability altogether.

Counterattack. When an organization is threatened with a patent suit, it can take a frontal approach – deny infringement, or argue that the patent is invalid. Such a lawsuit can take years and cost millions of dollars. But there are several patent jiu-jitsu moves that can be very effective in winning the day much more quickly.

---

[5] *Symbol Technologies, Inc. v. Lemelson Medical, Education & Research Foundation, LP,* 422 F.3d 1378 (Fed. Cir. 2005).

Unnamed co-inventor. It is difficult to determine who are the inventors of a patented invention, and mistakes are often made. If an organization is accused of patent infringement and investigation shows that there is an unnamed co-inventor, then the organization can approach the unnamed co-inventor and obtain a contingent license. The license essentially says "if I am found to be a co-inventor, I license my rights to you." Then, the organization may seek to have the unnamed co-inventor added to the patent. If this action is successful, then the newly added co-inventor becomes a co-owner of the patent, and the organization has a license to the patent.

In the 1990s, Barr Laboratories and the U.S. National Institutes of Health argued that the director of the National Cancer Institute, Sam Broder, was a co-inventor on Burroughs Wellcome's patent for using AZT to treat HIV/AIDS. The NIH gave Barr a contingent license, so that if the inventorship claim was successful, Barr could sell a generic form of AZT. However, the courts held that Dr. Broder was not a co-inventor.

I used that same tactic in a case in which a client was being sued by a competitor, who – suspiciously – had eliminated a co-inventor from the patent being contested. We found the outcast inventor, obtained a contingent license, and asserted co-ownership. The patent owner settled the case quickly.

Uncited prior art. Most patents are issued without a review of all relevant prior publications ("prior art"). Patent-office examiners review the literature, but their time is limited and they are not comprehensive. If an accused infringer does a more thorough search and finds prior art references that invalidate the patent claims, this provides leverage that can be used in several ways. The blunt approach is to wait until there is litigation, and use the references there. If the patent has not issued but is still pending, the concerned organization can send the reference to the patent applicant, who then becomes obligated to submit the reference as prior art to the Patent Office in the United States and several other countries. The hope is that the patent examiner will use the reference to reject the patent. However, patent applicants can often get around the reference through amendments and arguments.

For an issued patent, another approach in the United States is to file a reexamination request to the patent office, providing arguments directly to the examiner, who may then withdraw the patent and reject the claims. This leads to further prosecution. Many other countries permit opposition to a patent after it is granted. This permits the challenger to make the case that the patent claims are invalid.

TRADE SECRET STRATEGIES

The price of freedom is eternal vigilance

This quote, attributed to Thomas Jefferson, refers to the need for citizens of the United States especially in its fragile early days to guard their civil liberties or else lose them. A similar equation applies to trade secrets, even if the consequences are less dire for society at large. That is, innovators who hold trade secrets must never ever let down their guard. If anyone leaks or publishes a secret, intentionally or inadvertently, it is no longer a secret, and therefore has no further trade secret value. "Poof" and it is gone.

Therefore, anyone who wants to use trade secrecy to protect an idea or innovation must design and implement a plan for eternally retaining that secret. The information must be sequestered from the public and from any one in the organization who does not need it, or who may be a security risk. That information, when shared with anyone, must be marked confidential, and agreements must be in place for the select group that knows the secret, requiring them not to reveal it outside the secret circle.

Where possible, innovators use technical obstructions to prevent reverse engineering. Examples are "black box" electronic components that are difficult to reverse engineer; hybrid or genetically engineered crops that will not breed true after one generation, so that farmers can not keep or breed the plants; and flavor components such as those used to make "Coca Cola's" syrup. If (as is usually the case), the secret cannot be kept indefinitely, then these measures must prevail at least long enough to provide a competitive advantage until the next innovation can replace it.

Trade secrets vs. patents

The need for vigilance is one of many reasons inventors often favor patents over trade secrecy. However, an inventor who lacks the large amount of funding needed to patent an invention and then to enforce the patent may favor trade secrecy because of its low cost. Likewise, if it will be difficult to find infringers, as with inventive methods and software used only internally in a competitor's business, enforcement may not be feasible or necessary and trade secrecy is advantageous.

There is however a risk that a competition will independently discover the same invention, and seek a patent. This happened to one of my clients with respect to a new method of organic chemical synthesis used to make a pharmaceutical compound. We had to oppose a European patent and monitor the U.S. patent quite closely until we were satisfied that the competitor's patent would not block my client's method. The fact that my client had been using the method for years before its "invention" by the competitor was helpful in some countries (which allow a prior user to keep using an invention patented by another). But in the United States and many other countries, there is no prior user right. Therefore, the only way to preclude someone else from patenting such a method is to publish the method in a journal, on a website, or in the form of a patent – and that of course would negate any trade secret. Because such methods can not be safely kept secret, it may be worth obtaining a patent.

In 2007, decisions by the U.S. Supreme Court and other courts, pending legislation, and new patent rules have made patents harder to obtain, narrower in scope, and harder to enforce. As this trend continues, we may see an increase in trade secrecy for inventions that are relatively difficult to protect with patents and relatively easy to protect with trade secrecy, such as manufacturing methods and data processing algorithms. Society will lose access to such inventions, and the innovation cycle may slow.

TRADEMARK STRATEGIES

Branding

One aspect of trademark strategy is vividly illustrated by the practice of branding cattle. Cowboys on the range in the western United States, gauchos on the Pampas in Argentina, and Maasai tribal herders in the Rift Valley of Kenya and Tanzania all learned to brand (meaning burn) a distinctive mark into the hide of new calves in their herd, using a red hot iron. The brand allows the owner and neighbors to identify whose calf it is if it strays from the herd.

Cattle branding practices in the United States gave rise to an early kind of open access strategy. Samuel Maverick was a Texas lawyer who received 400 head of cattle in payment of a debt. He left them unbranded and wild on the open range. The other ranchers branded their cattle, but (the story goes), when they found an unbranded animal, they assumed it was one of Maverick's. He was therefore able to avoid the cost of branding, though his system was subject to abuse and would not work if anyone else tried to use it. The term "maverick" came to mean an independent person who refuses to abide by the dictates of his group.[6]

Mavericks may not do well in the marketplace. The modern innovator places a brand on a product, allowing consumers and competitors to recognize where the product came from. This helps the public to distinguish between uniformly good products of a particular brand that they want to buy and shoddy or dangerous products they want to avoid. Empowering members of the public to identify the source of a product helps reward the effort of those whose products are associated with high quality or other desirable features. Likewise, trademarks can serve as a disincentive against producing low quality, defective, or harmful products, because the producers may be liable to their victims, or at least lose future sales to unhappy consumers.

Move quickly and hold on

An innovator who has identified a desired trademark, and determined it to be clear of other similar marks, can hold onto that mark and preserve it for a long time. Most countries allow such speculative activity, where the applicant can protect trademark rights for years without any evidence that the trademark has actually ever been used in connection with a product or a service. In the United States, a trademark application can be filed if the applicant has a bona fide intent to use the trademark in commerce. With extensions, no evidence of use is required for about three years. In most countries, no evidence of use is required at all. If an applicant delays filing until after someone else files a trademark application, then the right to obtain a trademark registration may be lost, and the applicant may even be blocked from using that mark. Filing early and hanging onto a trademark is therefore a better strategy than waiting.

Trademark cluster

A trademark cluster or thicket exists when there are numerous related and similar trademarks covering a famous brand. It is relatively easy to build a trademark cluster because trademarks are relatively simple to create and to use, registering them is not as expensive as patents, and reserving domain names is extremely inexpensive. For example, a company may select a trademark and then seek trademark registrations on the mark for various goods and services, on various logos and variants of the

---

[6] Ross Shipman, "Samuel Maverick: John Howland's Texas Legacy," available at www.pilgrimjohn-howlandsociety.org/john_howland_texas_legacy.shtml, accessed January 13, 2007.

mark, and on a wide range of domain names related to the mark. Most internationally famous marks are protected by clusters of registered trademarks and domain
names.

COPYRIGHT STRATEGIES

Get it in writing

In the United States and elsewhere, an author generally owns copyright in his or
her works, with authorship and ownership indicated by the notice (© 2008 Michael
Gollin). For the author to transfer ownership, a copyright assignment needs to be
written. Oral agreements to assign are not binding – an oral agreement can only
provide a limited license to use the copyrighted work. A company that hires consultants as programmers, artists, and copy editors must be very careful to get written
assignments.

Open access

Many people confuse open source material such as software with material in the
public domain, but this is incorrect. As discussed earlier, open access licensing is an
important new intellectual property management strategy.

One fundamental principle stands out. Open access licensing is almost inevitably
built on a foundation of intellectual property. The basis for an open access arrangement is the existence of an underlying IP right. Open access licensing is not an anti-IP
approach, or one that creates an "IP-free" zone. An owner licenses users to access
the IP, but uses the IP right to force the downstream users to make their changes
accessible as well.

The counterintuitive essence of open access arrangements is that without the
underlying intellectual property right, downstream users could co-opt information
and material by adding their own innovative contributions, and then capture and
privatize the original material to use in their own activities without letting anyone
else use it. Ironically, therefore, intellectual property rights can be asserted, using
the open access model, to expand, not restrict, access, by forcing downstream users
to make their innovations publicly available.

The gold standard for this approach is Linux. The basics are simple and rely on
copyright law and trademark law. The software author (A) licenses a user (B) to use
a software program, and provides the source code, with permission to modify the
source code in any way – to fix bugs, or to add new functions. In exchange, user
(B) agrees that any new copyrighted software produced by B, based on A's work,
will be made available to other users (C), on the same conditions. That is, C, and
downstream user D, can use the source code, modify it, and write new variations,
provided that they make their new works available to others. The incentive is that
the open source community, working autonomously but in great numbers, is able to
fix and update open source programs, making them more robust and reliable than
many commercially available proprietary programs.

In contrast, a more traditional way to share information is simply to make it publicly available without restriction, so that it is truly in the public domain. Government

websites often provide unrestricted data libraries. Examples include the biotechnology databases maintained by the National Institutes of Health, such as the GenBank gene sequence database, which is used routinely by genomics researchers. Unlike open access licensing, there is no restriction on further discoveries made using such data, which can be protected as trade secrets, patents, or copyrights. Thus, although public dedication of information seems to be more open than using a licensing model, it can result in fewer innovations being accessible.

The open source model has been extended from software to publishing, through the Creative Commons and the Public Library of Science. These groups have in common a licensing approach that asserts copyright, but permits those accessing the work to use it for free, and to reproduce it and make derivative works, on condition that the original author receives recognition and the downstream user does not tie up rights or restrict access by others. This is, generally, the approach of scholars. Wikipedia runs on a similar license. A Wikipedia author A agrees to allow user B to modify A's text, but B must allow C and others to modify the text as well, to keep it accessible. Open systems of user generated content are somewhat socialist, in that participants give according to their abilities, and receive according to their needs.

The open source (or open science, or open access) approach continues to spread into other areas like research involving pharmaceuticals biotechnology, genetic resources, and agriculture. The open access model is particularly attractive to non-profit organizations because it minimizes their costs and gives some assurance that the innovation cycle will revolve with a high degree of public access. Other incentives for an open access innovator include creating a market for high value services (as with the companies that service commercial Linux systems), or undercutting a competitor (as with IBM's support of Linux as a way to keep Microsoft's market power in check).

So, open access licensing is one of many options in managing intellectual property, with advantages and disadvantages in any given situation. It is one of the choices that an IP manager should consider in deciding what to do with intellectual property to best meet the organization's objectives.

SUMMARY. IP management goals vary widely among organizations, but there are some common goals, strategies, and plans that are broadly applicable. Others are useful for a narrower range of organizations and IP types. Some of the general strategies described here include: switching from a do-nothing to a do-something organization, taking a minimalist approach, operating on a tight budget, using a burning stick, wearing a suit of armor and shield, growing an IP thicket, managing an IP forest, defending the Aleppo citadel, creating bargaining chips, establishing a relationship of mutual assured destruction, using a sword vs. a shield, and "the first one's free" – giving away rights and goods to establish demand. Patent-specific strategies include building picket fences, mazes, walls, and gates, setting up a supermonopoly, transitioning from patents to trademarks, and using patent jiu-jitsu – invent around, anti-invent around, the new submarine, staying out of treble trouble, and counter-attack. Trade secrets require eternal vigilance, and exercising judgment on whether to patent or keep the secret. Trademark strategies include branding, moving quickly to gain first rights and then holding on to build them, and growing a trademark cluster. Finally copyright strategies include confirming all transfers in writing, and using owner-driven licensing strategies such as open source/open access. This is the last chapter about planning. The next section relates to assessment.

11 Evaluating Internal Resources and the External Environment

The chapter describes the process of assessing IP rights, beginning with internal evaluation. We discuss timing, basic steps, and scope, and describe how to use a questionnaire, covering each type of IP asset (patents, copyright, trademarks, and trade secrets), as well as employment and other agreements. Next we address external evaluation: how to assess the external environment, by using public research tools, asking questions to others (as in due diligence), and monitoring the market to police rights. Some special concerns for public organizations and for developing countries are discussed.

* * * * * *

Ready, aim, fire! These are the three steps in managing IP strategically. An IP manager first gets ready by deciding on general goals, and ends by shooting – selecting and implementing a plan. In between comes the crucial step of taking aim, by assessing the situation and finding out the facts. The previous chapter described some of the available strategy options. This chapter presents a comprehensive approach for assessing IP – taking aim – as part of the process of deciding which option is best.

An IP assessment provides information vital to the management of the organization, to maintaining or improving its competitive position, and to its ability to continue to have access to the best creative content, technology, scientific materials, and collaborations. In theory, IP assessment should take place on a regular basis. In practice, the fact-finding process may be performed routinely, sporadically as the occasion arises, or not at all. An organization that does no IP assessment, in effect, shoots without aiming.

In my experience, most organizations do far too little IP assessment. Why? Many organizations lack the resources or the desire to conduct a thorough IP review, or they lack the will to see it through. They may not think it necessary. The process can seem daunting, even though it does not need to be and even though the rewards far outweigh the costs. Many IP managers lack the basic information to carry out even a simple IP assessment. Many people lack the knowledge and skills, but fortunately, the necessary skills can readily be learned.

A strategic assessment looks both inward and outward. Inwardly, the IP manager identifies the organization's own internal IP assets. Outwardly, the IP manager learns about the IP assets of outsiders – competing organizations and individuals in the competitive environment – to the extent that these may have an impact on the organization's own activities.

The first part of an assessment is an *evaluation* of internal and external IP rights. Evaluation involves asking two questions:

(1) What types of assets are there (secrets, patents, trademarks, or copyrights)?
(2) How strong are these assets in the three dimensions of exclusivity, geographical reach, and duration?

The second part of assessment is financial *valuation*. Valuation is the process of determining the cash equivalent of particular IP assets, groups of assets, and the portfolio as a whole. Evaluation is always part of an IP assessment. Valuation applies in a more limited set of circumstances. One common scenario for valuation occurs when an organization transfers intellectual property to someone else by sale or license, and the parties negotiate the financial terms of the deal. A second scenario may arise during litigation, when the parties calculate damages. The rest of this chapter details the evaluation process, and we will deal with financial valuation in the next chapter.

An IP portfolio can be evaluated similarly to the way accountants analyze corporations, public agencies, or households. Accountants group financial information into four basic categories: Assets, Liabilities, Revenue, and Expenses. In general, an IP manager follows a similar approach for intellectual property by compiling a list of IP assets and IP liabilities, a tally of IP-related revenues from assignment or licensing, and an expense budget showing the cost of creating IP assets, managing IP rights, and paying royalties or damages to others for use of their assets.

Of course, intellectual property is not money, and IP management is not financial management. It is often difficult to place a financial value on IP assets, because they are not liquid fungible assets. That is, a dollar is always worth a dollar, and a share of McDonald's stock has a market value, but each IP asset is unique, not readily transferred from asset category to asset category, or from organization to organization. Another difference is that the risks associated with various IP portfolios are hard to quantify, and insurance in the field is virtually nonexistent. Finally, there are few generally accepted accounting standards for intellectual property, so each organization tends to treat its own IP situation differently.

INTERNAL EVALUATION

Timing

When should an organization evaluate its own IP portfolio? At the least, a portfolio assessment is required the first time a strategic IP management plan is prepared, and then each time it is updated. Many organizations choose to update their IP portfolio regularly, and accounting standards may require it. An evaluation is usually required before (or as part of) conducting a financial valuation of an IP asset or portfolio.

IP portfolio assessment is much more difficult than balancing a checkbook or reading a corporate spread sheet, because financial accounting reduces every item to dollars, or Euros, or yen, while IP values may not be reducible to single monetary terms. Generally, the approach requires asking many questions to many people in the organization, including outside consultants such as patent and trademark law firms. Some organizations use form questionnaires customized for their purposes and distributed on a regular basis. (See Appendix C.)

The most highly managed organizations have in-house staff dedicated to collecting and updating portfolio information to keep it current. Those least involved in IP management approach the process in a more ad hoc fashion. For example, an investor may ask for a listing of all registered rights as part of due diligence, and the company then gathers the specific information, typically on a rush basis. But even though such information is specific, it may not be carefully considered or accurate. This type of reactive approach should not be confused with a strategic assessment, although it does present an occasion to begin acting strategically.

Basic steps

Assessing an organization's IP portfolio for the first time can be very time consuming. However, updating an existing portfolio is much easier. People use several different terms for compiling an IP portfolio – IP auditing, conducting an IP survey, compiling an IP inventory, or performing due diligence. Whatever the term, there are three basic steps that are required to gain comprehensive and useful information about an organization's IP assets, liabilities, revenues, and expenses.

(1) **Asset listing**. The first step in an IP evaluation is to list all the organization's registered IP rights. The list can be set up as a simple table or a more sophisticated database. This approach proceeds down a check list of each type of IP right for which there is documentation through the various legal regimes. The reviewer lists each patent, trademark, and copyright registration and application owned by the organization. Because this step is organized around the legal categories, the results may cut across all divisions, sectors, and programs. Trade secrets are not part of such an IP evaluation because they are not registered, but the most important trade secrets can be identified. If possible, the reviewer also identifies all major IP licenses by which IP flows in or out of the organization. However, many organizations do not keep track of licenses in a methodical way.

Most organizations can manage this level of evaluation. In my law firm, we routinely prepare and update lists of patents and trademarks for our clients, including U.S. and foreign applications, by family, with all relevant information including titles and inventors (for patents), marks and goods or services (for trademarks), filing dates, relevant serial numbers, and status.

(2) **Process review**. The second step is a process review. This approach seeks to determine what policies are in place for managing the organization's intellectual property, and what practices are followed. A process review is crucial to gather information about unregistered IP assets that may affect the organization's mission and operations – trade secrets, unregistered trademarks and copyrights, databases, biological and physical materials, and lower level agreements like those relating to confidentiality. In most organizations, it is impossible to list every trade secret, or all of the written works for which copyright might still exist, because there are so many. It might also be unfeasible to collect every agreement with a confidentiality clause.

As an alternative to listing all these assets, the reviewer can check to make sure that the organization is following sound practices with respect to IP. For example, with respect to trade secrets, are there employee confidentiality agreements? Are secret documents sequestered from nonconfidential materials? Are confidentiality agreements required in all partnering situations? Is there an invention disclosure program and is it being followed? Who is responsible for each of these measures? Every organization that manages IP has one way or another implemented some kind of IP management process, whether strategically or ad hoc, and this step simply codifies the existing process.

With respect to copyrights, the reviewer may check such basic measures as proper use of ®copyright notices on documents, photographs, software, labels, and web pages. Similarly, with trademarks, the reviewer makes sure that any slogan or distinctive image being used as a trademark is labeled with the ™ indication if possible, and if it is registered, that the ® registration symbol appears. There are many other items to cover in an IP process review, but these are some of the major points.

(3) **Project/Product review.** The third step in IP evaluation focuses on the organization's highest value projects or products. This approach cuts across the different legal doctrines (trade secret, patent, trademark, copyright), and complements the first two approaches. The main purpose is to make sure that the most important existing products are well-protected, and that protection is being built up for new planned products and projects. This approach allows the IP manager to scope out any IP clusters and thickets within the organization and to undertake management of the entire IP forest. In this process, the basic issue is not the entire set of what IP rights the organization owns, but which IP rights are most relevant to the organization's principal activities.

This third step of the internal evaluation, focused on products and projects, leads naturally to the outward review. Once the IP manager has identified the most important activities of the organization, and assessed the internal IP rights that protect them, the next task is to analyze what right the organization has to use that intellectual property. Is the organization blocked from carrying out those activities by IP rights of others, or does the organization enjoy freedom to operate?

An IP manager may skip or abbreviate certain parts of the process depending on the type of organization and the circumstances. For example, an open access nonprofit research organization may deemphasize trade secrets and focus on licensing. A software company in India may decide to focus on copyright. For most organizations, the best approach is to start with a comprehensive evaluation, and then pare back as appropriate.

Scope

The scope of an IP evaluation can be tailored to the circumstances, which are different when dealing with an individual, a nonprofit organization, or a commercial enterprise. For an individual the assessment process might seem trivial, but depending on the creative endeavors – for example with a celebrity – it may be more complex

When Tiger Woods measures his personal net worth, he must assess the trademark value of his name – and present that assessment in lawsuits over unauthorized use of the Tiger Woods name in product endorsements. Likewise, the artist Peter Max holds a vast array of copyright interests in his works that he uses in his studio work, reproductions, and shows. Some inventors hold title to their own patents and license them instead of assigning them to a corporation. However, as a general rule, most IP rights are held by the corporate entities or other organizations we have referred to as innovation communities.

Some readers may be surprised to learn that nonprofit organizations have many activities with significant intellectual property implications. Yet the fundamentals of assessing IP in both nonprofit and commercial organizations are more similar than one might think. The principal differences in the scope of the evaluations relate to the organization's mission – public purpose vs. profit-making – and the consequent financial implications.

The scope of an evaluation of internal IP assets and the external environment, for a nonprofit organization, depends on its structure, size, and mission, and the particular services and activities it undertakes. Some common IP-generating activities are as follows:

- Publishing
- Collecting and disseminating information from libraries and databases
- Maintaining websites
- Creating, performing, and presenting creative works
- Acquiring, maintaining, and improving genetic material, such as plants and microbes
- Researching and developing new technologies
- Licensing and collaborating with others
- Educating and training
- Sponsoring activities by others.

A commercial enterprise undertakes most of the same activities as a nonprofit, but in addition, sells products and services and uses production methods and marketing strategies for profit. The scope of an evaluation for a commercial venture as against a nonprofit is generally broader and involves more complex financial assessment (as is discussed below). But these are differences only in scope. The fundamental steps and questions of an IP assessment are the same for both types of organizations.

For example, for profit Google and nonprofit Wikipedia have completely different business and IP strategies. Google obtains revenue from advertising while Wikipedia survives by donations. But to the user, there are many similarities, and likewise a similar process can be used to evaluate the IP portfolio of either one – the review of copyright, secrets, trademarks, and patents, and licenses affecting the IP rights of either one. Both Google and Wikipedia work hard to understand the IP rights and restrictions in the content they obtain and present on their websites, trying to avoid infringing on outsider's rights. Both use legal stratagems to restrict the rights available to their user community. Both follow the ABCDs of IP dynamics. They make sure that they have proper access to the innovative material that comes in, to avoid liability, and that they protect what goes out, to advance their mission. This requires on-going IP assessment.

Likewise, the information to be collected about the R&D operation of a corporation is similar to that sought from a university laboratory. Both have to avoid infringing rights in the materials they obtain, the information they use and the experiments they carry out. Both seek to protect their rights in their innovations with a mix of patents, trade secrets, copyright, and trademark. Each uses a different mix and emphasis of course. A corporation has a higher degree of secrecy and restrictions while a university favors publishing and sharing. Each organization has different responsibilities in its community. But the scope of the evaluation, at its fundamental level, should be similar in either case, focusing on activities that are significant to the organization and its stakeholders (whether employees, consumers, shareholders, researchers, students, or the geographical region).

Groups with similar types of outputs or inputs have overlapping intellectual property concerns. And the similarities may be greater than the difference between for profit and nonprofit organizations. For example, although their strategies may differ widely, there are many similarities in the intellectual property assets of the website of a consumer product company and that of a scientific research institution. The people managing the two websites may have more IP issues in common with each other (relating to domain name and trademark protection, end user license agreements, and copyright clearance for software and content), than they do with other groups in their own organizations (like financial operations, human resources, or shipping).

The benefits of assessing IP assets in both nonprofit and for-profit settings can be readily appreciated from one example. RoyaltyPharma is an investment company that holds IP assets as collateral against which it is able to borrow and lend money at a profit. In 2005, RoyaltyPharma paid Emory University $525 million dollars in exchange for rights to receive royalties payable to Emory under several patents covering an HIV/AIDS drug. The Emory patents had been licensed to several drug companies, who also participated in the transaction. As a result, Emory's endowment grew dramatically and the broader Emory community in Atlanta benefited as well. RoyaltyPharma added the Emory royalty revenue stream to its portfolio, and was thereby able to increase its lending, and therefore its profit. Such a transaction requires a careful IP evaluation and financial valuation by both the nonprofit and the commercial venture.

Questionnaire

Because the different groups in an organization have widely disparate intellectual property assets, and operate in very different environments, it is wise for an IP evaluation to be broad. The IP manager should cast out a big net. The information-gathering net should include an internal questionnaire, complemented by research using public databases.

A questionnaire is the best tool for comprehensively assessing IP rights internally. An example of a comprehensive audit questionnaire is attached as Appendix C. Abbreviated versions of a questionnaire can be as short as one page, and a questionnaire can be completed by managers on paper or electronically. Alternatively, or in addition to written queries, a questionnaire can be a script used by an individual who collects the information in verbal interviews. The whole process can take anywhere from a couple of weeks to several months.

A short questionnaire may be limited to questions like the following, provided to give a general idea of the topics that are covered in more depth in more detailed questionnaires.

(1)   Who in the company is responsible for managing intellectual property?
(2)   Who are the company's external intellectual property advisors?
(3)   Is there a company intellectual property policy to protect trade secrets and require employees to assign intellectual property to the company?
(4)   What patents are in the company's patent portfolio?
(5)   What are the most valuable unpatented trade secrets of the company?
(6)   What are the trademarks of the company?
(7)   What are the copyrights of the company?
(8)   Does the company hold clear title to the patents, trademarks, and copyrights?
(9)   Have any licenses been given or received?
(10) Have any outsiders asserted that the organization is infringing their patents, trademarks, copyrights, or trade secrets?

A comprehensive questionnaire covers all these aspects of intellectual property. Only portions of it are likely to be pertinent to each of the respondents asked to fill it out. Nevertheless, such a questionnaire seeks considerable information and completing it requires a significant commitment of attention and time.

An IP evaluation seeks to identify unrecognized opportunities and potential problems related to intellectual property, and to handle them proactively. That is why candid information is required for the evaluation to be useful. However, some of the information may be sensitive, particularly as it relates to weaknesses in the organization's own IP portfolio and threats from the outside. For this reason, it is generally desirable to involve legal counsel, and to keep the answers to the questionnaire confidential and internal to the organization, and perhaps even safeguarded by attorney-client privilege. After an initial review, much of the information can then be disseminated more widely.

A threshold issue is how the IP manager can disseminate a questionnaire within the organization. In a small company, the IP manager has direct access to most of the relevant information, or can obtain it from the management team. In a larger organization, information needs to be obtained from various working groups. The best way to collect responses from groups across an organization is tailored to the organizational structure. This might mean going through regional offices, subsidiaries, divisions, or project teams or otherwise depending on the organization to obtain information.

To minimize disruption and internal resistance, it can be helpful to find an analogous existing process for reporting within the organization and to follow that. That is, an IP evaluation can be distributed via channels similar to those used for financial, legal, performance, or scientific audits and reporting.

The first part of the questionnaire serves to categorize each group by the inputs it uses, its activities, and its work product – according to the ABCDs of IP flow, from creator A to innovator B to recipient C, to end user D. Depending on the role of a particular group within an organization, it may access information about any of the following types of innovations:

- Raw materials and supplies
- Software
- Data
- Hardware
- Electronic and mechanical equipment
- Information posted on websites
- Printed publications
- Special biological or chemical materials
- Intellectual property licenses
- Music, literature, dramatic materials, graphic designs, and images.

The activities that each group carries out can be just as varied. They may include the following:

- Chemistry, biology, or physics research
- Mechanical or electrical engineering
- Artistic creation
- Procurement
- Manufacturing
- Marketing
- Installation and maintenance
- Information gathering
- Publishing
- Business and financial management.

Moreover, each group may have a different mix of outputs. The outputs can include any of the categories listed above as inputs, and also, generally:

- Commercial products
- Commercial services
- Supplies, software, databases, hardware, and other equipment for internal use
- Marketing materials
- Information posted on websites (e.g., publications, databases, software)
- Printed publications (published internally or by others)
- Scientific research results
- Artistic performance or display
- Biological or chemical materials
- Tests or analysis for others
- IP legal rights (licensing and business development).

These categories, or variations, can be presented as a checklist to the different groups of an organization. By checking off which of the above categories apply within a group, a leader can gain a quick perspective on the ABCDs of the group, providing a context for the questions that follow.

The body of the questionnaire focuses on the different types of IP rights – trade secrets, patents, copyright, and trademarks. The questionnaire gathers information about all three parts of the evaluation: registered rights in patents, copyrights, and trademarks; the policies and practices in place for IP management, in particular for trade secrets and employment relations; and a product-focused inquiry covering both internal IP protection and access to external IP rights.

Patents

Patents are granted by national governments upon application by an inventor describing the invention. Inventions may take the form of machines, compositions, and methods or processes. Special patents are available for designs and for plants.

Typically patents are coordinated by a single person or patent group in an organization. If an outside law firm handles the patent work, as is the case with many smaller organizations that lack in-house legal counsel, there must still be a point of contact – perhaps an administrator, or one of the executives within the organization who is responsible for maintaining the voluminous and complicated files, records, calendars, and budgetary information inherent in managing a patent portfolio. Indeed, the coordinator will typically be the IP manager or a supporting staff member. Larger organizations may have a decentralized approach to patent management, where each division, or campus, or office has independent authority to prepare and prosecute patent applications. But they will still generally have a central office that maintains the overall list of patents and basic information about them. In any of these situations, the first people to respond to the questionnaire should be the IP manager, the coordinator, or the central coordinating office, and they can answer many of the questions.

Some organizations defer to outside counsel in their home country to manage their patent portfolios, and in these situations, questions about the content of the portfolio are directed to outside counsel. Most companies work with several law firms, and in that case the inquiry about the contents of the patent portfolio must be sent to each of them. Likewise, in dealing with international applications, an inquiry may need to be sent to each foreign law firm or patent firm that is handling patent files for the organization conducting the evaluation. Often, one leading outside firm coordinates all international filings, and as part of that responsibility can handle any status inquiries and obtain any updated information from foreign patent firms around the world.

In sum, most patent related information can be obtained from the organization's internal coordinator and outside patent firms. But further patent-related questions should also be addressed to those who are more peripheral to the central coordinator, to find out if there are any "rogue" patent activities that are not known to the coordinator.

The starting point for assessing patents is to ask whether the organization owns any issued patents, or has filed patent applications on work done by the organization. The scope includes work done solely at the organization and work done jointly with others. The response to this inquiry will typically take the form of a list, table, or spreadsheet listing the patents and applications with the basic bibliographic information (country, serial number, reference number, title, inventors, original filing date, and issue date). It is also important to include information about other right holders – joint inventors, or licensees, or any people or entities other than the organization that may hold rights to the patent.

When dealing with the rights of outsiders (non-employees), it is important to review the internal procedures used to ensure clean chain of title from the original inventor to the organization. Employees will typically have a written agreement, and it is important to check whether outside inventors also have written agreements defining the rights of all the people and entities who helped to create the patented invention. Relevant agreements should be identified, including assignments and licenses. Finding agreements may require extensive work especially the first time an organization tries to assemble the information.

After identifying patents and patent applications, the next step is to consider whether the organization has an adequate invention disclosure program in place. Such a program includes: (a) standards for record-keeping (typically in paper or electronic laboratory notebooks); (b) an invention disclosure form to be completed by inventors who believe they have made an invention; (c) an IP review committee report that considers the patentability of invention disclosures and the value of the inventions to the organization or outsiders; (d) legal commitments in employment agreements; and (e) training and oversight to maximize compliance. The IP evaluation can identify gaps in the invention disclosure program, and can help find any unpatented inventions or ideas created in whole or in part by persons employed by or collaborating with the organization which may not have been previously reported. Often, an IP evaluation questionnaire will include a copy of the organization's invention disclosure form, to facilitate compliance by inventors. This can help identify inventions in new or improved equipment, materials, methods, and products.

The patent evaluation can also turn up potential infringements. In larger organizations, scientific staff members often know about outsider technology they may be using, and they may already have some information or concern about whether the technology is patented. Often they do not bring such concerns to the central coordinator, due to distance, cultural differences, or a lack of time or interest. One benefit of an IP assessment is that it provides an opportunity for staff to present any such issues so they may be resolved in an efficient manner. For example, a process change can be made to avoid a patent.

Because patent rights are legal constructs and it is difficult to define them without adequate expertise, people answering this part of the questionnaire should be directed to counsel or a central coordinator, rather than asking them to write their own conclusions on paper. Statements such as "we infringe this patent," or "I don't think this is patentable" can be extremely damaging if there is ever a lawsuit about the patent. Although such vulnerable statements may seem unlikely, or amusing to contemplate, on many occasions in patent litigations or in pre-litigation situations I have found myself commiserating with in-house counsel about just such memos and e-mails sent from one employee to another. We console each other, and then attempt to contain the resulting damage.

Trademarks

Trademarks help to identify the work and materials provided by the organization. Trademarks can be words, colors, symbols, logos, or designs. Trade dress is the ornamental design or shape of a product.

The starting point for a trademark evaluation is to compile, or update, a list of all registered and pending trademarks in all countries belonging to the organization. The process is similar to that for patents: Check with the internal trademark coordinator, ask outside counsel, and follow up with foreign law firms as needed to complete the international listing of rights. This process can be augmented by searching public trademark registries, by reviewing the organization's website and marketing literature, or by having an outside search firm conduct a search.

The next step is to have the organization's divisions, departments, and groups list any names, acronyms, words, colors, symbols, logos, packaging shapes, or designs used by that group, by which the organization and its products and services are known. It is helpful to ask for knowledge of any trademarks that have been registered in any countries, although this will generally be verified centrally by use of public information.

The organization's right to use trademarks can be verified by asking if any of them come from outsiders, and if so, whether the organization's use is pursuant to agreement. Potential infringement by outsiders can be identified by asking for knowledge of any outsider's use of trademarks that are similar to the organization's trademarks. This should include use that is authorized by license, endorsement, sponsorship, or the like.

Especially the first time a comprehensive evaluation is conducted, it is worth asking each group whether it knows of a policy or guide regarding adoption and use of names and logos on publications and in connection with new varieties, devices, projects, and other products and services. This would typically include a process for identifying potential marks, conducting a "knock-out" search for those marks which are already protected by others, doing a more comprehensive search on the remaining marks, selecting and seeking to register a mark, and monitoring its use within the organization and by others.

Copyright

Copyright exists for many forms of expression, including writings, photographs, drawings, software, web pages, and any other work which is "fixed" in a tangible medium. Rather than asking for each work, it is enough to ask for a list of *categories* of writings (books, journals, reports, articles, training materials), graphic works (photographs, slides, videos, drawings), web pages, and software created in whole or in part by employees (including works published by others) during the past several years. It may be helpful to specifically identify the most widely distributed works, and those which are otherwise important to the organization or its mission. If there are any copyright works, the next issue is whether applications for copyright registration been filed in any countries, and whether copyright registrations have issued. As with patents and trademarks, this inquiry may be augmented by searching public databases, and checking with outside counsel.

The next step is to find out if works the organization should own have been created by an outsider, in whole or in part – any outsiders, including consultants. If so, it is necessary to determine what licenses, assignments, or approvals apply, and what are the terms and conditions, in order to check ownership and freedom to use the works. It is also important to determine if any rights in the works been given to an outsider (completely or jointly with the organization). For example, has ownership of the work been sold or given to an outsider? Has an outsider been given the right to copy or distribute the work? Has an outsider been given the right to modify the work? Is there any outsider who may claim rights in an important work? Such rights may include the right to use or sell software, or a right to a royalty on the use or sale of that software.

As to the organization's policies and practices, some copyright-specific questions are helpful. Does the organization (or group) have a policy or guide regarding approvals, photo credits, copyright notices, etc. on works which it publishes? For example, has written permission been obtained from the authors of articles, images, and software to publish them, post them on a website, or otherwise disseminate them? Are approvals obtained from people whose images the organization publishes or otherwise uses?

Software licensing raises special issues, and an evaluation should cover proprietary software or databases obtained from an outsider. This should include generic operating systems and applications, as well as special or custom software, but the emphasis, as always, should be on the most important programs. The head of information technology may have a log of licenses and other records showing ownership or license to the software.

Trade secrets

Trade secrets, generally, are bits of valuable confidential information owned by the organization. Legal recognition for trade secrets requires that the owner take affirmative action to protect them. Trade secrets include unpublished data, formulas, methods of doing something, source codes, composition of materials, mailing lists, supplier information, employment records, and other information that is not available to the public and is not generally known outside of the organization. Given their breadth and pervasive nature, it is practically impossible to compile a list of all trade secrets in an organization. Rather, a process audit approach works best. In many countries, a claimant seeking protection under trade secret law must be able to show that self-help measures were taken, and so the mere act of assessing the trade secrets can strengthen rights in them. Again, this is why an IP assessment should involve legal counsel.

It is helpful to start by identifying confidential information that is of the highest importance to the organization and its mission. This might include, for example, databases, employee data, source code for software, formulas, methods, compositions, mailing lists, and financial data.

To track use of the information, the questionnaire should ask for circumstances when confidential information was disclosed to an outsider under a confidentiality agreement or as part of a government report. Any outsider that holds a license to confidential information, for example, as part of a collaboration, should be identified.

Any incident where valuable, highly confidential information was used by outsiders in a manner that was not authorized should be noted for follow up.

Some of the situations where trade secrets are most likely to be disclosed are in marketing materials and sales discussions, during purchase, in the course of collaborations, and in training sessions. Outright theft is rare, but the questionnaire should verify that confidential information is marked as such, that access is restricted to those who need to know it, that it is segregated from nonconfidential information (e.g. with passwords, or kept in locked offices or cabinets), and that it is disposed of in a manner to prevent disclosure. So-called "dumpster diving" – going through someone else's trash – is a common method of industrial espionage and journalism.

The final set of issues with trade secrets relates to the organization's use of confidential information provided by outsiders. Again, the terms of use should be identified, and it should be verified that the organization takes measures to maintain outsiders' confidentiality. If the organization has used the outsiders' confidential information to develop or improve methods, equipment, or materials, then a closer look may be necessary to determine whether the outsider has any rights in that improvement.

Many of these questions need only be asked the first time an evaluation is done. Later, the organization is likely to implement procedures that require confidentiality agreements with standard language whenever confidential information is received or provided to others. Thereafter, the task becomes primarily one of monitoring compliance with that procedure, and dealing with unusual situations.

Employment issues

Depending on the laws of the country in which an employee works and the employee's work status, the employee may have rights in intellectual property developed for the organization by that employee. Because of the ABCDs of transfer of rights in IP, it is important to address employment issues separately.

A good starting point is to confirm that all creative employees are subject to employment agreements which assign ownership of inventions, copyrightable works, and all other confidential information and trade secrets to the organization. The agreements should also provide for nondisclosure of trade secrets, and limit conflicts of interest that might arise when a former employee is working for competitors. Similar agreements should apply to officers and directors. It is worthwhile confirming that such agreements apply to each patentable invention, copyright work, and trade secret created at the organization. The evaluation can also find existing policies and training materials for employees, covering the use of logos and other trademarks, and rules about publications.

In particular, after identifying who the creators are or such works, the person assessing IP should determine if any of the people who created or contributed to the creation of the inventions or copyrights or trade secrets, are or were consultants or independent contractors, or held any posts with obligations to other organizations. If so, any agreements controlling the relationship should be identified.

Turning to the use of outsider's trade secrets, the questionnaire can ask if there are any projects which are likely to involve know-how, technology, and information obtained from the employees' previous employers, or other outsiders. The evaluation should confirm that the organization interviews new employees before they start performing work for the organization, to inquire as to whether there is any work or knowledge that they are restricted from using at the organization, whether the employees are subject to any covenants not to compete with former employers, or to inquire into any other agreements which assign rights in their work to the former employers. The evaluation should also confirm that the organization performs an exit interview when employees leave the organization, to request the disclosure and return of all intellectual property to the organization, and to advise the employee of the organization's rights in its intellectual property. If an organization, or its divisions, does not conduct such entrance and exit interviews, then steps should be taken to begin doing so.

Agreements

The final section of the IP evaluation questionnaire covers licenses and other agreements. Each division or group should provide a set of standard form agreements relevant to intellectual property. They should also list written licenses, biological material transfer agreements, software license agreements, and other agreements with outsiders to (a) take, borrow, purchase, or use; (b) give, sell, lend, or otherwise transfer intellectual property rights into or out of the organization. If there are too many to list individually, then the general types of agreements should be identified for follow up.

The agreements may cover transfers into or out of the organization, for any of the following: patent rights, copyrights, permission to use copyrighted material, trademark rights, rights to confidential information, and other intellectual property rights. It may be helpful to give a checklist of the types of agreements, because they may go by many different names in different parts of the world, and in different industries:

- Memoranda of understanding
- Letters of intent
- Employment contracts
- Consultant agreements
- Material transfer agreements
- Acquisition agreements
- License agreements
- Collaboration agreements
- Research agreements
- Research grant documents
- Management agreements
- Database agreements
- Supply contracts for critical software and equipment (leases, etc.)
- Assignments
- Releases.

Several additional questions help identify any restrictions on the organization's rights. Was any of the creative work funded by a government agency or a private investor, and if so, what IP rights did the funder receive in return? For any human or biological samples obtained by the organization, are all appropriate prior informed consents and approvals in place, and were any rights reserved by the provider of that material? Has the organization committed to indemnify any outsider for intellectual property infringement? Are there any research collaborations or joint ventures that include intellectual property sharing provisions?

The person responding to the questionnaire should be able to provide copies of the standard form agreements and of the more important executed agreements and grant documents. Many organizations build a table or spreadsheet or database of their licenses, and such a system is crucial in tracking licensing revenues, renewals, and so forth.

Conclusion of the questionnaire

It is wise to include open-ended questions at the end of the questionnaire. The person answering questions should be invited to mention to the evaluation coordinator any immediate pressing concerns about the organization's intellectual property or that of outside parties. If there are any issues outside the scope of the questionnaire, respondents should also be able to point out any other issues that they believe are important to the organization's mission and use of intellectual property. The answers to such open-ended questions can suggest areas for special attention and for staff training.

EXTERNAL EVALUATION: ASSESSING THE ENVIRONMENT

Although the best way for an organization to obtain information about its own intellectual property is to conduct a self-evaluation, the situation is reversed when finding out information about a particular competitor or the overall intellectual property environment. Here, the primary source for such information is public databases, and internal information is secondary.

Generally, information about outsiders can only be obtained from public sources. There are only two situations where it makes sense to ask outsiders directly for relevant information about their intellectual property. One is when negotiating an agreement such as a license, an assignment, or a merger, when the outsider has an incentive to be helpful and to cooperate with the information-gathering process referred to as "due diligence." The other is in litigation. In the United States and some other countries, the adversary is obliged to turn over relevant information. In litigation, the rules of discovery are very cumbersome, and any information that is obtained comes at great cost of outside counsel fees. Thus, even in negotiations and litigation, it is wise not to rely only on information provided by the outsider. Therefore, the gold standard for evaluating the intellectual property environment is the information found by using public information sources.

There is very good news in this arena. Modern life increasingly presents opportunities for finding relevant information on public databases, and IP evaluation is no different. Increasingly, vast amounts of information about intellectual property are available on publicly available databases. Government patent and trademark agencies around the world have posted publicly accessible websites with all relevant information, including issued and pending patents and trademarks. Copyright registrations are also widely available. Internet domain name registries quickly determine whether a new domain name is available, and if not, who owns it. The laws and regulations governing patents, trademarks, and trade secrets are widely accessible, and commentators have posted a huge literature of articles about what these laws mean for different groups of interested people, like the biotechnology industry, software companies, music publishers, and advocates for developing countries. Subscription services provide enhanced, more current, or easier to use versions of the same information. By the same token, it is harder to maintain trade secrets, as so much information finds its way out onto the World Wide Web.

This increased access to information helps fulfill one of the fundamental promises of the international system of intellectual property – the more access people have to innovations, the more quickly innovation itself advances. Even lay people can find useful information about their own intellectual property or that of others. However, a comprehensive analysis requires some training and experience.

Some of the many links and techniques for conducting IP research in public databases are listed in Appendix D. These include searching U.S. and WIPO records for patents, published patent applications, trademark registrations and applications, U.S. copyright registrations, and domain name registrations.

In patent lawyer conferences and articles, some people make the counter-intuitive argument that corporations should limit the amount of information they learn about competitors' patents, because learning about patents may bring negative consequences in efforts to obtain patents and avoid infringement liability: According to this "ignorance is bliss" approach, it is better not to know about prior art publications because patent applicants are required to disclose any prior publications of which they are aware to the U.S. Patent and Trademark Office and the patent offices in several other countries. If you do not know about the prior art, you need not disclose it. But a better approach is to learn about the prior art, and then structure a patent application to better define what is the new invention by distinguishing it from the prior art.

A second argument for ignorance is to avoid liability for willful patent infringement in the United States, where infringement damages may be trebled if the infringer knew about a patent and nevertheless willfully violated it. Without knowledge of the patent, there is no willfulness. But the best way to avoid any liability at all is to learn about relevant patents, and take steps to avoid infringing them, including taking out a license if necessary. So, the more information that a company has available about intellectual property, the better it is able to plan and implement a strong strategy.

IP due diligence

As discussed above, organizations should review their IP assets and the IP environment on a regular, periodic basis. However, many organizations have not made IP evaluation as routine as financial auditing, and instead they review their internal and external intellectual property landscape only in reaction to a particular event. For example, many companies consider the IP landscape only when launching a new product. Also, organizations generally react promptly with some sort of investigation when they receive an infringement notice letter from a competitor. But the most common trigger for IP evaluation is due diligence in negotiating a transfer of IP rights, such as by license or assignment, or in purchase or merger discussions.

Generally, any party that is considering acquiring rights from another conducts some sort of due diligence. When buying a house, we do a title search to make sure the seller actually owns all the rights. When buying a business, the acquirer reviews the financial statements and other records to make sure of the assets that are being purchased. IP due diligence is simply an extension of this approach.

The entity acquiring IP rights, or investing in a company that holds IP rights, typically asks basic questions: what are the assets, how strong are the exclusive rights, and is there freedom to operate? The questions differ slightly for patents, trademarks, copyright, and trade secrets.

Patents

Assets

What U.S. and foreign patents and patent applications (provisional and regular) does the organization own? What types of licenses for the patents and patent applications does the company hold? Is the chain of title clear for all patents and patent applications?

Exclusivity

Do the claims of the patents cover the subject matter that the acquiring company considers to be commercially significant? That is, do they cover the products or services that the parties intend to commercialize? Do they cover products or services that competitors would likely try to commercialize? How significant are any weaknesses of the patents? Can they be cured? Consider any ownership rights of consultants, independent contractors, employees, former employees, strategic partners, and government agencies, in terms of their impact on both exclusivity and freedom to operate.

Freedom to operate

Are there any third party patents that might cover what is being sold or practiced by the organization?

Trademarks

Assets

What U.S. and foreign trademarks and applications does the organization own? What types of trademark licenses does the company hold? Is the chain of title clear for all trademark assets?

Exclusivity

Do the trademark registrations and applications cover the products and services being sold by the selling company? Do they cover the products or services that the acquiring party intends to commercialize? Do they cover products or services that competitors would likely try to commercialize? Are there important trademarks that are currently being used or intended to be used for which applications have not been filed in key countries? What steps can be taken to fill any gaps in the trademark portfolio? Consider ownership rights of consultants, independent contractors, employees, former employees, strategic partners, and government agencies, in terms of their impact both on exclusivity and freedom to operate.

Freedom to operate

Are there any trademarks of others that might cover what is being sold or practiced by the organization?

Copyrights

Assets

What U.S. and foreign copyright registrations and applications does the organization own? Is the chain of title clear for all copyright registrations and applications?

Exclusivity

Do the copyright registrations and applications cover the works being distributed by the selling company? Do they cover the works that the acquiring party intends to commercialize? Do they cover works that competitors would likely try to copy? What unregistered copyrightable subject matter does the target company own (e.g., software, text, graphics, websites, databases, compilations)? Should these works be registered?

Freedom to operate

Consider ownership rights of consultants, independent contractors, employees, former employees, strategic partners, and government agencies, in terms of their impact both on exclusivity and freedom to operate.

Trade secrets

Assets

What inventions are being held as trade secrets?

Exclusivity

How is the secrecy of the trade secrets being maintained? What is the policy of the company governing internal use of trade secrets and external disclosure?

Freedom to operate

Does the company take steps to avoid using trade secrets received from others under confidentiality agreements, and from new employees bringing information with them from a former employer?

Policing IP Rights

An organization that wants to prevent infringement of its IP assets must police those rights. Some types of IP are easier to police than others. For example, trade marks are relatively easy to police. Anyone marketing products or services using an infringing trademark leaves a clear trail – on the internet, in print advertisements, and in telephone listings. For a fee, professional trademark monitoring services can scour all publicly available data sources and report any questionable activities to the trademark owner, who can then consider how to proceed. Copyright owners may set up elaborate procedures to identify people infringing their copyrights in music and video by using file swapping services.

But policing patents can be more difficult. Patent owners may have to buy a competitor's product and analyze or reverse engineer it to determine if it infringes a particular patent. Patents claiming methods for making products are even harder to police because the owner may need to gain access to a competitor's factory to find out if the patented process is being used. See Chapter 14 for more details.

Evaluation for public organizations

The evaluation process just described is most applicable to private businesses. Whether privately held or publicly traded, whether local or multinational, a primary concern of corporations is to build assets and avoid liabilities. The main limits a corporation is likely to place on IP evaluation are those dictated by resources – staff time and expense. In the case of due diligence, calendar time is important too, because a transaction may have a deadline and collecting some of the relevant information may take longer than is available.

Public organizations, including nonprofit groups and government agencies, generally expend less effort on evaluation and scrutiny of intellectual property. The funding sources and purposes of universities, research institutions, and government agencies are public, and their strategic interests are more subtle than the corporate interest in maximizing assets and minimizing liabilities. As a general rule, therefore, public organizations have less intense interest in protecting their IP assets than do for-profit corporations, and the purposes of evaluation for public organizations also diverge.

With respect to trade secrets, public entities, both governmental and nongovernmental, generally are more interested in publishing new information than in maintaining confidentiality. But public organizations need to maintain confidentiality in financial and personnel information, and to protect any trade secrets they receive from members of the public. Privacy laws increasingly mandate such trade secret protection. They therefore need to monitor their procedures for maintaining confidentiality.

The role of copyright is also limited for public organizations, because they are more concerned with disseminating their publications than profiting from them. For example, the U.S. government, by statute, is not permitted to use copyright law to protect its publications – they are in the public domain with respect to copyright. International and private philanthropic nonprofit organizations generally do not register copyrights or spend much effort evaluating the copyrights of others – although it is important for such entities to control their internal procedures to avoid infringement. International organizations like the United Nations and its affiliate organizations such as the World Health Organization and the World Intellectual Property Organization sometimes use copyright notices, but do not stringently restrict reproduction of their publications and so do not monitor for purposes of policing their rights.

Trademarks, too, have little relevance for national government agencies, which do not sell products or services. However, trademarks are vital for nonprofit organizations, which use them to protect their own identity and to distinguish their services and activities. For example, the Smithsonian Institution name and its sunburst trademark are well-known, and are used or licensed for magazines, souvenirs and gifts from the museums, and so on. Such organizations may employ sophisticated trademark policing efforts to protect their names and logos. But on average, nonprofit organizations have less active trademark portfolios than similarly sized profit-making organizations, and the need for evaluation is therefore less.

Finally, some public institutions are very active at patenting their innovations. For example, in the United States, under the Bayh-Dole Act of 1980, universities receiving public grant money may file patent applications on inventions made by their faculty members, for purposes of licensing them out to commercial entities. The University of California and Massachusetts Institute of Technology top the list of university patent owners. Universities can have extensive patent portfolios they evaluate and track carefully. There is rarely any need for universities to routinely evaluate the IP rights of others. Instead, universities generally require their licensees to police and enforce the licensed patents.

Evaluation for developing countries

Strategic assessment of IP is important to IP management in developing countries, as it is in developed nations. Some general differences between assessment in poorer countries and wealthier countries are as follows.

In wealthier countries, innovation is generally broader and more rapid, and may involve fundamental products or information. In developing countries, innovations usually occur at a slower pace and are incremental – a translation of a book or software, an adaptation of a mechanical or electronic device to local conditions, or a trademark for local markets. In wealthy countries, IP rights are generally stronger and easier to enforce than in poorer countries, and the stakes (and damages) are higher. And the level of professional knowledge, including business management and legal skills, is generally higher in wealthier countries.

But these generalizations aside, there are great advantages for organizations in developing countries who conduct evaluation of their own IP and that of others. Indeed, for any organization that has never conducted an IP evaluation, the first evaluation may bring immediate opportunities to improve the organization's ability to achieve its mission, and the costs may be low if the organization does not have extensive IP assets. Several illustrations show how IP assessment can proceed in developing countries.

The CGIAR Centers. The Consultative Group on International Agricultural Research (CGIAR) is a strategic alliance of fifteen international agricultural research centers (known as IARCs, or Centers), and donor governments and philanthropic organizations. In 1999, the IARCs conducted their first-ever IP evaluations.

The IARCs are organized as international organizations and are located in developing countries on every continent, with headquarters based in Benin, Nigeria, Kenya, Syria, India, Sri Lanka, Indonesia, Malaysia, Philippines, Mexico, Peru, and Columbia, as well as the United States and Italy, and they conduct agricultural research in crops relevant to poor farmers, with a combined budget exceeding US$450 million in 2006.

During the 1990s, with the rise of genomics and agricultural biotechnology, the IARCs faced mounting concern that (a) they were not managing their own IP assets wisely, and (b) they may be liable for infringing IP rights of others. The IARCs historically viewed their innovations as public goods available for farmers to use without cost, but they recognized that the university technology transfer model in the United States under the Bayh-Dole Act might apply in some situations – where IP rights are used to stimulate investment in technologies necessary to bring them to market. They also recognized that the IP rights of others might block their research and the ability of their farmer constituents to use and sell improved crops.

To address these concerns, in 1999 the CGIAR provided funding for each of the IARCs to conduct a comprehensive IP audit to consider their IP management practices, and to evaluate and eliminate potential risks to the IARCs and their partners. (I conducted the IP audits at five of the IARCs.)

The audits had concrete results. As reported in the 1999 annual meeting of the CGIAR, no "inappropriate activities" were identified, and this satisfied donors that they were not funding infringement. Also, the IARCs recognized the importance of managing their IP assets more wisely. Several set up their own IP management offices, and the CGIAR established a system-wide central advisory service on IP (CAS-IP).[1] They hired IP professionals and are incorporating IP analysis and management into their strategies and budgets.

The IARCs, with their first IP assessments, were able to begin the process of defining IP strategies tailored to their missions. The IARCs have not copied the traditional approach of universities, which focuses on protecting and transferring IP. Rather, to oversimplify somewhat, the IARCs treat plant seeds and other genetic material they hold as common property, in trust, and they are moving in the direction of an open science approach to their research results, with limited intellectual property protection, and a licensing strategy of requiring recipients to make their innovations publicly accessible, too. But they recognize that even this open approach requires IP management expertise.

PIIPA Projects. PIIPA (Public Interest Intellectual Property Advisors, Inc.), the global nonprofit organization, helps developing countries and public interest organizations seeking expertise in intellectual property matters to promote health, agriculture, biodiversity, science, culture, and the environment. As founder and Chair of PIIPA's governing board, I have worked to distinguish PIIPA from other organizations involved in policy advocacy and training activities. Instead, PIIPA provides practical assistance in the form of worldwide access to IP professionals who can advise and

---

[1] Egelyng, Henrik, "Evolution of Capacity for Institutionalized Management of Intellectual Property at International Agricultural Research Centers: A Strategic Case Study," *AgBioForum*, 8(1): 7–17 (2005), available at. http://www.agbioforum.org/v8n1/v8n1a02-egelyng.htm, accessed November 29, 2006.

represent clients pro bono publico (as a public service). Many of PIIPA's projects involve IP evaluation.

For example, the International Alpaca Association is a nonprofit association based in Peru representing individual breeders and companies processing Alpaca fiber. PIIPA's IP professional volunteers are assisting the association in opposing an application by a US farm to register the certification mark "Alpacamark" in the U.S. In another project, PIIPA volunteers helped LightYears IP work with Ethiopian coffee growers to develop trademarks for the varieties of specialty coffee grown there. A third project involved Ibis Reproductive Health, an organization seeking to expand availability of anti-HIV technology to females in Zimbabwe and South Africa where women and girls are highly vulnerable to HIV/AIDS. PIIPA volunteer IP professionals evaluated whether products involved in a clinical trial were protected by third-party patents, and how to make the study products more widely available. PIIPA volunteers also helped the Agricultural Technology Foundation evaluate whether any patents blocked development of corn varieties that could be treated with an herbicide that can kill a troublesome weed called *Striga* that especially affects poor farmers. Likewise, PIIPA volunteers helped Public Intellectual Property Resource for Agriculture conduct patent evaluations relating to various crops grown in the developing world for subsistence or export.

In each of these cases, organizations working in developing countries sought assistance in managing their IP. With PIIPA's help, they were able to find professionals who conducted evaluations of patents, trademarks, and other IP assets of the organizations and related outsiders. These evaluations helped the developing country organizations to achieve their goals.

Beijing Olympics 2008. When the Olympics come to town, they bring an army of trademark and copyright lawyers trying to prevent sale of counterfeit merchandise with unauthorized five-ringed Olympic logos, and distribution of unauthorized recordings of the sporting events. Multinational corporations pay sizable sponsorship fees for the right to sport the Olympic rings, and broadcasters pay for exclusive access to the recordings, and they frown on infringement.

The perception of lax IP enforcement in China is a hot political topic, so it will be interesting to see how far China in general, and Beijing in particular, goes to crack down on IP piracy. A key component in enforcing rights is monitoring and evaluating potential infringement. The Olympic organization and the licensees of the trademark and copyrights associated with the Olympics will take steps to track down and stop any infringement. One possible side effect of stepped up enforcement for the Olympics may be that other IP holders will better be able to evaluate potential infringements in other areas – such as software, automobiles, and pharmaceutical technology – and take steps to enforce rights. Motion picture studios and the recording industry would certainly be pleased if the active Chinese market in unauthorized recordings was shut down or constrained.

SUMMARY. IP evaluation – conducted as part of IP assessment during planning, auditing, or due diligence – is the crucial link between understanding an organization's mission and coming up with a suitable IP strategy. It is also a key part of the process of implementing that strategy, because organizations need to monitor their IP assets and police them as well. The first step in assessing IP rights is an internal evaluation conducted when needed, preferably on a regular schedule. The basic steps include listing all registered IP assets, checking procedures for protecting unregistered rights, and reviewing protection for the most valuable products. The scope of an internal evaluation can be custom tailored, but conveniently employs a questionnaire to organize the inquiry, covering each type of IP asset (patents, copyright, trademarks, and trade secrets), as well as employment issues and agreements. The second step is an evaluation of the external environment, studying the IP rights of others to avoid facing liability for infringement. This is typically done using public research tools, and private investigators of market activity. In due diligence, the evaluator may ask questions to the other party to help determine what assets are involved, how strong are the exclusive rights, and if there are any third party rights to avoid. Public organizations have particular concerns – for example, trade secrets may be less important. Developing country organizations are new to IP management and generally require more technical assistance in how to proceed. Finally, evaluation leads, in some cases, to the need to determine the financial value of IP assets, a topic dealt with in the next chapter.

12 Placing a Financial Value on Intellectual Property Assets

Financial valuation of IP assets is crucial in many circumstances, such as managing an IP portfolio, acquiring IP rights, and calculating prospective damages in an enforcement lawsuit. This chapter presents some threshold questions — the purpose for a valuation, the owner of the assets, and the type of assets — which help when selecting the valuation approach to use. There are four basic approaches, each with strengths and weaknesses in any given situation. First, the cost approach (sunk cost or replacement cost) is perhaps the simplest — how much money did the asset cost to produce, or how much would it cost to replace it. However, cost has little relevance in setting a market value. Second, the income approach focuses on net present value or discounted cash value, and applies only to assets with actual or predictable revenue streams, such as a running royalty. Third, fair market value is determined by reference to comparable assets. Finally, there are hybrid methods, such as rules of thumb for royalty percentages, and approaches for special valuation situations such as converting IP assets into securities. Several techniques can be combined to gain confidence about the value of an IP asset. The financial value of any bundle of IP rights is subject to much debate but ultimately most organizations care about the results, and so IP valuation is an important skill to master for individuals, organizations, and nations.

* * * * * *

THE IMPORTANCE OF IP VALUATION

Everybody interested in intellectual property, whether for profit or not, in rich or poor countries, needs to be able to measure what an IP asset or portfolio of assets is worth, in dollars, euros, rupees, renmimbi, or pesos. Much of the preceding discussion has focused on qualitative aspects of intellectual property and the systems supporting it. Where does intellectual property come from, how does it grow and how is it bundled together? How does the IP system benefit society? What are the goals and methods for managing IP in individual organizations? Here, we turn to *quantitative* valuation of IP – measuring how much it is worth.

It is important to understand valuation concepts because the valuation of IP serves as a measure of its IP's influence in the economy. And valuation is a key tool for strategic management of IP.

As Voltaire wrote, "When it's a question of money, everybody is of the same religion." Business organizations manage intellectual property to maximize profit by increasing their assets and reducing their liabilities. These organizations link IP and money with clear, direct, and strong connections. The stakes are enormous. Intellectual property makes some companies rich, and costs other companies fortunes.

A compilation of patent and copyright licenses and damages awards since 1985 shows 14 transactions worth more than $500 million, 73 transactions worth $100 to $500 million and 157 transactions worth $10 to $50 million, based on media reports.[1] Most of these occurred since 2000. The two biggest amounts were for broadcast copyright/trademark agreements for Major League Baseball ($2.5 billion) and NCAA basketball ($1.725 billion). The top technology valuation listed is the $1 billion that Qualcomm paid in 2000 to acquire SnapTrack and its portfolio of 50 patents covering wireless geological positioning system (GPS) technology, which was widely licensed in the industry and is reportedly now used in 150 million wireless devices. The second largest IP valuation is the $873 million damages award from Eastman Kodak to Polaroid in 1991, relating to instant photographs (in the predigital camera days). Eastman Kodak never fully recovered from that loss, nor has its hometown (mine, too) of Rochester, New York. The largest IP valuation listed in life sciences was a $505 million patent and license damages award from Roche to Igen for electrochemoluminescence imaging technology used in diagnostics, in 2002. The award was reduced to $18 million, but Roche acquired Igen the next year for $1.25 billion, in order to gain the right to continue using the technology.[2]

Money makes the world go round, in rich and poor countries, and IP helps corporations make money. That money, in turn, serves as an incentive and reward for innovation.

But the religion of money is not quite the same for nonprofit organizations. There a comment by Jonathan Swift may be more appropriate: "A wise man should have money in his head, but not in his heart." Like corporations, nonprofit organizations are wise to manage IP to increase their assets and reduce their liabilities. However, by definition, nonprofits are organized to pursue objectives other than profit, such as education, public health, environmental protection, or alleviation of poverty. So, nonprofits and public agencies manage IP for a broader range of purposes than just "making money."

For example, they may choose to manage IP for purely nonfinancial purposes, the most common approach being to openly publish information without restriction, as with the U.S. National Center for Biotechnology Information, through which the National Institutes of Health publish extensive genomic and proteomic data, as well as abstracts of scientific journals. Second, they may use open access licensing to promote an accessible domain in innovations building on their own.

Third, they may protect and license IP to earn money to support their public, nonfinancial purposes (by licensing patents, trademarks, and copyrights, and using that revenue for public purposes, in turn motivating employees to be creative). Fourth,

[1] Gregory Aharonian, "Patent/Copyright Infringement Lawsuits/Licensing Awards," available at www.patenting-art.com/economic/awards.htm, accessed December 4, 2006.
[2] Aaron Bouchie, "Roche and Igen in Shotgun Wedding," *Nature Biotechnology* 21:958 (2003)

they may use IP as a tool to induce others to invest their money into an innovation that it can be developed into a marketable product. For example, these last two purposes were achieved when the U.S. National Institutes of Health patented Taxol and licensed the patent to Bristol-Myers Squibb. The drug company invested many millions of dollars in the clinical trials and product development necessary to obtain regulatory approval and to bring the drug to market.

Valuation of intellectual property is increasingly important around the world, but the approaches differ. Developing countries have been placing an increasing value on their domestic cultural innovation, such as traditional medicines and foods and music. Biodiversity-rich but financially poor "source" countries have begun to bargain with foreigners seeking access to their plant and genetic resources under the 1992 Convention on Biological Diversity, which established the international rule that genetic resources are the sovereign property of individual nations, not the common heritage of humanity. Source countries tend to place a high value on their biodiversity and traditional knowledge, arguing that the collector may identify a valuable chemical or gene that could be the next blockbuster drug and create a huge income stream.

The researchers seeking access to those biological resources argue that the likelihood of any income at all is vanishingly small, that the cost of research is extremely high, and many other innovations are required beyond the source country's inputs. For accessing genetic resources, there is still no standard pricing model on which source countries and recipients agree.

Economists, accountants, business managers, judges, and lawyers have come up with numerous and complex valuation methodologies for IP assets in different settings, described in an extensive literature of books, articles, and court decisions.[3] Despite the differences between profit-making companies and nonprofit organizations, and rich and poor countries, and despite the wide range of business situations and types of IP assets, we can extract a common set of fundamental concepts and basic approaches that can be used by most IP managers. As one author stated, "When

[3] Joseph Agiato, "The Basics of Financing Intellectual Property Royalties," in Bruce Berman (ed.), *From Ideas to Assets: Investing Wisely in Intellectual Property* (John Wiley & Sons, 2002); Wston Anson, ed. *Fundamentals of Intellectual Property Valuation: A Primer for Identifying and Determining Value* (American Bar Association, 2005); Alexander Arrow, "Managing IP financial assets," in Bruce Berman (ed.), *From Ideas to Assets: Investing Wisely in Intellectual Property* (John Wiley 2002), chapter 5; L. M. Brownlee, *Intellectual Property Due Diligence in Corporate Transactions: Investment, Risk, Assessment, Management* (West 2002); Lanning Bryer and Melvin Simensky (eds.), *Intellectual Property Assets in Mergers and Acquisitions* (Wiley 2002); David Burge, *Patent and Trademark Tactics and Practice*, 3d ed. (Wiley: 1999); Jay Fishruck, "Royal(ty) succession: The evolution of IP-backed securitization" in *IP Value, 2007*, p. 17, available at http://www.buildingipvalue.com/07intro/p.17–21%20Intro,%20Moody.pdf. Accessed March 31, 2007; William Finkelstein and James Sims, III. (eds.), *The Intellectual Property Handbook: A Practical Guide for Franchise, Business and IP Counsel* (American Bar Association, 2005); Chris Fitzsimmons and Tim Jones, *Managing Intellectual Property* (Capstone Publishing, 2002); John Hillery,. "Securitization of Intellectual Property: Recent Trends from the United States" (March 2004), available at http://www.iip.or.jp/e/paper.html; Jackson Knight, *Patent Strategy for Researchers and Research Managers* (John Wiley, 1996); Baruch Lev, *Intangibles: Management, Measurement, and Reporting* (Brookings Institution Press, 2001); Baruch Lev, Paul Flignor, and David Orozco,. "Intangible Asset & Intellectual Property Valuation: A Multidisciplinary Perspective" (June 2006 IPThought.com); Alexander Poltorak and Paul Lerner, *Essentials of Intellectual Property* (John Wiley & Sons, 2002); Richard Razgaitis, *Early-Stage Technologies: Valuation and Pricin.* (John Wiley 1999); Gordon Smith and Russell Parr, *Intellectual Property: Licensing and Joint Venture Profit Strategies*, 2nd ed. (Wiley, 2000)

valuing intellectual property, the 'devil is in the concepts, not in the details.'"[4] Once the reader understands the conceptual framework for valuation, the details of specific methodologies will fall into place.

THRESHOLD QUESTIONS

To act strategically in placing a financial value on IP assets, the first step is to ask some threshold questions. The answers then help in selecting an appropriate methodology.

First, **what is the purpose of the valuation?** Why place a value on the asset? The purpose may be to provide pricing information in a transaction, such as a license, a collaboration, or a purchase or sale of intellectual property rights, or of equity in a corporation. It may be to satisfy financial or tax reporting requirements, following specific valuation methodologies. It may be necessary to calculate damages in a pending or threatened litigation, or to distribute assets in a bankruptcy, where the valuation rules depend on the law in the particular jurisdiction. Which methods to use, and how to apply and prioritize them, will depend on the purpose of the valuation.

Second, **who owns the asset?** If the asset is owned by the person conducting the valuation, the valuation serves to measure the owner's net assets and leverage over competitors. If the IP asset is owned by someone else, then the valuation may be part of competitive intelligence, such as estimating the risk of infringement damages, or preparing to make an offer for a license, or obtaining information as part of due diligence in a transaction.

Third, **what is the asset or portfolio being valued?** In legal terms, the IP assets are patents, trademarks, trade secrets, and copyrights. In business terms, the assets may be given a value in reference to the products or services, or divisions, to which they relate. In financial terms, the assets may be considered capital, collateral, expense items, or something else. For each valuation methodology, it is very important to look at the IP assets as bundles of rights – an innovation forest. It is also necessary to consider each type of IP right individually and also in connection with each type of product or service to which it applies.

With a goal in mind, and a sense of the IP portfolio under consideration, an IP chief can select a valuation methodology. To simplify, most of the valuation methods can be placed into four basic categories:

(1) Cost approach.
(2) Income approach.
(3) Market approach.
(4) Hybrid methods.

Fortunately, each of these methods is applicable in for-profit companies and nonprofit organization alike, and in developed or developing countries. Each method has some relevance to each of the different types of IP, and in different industrial sectors. Unfortunately, there is no single method that works best in all situations.

---

[4] Weston Anson (ed.), *Fundamentals of Intellectual Property Valuation: A Primer for Identifying and Determining Value* (American Bar Association, 2005), p. 29.

Table 12.1. Valuation of IP assets for a medical information website company, using various approaches

Financial facts	$	Cost valuation	Income valuation	Market valuation	25% rule
Investment					
Creative	1,000,000				
Marketing	500,000				
IP					
Trade secret	10,000				
Patent	200,000				
Copyright	5,000				
TM	25,000				
license costs	25,000				
		Total $1,765,000			
Revenue					
sales (profit margin 50%)	500,000/yr		NPV ~$1.93M over 10 years		
license (royalty 5%)	150,000		NPV ~$1.16M over 10 years Total $3.09M		
Competition					
Rejected offer to buy assets	$2,000,000			>$2M	
Market valuation of licensee company ($5M sales)	10,000,000			<$1M	
Profit margin 25%					6.25% royalty

Each approach has flaws. It is often necessary to run through many approaches to come up with a range of values, and then work towards a figure that fits best in a particular set of circumstances.

To provide the reader with an understanding of the fundamental principles and dynamics of IP valuation, we define each valuation approach, describe a method for using it to prepare an IP valuation, and identify some of the strengths and weaknesses of each. A simple illustration of each valuation approach is provided in Table 12.1.

COST (SUNK OR REPLACEMENT)

What was the cost of acquiring an IP asset or portfolio? In a historical (or sunk cost) approach, an IP owner may tally up the actual costs incurred to create and protect an IP asset. These may include actual research costs, equipment, labor, supplies, marketing, and overhead. Cost-based valuation is a traditional method for tangible assets and is used to set prices for many tangible products on the market – the manufacturer tallies the costs, adds a desired profit margin, and thereby sets a target price.

Sunk costs vary greatly for different types of IP assets, and in different parts of the world. For trade secrets, the sunk cost includes not only the research cost in creating the secret, but also any special equipment, software, or other measures used for security, and also the time value of the management and legal labor in identifying and protecting the secrets, including preparing confidentiality agreements and possibly, enforcing the trade secrets in court. This may be a relatively low number, but depending on the amount of research underlying the secret it can be substantial.

For patents, the sunk costs are typically more substantial. As with trade secrets, they include the costs of registering the patent (patent prosecution), in addition to research costs and whatever ancillary steps were needed to maintain trade secrecy prior to patent publication. Patent prosecution can be quite expensive. It includes in-house staff time spent preparing an invention disclosure and evaluating it; the cost of patent counsel in preparing and filing a patent application in a first country (typically $4,000 to $20,000); the cost of refiling the same application in foreign countries (averaging about $5,000 each); and the cost of the administrative procedures through examination, issuance, and payment of maintenance fees (ranging from $3,000 to $20,000 per country over the lifetime of the patent). For a single patent in one country, the sunk cost may be $25,000. For an international portfolio based on one invention, the sunk cost may be $100,000 or much more. For an international portfolio of a dozen patents, the prosecution costs can exceed $1 million. If there has been any expense for licensing activities, or enforcement litigation, that amount may be included in the sunk cost (and may add millions of additional dollars). Universities and the government agencies such as the U.S. National Institutes of Health generally expect to be reimbursed for sunk patent costs when they negotiate to grant a license. The sunk costs are used as a measure of how much the licensee should pay up-front, with royalties to follow on eventual sales.

For copyrights, the sunk cost involves the cost of creating the work and protecting the copyright. There is no real cost to place a copyright notice on a work. The cost of registration can be less than $100, or more in complex cases such as those involving multiple authorship or computer software. Sunk costs may also include the cost of licensing and enforcement programs.

For trademarks, the sunk cost includes expenses in selecting the mark, including artwork for a logo; clearing the trademark (searching for similar marks already in use, about $1,000 to $5,000); filing and issuing a trademark application in a first jurisdiction ($1,000 to $5,000); and filing trademark applications in other countries (about $2,000 each, on average). If the trademark is opposed, the cost of defending it should be added. As with other IP assets, the sunk costs may include the cost of licensing and enforcing a trademark through an infringement action in court.

Table 12.1 illustrates cost valuation. In this hypothetical, a medical information website has been in business for several years. The cost of the creative work needed to create the data processing tools, obtain links to the necessary data, and design and operate the website to date is $1,000,000. The cost of marketing the business to date is $500,000. The costs for protecting intellectual property include $10,000 for trade secrets (e.g., for confidentiality agreements, segregating secret information); $200,000 for patents (two in the United States, filed in the twelve biggest global economies); $5,000 for copyright registration and consultant agreements; $25,000 for international protection of four trademarks; and $25,000 legal costs for entering into a license with another website that is using some of the data and data processing tools. Here, the sunk cost totals to $1,765,000 and that is the sunk cost valuation of the company's IP rights, with $265,000 of that being IP-related expenses.

Perhaps the greatest strength of the sunk cost approach is that it is relatively easy to calculate. It is based on objective facts about expenditures, which most organizations monitor and maintain in their accounting records. Cost approaches can be useful with early stage innovations. Before an innovation is adopted by the market, there is limited data about the income or market value of the innovation, so it is relatively difficult to use the income and market approaches.

However, there are numerous weaknesses to the sunk cost approach. First, it may undervalue the IP asset. Assuming reasonable decision-makers (above all a competent IP manager), then a decision to protect the IP asset, for example, may be based on a prediction that the asset is be worth more than the cost of obtaining it. If that prediction holds true, then the sunk cost approach undervalues the asset.

Second, the sunk cost approach has no bearing on what an outsider might be willing to pay for the asset. The value of an IP asset or portfolio to a licensee or buyer may be much more or much less than the sunk cost. By way of analogy, back in the 1980s, I bought a rustic vacation cabin in the Catskill Mountains north of New York City, as an investment. My sunk costs included the cost of purchase, repairs, tax, and so on. Because of a general bust in real estate values around 1990, I ended up selling the cabin at a substantial loss. The buyers told me that my sunk costs were irrelevant to the amount they were willing to pay. The situation is no different for IP which has not fulfilled the owner's hopes for appreciation in value. The world's patent offices are full of worthless patents the owners paid a small fortune to obtain.

The sunk cost approach has been used by U.S. corporations to place a value on IP assets they donate to charities. However, the Internal Revenue Service has questioned whether such valuations are relevant, and looks instead to fair market value, as is the case with almost all in-kind contributions to charity.

Replacement cost is another cost-based valuation method that asks the following question: How much would a competitor need to spend if they were to create the asset themselves? This question strays from the straightforward fact-based methodology of the sunk cost approach, and requires some hypothetical calculations. However, it can be a useful measure of damages. For example, an engineering services company may create a specialized new software program, protect it with copyright, and provide it to customers as part of a service contract without a separate fee. If someone makes an infringing copy of the software, one measure of damages would be the cost that the infringer would have incurred to write the program itself – the replacement cost. A strong piece of evidence affecting damages would be the creator's sunk cost, but the infringer's hypothetical costs might be much more or less than the creator's actual cost.

INCOME (NET PRESENT VALUE OR DISCOUNT CASH VALUE)

The income or cash value model for IP valuation focuses on the revenues an owner can obtain from an IP asset, rather than its cost. The first step in identifying a cash value is to estimate how much revenue a particular IP asset will bring to its owner over the lifetime of the asset. Using simple financial calculations, a stream of revenue in future years can be converted into net present value (NPV) or discounted cash flow, which represents the cash value of an IP asset based on the income it can produce.

Two of the variables in a NPV calculation are: (a) the total future income attributable to the IP asset (as opposed to other IP assets and product features); (b) the timing and duration of the income stream; and (c) the discount rate, which can be based on the prevailing interest rate at the time, or a rate of return that an investor expects to receive, and other risk factors. NPV calculations (performed with easily available software spreadsheet templates) measure the time value of money.

In a simple example, you have a contract that will pay you $1 million in one year, and the interest rate is 10 percent. Your contract therefore has a net present value of $909,090. In a slightly more complex example, a potential purchaser of a portfolio of musical recording copyrights calculates that a popular musician will sell $10 million in recordings each year for the next 10 years, earning $1 million in copyright royalties each year. If the interest rate is predicted to be 2 percent, the net present value is $8,982,586. At 5 percent interest, the NPV is $7,721,735. If the expected interest rate was 10 percent, the NPV would decrease to $6,144,567. Based on the income approach alone, assuming interest rates would remain between 2 percent and 5 percent, the purchaser would be very interested in a purchase price below $7.5 million, and would be uninterested in a price over $9 million. This is a simplified version of David Bowie's 1997 sale of $55 million in bonds based on future royalties from his existing albums and future recordings.

A simple income valuation approach is illustrated in Table 12.1. Here, the medical information website company receives $500,000/yr for sales of subscriptions and advertisements, with a profit margin of 50 percent ($250,000/yr). It also receives $150,000 in royalties from its license to a competitor, at a rate of 5 percent on sales of $3 million. If we assume the business will be able to continue at this rate for 10 years, neither increasing nor decreasing in volume, and assuming a 5 percent interest rate, the NPV of the profit stream is about $1,930,000, and the NPV of the license royalty revenue is about $1,160,000. The total NPV of the income of the company would be about $3,090,000. Thus, the NPV based on the income method is between about $1.2 million and $3.1 million. This figure brackets the total sunk cost calculated above (about $1.8 million).

The main strength of income valuation is that the NPV figure is the number that attracts the most attention from investors, purchasers, licensees, and others interested in obtaining rights under an IP asset in order to make money. The income approach works well where there is a clear predictable cash flow from licensing an IP asset.

In another example, assume a university owns a patent on an approved pharmaceutical product, licensed to a drug company for 10 percent of net sales for the life of the patent, which is 10 years from the contract date. If drug sales are steady at $1 billion per year, then the university can expect $100 million in royalties per year. If the discount rate is projected as 10 percent, the net present value of the patent is therefore about $614 million. This is approximately what happened in July 2005 when RoyaltyPharma agreed to pay Emory University $525 million to buy out the royalties payable under a patent for emtricitabine, an antiviral HIV drug.[5] According to Emory's published financial statement for 2005, after payment of fees and the inventor share, the transaction netted the university $320 million for the year.

One weakness of the income approach is that it does not apply well to most IP assets because usually there is no predictable revenue stream attributable to an IP asset. It is inherently more difficult to estimate future revenues for an IP asset than it is to tally past costs, as with the sunk cost approach. It is difficult to unbundle IP assets and estimate the amount of revenue to be attributed to a particular IP asset in any given set of circumstances. For example, for a flat screen computer monitor containing a patented liquid crystal arrangement, what portion of sales should be attributed to the patent, as opposed to the brand name, or other product features? It is also difficult to predict market behavior, such as the possibility that another type of screen (such as a plasma screen) may take away market share. Finally, predicting interest rates is notoriously uncertain, so selecting the appropriate discount rate requires guesswork.

Decision trees can help in an income valuation. Many analysts use decision trees to conceive various possible scenarios with the percentage likelihood of each, and to calculate the ultimate value of an IP asset. An exemplary decision tree is shown in Figure 12.1. Based on estimates of the probability that different milestones (forks) will occur along the path of bringing a potential new drug to market, the probability of the different endpoints can be calculated. With further assumptions about the value of the outcomes (blockbuster drug, drug with generic competition, or no marketable drug at all), the net value of the drug per year can be calculated, and from this a discounted net present value can be derived. Although the potential market is huge, the discounted value of the invention is much smaller.

For the example shown, if a university researcher invents a new antiviral compound that shows activity in mice, and tries to place a value on the resulting patent application for purposes of licensing, we could assume (or estimate) that the licensee has a 10 percent chance of success in human clinical trials, leading to FDA approval and the possibility of sales, with a 90 percent likelihood of failure. We could also factor in a 50 percent chance that a strong patent will issue, barring generic competition, and assume that the annual market for sales of the drug would be $500 million with a patent, with profit of $200 million (a 40 percent profit margin). Without a patent,

[5] Joseph Agiato, "The Basics of Financing Intellectual Property Royalties," in *From Ideas to Assets*, chapter 19.

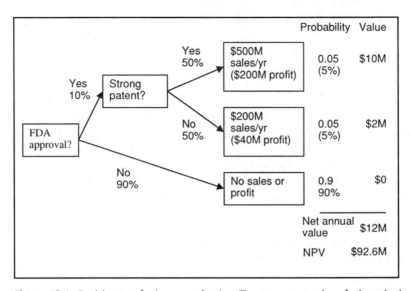

Figure 12.1. Decision tree for income valuation. The net present value of a hypothetical drug lead is calculated based on the probabilities of FDA approval and patent issuance and assumptions about sales.

because of generic competition, sales would be $200 million, with profit of $40 million (a 20 percent profit margin) without it. Using these assumptions, calculating the likelihood of the various scenarios, we can predict that there is a 90 percent chance of no FDA approval (a probability of 0.9), with a resulting profit of zero dollars. There is a 5 percent chance that the drug will be approved with a strong patent, with a profit, discounted for probabilities, of $10 million per year. There is a 5 percent chance of FDA approval without a strong patent, with a discounted value of $2 million per year. Adding up the possible outcomes (amounting to 100 percent), the annual profit discounted for probability, would be $12 million per year. (See Figure 12.1.)

The total NPV assuming all these contingencies could then be calculated based on the number of years until market approval, the lifetime of the patent, the prevailing interest rates, and other risk factors. Assuming 10 years patent life and a 5 percent interest rate, as above, the NPV would be about $92,652,000. Changing any of the assumptions would change the valuation accordingly.

One clear conclusion from such a decision tree is that the actual value of a lead compound is much less than that of an approved compound, because of the low probability of success. Conversely, as milestones are reached (patent issuance, regulatory approval, court judgment), the value of the asset increases dramatically. Another conclusion to draw is that the valuation depends heavily on assumptions that may be totally wrong.

A further example of the importance of time and projected sales volume in IP valuation can be found in the *NTP v. Research in Motion* (Blackberry) case. After trial in 2002, the court awarded $23 million in damages based on a reasonable royalty approach. Damages were increased to about $60 million and interest in 2003 due to willful infringement. The parties discussed settlement for $450 million the following year, and RIM set aside an accounting reserve fund ("war chest") in that amount. The parties ultimately settled for more than $612.5 million on March 3, 2006. The growing amount of the settlement payment was not due to any change in the royalty rate or valuation approach, but rather was primarily due to much larger sales of Blackberry services during the intervening period, along with a rapidly growing subscriber base. NTP ultimately was able to share in RIM's success in the 4 years between the trial and the settlement.

A variant type of income-based valuation is so-called relief from royalty modeling. This method is particularly relevant to an organization deciding what price to pay someone else for purchasing rights to their IP assets. Here, the question is, if no purchase is made, how much would the organization have to pay to the asset owner as royalties, as a potential licensee? The income approach is then used to quantify the net present value of what the owner would have to pay to license the technology.[6] Alternatively, what would be the measure of damages that the prospective purchaser would likely have to pay? In the example above, where Roche agreed to pay $1.25 billion to acquire Igen after losing an IP lawsuit, relief from royalty pricing was certainly a relevant model, because by acquiring Igen, and its IP assets, Roche was able to avoid paying royalties on all future sales of the ECL diagnostic product. In such a case, the parties perform extensive economic modeling of the value of the relevant patents and licenses as part of the damages calculation in the lawsuit, so they have plenty of information to use in settling on a price.

MARKET VALUE (COMPARABLES)

In fair market valuation, the monetary value of an IP asset is based on similar transactions involving similar assets. For example, a McDonald's franchise can be viewed as a combined license of the arches trademarks, the trade secrets about food preparation and service, and copyright in the various printed materials, along with a food and equipment delivery contract. The value of the IP assets in one franchise can be determined based on the value in a similar transaction.

A simplified market valuation for the medical information website is shown in Table 12.1, above. In this scenario, the licensee competitor last year offered $2,000,000 to buy the patent portfolio, copyrighted software, and associated trade secrets (but not the trademarks). The company being valued rejected that offer, thinking the value was higher. Based on this offer and rejection, the market valuation suggests that the IP rights are worth more than $2,000,000. Also, the licensee competitor had a market valuation of $10,000,000 at the last financing round, based on $5,000,000 in sales. Based on that data, and a sales volume one tenth the size, assuming the same profit margins and growth, the total value of the website business in question would be $1,000,000. The value of the IP assets, without the business itself, would presumably be worth less than $1,000,000. Market valuation is not much help here.

---

[6] Michael Lesinski, "Valuation of Intellectual Property Assets," in Bryer and Simensky (2002), p. 4.10.

The sunk cost valuation was about $1.8 million, and the income valuation was about $1.2 to 3.1 million. This market valuation did not give any basis for a particular figure within that range or outside of it.

One of the strengths of fair market valuation is that it is well-established in economic theory, legal doctrine, and in day to day life, in all parts of a market economy. The methodology of appraisal using comparable sales is familiar to anyone who has bought a home. If an identical house just sold in your neighborhood for $250,000, then your home is worth $250,000. If your house has an extra bathroom, then the value of your house might be $10,000 higher. In an even simpler example, if you want to buy a new car, or desktop computer, or a copy of this book, you can compare prices at various online vendors and come up with a reasonable idea of the fair market value of the item. Stock prices, too, are set based on daily trades of other such securities.

One problem with using comparable transactions in IP valuation is that many IP assets, by their very nature, are unique, so that no direct comparison can be made. There is no established market for most IP assets, so often there is almost no data at all.

Another problem is that many IP transactions are secret. The parties to an IP transaction are usually sophisticated enough to recognize that there are trade secrets both in the underlying technology and in the business terms of the agreement, and they agree to keep the terms of the agreement secret from the public. Much of the available data about IP transactions comes from published court opinions (and even there, details may be kept confidential by a judge), also from press releases and annual reports by publicly traded corporations, and from special industry reports and surveys (such as the Association of University Technology Managers annual survey of patenting and licensing activity).

HYBRID METHODS

A variation on income valuation is the use of hypothetical royalty negotiations to establish value. This approach conjures up a scenario of a willing buyer and a willing seller – a scenario that may make more sense in a friendly negotiation than in a high-stakes litigation, where it is often used.

A reasonable royalty is one measure of damages awarded in infringement litigation enforcing patents, trade secrets, trademarks, or copyrights. To determine a reasonable royalty, the courts typically imagine a hypothetical negotiation between a willing buyer and a willing seller of the IP asset. The willing buyer-willing seller model is used for example in patent infringement litigation to determine what would be a reasonable royalty to assess as damages. For example, in the United States, courts assessing damages for patent infringement generally apply the fifteen "Georgia-Pacific" factors to help decide what the result of the hypothetical negotiation would have been, and thus to determine a reasonable royalty in a patent case.[7] The factors are:

---

[7] These fifteen factors were first set out by a trial court judge in the seminal case of *Georgia-Pacific Corp. v. U.S. Plywood Corp.*, 318 F. Supp. 1116 (S.D.N.Y. 1970), and have been accepted by higher courts, even in contexts other than patent infringement.

(1) Established royalties, actually received by the patent holder for licensing the patent
(2) Royalty rates paid by licensees of comparable patents
(3) License scope (exclusive vs. nonexclusive, field or industry of use, geographic restrictions)
(4) Patent owner's licensing practices (active licensing, no licensing)
(5) Commercial relationship between the patent owner and the licensee (competitors, collaborators, contractors)
(6) Effect of infringement on sales of other products
(7) Duration of the patent and term of the license
(8) Profitability, success, and popularity of products made under the patent
(9) Advantages of patented products over prior art
(10) Nature and benefits of the patented invention and commercial embodiments
(11) Extent of use by the licensee and value of that use
(12) Customary rates in the industry for similar inventions
(13) Share of the profit attributable to the invention relative to unpatented elements added by the infringer
(14) Expert testimony
(15) Ultimately, the amount that a reasonable licensor and licensee would have agreed on for the license, immediately prior to the infringement.

Over the past decade there have been several well-known efforts at auctioning IP assets, first the Patent License Exchange, and more recently Ocean Tomo. Auctions, although fascinating, remain a vanishingly small part of the valuation options for IP assets

One of the more ambitious efforts to define a new IP valuation method is the use of the Black Scholes option pricing formula, or Real Options Theory.[8] This Nobel prize-winning economic model is used by securities analysts to provide a fair price for stock options, and has been crucial to the growth of derivatives trading and hedge funds in financial markets. Call options are the right to buy a stock in the future at a set strike price. If the stock price in fact is higher at that time, then the value of the call option will be the difference between the actual stock price and the strike price. If the stock price is lower than the set strike price, the call option will have zero value. Like call options, patents have huge potential value but a high likelihood of having zero value. Alexander Arrow, Nir Kossovsky, and colleagues at the Patent & License Exchange in about 2000 developed patent valuation tools based on this approach, including their Technology Risk-Reward Unit (TRRU) Valuation model. To place a value on a particular patent, this model uses the Black-Scholes formula with inputs adapted to patents: the remaining development cost of the product, the remaining development time, and the market value of "pure play" nondiversified companies that only sell products in the same niche as the patent.

Despite its complexity, Real Options Theory has some advantages over conventional approaches where buyers and sellers do their own valuation modeling and then argue over the differences. A seller tends to focus on the reward of a return on

---

[8] Alexander Arrow, "Managing IP Financial Assets," in *From Ideas to Assets*, chapter 5.

the investment of sunk costs in the IP asset, and a buyer tends to focus on the risk of investing more and failing to earn a return on the investments. If Real Options Theory valuation can create an objective, somewhat more automatic estimate of the risk-reward ratio, one that is acceptable to buyers and sellers of IP assets, and traders in financial markets, then adoption of such a valuation approach could reduce transaction costs and increase the liquidity of patents (and other IP assets). But the model has not yet been widely adopted.

Rules of thumb

Experienced IP managers and professionals use rules of thumb to estimate the value of IP assets. A rule of thumb is a simple, easy to remember guideline that serves as a shortcut to reach an approximate value that may be useful, but is not very accurate. Some call them "guestimates." By using a rule of thumb, an IP manager or a negotiator trying to put together a deal can quickly get a rough idea of the value of an asset, with numbers that can be run in one's head and without extensive data gathering and calculation.

A leading rule of thumb is the use of established royalty rates in a particular industry. Using a royalty rate to define the value of a license is often more logical and fair than, say, payment of a flat fee, because the licensor and licensee share the risk of failure and the benefits of success. Another virtue of royalty based valuation is that no data is required other than the sales volume – which is the most commonly tracked financial statistic in businesses around the world.

However, the ideal of an "established rate" is elusive in practice. Because the actual licensing terms across an industry are often kept secret, it may be hard to obtain objectively verifiable data that would allow a wide range of people to agree on what is the established rate. Instead, experienced professionals may aggregate their own experiences to come up with a general idea of what their clients might expect in the industry. A large corporation, too, can aggregate data from all of its own transactions with different organizations to come up with its own view of an established royalty rate.

In the absence of data about established rates, the crudest rule of thumb is to assume that 5 percent of gross sales amount is a reasonable royalty to pay for a license. The 5 percent rule can also be used to estimate income valuation (calculating the net present value of a 5 percent royalty over a set period of time.)

The 5 percent rule is a popular – if flawed – starting point in negotiations where there is little data about comparable transactions, income streams, or costs. For example, in the 1990s there was little comparable information about royalty rates for biodiversity prospecting agreements, in which a researcher obtains access to plant or other biological resources in a source country in exchange for a share of the resulting benefits. In my experience with many source country negotiations, the 5 percent rule of thumb was often used as a starting point. However, the range of royalties to which parties have actually agreed is in a vastly broader range – 0.025 percent to 10 percent.[9]

[9] Kerry, ten Kate and Sarah Laird, *The Commercial Use of Biodiversity: Access to Genetic Resources and Benefit Sharing* (Earthscan, 2000), p. 252.

There is no sound theory behind the 5 percent rule. It only applies directly to license transactions with royalties, not to purchase of assets. When several IP rights are involved, the royalty for any one of them may well be less than 5 percent to avoid stacking the royalties too high. The reality is that in different situations and industries established royalties may range from as low as 0.01 percent to as high as 50 percent. Ultimately, the 5 percent rule is of little help.

Another rule of thumb is called "the 25 percent rule." This is most often applied when two parties are setting a royalty rate in exchange for licensing an IP asset. The basic principle is that the profit attributable to the intellectual property should be split between the IP owner (licensor) and the licensee. Specifically, the 25 percent rule holds that the licensor should get 25 percent of the profits, while the licensee gets 75 percent. For example, a publisher wants an author to write a book and assign the copyright to the publisher. The publisher plans to sell the book for $10. The costs (editing, printing, and marketing) are $6, so the profit margin is $4 (40 percent). Under the 25 percent rule, the author would get 25 percent of the profit, or $1. This is equivalent to a royalty of 10 percent of the sales price. In practice, authors' royalties may be higher or lower than 10 percent, but the 25 percent rule serves as a good rule of thumb because it falls within the reasonable range of author's royalties.

In another example, assume that a university licenses a new chemical compound patent to a pharmaceutical company, which then sells the drug at an 80 percent gross profit. The 25 percent rule would give the university a 20 percent royalty – higher than many, but still within the range of experience, and reportedly the rate that Emory University received for emtracitibine before selling the royalty stream to RoyaltyPharma.

An example of the 25 percent rule is shown in Table 12.1, above. In this scenario, the profit margin of the licensee competitor is 25 percent, only half the profit margin of the company in question. One reason for the lower profit margin is that the licensee is paying 5 percent of its sales in royalties. But whatever the reason for the lower profit margin, if we use the 25 percent rule, we come up with 6.25 percent of sales. By this calculation, the current 5 percent royalty rate may be on the low side.

The basic premise in the 25 percent rule is quite sound – that a reasonable business would not use an IP asset that did not increase its profit margin, and that the licensor and licensee should split the increase in profits. But implicitly, the 25 percent rule of thumb is based on two further assumptions: (1) that the licensee's right to use the IP asset actually does increase the profit margin, and (2) that the innovator's fair share of the profits is 1/3 of the licensee's increased profits (25 percent compared with 75 percent). A key problem with the 25 percent rule lies in the difficulty in calculating profits. There may be different opinions about whether to count fixed costs as well as marginal costs and overhead. The more costs that are included, the narrower the margin, and hence the lower the royalty calculated using the 25 percent rule. A second problem is in the split between the innovator and the licensee. Rather than taking 25 percent of the profits, the IP owner might reasonably expect one third, one half, three-quarters or some other fraction of the profits in a given situation. Third, the success of a product, may depend on several innovations, so no single one of them deserves 25 percent of the profits.

Special valuation situations

Often the IP owner is not the original creator of the asset but someone who bought it or licensed it from the creator. Qualcomm paid $1.25 billion to purchase SnapTrak. Research in Motion paid NTP $612 million as a settlement and patent licensing fee for the Blackberry personal digital assistant. Such a situation can be analyzed by a sunk cost, income, or market method. The purchase price paid for the asset might be considered as one kind of sunk cost for the purchaser in future calculations. Or the purchase price can be used in a market approach, to determine the fair market value of the asset. For a license, the royalty payments can be used to determine a market value for a similar license, or to calculate the expected income stream from the license, in an income method.

In infringement litigation, at least in the United States, the measure of damages is slightly different for each type of IP asset. With patents, the owner may recover at least a reasonable royalty. NTP's award against Research in Motion for the Blackberry was based on a reasonable royalty. The owner may also recover lost profits from sales of the product in competition with the infringing product. And if the infringement was willful, the owner may be able to recover treble damages and attorney fees. Injunctive relief (a court's order that the infringer must not sell the infringing product) is not included when calculating damages, but the IP owner certainly gains financial value by winning an injunction, as witnessed by Roche's purchase of Igen in order to get out from under an injunction.

For trade secrets, the measure of damages may include the replacement cost, reasonable royalty, and the lost profits suffered by the owner or gained by the infringer, depending on which is the larger number. For trademark infringement, the damages are similar, although punitive damages and attorney fees may also be available for willful infringement (such as counterfeit). For copyright, in the United States, the owner may recover actual damages (such as lost profits), or instead may elect statutory damages in an amount of $750 to $30,000 per infringement, or up to $150,000 if the infringement was willful.

In licensing negotiations, even if there is a general agreement about the value of a license, there are many ways to structure the transfer of value from the licensee to licensor. For example, there may be a fixed up front payment, and if that is the only payment, the license is referred to as "paid up." There may be fixed periodic payments, such as annually. There may be a royalty based on percentage of sales or on a fixed amount per unit sold. The royalties may start out high, to help the innovator recoup investment, and then drop down on higher sales volume. Or they may start low to help the licensee establish a market, and then ramp up later after the profit margin increases. And there may be a minimum amount of royalties payable each year in order to protect the licensor from a situation where the licensee fails to make any sales.

In IP transactions involving universities and public agencies, the non-economic terms of a license may be as important as the financial terms. For example, public sharing of data may be paramount to a university, even if a company is willing to pay for an exclusive license. Universities and the National Institutes of Health also have policies for public access to research tools – innovations that help researchers, as opposed to innovations with immediate commercial value, and these policies may be more important than financial valuation.

Monetizing IP assets – converting them directly into monetary assets that can be traded on financial markets – is an increasingly popular strategy. IP owners have long used their IP assets as collateral security against loans – so called debt financing for the IP owner. The newer variations over the past ten years use IP assets to back securities that are then issued to the financial markets – so-called equity financing, because the investor holds a share of the asset. As we have seen, IP valuation is subject to much uncertainty. Even with income valuation based on existing royalty streams, there are numerous risks, such as loss of patent validity, competing products, changes in pricing, and so on. Therefore, companies like RoyaltyPharma have learned to assemble a diverse pool of assets with a combined valuation far in excess of the value of the securities they sell on the financial markets. In other words, they over-collateralize and diversify their portfolio. This serves as insurance against the loss of any one asset, and protects the company and its investors in the event the IP valuations are wrong – even if they are far wrong – with a combined valuation far in excess of the amount of debt that that they have securitized.

Economics provides a final example of a special IP valuation situation. Several years ago, economists began to use patent counting as a proxy for innovativeness. Economists like to use such data because it is readily available from public databases such as the U.S. Patent and Trademark Office. (See Appendix D.) In microeconomics, one can count the number of patents (or trademark registrations or copyright registrations), issued to a particular company, and then can draw certain conclusions about how innovative the company is. By comparing these figures to those of competitors, over time one can judge the competitive posture of the companies. Going further, in macroeconomics one can derive certain conclusions about the innovation level of an industry, or a nation, or a region, by looking at the number of IP assets issued over a period of time.

However, raw patent counts are very limited in their usefulness. They equate trivial innovations or patents with valuable ones. Some patents are extremely valuable (such as the six NTP patents used to force Research in Motion into paying more than $600 million to settle infringement claims), but most patents have little or no value at all. On a macroeconomic basis, within an industry, in a single country, raw patent counts may be useful for observing trends over time, but they may not be much help in comparing, say computers and biotechnology, or activity in the United States and Brazil.

IP valuation methods can be combined with patent-counting methods to improve economic analysis of innovation. Economists have tried to assess the value of patents, rather than their sheer numbers, for example, by considering forward citation – a count of how often a company's patents are cited by other patents (a statistic also available from public data).[10] Similar approaches can be used in microeconomic analysis of individual organizations, looking at the value of their patent or trademark portfolio, rather than the raw numbers.

---

[10] Francis Narin, Patrick Thomas, and Anthony Breitzman, "Using Patent Indicators to Predict Stock Market Performance," in *From Ideas to Assets*, chapter 14.

From a social perspective, some might argue that the value of IP rights to one organization can also be seen as a representation of the cost those assets impose on consumers, competitors, researchers, and society at large. That is, if my patent and trademark portfolio permits me to charge a premium over my competitors, and therefore has a value calculated at $5 million, that figure also reflects the extra cost paid by consumers due to lack of competition. Patents permit pharmaceutical companies to earn extra profit before a generic company introduces a competing product, and that profit is also a measure of the extra cost of exclusivity to patients. One man's meat is another man's poison. The innovator's value is the consumer's cost. The question is whether the extra cost is worthwhile in promoting innovation.

Valuation as a measure of driving force of the IP system

IP valuation is a crucial tool for any organization in managing its intellectual property. Valuation practices can help identify strong developmental and management strategies, and can help owners to track their assets and establish their investment priorities. They help organizations assess the risks they face from competitor's IP rights. And they provide a measure of whether a strategy is succeeding or failing.

Valuation practices also illuminate the incentive and reward system of intellectual property laws and practices around the world that helps drive innovation through its cycle. The economic value of IP assets to their owners provides one measure of the force that intellectual property exerts, and hence its influence on the flow of innovation. The tools of IP valuation show what assets are economically worthwhile, and which (the majority) are not. IP provides value to its owners, and that value can be measured. Even in nonprofit organizations, financial measures are easier to grasp than qualitative descriptions of the noneconomic value of IP assets in terms of the exclusive control they provide.

SUMMARY. An IP manager needs to know the financial value of a particular IP asset or an entire portfolio in situations including managing, acquiring, or selling a portfolio, or predicting the damages that might occur in an infringement lawsuit (from the perspective of a plaintiff or a defendant). An IP manager should prepare for a valuation by asking the "W" questions – why proceed, who owns the assets, what type of assets are involved, when is the relevant time period, and where is the focus of the valuation. The answers to these questions shape the valuation process, which includes one or more of the four basic approaches. These approaches can apply in industry, the nonprofit sector, and developing countries. Examples are provided in Table 12.1. The cost approach (sunk or replacement) is simple and attractive to an owner, because it is based on how much money the asset cost to produce, or how much it would cost to replace it. However, a buyer or investor cares more about revenue potential or market value. The income approach focuses on net present value or discounted cash value of an IP asset with a predictable revenue stream, such as a running royalty on a drug. The income approach is not very helpful in situations where there is no predictable revenue directly linked to an IP asset. The fair market value, based on comparable assets, makes sense when buying or selling an IP asset, but it has limited applicability because each IP asset may be unique. Finally, many people use hybrid methods, such as the reasonable royalty method for calculating patent damages, the 25 percent rule for royalty percentages, and approaches for special valuation situations, such as litigation, converting IP assets into securities, biodiversity prospecting, and nonprofit settings, such as open source licensing. By using several techniques, the IP manager may produce a range of values, with some confidence that the value of an IP asset or portfolio, is within that range. The IP system exerts a driving force on individuals, organizations, and nations seeking to generate financial value, and the actual value of IP assets, as difficult as it may be to ascertain, is a good measure of that economic force. Value generation is one of the principles underlying implementation of an IP strategy, the topic of the next section.

13 Accessing Innovations of Others

This section presents a systematic approach to implementing an IP management strategy, the last stage of strategic management. The process of identifying a strategy and assessing internal resources and external challenges can greatly simplify the task of implementation, and can give confidence to the person in charge. With a sense of purpose and knowledge of the facts, an IP manager can proceed through a step-by-step system using decision trees to decide how to manage innovations that are important to the organization. This chapter focuses on how to access innovations of others without creating liability for infringing IP rights. The first step is to screen innovations to decide whether innovations by outsiders are involved. If so, the second step is to determine whether access is readily available on reasonable terms, in which case a pathway exists for using the innovation. When access is not readily available, a more complicated series of decisions follows, trying to find the path of least resistance – to wait for IP rights to expire, use the innovation in countries without relevant IP rights, find an alternative, or probe for a bargaining chip such as a legal defect, fair use, blocking IP rights, or a compulsory license. Upon evaluation of the circumstances, the organization may choose to use the innovation without permission or to challenge the IP right in court, but these options require especially careful analysis because of the cost and potential liability involved.

* * * * * *

IMPLEMENTATION AS PART OF PLANNING

To recap, management of intellectual property boils down to this: Organizations need to cut through the complexity of intellectual property issues by coming up with a strategic plan to protect their own assets and to respect those of others. The strategic planning process is always as follows:

- Define the organization's goals.
- Assess internal resources.
- Evaluate the external environment.
- Form a simple, long-range plan consistent with resources, environment, and goals.
- Implement the plan.

Each organization needs its own strategic plan, based on its overall mission, its particular IP assets, staffing, and resources, and its competitive environment. The plan may be like one of those discussed in Chapter 10, or it may be a new one. But whatever plan is adopted, it is of no use unless it is carried out.

This chapter focuses on implementation. Implementation refers to the concerted actions taken to carry out a strategic plan. There are two parts to implementing a strategic plan for managing IP. The first is accessing the intellectual property rights of others without disruption or liability. The second is protecting the enterprise's intellectual property assets in a way that furthers the organization's goals. Both parts need to address all types of intellectual property – trade secrets, trademarks, copyrights, patents, and related rights. One or another of these assets is typically most important to a given organization, but implementation is required for all of them.

SIMPLIFY, SIMPLIFY

The key to success in implementing an IP strategy is to find a simple path. "Simplify, simplify," as Henry David Thoreau once reminded us.[1]

Implementing a strategy can be daunting. The IP manager must select the innovations to protect, choose the right type(s) of IP protection, and then conceive and coordinate the steps taken over an extended period, to achieve such protection. The IP manager must also determine whether any of the organization's activities infringe the IP rights of others. If so, the IP manager must find ways to avoid these outsider rights. The questions, decisions, and acts required to protect and respect IP rights can be extremely complex. Laws, business practices, and technical details are in many cases so arcane and cover so many specialties that even smart, experienced professionals get lost or overwhelmed.

The tasks of implementation can be reduced to three basic steps. First, screen innovations for access or protection. Second, access desired innovations from outsiders. Third, grow and harvest IP rights from innovations inside the organization.

1. Screening innovations

Screening innovations is the first step in implementing an intellectual property management plan. The screening process can be shown as a decision tree. (See Figure 13.1.)

As a starting point, the IP manager identifies a particular innovation that is important to the organization. The innovation can be anything that will be used by the organization, or sold by it. The innovation may be specific, such as a computer software program, a pharmaceutical formulation, a portable drill, a bacterial culture, a book, or a song. Or the innovation may be much broader, such as Toyota's synergy

---

[1] "Simplicity, simplicity, simplicity! I say, let your affairs be as two or three, and not a hundred or a thousand; instead of a million count half a dozen, and keep your accounts on your thumb-nail. In the midst of this chopping sea of civilized life, such are the clouds and storms and quicksands and thousand-and-one items to be allowed for, that a man has to live, if he would not founder and go to the bottom and not make his port at all, by dead reckoning, and he must be a great calculator indeed who succeeds. Simplify, simplify." Henry David Thoreau, *Walden, or Life in the Woods* (1854).

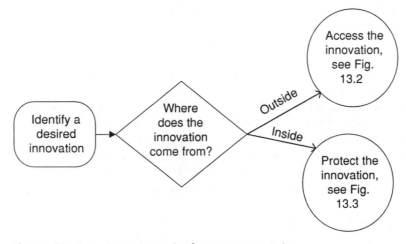

Figure 13.1. Screening an innovation for access or protection.

hybrid drive system, a new technique for identifying DNA sequences, or a combined music delivery and listening system like Apple's iTunes and iPod.

The first question is where does the innovation come from? The answer is eitherr that the innovation comes from inside the organization, or outside the organization, or both. Innovations arise from the creative work of individual people. The creative work of one person flows together with other creative work, from other people, and over time.

If the innovation was created by outsiders (anyone without an obligation to transfer IP rights to the organization, such as independent individuals and employees of other organizations), then the next series of tasks relates to finding a way to gain access to the innovation without creating legal liability. This leads to the initial phase of the decision-making pathway for accessing innovations from others as shown in Figures 13.2 and 13.3. Protecting innovations by insiders is discussed in Chapter 14.

2. Accessing an outsider's innovation

Since an enterprise's value is basically the total of its assets minus its liabilities, it is just as important to avoid catastrophic liability and disruption as it is to increase the value of its assets. Therefore, organizations must be careful to respect the IP rights of others. If an IP right is (or may be) asserted against an organization, then the organization must itself determine if there has been or will be any infringement. That is, do the IP rights affect the company's work, and if so, is there any reasonable way to gain access to the innovation anyway? The process of identifying how to access an innovation is often referred to as a "freedom to operate" analysis.

Intellectual property rights can exert a chilling effect far beyond their proper scope. For example, as I have often witnessed, a scientist or engineer may find a patent on a desired technology, read the broad discussion of technology in the description, and conclude that the patent excludes him or her from the entire field. But closer examination may reveal that the claims of the patent are limited to very specific circumstances, such as particular times, temperatures, or components, so the scientist can find a way to use the technology without infringing. In another scenario, a developing country's health agencies may complain that U.S. patents claiming a pharmaceutical product block the agency from using the drug in that country. A more careful analysis then reveals that there are no relevant patents in that country that would block access to the drug, so the drug can be made there, or imported without permission from the patent holder.

With copyright, some people ignore even the most legitimate rights of others, copying and selling pirate movie DVDs and music CDs, and downloads of pirate software. At the other extreme there is a chilling effect among people who in good faith would like to use copyrighted materials but are uncertain about whether they can properly do so under the doctrine of fair use. For example, there has been an ongoing discussion at Wikipedia since 2001 titled "Avoid copyright paranoia," where users have been debating among other things whether the Wikipedia site should remove material that is merely suspected of being in violation of copyright, or should wait until an owner asserts infringement.[2]

Ignorance and confusion are the main reasons that IP rights can exert a chilling effect beyond their legitimate reach. With care and experience, it is often possible to find ways around many intellectual property rights. No IP right is water-tight. All have limits.

IP rights balance exclusion with access. Therefore, the discovery that there are (or may be) IP rights covering an innovation is not the end of the story. The existence of IP rights owned by someone else does not necessarily preclude access to the innovation. If the organization can gain access to the innovation on reasonable terms, then the existence of IP rights is not a problem. Skillful management can often lead to access to the underlying innovation. The following discussion lays out a roadmap for gaining access to innovations with minimum risk and cost.

WHEN ACCESS IS READILY AVAILABLE

A relatively short decision tree is appropriate for accessing an outsider's innovation when access is readily available. (See Figure 13.2.) The first question is whether IP rights block access to the innovation. This requires some research, either as part of a routine assessment, or in a special search. If there are no applicable IP rights, then the organization can use the innovation freely. That is one happy ending of the inquiry.

Examples of innovations not protected by IP rights include the image of Leonardo da Vinci's Vitruvian Man used on the cover of this book; facts reported in numerous sources; old works like Shakespeare's plays, and books from the nineteenth century; technology described in expired patents; abandoned or generic trademarks like cellophane; and music and video sites on the Internet full of free files donated by their creators.

[2] http://meta.wikimedia.org/w/index.php?title-Avoid_Copyright_Paranoia&dir-prev&action-history, accessed December 10, 2006.

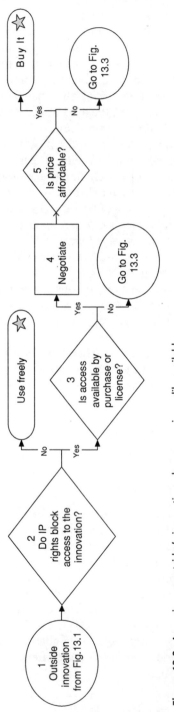

Figure 13.2. Accessing an outsider's innovation when access is readily available.

The first sale doctrine also expands the field of accessible innovations. As a general rule, when the holder of an IP right sells a product embodying that right, the sale transfers to the buyer all IP rights necessary to use and to resell the product, and extinguishes all rights to exclude subsequent users of the product. Accordingly, if a patent owner sells patented goods to a wholesaler, the wholesaler is free to resell to a retailer, who can sell to the consumer, who can resell the product on eBay, or give it away, and the IP rights do not block these further sales. The first sale doctrine is subject to exceptions, however, such as limitations in the original purchase agreement.

If it turns out that there are IP rights covering the innovation, then further work is needed. The bad news is that the pool of innovation that is completely free of IP rights is increasingly small. Most innovations have at least some degree of IP rights associated with them. The next question (Figure 13.2, box 3), therefore, is whether access is available by purchase or license. The good news is that most often, the answer is yes. If so, then the organization seeking access can negotiate to find out the price of access (Figure 13.2, box 4), and if it is affordable (Figure 13.2, box 5), go ahead and pay it. In many cases the price is minimal or reasonable. This is another happy ending.

For example, most of us are willing and able to gain legitimate access to the software on which our computers depend, typically an operating system from Microsoft or Apple, purchased as a bundle with the computer, or from a store, or from the manufacturer. If the operating system is Linux, then the price of access is our agreement to abide by the Linux open source license. Likewise, when we download Adobe Acrobat or other "free" software, the price of access is that we click "I agree" when we are presented with the terms of software license. If we like a particular song or video and want a copy on our computer or personal music player, then we can purchase a CD of the song, or download it from a music service. If a plant chemist wants to gain access to plant material in the Amazon, she may negotiate the terms of access, which may include training local scientists, acknowledging their contributions in publications, and providing payment towards conservation of the region. If there is a patent on a new antibiotic that we need to cure a case of drug resistant pneumonia, we do not much care so long as we can buy the drug from the manufacturer at an affordable cost, which is often subject to price control or insurance reimbursement.

WHEN ACCESS IS NOT READILY AVAILABLE

There are many circumstances that may lead an organization to conclude that access to an outsider's innovation is not readily available. In some circumstances, no license is available. The IP owner may choose to exert exclusive control over the innovation, without offering access at any price. A software program may be secret and unavailable for purchase or license in the market at an affordable price. Or the cost of access by permission (a license) is too high. A music lover may decide that the cost or inconvenience of downloading a song legitimately from a music vendor is more than she is willing to pay. The plant chemist may give up trying to negotiate the bureaucracy of the Amazonian country where the desired plants are found. A patient in that country may not be able to obtain the new antibiotic because it is not for sale there, or the price is too high and beyond the reach of the patient.

When access to an innovation is not readily available, as shown in Figure 13.3, the task is to seek weaknesses in the scope of the IP rights. If a weakness is found, then access can be had despite the IP owner's refusal to grant permission at the outset.

The first question in accessing a protected innovation is whether the duration of the IP right is short. (See Figure 13.3, box 2.) If so, then the organization may simply wait until the IP right expires, and then use the innovation freely. For example, a patent on a drug may be set to expire in two years. If it will take a generic company one year to develop a generic version of the drug, and a second year to gain regulatory approval, then there is no reason to challenge the patent. It will expire about the time the generic drug is ready for market anyway. In another example, someone who receives a trade secret from a competitor may be bound by a confidentiality agreement not to use the secret for a given period of time, but if the secret is published, or after the period set in the agreement, there may be no further restriction on the recipient's right to use the information. However, with trademark rights (which can last forever), and copyright (which can last almost that long), waiting is seldom an appropriate choice, and it may not be suitable with patents and trade secrets as well.

The second question: Is the geographic scope of the rights limited? (See Figure 13.3, box 3.) If so, then a competitor may use the innovation in the IP-free zone. The "off-shoring" of IP infringement can be a very effective business strategy. Research in Motion argued (unsuccessfully) that it was not subject to NTP's patents in the Blackberry case because much of the signal processing was carried out in Canada, not in the United States. Microsoft convinced the U.S. Supreme Court that its overseas activities were not subject to U.S. patent law when Microsoft made a "golden master disk" in the United States, exported it, and reproduced the software outside the United States.[3]

This approach can also be attractive in developing countries. If a drug is covered in patents in the United States, Europe, and Canada only, then a competitor in Argentina may set up a manufacturing facility there, and sell the drug throughout Latin America, Africa, and Asia. In countries where a famous trademark is not registered, a local company can use the trademark to market its own products, to attract local customers. With trade secrets, this approach is not likely to be available, because the person accessing the secret either received it from the owner subject to the terms of a confidentiality agreement, which would apply everywhere, or the person obtained the information from a public source, in which case it is not secret, or the person obtained the information surreptitiously, in which case its use is not authorized anywhere. With copyrights, also, global rights attach at publication, and so books, music, videos, and software are subject to copyright everywhere.

The next step in trying to find access is to ask if there are alternatives to the innovation that is blocked by IP rights (Figure 13.3, box 4). If so, and if the person seeking access is satisfied with the alternative, then there is another happy ending (for that person). If one trademark is registered, then the organization may be able to use a variant that is sufficiently different to avoid infringement. If a modern translation

[3] *Microsoft Corp. v. AT&T Corp.*, 127 S.Ct 1746 (2007).

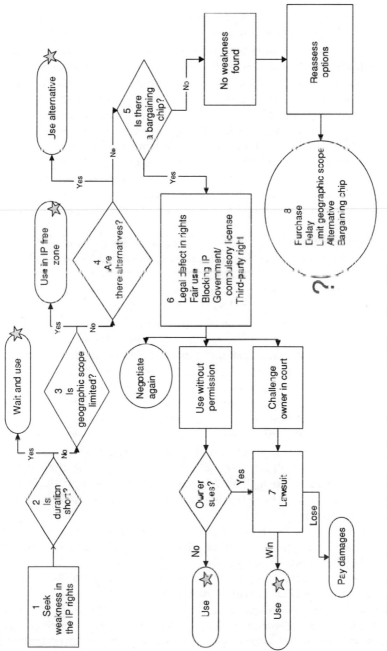

Figure 13.3. Accessing an outsider's innovation when access is NOT readily available.

of an ancient text, or an adaptation of a Shakespeare play, is subject to copyright, then the person seeking access may try to use the original text for which copyright expired.

In a patent case in the 1990s, my client was among several companies selling a topical anesthetic cream containing purified capsaicin, used to treat arthritis. A competitor, the maker of Zostrix brand cream, was able to obtain a patent to a formulation of the cream. My client decided to stop selling the product because the profit was too low to make it worthwhile to challenge the patent. Another company found an alternative – capsaicin is the purified active ingredient in hot peppers, and the patent did not cover use of less pure preparations, like capsaicin oil.

In another example, Indian intellectual property rights advocates became furious in 1990 when W.R. Grace obtained patents on a storage-stable oil extract from the neem tree, sold as an organic pesticide. The U.S. patent survived challenge in 1995, because there was no prior publication of the claimed method and extract. Antibiopiracy advocates argued that the patent would prevent Indian farmers from carrying out their ancient tradition of making a simple mixture of neem and water and spraying it on their crops.

There were two flaws in that argument. First, there was no counterpart patent in India. Second, the farmers, and anyone else, remained free to use the older, traditional water extract of neem. But they were not able to use the newer extract. A deeper concern was why a foreign research company made the innovation, rather than Indian researchers working with local farmers. The European patent was invalidated in 2005 based on evidence that an Indian company had made the same extract several years before the patent was filed, which was grounds for revocation in Europe, but not in the United States. The upshot is that the traditional methods can be used anywhere, the newer methods can be practiced in India and Europe, and the U.S. patent excludes access to the technology in the United States.

"Designing around" a patent is another alternative. In designing around, a company discovers a patent that relates to a project that the company is trying to pursue. Patent counsel reviews the patent, and determines that the claims are limited to specific ranges or sizes of components, or they require certain steps, that the company does not need to use. By selecting other components and materials and steps outside the ranges of the patent claims, the company is able to find an alternative to the patented invention – a happy ending for the company, in that they can access what they need to access.

If there is no adequate alternative, then a more complex quest begins, to find a legal bargaining chip to be used as leverage. (See Figure 13.3, box 5.) There are several kinds of bargaining chips to consider. (See Figure 13.3, box 6.)

The first bargaining chip is a legal defect in the IP owner's rights. There are many types of legal defects, but here are some generalized examples. A trademark may be overbroad, or may not cover the type of products in question. The owner of a putative trade secret may actually never have taken steps to keep it confidential, or parts of it were published, or publicly known. The person asserting copyright may not have been the author, or may otherwise lack the right to assert the copyright. A patent may be invalid based on prior art that the patent office failed to consider, or it may have been obtained through deception. These issues arose with the challenges to the neem extract patents in the United States (unsuccessful) and in Europe (successful).

A freedom to operate analysis is a defensive study of whether anybody has patent rights blocking an organization from doing what it needs to do. In some areas like agricultural biotechnology and some fields of electronics, there is a growing thicket of patents that can seriously interfere with the ability to commercialize a product. There may be a dozen different patented aspects of a technology, such that the path to market must pass through the thicket by maneuvering around all the obstacles or else by cutting them down. That can involve extensive analysis of numerous patents, at significant cost in time and money.

A second bargaining chip is fair use. This is a body of legal doctrines that identify circumstances where a person may use an innovation subject to IP rights without being liable for infringement. The legal subtleties of fair use are quite extensive, and the following summary is intended to provide only an overview, not any specific legal analysis.

The most extensive possibilities for fair use exist with copyright. In the United States, the determination of whether use of a copyrighted work is fair use requires consideration of four factors:[4]

(1) the purpose and character of the use, including whether such use is of commercial nature or is for nonprofit educational purposes;
(2) the nature of the copyrighted work;
(3) the amount and substantiality of the portion used in relation to the copyrighted work as a whole; and
(4) the effect of the use upon the potential market for or value of the copyrighted work.

Contrary to popular belief, there are no set rules about what is and is not fair use. There are exceptions to every rule of thumb, depending on the facts and circumstances of each use. Nonetheless, as a general matter, looking at each of the four factors, fair use is most likely to be found for (1) nonprofit, academic, or artistic use of (2) a factual report, (3) in a small amount, (4) with citation of the source. Fair use is less likely to be found for (1) commercial use of (2) a fictional or novel creation, (3) in substantial portions, (4) sold in competition with the original work.

Doctrines of fair use exist with trademarks, too. One type of fair use precludes a trademark owner from monopolizing all use of descriptive terms – like BOSTON MARATHON in a report about the marathon. "Nominative" fair use occurs if one company uses the trademark of another company's product solely to refer to that product, without suggesting endorsement – for example, in product reviews, comparisons, and marketing literature by sellers of that product. And trademark parodies and artistic expression can also be fair use – such as a series of photographs showing Barbie dolls baked into different types of food.

Fair use does not generally apply to patents. However, scholars and policy activists have seized on fair use doctrine as a possible way to reform patent laws, to regain a desired balance between exclusive rights as an incentive for innovation, and

---

[4] Section 107 of the Copyright Act, 17 U.S.C. §107.

access to innovation in the public interest.[5] The most common rallying point in the United States is for a research use exemption from patent liability. Even academic researchers are generally subject to liability for patent infringement, including damages and an injunction blocking their activity. A research fair use exemption would permit academic researchers to use a patented invention for academic purposes without facing liability. In coming years, patent fair use may become one more bargaining chip in gaining access to an innovation.

There is no established trade secret fair use. There are very practical limitations on trade secrets – they need to have been kept secret, and they must have value in their trade. Under Article 39 of the 1995 WTO Trade-Related Aspects of Intellectual Property Rights (TRIPS) Agreement, trade secret laws must give the owner of confidential information the right to prevent it from being disclosed, acquired, or used by others without consent, for example by breach of contract or breach of confidence, or otherwise in a manner contrary to honest commercial practices, or by misappropriation. Generally, trade secret laws and agreements do not apply to information that has been made public, or is developed independently. Also, governments may require confidential data, for regulatory approval of a drug or approval of a pesticide for agricultural use, but the government must protect that information. Such limitations tend to maintain the balance between exclusive rights and public access without need for the additional legal doctrine of fair use.

A third bargaining chip is obtaining a compulsory license, or government right to use the innovation without the IP owner's permission. A compulsory license applies to acts by private parties. Under copyright laws, for example, there are extensive systems permitting the use of copyrighted works without the owner's permission. For example, radio stations may play musical recordings without permission, and then pay a preset fee which is distributed to the artists. With patents, under Article 31 of the TRIPS Agreement, countries may permit the unauthorized use of a patented invention in a single country under certain circumstances: a failed negotiation with the owner or a national emergency; a case-specific review by the government; and adequate remuneration.

As for government use, in the United States, a federal statute permits the government and government contractors to use patented inventions without permission, upon payment of a reasonable royalty.[6] Here, the government may either use an innovation, or permit others to use it, without the owner's permission. Further, the doctrine of sovereign immunity is recognized in international law and in many legal systems as blocking legal claims against a sovereign government without its consent, though the relevance of this doctrine to limit the reach of intellectual property rights is still being explored in different countries.[7] In the United States, individual states have been held to be immune from patent and copyright claims, in the *Florida Prepaid* decisions by the U.S. Supreme Court. National and international government agencies, and corporations and nonprofit organizations under contract with these

[5] Maureen A. O'Rourke, "Toward a Doctrine of Fair Use in Patent Law." *Columbia Law Review* 100(5): 1177-1250 (June 2000).

[6] 28 U.S.C. §1498.

[7] Akihiro Matsui, *Intellectual Property Litigation and Foreign Sovereign Immunity: International Law Limit to the Jurisdiction over the Infringement of Intellectual Property* (Institute of Intellectual Property, 2002), available at http://www.iip.or.jp/e/summary/pdf/detail2002/e14_20.pdf, accessed December 10, 2006.

governmental agencies may find that they are entitled to use a particular innovation without permission from the owner of IP rights.

A fourth bargaining chip is a blocking right. The organization seeking access identifies a patent, trademark, or other IP right that it holds, which the other IP owner is infringing. This blocking right provides leverage over the outside IP owner. For example, company A owns a patent on a group of chemical compounds with desirable properties. Company B obtains a patent on a new, unique compound that falls within the patented group, but is patentable because of its special properties. If company A asserts its patent against company B, company B may be able to strike a bargain, if company A wants the right to use the unique compound.

In another example of a blocking right, a strategy employed in my firm, company A holds a trademark registration XYZ in one country, and company B wants to use a similar mark, XYYZ. Company B may obtain trademark registrations in several other countries of interest to both A and B. Then, if company A asserts its trademark rights for XYZ, company B can assert its rights for XYYZ, and perhaps force a settlement.

A blocking right does not have to be the same type of IP. If organization A threatens or accuses organization B with infringing its trademark, B can challenge A by asserting a blocking patent. Beyond IP rights, B may assert other legal claims as well, such as breach of contract, or anticompetitive activity by A.

A fifth way to find a bargaining chip is to search for a third party IP right that could either block the IP owner or provide access. For example, in two cases I have dealt with, the patent owner failed to include in the patent a co-inventor who was not in the same organization. We obtained rights from the unnamed co-inventor, and then instituted proceedings to have the co-inventor joined to the patent. This approach results in joint ownership, and the patent owner can not then assert the patent against the co-inventor, or against the organization to whom the co-inventor assigned his or her rights.

If the search for a bargaining chip has been successful, then the path toward access continues down one of three forks. First, the access seeker may try to negotiate again, returning to the position of box 4 in Figure 13.2. If a fair deal can be worked out with the increased leverage, this is a happy ending. Second, the access seeker may feel in a strong enough legal position to now go ahead and use the innovation without permission. If the IP owner does not sue, then this too is a happy ending for the access seeker. However, if the use is unauthorized, the owner may assert its IP rights in a lawsuit (Figure 13.3, box 7).

The likelihood of such a suit may be high or low. Indeed, for the millions of copyright infringers worldwide engaged in unauthorized file-swapping of movies and songs through the Internet, and for the smaller but large number selling unauthorized DVDs of movies and CDs of music and software, this is the path that they have chosen. They assume that the chance of an enforcement lawsuit is so remote that there is no need to worry about it. There have been enforcement actions against thousands of people in the United States, including college students, with settlements and damages of several to many thousand dollars, but this is a very small percentage of the whole. Anti-piracy campaigns in China and elsewhere also reach a small sliver of the infringing market. Such actions are effective, however, in raising the risk of infringement, and thereby they decrease unauthorized copying, by convincing some people to buy authorized copies of movies and music.

The third option is to be proactive, not waiting for the suit, and challenging the IP owner in court or in another forum. For example, with patents and trademarks, it may be possible to oppose issuance or registration in the national patent and trademark office, or alternatively to challenge the validity of the patent or trademark in court. It generally requires an administrative proceeding to obtain a compulsory license to a patent. In some circumstances, a copyright user may seek a declaration that its use is fair use.

If there is a lawsuit or other legal proceeding, and the judgment favors the access seeker, then there is another happy ending. However, if the access seeker loses, then this may be a very unhappy situation indeed. Loss of an intellectual property lawsuit can lead to injunctions and potentially to huge damages or settlements, as with *Polaroid v. Kodak, NTP v. Research in Motion* (Blackberry), and *Igen v. Roche*, where each of the defendants ended up paying more than a half billion dollars to resolve the dispute.

If the quest for a bargaining chip fails (Figure 13.3, box 5), and no weakness in the IP right is found, then the access seeker needs to reevaluate options that were previously considered (box 8). The access seeker may decide to pay what the IP owner is asking for a license or sale, even though it is more than originally planned. (See Figure 13.3, box 5.) The access seeker may decide to delay entry into the market for a longer time than originally planned (Figure 13.3, box 2) or to limit the geographical scope of activities (box 3). It may be necessary to look farther afield for an alternative to the desired innovation (box 4), or to find a bargaining chip (box 6). The access seeker may decide to infringe the IP right, accepting the risk of damages (box 7). Finally, if there is no viable alternative, a sound decision may be to drop the project and invest elsewhere. By the time an access seeker has moved through the entire decision-making process, however, the chances are very high that a good path can be found to reach a happy ending, with sufficient access at an affordable price to meet the organization's goals.

SUMMARY. Each organization needs its own strategic plan at any given time, and a simple process for implementing that plan. By following the decision trees in this chapter, anyone can take systematic action consistent with an overall plan. There is no need for confusion, and ignorance is not a wise alternative to finding a legitimate path with no liability, or an acceptable calculated risk. In many cases, innovations can be acquired without infringing the IP rights of an owner – by purchase, by paying a reasonable fee, or by accepting other reasonable terms – and most IP rights are transferred this way. However, inconvenience, cost, or nonfinancial restrictions may preclude an agreement with the IP right holder, in which case a path to circumvent the IP rights is required – waiting until the IP right expires, proceeding in an "IP-free zone," finding a technical, commercial, or creative alternative to the inaccessible innovation, proceeding based on fair use, obtaining a compulsory license from the government, or asserting a blocking IP right, if necessary going out to third parties to acquire it. By methodically exploring these alternatives, an organization can usually find a low-risk path to use the necessary innovations. If need be, that path may involve litigation in selected jurisdictions around the world, if the potential rewards exceed the predicted risk of liability.

14 Acquiring and Policing Intellectual Property Rights

This chapter presents a first decision tree approach for protecting innovations with IP rights, and a second one for enforcing them. The process begins with the internal innovations identified in the screening step in Chapter 13. Next comes innovation triage, sorting innovations according to their value to the organization and the urgency of protecting them. The next step is a methodical approach to making decisions about protecting individual innovations as IP assets, with specifics for protecting trade secrets, copyright, trademarks, and patents. A similar approach is described for managing a portfolio of existing IP assets. The second part of the chapter describes enforcement and policing an organization's IP rights against infringement by outsiders, including a process of enforcement triage for each type of IP asset.

* * * * * *

PROTECTING INNOVATIONS FROM INSIDE THE ORGANIZATION

When screening innovations that are important to the organization, the first step is to identify where the innovation comes from. We turn now from innovations that come from outside the organization to the task of protecting and enforcing innovations that come from inside the organization.

For innovations created by insiders (that is, people under an obligation to transfer their innovations to the organization, people such as employees and consultants under appropriate contract), the next series of decisions go toward protecting the innovation with IP rights. If an innovation was created by the combined efforts of insiders and outsiders, it may be desirable to break down the innovation into smaller parts, some from inside and some from outside, and deal with the rights that way. Alternatively, there are techniques for resolving joint innovations, dealt with below.

As when accessing innovations from others, there is a logical decision-making process for protecting innovations in line with an overall strategic plan. Each of the individual acts required to implement that plan can be complicated, time-consuming, and expensive, and may require the concerted actions of several people. Before committing to such an effort, it is wise to make sure that the benefit outweighs the cost. The best way to do that is with a triage process.

Encouraging innovation is a policy challenge in different countries and a management challenge for corporations in various industries, nonprofit organizations, and government agencies. In nonprofit organizations, funding for creative work comes from governments, philanthropists, and market forces that provide grants, and awards. Much of the incentive for creative individuals in nonprofit organizations is nonpecuniary – the admiration and respect of peers, and the personal satisfaction that comes from setting and resolving difficult problems and having a positive social impact. For the organizations, the primary motivators are the desire to achieve their public mission, and to earn prestige.

In for-profit organizations, incentives for creativity are provided by investors and employers who pay salaries and provide resources to people who have the potential to be creative. Because of the need for a return on investment, corporations generally focus these creative efforts in areas that are likely to produce valuable innovations. We will not address in any further detail the task of encouraging innovation within an organization. Here, we deal with the framework for managing innovations as they are born unprotected into the world.

INNOVATION TRIAGE

Innovation triage is a process in which the IP manager considers the value of an innovation, and flags it for a high investment in IP protection, a lower level of investment, or no investment at all. Innovations are also identified by whether action needs to be taken immediately or later. (See Figure 14.1).

Beginning with an innovation that has been tentatively identified as desirable, the IP manager asks whether the innovation advances the organization's goals (as identified in the first stage of the strategic planning process). If so, the innovation may be dubbed a central or "core" innovation. The second question is whether the innovation would have a high value to outsiders. If the answer to both questions is "yes" then the innovation should be flagged for the highest level of investment. For example, assume that a biotechnology company identifies a new gene called MS1, associated with multiple sclerosis, and a compound, called anti-MS1, that inhibits the activity of that gene. The discovery of MS1 is valuable to the company, because it may justify manufacture of the pharmaceutical product anti-MS1, the inhibitory compound. The discovery of MS1 is also valuable to other biotechnology companies, because with that new knowledge, they may seek to find other compounds that inhibit the MS1 gene. This qualifies MS1 for a high level of investment in IP protection.

An innovation that is valuable to the organization (a core innovation), but not valuable to others, should be flagged for a lower level of investment in IP protection. For example, a manufacturer may improve a production line by eliminating a toxic chemical, or a telecommunications company may find a faster, more efficient way to process subscriber data – such innovations may be very valuable for their own organizations but currently irrelevant to other companies.

If the innovation has no value to the organization (a noncore innovation), but has high value to others, then it too might be flagged for a lower level of investment in IP protection. Such innovations may still be valuable. For example, all patents obtained by universities would fall into this category because universities do not commercialize their own inventions but rather license them to others. A company may change its focus and decide that innovations that were initially thought to have high value to

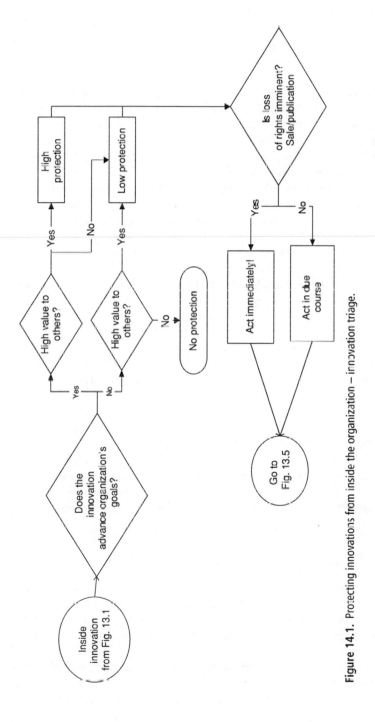

Figure 14.1. Protecting innovations from inside the organization – innovation triage.

the organization are no longer a priority and so should be sold to someone else. For example, a company that initially invested in research in a particular technology or a music publisher or book publisher who has built up a catalog of works may decide to sell that line of business and the associated IP rights. In that case, it is worth maintaining the IP asset, but with a lower level of investment than that accorded core innovations with value to others.

Some innovations that were initially identified as desirable may, on closer inspection, turn out to lack value either to the organization or outsiders. Such innovations should be flagged for no investment. They will either fall into the public domain, or remain secret, but they are not worth the investment of effort or concern from an IP management perspective. Mistakes can be made here, and often are, when the true value of an innovation is overlooked.

For those innovations that are flagged for IP protection, at a high or lower level of investment, the next question is whether there is any imminent loss of rights. If there is, immediate action is required. If not, then the IP manager may wait and take action in due course. For example, a trade secret may be threatened by a plan to post a formulation or a method on a marketing website, or to present the information at a conference, or to a customer, or in an article.

The same risk of losing rights applies to patentable inventions, because in most countries (the United States being a notable exception), the right to obtain a patent vanishes on the day the invention is made public. In these situations, where a decision has already been made to protect the innovation, the IP manager needs to act immediately. Also, when a marketing campaign is being mounted for a new product and a trademark is found that is desirable, it is important to move quickly to protect the trademark, and associated domain names, in order in turn to protect the investment in the marketing campaign. Otherwise, someone else may adopt the same trademark and force the organization to change its own.

The specific actions to be taken differ depending on the type of innovation and the level of protection desired, but it is important to keep in mind that timing is a separate issue in innovation triage. It seems counterintuitive, but because of the time-sensitivity of many types of IP protection, a lower value innovation flagged for a lower level of protection may require action *before* a higher value innovation flagged for higher protection, if immediate action is required to protect the low value innovation.

Protecting innovations as IP assets

The next step, after triage into high and low levels of investment, and immediate or eventual action, is to choose the right path for IP protection (Figure 14.2). Again, the inquiry turns back to the nature of the innovation as determined by triage. The task is to identify which type of IP rights apply to the innovation, and to decide how to protect those rights.

Although one premise of this book is that certain concepts and strategies are common to all types of intellectual property, there are also many crucial differences between them. Focusing on the principles common to all of them can help an IP

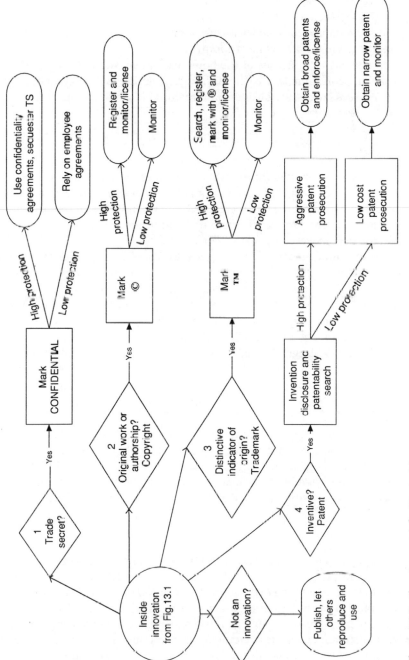

Figure 14.2. Choosing a path for IP protection.

manager to form an effective strategy. But noting the differences is also crucial in implementing that strategy.

The laws governing each type of IP differ from country to country, but the following description – somewhat simplified – follows the general principles of intellectual property law and is consistent with the standards set forth in the international TRIPS Agreement and the laws of most countries.

This summary, as with the rest of the book, cannot substitute for legal advice from competent professionals in each relevant jurisdiction. But it can help the IP manager make some necessary business judgments and can frame the issues for a professional to evaluate more closely.

Trade secrets

The first question is whether the innovation qualifies for trade secret protection (Figure 14.2, box 1). According to Article 39.2 of TRIPS, trade secret protection applies to information that is secret, has commercial value because it is secret, and has been subject to reasonable steps to keep it secret. If the innovation does qualify as a trade secret, then the IP manager must act to keep it secret.

Trade secrecy is protected by self-help measures. There is no administrative procedure for obtaining trade secret protection, and the protection is, in effect, international, because the secret is protected in any country where it is not known. The self-help measures always include, at a minimum, preventing publication of the information, and restricting access to it, for example by marking any documents that include the information as "CONFIDENTIAL."

If the trade secret is flagged for high investment (like the famous Coca-Cola formula, or the yeast used in brewing Guinness stout), then additional measures are called for. These may include limiting access within the organization to only those who need to use the information in their work, and sequestering the information into special limited access files, or safes. Any plans to share the information with outsiders are carefully structured, and require a strong confidentiality agreement, sometimes referred to as a nondisclosure agreement (NDA) or confidential disclosure agreement (CDA). By contrast, if the innovation is a secret of low value, then no further measures are required. The IP manager can just rely on existing employment agreements that commit employees not to disclose or use confidential information.

Copyright

The second question to be asked is whether the innovation is subject to copyright protection (Figure 14.2, box 2). In the United States, copyright applies to original works of authorship. According to the Berne Convention on Copyright, Article 2(1), copyright applies to literary, scientific, or artistic productions, in any form of expression, such as books, lectures, dramatic, musical, or choreographic works, movies, drawings, architecture, sculptures, photographs, and maps. The TRIPS Agreement, articles 9 and 10, adds that copyright applies to computer programs and databases as long as the selection or arrangement of the database contents constitute intellectual creations, but that copyright does not apply to ideas, methods, or concepts.

Copyright attaches to a work from the moment it is published, and is international in scope. Although no formal procedures are required, the formality of a copyright notice somewhere in the work is very helpful and always advisable, because it informs the public that the work is protected by copyright, may scare away infringers, and prevents the "innocent infringer" defense. It also identifies the copyright owner and the year of first publication, making it easier for interested parties to seek permission to use the work. A copyright notice typically is in this format:

© [Publication year] [Owner].

If the work has been flagged for high investment, then the IP manager should take further steps. First, registering the copyright in the work is required in the United States as a prerequisite to enforcement and helps prove ownership in other countries. Second, the IP manager may monitor the market to find any unauthorized copying, and may also actively license the work in exchange for compensation. Alternatively, the IP chief may use an open access type of license, imposing obligations on the licensee without receiving any payment.

If the work has been flagged for low investment, no special activity is required.

Trademarks

The third question is whether the innovation is subject to trademark protection (Figure 14.2, box 3). Under U.S. law, trademark rights apply to any distinctive indicator of origin. Under the TRIPS Agreement, Article 15, trademark registration must be available for any visible sign capable of distinguishing the goods and services of one undertaking from those of other undertakings, such as words including personal names, letters, numerals, figurative elements and combinations of colors. Distinctive smells and sounds can be registered as trademarks in some countries.

In most countries, trademark protection requires an administrative proceeding in which an application is filed with the national trademark agency, and if the application is approved then the trademark is registered. Typically, trademark registration is obtained country by country. A European Community Trade Mark can be obtained, and the Madrid Protocol can be used to file applications simultaneously in many countries, but trademark rights still arise under the laws of each individual country. In the United States, UK, and many common-law countries, including former British colonies, some trademark rights attach to a distinctive word or logo automatically when it is first used in association with goods or services. To gain rights based on use in these countries, it is generally helpful to have a ™ symbol on the shoulder of the mark, prior to registration.

If the trademark is flagged for high investment, then the best practice is to conduct a search for similar marks, and to file at least one initial application to register the mark, then pursue that application through to registration, which can take anywhere from one to three years. At that point the ® symbol can and should be used. As with copyrighted works, it is desirable to monitor any infringements and to license the trademark if the circumstances are appropriate. If the trademark is of low significance, it may be appropriate not to file an application to register the mark, but non-action poses several risks. For example, if no "freedom to operate" search has been performed, and someone else owns rights to the trademark, it may be necessary to change the mark to avoid infringement. Also, even in common law countries, it is harder to enforce an unregistered mark than a registered mark against someone who uses a similar mark.

Searching trademarks and preparing applications, prosecuting them through to registration, enforcing them, and managing international trademark portfolios, require a high degree of expertise, and the costs can be substantial. When compared to patents, however, trademarks are inexpensive.

Patents

The fourth question is whether the innovation is an invention subject to patent protection (Figure 14.2, box 4.) The TRIPS Agreement, in Article 27 provides that patents are available for any inventions whether products or processes, in all fields of technology without discrimination, subject to the normal tests of novelty, inventiveness and industrial applicability, and without regard to the place of invention.

Countries are permitted three exceptions to patentability. One possible exception, rarely applied, is for inventions that are so contrary to the public interest or morality that their use is forbidden, such as those that are dangerous to human, animal, or plant life or health, or seriously prejudicial to the environment. The second exception is for diagnostic, therapeutic, and surgical methods for the treatment of humans or animals, and many countries have some form of this exception. The third possible exception (Article 27.2) is for plants and animals other than microorganisms and biological processes for producing plants or animals. If plant varieties are excluded from patent protection, the country must provide an effective *sui generis* (specific) system of protection, such as plant variety protection.

Protecting patent rights and then maintaining or expanding those rights, demands considerable amounts of attention and resources. The first step is to have the inventor write a full, detailed disclosure of the invention. An invention disclosure form like the helps to ensure that all relevant information will be collected in one place, efficiently.[1] The form should ask the inventor to provide the following information: the general nature of the invention including its potential market, a detailed description, with examples, identification of relevant prior art – that is, pre-existing technology – and relevant public disclosures, distinctions from prior art, and the personal information necessary for filing an application and avoiding later complications, such as the inventor's name, address and citizenship The invention disclosure can provide the basis for an independent search of the prior art to assess whether there is indeed an invention being described, and if so, how broad it is in contrast to the prior art. A marketability assessment can also be done.

Without a thorough invention disclosure, it is difficult to predict the kind of patent coverage that can be obtained, and whether it will be valuable. Only with that information can an intelligent decision be made as to whether to file a patent application, and what to do with it once it's filed and issued. For example, a patent application

---

[1] See, for example, "Invention Disclosure Questionnaire" available at http://www.venable.com/ publications.cfm?action = view&publication_id=900&publication_type_id=2&practice_id=40z,accessed October 15, 2007.

would be handled differently if intended for commercial exploitation, for use as a tool to block competitors, for licensing, for holding for future development, or for sale.

Typically, it takes anywhere from a week to six months from the time the inventor first presents a disclosure to the time a patent application is filed (although I have had to file applications on the same day in emergency situations where a description of the invention was about to be published). Generally, filing a first patent application with a national patent office preserves rights to the invention worldwide for one year. The application is then considered to be "patent pending" and is examined through administrative proceedings at the patent office called "patent prosecution." Eventually – anywhere from a year and a half to four years later, or much more – the application is allowed (hopefully) and the patent issues, thus perfecting the owner's rights. Throughout that entire time, questions of patentability and value need to be asked over and over again, at each step of the way.

In some cases, where the invention merits a high investment in protection – such as if there is an immediate market or a close competitor – the best implementation approach for protection may be to prepare a thorough patent application (at relatively high cost), and then to move quickly with parallel patent prosecution in many countries, to seek the earliest possible patent issuance. In many cases, however, the best approach for pursuing patent protection is to move more slowly, preserving the maximum scope of rights for the longest period of time at the minimum cost. Under this implementation approach, costs are postponed until the business prospects become clearer, and a no-go decision can be made at any stage for any given country, thus conserving funds. As new inventions are made, new provisional applications can be filed, and the process continues. This way, rights are preserved economically. If the business prospects look positive or if a competitor is found to be infringing, then the organization can pursue a patent aggressively to obtain issuance in a given country.

In one example of this approach, a provisional patent application may be filed in the United States at the beginning of year one. The application may be short (and inexpensive) or long (and more expensive). This preserves rights in the described invention in the 169 member countries of the Paris Convention. At the end of year one, an international patent application is filed under the Patent Cooperation Treaty (PCT), preserving rights in the 132 member countries. An application would need to be filed in Taiwan at the same time, as it is not a member of the PCT. Two and a half years from the original filing date, national applications are filed in national patent offices in the United States and those foreign countries in which the invention appears to be valuable. Examination of the applications often leads to rejections and amendments prior to patent issuance.

Costs escalate dramatically throughout this process. Current estimates are as follows.[2] Drafting and filing an initial patent application in the United States may cost $5,000 to $20,000. Patent examination usually costs $5,000 to $15,000 in the United States. Preparing and filing a PCT international application may cost an additional $5,000 to $20,000. Filing national applications may cost $5,000 to $10,000 each, and

---

[2] Costs are based on the AIPLA Report of the Economic Survey 2007 and personal experience.

there may be five, ten, or more of them. Prosecuting national applications can cost $5,000 to $10,000. Prosecuting each of the applications can be delayed and done slowly, postponing expenses, or it can be pursued earlier and more aggressively, at higher cost. Annuities (the annual maintenance fees required to keep an issued patent alive in any given country) may rise from a few hundred dollars per year up to thousands of dollars for each patent, on average totaling $15,000 per country through the full 20-year patent term. At each point, depending on the perceived value of the application, the IP manager must decide whether to continue to preserve rights, to push to perfect rights, or to drop the application altogether.

A competent patent attorney knows tactics for moving slowly, preserving rights for a long time, or moving quickly, pushing to perfect rights by obtaining allowance and following the formalities so that a patent office will finally issue a patent. Generally, the inventor and the IP manager consult with the legal practitioner to choose the right tactics, and the practitioner then carries them out.

Managing an existing IP portfolio

Once innovations are converted into IP assets they become part of an organization's IP portfolio. Different steps are required to manage a portfolio – pruning, maintaining, or expanding rights through coordinated action taken over time.

IP portfolio management is much like forestry management. A forester plants new trees on a regular basis, and stakes and supports young saplings so they can grow strong. During periodic inspections, weak branches are pruned off and crowded or diseased trees are cut down. The forester then harvests trees in their prime to be sold for lumber or firewood. The forester may meanwhile leave snags (dead or dying trees) to return to the soil, or may haul them away. Likewise, an IP manager protects innovations as new IP assets, supports them so they grow stronger, prunes weak assets, enforces or licenses valuable ones, and plans ahead, anticipating the expiration of the older assets.

IP portfolio management should be performed on a regular periodic basis, such as monthly, quarterly, or at least annually, depending on the nature of the organization. Each time it's performed, IP portfolio management requires current, comprehensive information about all of the organization's IP assets. An organization that has already carried out a strategic assessment process, as discussed in Chapter 8, will have a list of its IP assets and some information about the organization's goals, its policies and practices relating to IP, its important products and services, and its relations with outsiders. All the information obtained during that strategic assessment is useful to IP portfolio management.

The first step in managing a portfolio is to break down the current IP assets into different categories for further analysis. (See Figure 14.3.) They may be grouped by the kind of asset. They may also be grouped by different business lines, divisions, or profit centers, different countries, or otherwise. In practice, once such business-line groupings are made, IP managers will nevertheless further sort the assets within each group into trade secrets, copyrights, trademarks, and patents, because each of these types of assets is subject to different legal principles, and requires different practices to protect them.

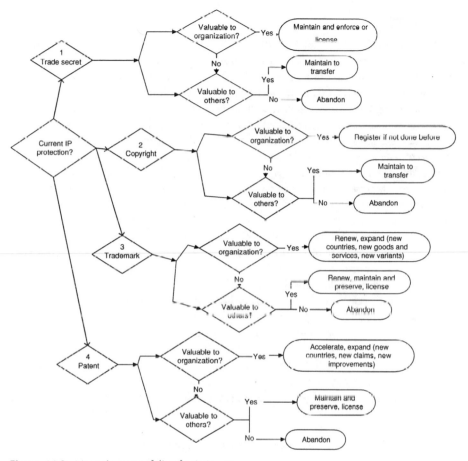

Figure 14.3. Managing a portfolio of existing IP.

Second, the IP manager should repeat the process of innovation triage for new innovations. Triage is common to all of the four main kinds of intellectual property. Decisions made earlier need to be re-assessed at each point in the management cycle. Strategies can evolve, and facts can change. If an organization decides to change its direction, an innovation asset that was central to the organization's business plans in one cycle may become less important in the next cycle, and an innovation that was less relevant may become much more valuable. Likewise, a competitor's activities may change. If competitors converge on a particular innovation, an asset that was of low value to them may suddenly have a higher value. If an asset is originally thought to have high value to collaborators and yet efforts to find a collaborator or licensee ultimately fail, then the IP manager must conclude that the asset's value has lowered.

So, existing assets must again be subjected to triage, categorizing them as assets worthy of high levels of protection, lesser protection, or none at all.

Trade secrets

Turning now to trade secrets, information that remains secret and is valuable to the organization needs to be kept confidential, and efforts to restrict disclosure, to monitor use, and to enforce or license the information should be continued or expanded (Figure 14.3, box 1). If the information is no longer important to the organization, it may be worth seeking someone else who would be willing to buy or license it. If no one will, then no further investment in protection is warranted. Also, if a strategic decision has been made not to maintain trade secret protection, then related efforts to maintain trade secrecy can be abandoned. (Strictly speaking, trade secrets are not abandoned, they are merely no longer kept secret.) The information can be actively published, allowed to leak into common usage, or left to be forgotten.

From society's perspective, the last option is the worst, because it leads to loss of the innovation itself. The situation arises with loss of traditional knowledge. Indigenous people may know vast amounts of information about particular plants, their locations and growth habits, and their practical uses in medicine and otherwise. Traditional farmers tend to know about wide varieties and strains of crops, including how they grow under different soil and climate conditions. Traditional stories, songs, dances, crafts, and art may similarly be known or closely held by only a few. Unless such information is passed on to future generations or is published, it is lost to society. It is better for society when such people continue to use such knowledge in their work, than if the information is kept secret, abandoned, and lost, no longer available to the creative endeavors of future generations. This is one of the ways in which innovations may become truly inaccessible.

Publication benefits society by keeping the information available and reducing risk of loss. We automobile drivers know less about horses and buggy whips than our ancestors did 100 years ago, and my children will never need to learn how to replace a typewriter ribbon. But if we needed such knowledge we could find it.

Copyright

Several options are available for copyrighted works that remain valuable to the organization (Figure 14.3, box 2). Supplementing a copyright notice by registering the work in the United States should be considered if it has not been done before, to perfect rights. If new editions, adaptations, translations, or other derivative works have been produced, they should be considered for protection as well. Use by others should be monitored and rights licensed or enforced if necessary. With copyrights of lower value to an organization, but valuable to other organizations, it is worth exploring possible interest in licensing, and monitoring for infringement by others. Not much additional effort is required because copyright is international and persists in a work for so long (50 to 95 years after creation, or longer, depending on the country and when the work was created).

For copyrighted works that have no great value to any one, the owner may dedicate the work to the public, affirmatively disclaiming any copyright. This approach is rare because there is no incentive for the copyright owner to make the effort to do so. Most such valueless works become orphaned, out of print, unavailable. They remain under copyright protection, but no longer part of other people's creative endeavors.

From a social perspective, as with lost trade secrets, this can present a problem, the scale of which is revealed by Google's effort to scan all of the world's 32 million catalogued books, to make them available for online searching. About 10 percent of the books remain in print, available for purchase, and licensed to Google. About 15 percent are in the public domain, available for free copying and scanning. But about 75 percent are orphans for which permission for copying is required under copyright law but is not readily available.[3]

Trademarks

Trademark management is somewhat more complex (Figure 14.3, box 3). For the most valuable marks, rights can be extended by continuing to prosecute pending applications in order to receive new registrations, by renewing existing registrations as required – every 10 years in most countries, although there are other requirements as well, such as maintaining continued use of the trademark – by filing trademark applications in additional countries as the marketing effort expands, by reserving additional domain names, by filing new applications on additional goods or services as usage expands, and by filing new applications on variants of the name or logo as they change over time due for example to new marketing efforts. An old trademark like Johnson & Johnson, Kodak, or Coca-Cola, is updated every decade or so, resulting in new marketing campaigns, new packaging, and new trademark filings worldwide. The older marks are usually maintained in some fashion, for continuity, and to limit the chance of infringement.

As the organization expands its international family of registrations for a particular trademark, the possibility of an opposition proceeding increases, because the new trademark may resemble one already in local use somewhere else. A local trademark owner may try to block registration of the new mark. It may take years to win an opposition. They are often resolved with a settlement whereby the two parties agree on how to limit their use of the marks, so they can coexist in the local market without confusing the public.

For trademarks that are less valuable to the organization but valuable to others, it is worthwhile to perfect and renew registrations, but perhaps not to invest in expanding rights. A licensing or franchising campaign may be appropriate, converting other people's interest into collaborations or revenue.

Trademarks that are not in use and have lost value both to the organization and others may be abandoned. Registered marks and pending applications are treated as abandoned by trademark agencies around the world when a deadline is not met, and this is the most common path to abandonment.

However, trademark rights may persist for a long time. Pan American World Airways went bankrupt in 1991, but its famous PAN AM and globe trademark lives on. In 1993, those trademark rights were bought at auction for $1.3 million. The trademark rights have changed hands since then, but according to the USPTO website, the current owner has maintained the oldest registration (from 1957), and has filed new applications in the past couple of years covering rail service, as well as merchandise

---

[3] Kevin Kelly, "Scan This Book!" *New York Times* (May 14, 2006).

like luggage, clothing, and coffee mug trinkets. Corporations may come and go, but a strong trademark can last forever.

Patents

Patents are the most demanding IP asset to manage, due to their complexity and the many differences remaining in how different countries treat them (Figure 13.6, box 4). For the most valuable inventions, there are several measures the owner can use to accelerate prosecution to perfect rights, getting patents issued earlier in more countries. Many decisions are time sensitive. That is, patent laws set critical deadlines for action, and if the necessary filings are not made in time, rights are lost in one or more countries. A first patent application must be filed before the invention is published, or in most countries patent rights are lost. Applications filed before the anniversary of the first application are treated as if they were filed on that day under the Paris Convention, but thereafter, rights are lost. An international application filed under the Patent Cooperation Treaty keeps the application alive until $2 \frac{1}{2}$ years from the earliest filing date, but at that time rights are lost in any country in which no further national application has been filed. Annual maintenance fees are required in most countries. Each of these deadlines, and many more, must be tracked for each patent and application in a portfolio. Large patent portfolios require frequent review so that filing decisions can be made in a strategic manner.

Another way to expand patent rights is to pursue different or broader patent claims. A patent application is usually filed with a variety of claims covering different aspects of the invention and having different breadth. A typical patent application will include claims for a thing (a composition or manufactured article), a method of making it, and a method of using it.

For example, if a biotechnology company discovers a new vaccine against a potent influenza virus, the company may file a patent application with claims to (1) the particular viral protein VP that is used to stimulate immunity in a patient, (2) the genetic sequence of DNA (gene) that encodes the VP protein, (3) a vaccine combining the VP protein with other components that make the vaccine more potent, (4) a method of vaccinating people by injecting the VP vaccine, (5) a method of making the VP vaccine by modifying bacteria with the VP gene to produce the VP protein, and (6) bacteria modified with the VP gene. A patent office may limit prosecution to one or two of these types of claims in one patent application, requiring the owner to refile the application to seek patents on the other claims.

Also, one characteristic of a valuable invention is that the inventors continue to develop the technology that led to the original filing of a patent application. As they continue their research, they will likely discover improvements. Such improvements might then be considered for protection in some fashion, as trade secrets or possibly as new patent applications.

Frequently, inertia and an "arms race" desire to have many patents drives an organization to file a new application for every disclosure in hand. Also, once an initial patent filing has been made, it is hard for somebody to take responsibility for the decision not to maintain it. Yet a lot of money can be saved by pruning applications at appropriate times.

A key decision point comes when foreign applications need to be filed (usually 2 $\frac{1}{2}$ years after the first filing date). Organizations typically choose three to ten countries, which may cost $10,000 to $60,000 just for the filings, and then that much again through the lifecycle of the patent. Some companies maintain a list of countries where they always file regardless of the technology. This could include each country where the company has research, manufacturing, data processing, or sales operations, and also where major competitors are located. But smaller organizations rarely inquire carefully enough into patentability or marketability in a particular country, which is surprising for such a crucial and expensive decision. For these reasons, a periodic patent portfolio review is highly advisable, a time when decisions can be made for all patents at once, so the priorities and budget may be aligned. Certain applications can be pruned or at least put "on probation," to be killed in the next meeting unless a compelling case is made to retain them. Even a weak patent application should sometimes be maintained, so the technology can be marked as "patent pending." This designation may inhibit competitors who do not know there is little intention to pursue the patent.

For patents of less value to the organization, but still valuable to others, a reasonable approach is to perfect pending applications, so that they issue, but not to invest in new filings, and not to file a broad range of foreign applications at great expense. Some effort at divesting such patents is worthwhile, given the substantial annual costs of maintaining them. There is no single effective way to find a licensee or purchaser of a patent, but in most cases the dedicated efforts of a talented business development professional is the best approach.

For patents with no value to the organization and unlikely to be valuable to outsiders (especially after a concerted effort at licensing or sale has failed), abandonment is the best option. There is usually no advantage to deliberate abandonment. Because of the time-sensitive nature of patents in most countries, a decision to be passive – that is, not to respond to any deadlines – leads to abandonment relatively promptly, usually within a year. Notably, there is no social loss in abandoned patent applications. Because one of the fundamental requirements for a patent is an enabling description of the invention, the publication of a patent preserves the underlying innovation for future innovators to use and develop further.

ENFORCEMENT

The hieroglyphic confidentiality promise made by chief scribe Irtisen to his Pharaoh Mentuhotep 4,000 years ago did not prescribe the penalty for disclosure of his secret methods, but we can imagine that if he did disclose his secrets to rivals, the punishment would have been death. The Venetian patent statute of 1474 is kindly by comparison – it explicitly provides only that infringing devices must be destroyed and the infringer must pay 100 ducates. Present day enforcement of IP rights falls somewhere between the two in severity, and remains a great concern to IP owners and infringers alike.

Enforcement is the ultimate test of the exclusive rights provided by intellectual property. Intellectual property fosters creative acts, promoting their broader adoption in the marketplace, and providing for the fruits of innovation eventually to become accessible to the broader society, enabling new creativity, completing the innovation cycle. The effective resolution of IP disputes is vitally important not only for IP owners and those trying to access innovation, but indeed to the operation of the entire IP legal system. Enforcement of IP rights is inevitable and necessary. This is because IP rights invariably require a balancing of contradictory forces – the right of the owner of an innovation to exclude others, and the right of others to have access to the innovation. Often the balance needs to be tested, and this is when disputes occur.

Today, litigation over intellectual property rights is a big business. At the New York Intellectual Property Law Association's Annual Black-Tie Dinner in Honor of the Federal Judiciary, more than 3,000 local patent litigators and other intellectual property attorneys gather with federal judges at the Waldorf-Astoria, dressed in tuxedos and evening gowns, with vast power and money on display at the law firm hospitality suites scattered throughout the hotel. IP litigation receives increasing attention in industry and the media, largely because damages can be so high and the impact of injunctions so powerful that the results of a lawsuit can determine the fate of a company or a technology.

Cynics say that the task of policing IP rights is important primarily to the intellectual property attorneys who handle litigations. The cost of enforcement is generally very high, though it could be reduced by procedural reform. Costs could also be reduced by altering the strategy and tactics employed by judges, lawyers, and parties on both sides. But enforcement of IP rights is always complex anyhow, because it must balance not only the interests of the two contesting parties, but also the wider public interest in making the system work effectively, by correcting mistakes that occur when IP rights are too broad or not broad enough.

There is really only one reason for an organization to build and maintain a portfolio of IP assets – to gain control over innovations that come from inside the organization or are obtained from outside. If no control is desired, no IP rights are required, or, if IP rights exist, they are simply not enforced or asserted. But if control is desired, an organization can do two things to help achieve its goals.

First, the organization can let others have access to the IP rights, but only in exchange for some consideration of value. That consideration is generally money, but it can also be a commitment to develop the innovation further, or merely a promise to keep further improvements accessible (as with open access "copyleft" licenses).

A second way to control others' access to an innovation is to block them altogether, preventing them from competing. This allows the owner to exert control over the market for the innovation and to affect the way the innovation cycle moves forward. Exclusivity allows an innovator to charge more money for its product or services than would be possible if others could copy the innovation. Coca-Cola costs more than a store brand cola. Pharmaceutical innovators charge more before their patents expire, when generic competition begins. Blocking others may also be used to limit the way in which a creative work is reproduced for aesthetic, political, or other reasons – like movie producers preventing their classic black and white movies from being "colorized."

It is often said that intellectual property rights confer monopolies on their owners, but this is not strictly true. A monopoly exists where there is only one seller for a good or service over a prolonged period, and no close substitutes exist. An intellectual property right such as a patent, copyright, or trademark, does not meet all these criteria. First, if the owner is unsuccessful in selling the protected goods or services, there is no monopoly. Second, if the owner does sell products or services protected by IP rights, it is still possible for competitors to sell similar products or services that do not infringe the IP rights, or to challenge the IP rights, or otherwise to access the innovation. (See Figure 13.3.) Nevertheless, even without a classic monopoly, using IP rights to block competitors outright is, by definition, anticompetitive. As a result, the owner of the IP right may be the only one using the innovation, and if that owner does not use it, then access by others may not be available at all.

Implementing a strategic IP plan involves much more than litigation. In addition to building a portfolio and accessing innovations from others without infringement, implementation requires policing activity – searching for infringers, contacting them and trying to convince them to stop their activities, negotiating settlements, and filing lawsuits if necessary. Litigation is a last resort because of its cost and uncertainty.

This section summarizes the basic questions and decisions that an IP manager must ask in policing IP rights. All these issues revolve around the possibility of litigation, but do not necessarily include litigation.

Enforcement triage

Exerting control over the acts of others is one way to define enforcement, or policing, of IP rights. The first phase of IP enforcement may be called enforcement triage. (See Figure 14.4.) Triage can be triggered by undesired activity by a competitor. If there is competitive activity in apparent violation of the organization's IP rights, then the next question is whether the activity is licensed. This may be more difficult to ascertain than one might think.

In many cases it will be apparent whether or not the competitor holds a license. However, with broad licenses (such as click-through software licenses for on-line downloads), the owner would not necessarily know if the competitor has a license. Also, "licensed activity" includes implicit licenses. For example, the "first use" doctrine provides that once a product embodying an IP right is sold, further sales of that product carry an implicit license to use the IP. That is, as a general matter, the IP owner who sells a product to a wholesaler cannot thereafter use the IP rights to control how the wholesaler, or retailer, or customer user uses the product. The product may also be subject to compulsory licensing, or a government license. If there is a license, then the next question is if the licensee is operating within the scope and terms of that license, in which case there is no infringement, and the competitor's activities must be accepted, or whether the license needs to be renegotiated to allow the competitor's apparent unlicensed activities.

For example, my first individual client when I was fresh out of law school in 1984 was Andrew Moore, a gifted photographer and college friend who had licensed some photographs of Manhattan's old South Street Seaport to a magazine. The magazine

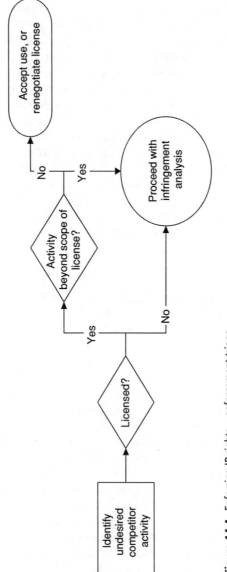

Figure 14.4. Enforcing IP rights – enforcement triage.

printed the photographs but did not pay the license fee. The magazine's use of the photographs without payment was beyond the scope of the license, and was in effect unlicensed, so we accused the magazine of copyright infringement. The settlement, unsurprisingly, was that the magazine promptly paid my friend the agreed upon license fee, eliminating the infringement.

If there is no license, or if the competitor is engaged in activity beyond the scope of the license, then the next step is to conduct an infringement analysis. This involves two basic issues: validity and infringement.

First, the IP manager should consider once again if the IP right is valid. If not, then no IP rights apply, and there are no legitimate rights to enforce. If putative secret information was actually publicly available, there is no valid trade secret. If a patented idea was actually already part of the prior art (the accessible domain), then the patent is invalid and there should be no patent-based exclusivity. If a copyrighted expression was copied from someone else, there can be no copyright-based exclusivity. If the word or logo used as a trademark is confusingly similar to one that was previously used or registered, then they cannot serve as a trademark. In these circumstances, the IP owner may need to back down.

On the other hand, exclusivity is appropriate if there was a legally cognizable innovation (a secret, an invention, an original work of expression, a distinctive indicator of origin), and the innovator took the necessary steps to protect it as an IP asset. If so – if the strategic planning and protection of IP rights was successful – the innovator should then be able to enforce its IP rights. In the following discussion, we assume that the IP rights are valid and enforceable.

Second, the IP manager must consider the issue of infringement. Did the accused infringer actually engage in activity that violates the exclusive rights defined by the IP asset? If not, then the owner of the IP right can not restrict the activity, and the accused infringer is free to carry on. If the accused infringer actually has improperly acted within the IP domain of the accuser, however, then the basic premise of the global network of national IP systems is that the owner must be able to stop the infringer's acts. If not, then the IP right has no value, no force or effect, and the incentive/reward system fails.

When reviewing information about possible infringing activities by others, an IP manager needs to consider specific rights over specific innovations, as granted by individual countries. This leads to decisions on whether to enforce these rights, or not. (See Figure 14.5.)

Trade secrets

First, the IP manager should consider if there has been any misappropriation or theft of trade secrets (Figure 14.5, box 1). The IP manager may become suspicious if a key employee leaves to join a competitor, or if a customer mentions that a competitor has suddenly duplicated a secret method.

A key question in this determination is whether the competitor had access to the secret information, either from the organization, or from an intermediary to whom the organization may have disclosed the secret information. If not, if the competitor developed the information independently, then there can be no trade

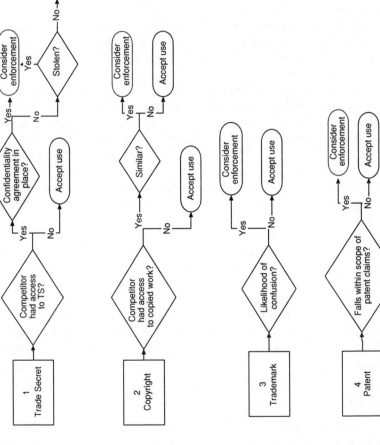

Figure 14.5. Enforcement of IP rights for specific types of IP.

secret violation. The IP owner must accept such use. There is no valid enforcement claim. For example, many soda companies make and sell colas. If Coca-Cola discovers that one of them is completely identical to Coca-Cola in every way that can be measured, that does not necessarily mean that the Coca-Cola formulation has been leaked by a Coca-Cola executive, or stolen from its safe in Atlanta. Rather, more likely, the competitor used modern analytical equipment to determine the contents of Coca-Cola, and then independently formulated a soda that was not just close, but identical. Trade secrecy gives no protection against such reverse engineering.

If records and discussion with staff show that the putative infringer did obtain the information from the organization, then further inquiry is required. If there was a confidentiality agreement, such as an employment agreement, then the rights of the putative infringer will depend on what is stated in the agreement. If the offending acts breach the terms of the confidentiality agreement, then enforcement for misappropriation is a viable option.

If the competitor obtained the information from someone who had not signed an agreement, it is possible that the information was not actually sufficiently protected as a secret, the evidence of this being that it was made available properly, with permission and without restriction. If so, there is no possibility of enforcement, and the IP owner must accept the use. However, if the accused infringer stole the information, that is, obtained it surreptitiously without permission, then enforcement is possible.

In deciding whether to enforce trade secret rights, the IP manager must consider a series of legal issues analogous to those the accused infringer would have to confront if sued. Those issues include legal defects in the trade secret, and the possibility that the accused infringer will assert a counterclaim. Other issues to consider include the place or places where lawsuits might be filed, the amounts of damages, and the costs, which might be in the range of $50,000 to 100,000 in the United States. Costs can be even higher, into the millions of dollars, as with the international civil and criminal case against Jose Ignacio Lopez de Arriortua, the Volkswagen executive accused of stealing General Motors's trade secrets. As with all litigation, the IP owner should consider approaching the accused infringer to see if an adequate settlement is possible.

Copyright

The pivotal issues are somewhat different when assessing whether there has been a copyright infringement (Figure 14.5, box 2). Copyright law does not require proof that copying was intentional. Generally the plaintiff must prove both access and similarity. That is, the competitor must have had access to the owner's work. If there was never any access, then the competitor could not in fact have copied the work, and there is no infringement. Then again, the accused work must also be similar to the protected work. If so, a copyright claim can be made in an appropriate court.

In a famous case against George Harrison of the Beatles, a court found that the 1970 hit song *My Sweet Lord* had a melody with motifs similar to the Chiffon's 1963 hit *He's So Fine*. Access was proven by evidence that the earlier song had been played frequently on English radio, and Harrison acknowledged he had heard the earlier song.[4] In a bizarre twist, Harrison's agent secretly agreed to buy the company that owned the rights to *He's So Fine* to sell it in turn to Harrison to end the lawsuit. A later proceeding found the agent liable to Harrison for breach of client confidentiality.[5]

As with trade secrets, enforcement of copyright requires careful consideration of many legal issues. Some are specific to copyright. The plaintiff needs proof of ownership, which is satisfied in the United States. by a copyright registration, and copies of any assignments, licenses, or other ways to establish there are no defects in legal title.

Other issues are not specific to IP enforcement, and apply in any lawsuit. The appropriate jurisdiction must be selected, typically a place where the defendant resides or does business. The various litigation approaches should be considered, along with their costs – fast, or slow, with motions or straight to a trial – and the potential damages. Costs tend to be in the range of $100,000 to $400,000 in the United States and the UK, or more with a complex case. Damages could be up to $150,000 for statutory damages in the United States, or as high as the lost profits due to the infringement. The defenses that the infringer might raise include legal defects, fair use, government or compulsory licenses, and various IP law or other types of counterclaims. An enforcement plan should be established taking all these factors into consideration. It is generally wise to give notice to the competitor and a last chance to explore the possibility for settlement.

Trademarks

The main issue in weighing the merits of a trademark enforcement claim is whether the competitor's trademark, used on the goods or services in question, creates a likelihood of confusion with the IP owner's trademark in a particular country (Figure 14.5, box 3). If there is no likelihood of confusion, then a trademark infringement claim will not prevail and the trademark owner may have to accept the other party's use. If there is a likelihood of confusion, then enforcement is possible.

Again, as with trade secret and copyright claims, the trademark owner needs to consider the location of the infringement, the costs and damages, and legal issues including possible defects in the trademark claim and various counterclaims. A trademark infringement action in the United States can cost each litigant $100,000 to $250,000 (or up to $1,000,000 in a complex case) before damages awarded or a settlement reached. Settlement discussions are often fruitful in trademark disputes because uncertainty can harm both parties, and both can benefit from a coexistence agreement defining how each party may use its trademark so that no confusion results.

Patents

The central issue with patent infringement is whether the competitor's activities (making, using, selling, importing, or offering a product or service for sale) falls within

---

[4] *Bright Tunes Music Corp. v. Harrisongs Music, Ltd.*, 420 F. Supp. 177 (S.D.N.Y. 1976).
[5] *ABKCO Music Inc. v. Harrisongs Music*, Ltd., 722 F.2d 988 (2d Cir. 1983).

the scope of the issued patent claims in any particular country. If the patent owner believes that the competitor's actions fall within the scope of a single claim of a single patent, then there are grounds for an infringement action no matter how many other claims and other patents are not infringed. To avoid damages and injunctive relief for infringement, the competitor must stay clear of every single claim.

For example, in the *Polaroid v. Kodak* case over instant image cameras, Kodak was successful in invalidating most of the patents that were asserted against it, and was held to infringe a limited number of claims involving a smaller number of patents. But the few remaining claims were sufficient to support an injunction forcing Kodak to pay $909 million, to recall all its instant cameras from customers, and to drop out of the instant image business. On the other hand, treble damages were avoided – Polaroid had been seeking $5.7 billion during the 1980s) because Kodak's counsel had reviewed 250 Polaroid and other patents, and rendered 67 written opinions of noninfringement. Only seven patents were found to be infringed. But the cost of these infringements was substantial.[6]

The legal, technical, and economic issues in patent litigation are far more complex than with other types of IP. The stakes are obviously far higher. Therefore, in the United States, few patent lawsuits can be resolved for less than $250,000, and many cost $2 million or more, as much as $10 million.

A patent suit usually resembles three dimensional chess. Every possible defect in the patent is usually contested in detail, including additional prior art that was not considered during patent prosecution, and matters such as improper claim language and inequitable conduct by the patent applicant. During the *NTP v. RIM* Blackberry litigation, Research in Motion, the Canadian defendant, was able to convince the USPTO to reexamine the patents, to convince the Canadian government to lobby on its behalf at the USPTO, and to scare the Sergeant at Arms of the U.S. Congress into sending a letter to the court pleading that any interim injunction should not affect members of Congress and their staffs due to the importance of Blackberry devices to the legislative process (with members of Congress so often absent from the Capitol). International campaigns to enforce patents in different countries are even more complex, because of the different laws, proceedings, and risks that an admission of guilt in one country may damage the case in another country.

Other rights

A comprehensive overview of IP management should at least mention the existence of other rights, beyond the four main types, that may affect innovation. There are quasi-trademark rights relating to domain names and geographical indications of origin. IP assets may be at issue in breach of contract disputes involving licenses, confidentiality agreements, and biological material transfer agreements. Plant variety certificates, design patents, and database rights can all be used to limit access to innovations, and owners should manage and enforce them carefully, following a similar decisionmaking process as that outlined above.

---

[6] *Polaroid Corp. v. Eastman Kodak Co.*, 16 U.S.P.Q.2d 1481 (D. Mass. 1990), *as corrected*, 17 U.S.P.Q.2d 1711 (D. Mass. 1991).

SUMMARY. The many complex issues involved in protecting internal innovations with IP rights can be simplified by a methodical approach using decision trees. The first step is to identify important innovations that come from inside the organization (from employees and consultants). The second step is innovation triage, sorting a innovations according to their value to the organization and the urgency of action, to decide how much effort to invest, and when action is required. If IP protection is worthwhile, then a series of steps can be taken to decide how best to preserve and perfect IP rights in a cost-effective manner. This means choosing a path for protection: trade secrets for confidential information; copyright for original works of authorship; trademark for distinctive indicators of origin; and/or patents for inventions. Different steps are required to create each type of IP asset, and aggressive or low cost approaches can be used for each. Trade secrets require self-help measures. Copyright protection generally requires notice and monitoring. Trademarks generally require registration, and so do patents. A different set of decisions must be made in managing a portfolio of existing IP assets. Here, the thrust of implementation is to perfect, expand, renew and maintain the most valuable IP rights, while delaying action, minimizing cost, or pruning (abandoning) the least valuable assets. Finally, enforcement and policing of IP rights includes a process of enforcement triage for each type of IP asset. Many other IP management decisions revolve around the question of whether a court would find that a given activity infringes a particular IP right. It is generally desirable to be proactive, monitoring activities to find infringement, and possibly establishing contact with potential infringers to see if a nonlitigious resolution is possible. When an IP manager identifies an undesired competitor activity, a triage step helps determine whether the activity is licensed or otherwise permitted, and if not, whether any infringement of any type of IP right has taken place. If the basic elements of infringement can not be proven, IP law will not help the owner prevent the offensive activity, but if infringement can be demonstrated, then the owner should consider the possibility of enforcing rights, seeking damages and an injunction. Different proof is required for each type of IP asset, and overlapping, but different types of remedies are available. Enforcement of IP rights is perhaps the most visible part of the IP system, but it can best be viewed as just another tool for implementing an IP management strategy.

15 Doing Innovation Deals

This chapter relates to transferring IP rights to implement a management strategy. It begins with the basic elements of making deals relating to intellectual property. It continues with the principles of owning innovations, including how to acquire ownership of IP assets, and what ownership means. The next section describes transferring rights in intellectual property to implement a strategic plan. Assignments, licenses, and other types of transfer are described. Details for transferring each type of IP assets are given – trade secrets, patents, copyright, and trademarks. There are reasons for an owner to license out, but also some disadvantages. The final section outlines the pivotal terms and conditions in IP transfer agreements, both noneconomic (granting clause, exclusivity, field of use, and so on), and economic terms. This chapter concludes with some general advice on how to approach IP deal-making.

* * * * * *

In 1995, I traveled to Verata village in Fiji, put on a local sulu sarong skirt, and sat cross-legged on straw mats in an open thatched meeting shelter with community leaders and other outsiders. Our host, Bill Aalbersberg, speaking Fijian, recited the terms of a biodiversity access- and benefit-sharing agreement that had been negotiated during the preceding week. The villagers planned to collect plants and marine invertebrates in collaboration with biologists from the University of the South Pacific, then to provide them to Smith-Kline Beecham for pharmaceutical research, in exchange for payments, training, and a royalty on sales of any resulting products.[1] We all drank yaqona (kava kava) from a coconut shell in ceremonial fashion and clapped hands, as a way to formalize the deal. As I sat and listened, and tasted the mud and pepper flavor of the powdered-root-in-water brew, I realized that the formalities surrounding an intellectual property agreement may vary widely around the world, but the basics remain the same.

In the revolutions of the innovation cycle, some innovations are passed from the creator to other entrepreneurs, and on into society. The creator's original rights to the innovation can be abandoned, shared, protected as intellectual property, or grown and developed further and combined with other innovations. Or they can be harvested as it were, either by marketing the innovation while enforcing exclusive rights to it, or by transferring those rights to someone else. This chapter focuses on the last option, transferring rights.

[1] William Aalbersberg, "The Development of Bioprospecting Agreements In Fiji, BCNet 1999" available at http://www.worldwildlife.org/bsp/bcn/whatsnew/biosprosfiji.htm, accessed December 14, 2006.

BASIC PRINCIPLES OF IP TRANSACTIONS

IP transactions follow the same basic principles as trade in anything else – trees for example. People have long been trading, buying, and selling lumber and firewood, fruit, nuts, whole plants and plant parts, such as bark. Spice is made from the bark of the cinnamon tree. In Fiji and the South Pacific islands, beautiful geometric paintings are made from mulberry bark tapa cloth. Birch bark has been used for canoes, and aspirin derived from medicinal use of willow bark. The intellectual property rights symbolically described as innovation trees, and forests of them, can likewise be harvested and used or sold, in whole or in part.

What sets IP transactions apart from others is their intangible subject matter. There are special ownership concepts that apply to intellectual property, including the legal rights that an IP owner possesses and the limitations on those rights. Most people grasp the legal process by which they acquire rights to tangible things – by buying or renting their homes, their cars, their clothes, their books, their computers, their food and medicine. Fortunately, those same principles apply to assignments and licenses of trade secrets, patents, trademarks, copyrights, and related rights.

Deal making basics

A moment's thought informs us that despite what is generally believed, the world's oldest profession is deal-making. Civilization would not have developed without trade. Communities would not exist, nor would nations. Deals make the world go around. Except for language barriers and security issues, anyone can walk into a market in any community in the world – Manhattan, Lima, Nairobi, Geneva, Mumbai, Beijing, or a village in Fiji – and make a deal with a local merchant for food, a tool, or a handicraft. The same has been true for millennia. Although there are differences in prices, customs, and rules, the basics of this simple trade are the same. You give something to the merchant, the merchant gives you something in exchange, and both of you agree to the terms. The most sophisticated financial transactions follow the same structure. There is an agreement between two or more parties, and an exchange. And the same dynamic underlies every IP agreement, however complex its language may appear.

The main difference from deal to deal is what each side gives the other. In countries whose law derives from British common law, the "something" that is given is called "consideration." That is what law schools teach – a contract is formed between two people when there is consideration and mutual assent.

By focusing on consideration, it is possible to strip away the complexity of an IP agreement and reveal the basic structure of the deal. At the simplest level, there are five different types of consideration that can flow to or from each party:

(a) Giving something,
(b) Doing something,
(c) Promising to give something,
(d) Promising to do something, or
(e) Promising not to do something in the future.

Every transaction can be understood as an exchange of one or more of these types of consideration. For example:

(1) I give you A and you give me B. Example: You pay money and receive this book, or a compact disk with a recorded song, or a bottle of antibiotic pills.
(2) I do C for you now and you promise to do D for me in the future. Example: I hire you in exchange for your promise to assign your future inventions to me. I design your website on condition that you display my logo on the finished Website.
(3) I promise to give you E in the future, and you promise to give me F in the future. Example: I subscribe to your monthly magazine for 3 years, under an installment plan with annual payments.
(4) I promise not to do G in the future, and you promise not to do H. Example: Our two software companies cross license their copyrights, promising not to sue each other for infringement.

In addition to consideration, for a contract to be binding such that a court would enforce it, there must be some manifestation of agreement, or mutual assent. In essence, this simply means that there is evidence that both parties made a commitment to the same terms. That is, neither party has taken something from the other by force or deception. Both willingly give their informed consent.

In the simplest deal, the parties actually swap money for merchandise, hand to hand. Agreement is apparent and there is no need for enforcement because the deal is done. But in most deals, at least one person has an obligation that lasts beyond the moment of agreement. The assent can be evidenced by anything from a nod, a handshake, a verbal agreement, a simple piece of writing, or an elaborate contract, negotiated by lawyers and signed with witnesses.

Most written agreements include "magic" legal words like the following:

NOW THEREFORE, in consideration of the mutual promises, benefits and covenants set forth herein and for other good and valuable consideration, the receipt, adequacy and sufficiency of which are hereby acknowledged, the Parties intending to be legally bound, hereby agree as follows: . . .

But as noted above, arrangements can differ markedly, such as drinking yaqona in Fiji, sending facsimile copies electronically, or increasingly the use of e-mail confirmations and click-through "I agree" e-commerce contracts. Some IP contracts need to be in writing to be recognized in certain countries, and some need to be witnessed by a notary public, while others can be based on oral promises. Written agreements are always desirable because they force the parties to confront and decide all important issues, and reduce the likelihood of later disagreements about what the parties meant to do. Written agreements also help overcome local differences between countries and states about what terms might be implied by law.

ACQUIRING IP OWNERSHIP

One of the legal rights generally bundled together as "property" is the right to acquire ownership, along with the right of possession, exclusion, improvement, destruction, and transfer. Like other property, IP assets can be acquired and transferred.

There are essentially only two ways to acquire ownership of intellectual property. The first applies to the creator and derives from creating the underlying innovation. The act of creation does not, by itself, establish ownership. A creative person who wants to own an innovation can take steps to make certain that the ownership is recognized by law. To own a trade secret, the creator restricts access to the secret information or material. To own a patent, a creator applies for a patent and prosecutes it to issuance. To own a trademark registration, the creator files an application and registers the mark. To own a copyright, the creator publishes a copyrightable work.

Creative acts produce ideas. To put the ideas to work as intellectual property requires additional legally recognized acts. By taking these acts, the creator of an innovation becomes the owner of the associated IP rights.

The second way to acquire ownership in IP is by agreement with someone else who already owns the rights. The creator of an innovation that has been or can be protected as an IP asset can transfer the IP rights to someone else. In the most common type of IP transfer agreement, the creator is an employee who has agreed, in advance, to transfer all work-related intellectual property to the employer, from the time of its creation. The employer then stands in the shoes of the employee in maintaining secrecy, filing patent or trademark applications, or publishing copyrighted works.

IP rights can also be transferred further downstream, between people who have no connection with the creator. Thus, as a general rule, the owner of an IP right can be either the creator, or someone to whom the creator transferred rights, or someone downstream – A, B, C, or D.

A well-run innovative organization has partnering relationships with people and organizations with which it works, including suppliers, customers, licensees, licensors, collaborators, investors, donors, franchisees, and affiliates. Employees and consultants fill a special role, given their close relationship. All of these relationships involve transfers of IP rights.

The dynamic of any such relationship, from the perspective of IP rights, can be defined in terms of who owns what rights, which rights are being transferred and which retained, and what becomes of any new rights that are created as a result of the relationship. The balance of rights between the parties may be different for inventions, secrets, trademarks, and copyrights in software, literature, data, and so on.

OWNING INTELLECTUAL PROPERTY RIGHTS

In colloquial use, people say that they "own" information, ideas, inventions, technology, songs, and other intangible innovations, just like owning tangible things – food, books, computers, or houses. But strictly speaking that is not correct. Ownership applies not to innovations themselves, but rather to specific bundles of IP rights. That is, an individual or organization may own trade secret rights in confidential information (the right to condition disclosure on consideration, and to prevent others from disclosing it), a patent (or the right to obtain a patent) on an invention, a copyright on a published work, and a trademark restriction on a commercial symbol. IP ownership is best understood as it applies to the individual legal assets created by applying IP law to the fruit of creative acts, rather than the creative acts or the products themselves.

We refer, then, to owning specific patents, copyrights, trademarks, and trade secrets. Typically an IP owner holds rights to a portfolio of these assets. Patents and trademarks are government-recognized assets, identifiable by their government-issued serial numbers. Owners of these IP assets can list them by number, and can prove ownership by various means such as a certified copy of the registration and an assignment recorded at the national patent and trademark office referring to the registration number.

In the narrow sense, one can own patents, not inventions. Patent rights extend only to national boundaries. So instead of owning an invention, an organization can own an international family of related patent applications and patents in many countries. Some families of patents on a single invention exist in only one or two countries. Many cover about a dozen countries, typically the wealthier ones – such as the United States the most affluent countries of Europe, Japan, Canada, and Australia. Other common countries for patent filings include Korea, Brazil, China, India, Israel, Russia, and South Africa. Some patent families include as many as 50 or 100 countries, but there are very few that extend to all the countries of the world that issue patents.

Sometimes a single patent application may give rise to two or more patents in particular countries, depending on the breadth of the invention. Each patent in each country represents a separate asset held by its owner. The scope of rights that each patent conveys can only be determined by reviewing the patent claims there, which may differ from the scope in other countries.

Likewise, one does not own a logo, but rather trademark rights that must be protected in each country. In most countries trademarks are protected solely by registering them, but in many former English colonies and other countries, like the U.S., rights can also arise based on actual use of the trademark in commerce in that country. Many trademark registrations are limited to one country. Some families of trademark registrations include a few countries, some extend to 10, 20, or 50 countries, and a few to most of the countries of the world.

A consequence of the national limitations and variations of patent and trademark rights is that there is an "IP-free zone," or accessible public domain, in numerous countries for many inventions and trademarks. No one owns rights to inventions and trademarks which are unprotected and accessible for use in those countries. Such IP free zones may be thought of as public domains with respect to a particular type of IP right, though limited to one country.

So the correct way to describe ownership of a patent or trademark is to say that company X owns patents on innovation Y in countries A, B, and C, or that company X owns registered trademark Z in countries D, E, F, and G, with serial numbers listed. Ownership rights are limited to those assets in those countries.

Copyright ownership is somewhat different because rights extend internationally in most countries upon publication of the copyright work in one country. One can refer to owning copyright in a work without referring to national rights. Trade secrets extend globally, in principle, too. If the Coca-Cola formula is secret in Atlanta, Georgia, it is probably secret everywhere else.

In other words, ownership of patent and trademark rights refers to individual government-identified assets in specific countries. Copyright ownership refers to global rights in a particular work, and trade secret ownership refers to the right to keep information secret globally.

Owning an IP asset is different from owning stock in a corporation that owns an IP asset. A stockholder of a company owns a share of all the assets of the company, including its buildings and bank accounts, and its IP rights, as well as a share of all liabilities. IP assets on the other hand can be created, bought, or sold separately from corporate stock. And nonprofit organizations have no stock, but can own valuable IP rights. Universities may hold royalty-producing patents, and those assets can be transferred.

Owning an IP asset is also different from owning an object embodying that asset. If I buy a drug made by a secret method, I own the drug, but not the secret method. If I buy a book, I own the book without owning the right to copy it. If I buy a patented electronic device, I own and can sell the device separately from the patent rights. If I select the trademark SNAP for a mousetrap, again I can sell the product without giving away my trademark rights.

TYPES OF TRANSFER

IP rights can be transferred by assignment and by license. The distinction is generally quite simple. If all rights in an IP asset are transferred, the transaction is considered to be an assignment. If less than all the rights are transferred, that is generally referred to as a license.

There are some variations, like assignments including a promise to assign rights that arise in the future, and those that reserve a security interest or promise of royalty payments. There are some important differences also in the nature of the rights transferred, the consequences of the transfer, and the formalities required to effect the transfer, depending principally on the nature of the IP asset, and the business terms involved in the agreement.

In all types of IP transfer, the Latin adage learned in law school holds true:

Nemo dat quod non habet – You can't give what you don't have.

In other words, no one can transfer out rights that are superior to or more extensive than what they have obtained. For example, if A has only licensed a copyright to B, B can not give an assignment to C, because B does not have an assignment to give.

Assignment

IP rights are assigned most commonly in connection with employment agreements, where employees (assignors) assign all inventions, copyright works, trade secrets, and other similar rights to their employers (assignees). Specific IP assets can also be assigned as part of an arms length agreement between independent parties of equal bargaining power, for example by two parties who decide to assign their rights to their joint venture.

Assignment can occur when one company merges into another. In a merger, the surviving company usually receives all of the IP assets (and other assets) of the company being absorbed, which ceases its corporate existence. Similarly, in an acquisition by purchase of assets, one company buys the assets of another, including its IP assets, and they are all assigned, in bulk. By contrast, when one company acquires another company's stock, that other company retains all its assets, including its buildings and its IP assets, and no transfer of IP rights takes place.

In an assignment, the owner of a patent, trade secret, trademark, or copyright executes a document transferring "all right, title, and interest" in the IP asset to the assignee. The minimum documentation for this transaction is a recordable assignment form, which simply identifies the asset or assets involved, the owner, and the assignee. It is signed only by the assignor (unlike most agreements which are countersigned).

A novel way to transfer IP assets is by auction. The auction may be via Internet or a live auction such as those run by Ocean Tomo since 2006. The owner of an IP asset signs a contract committing to sell the asset to the highest bidder if the bid exceeds an agreed upon minimum price. After the auction, the owner assigns the asset to the winning bidder. The auction house may receive a commission from the seller and the buyer.

But many assignments take place in the context of a larger transaction, such as an employment agreement, or a merger or acquisition. These usually rely on a separate business contract that precedes the recordable assignment and sets forth both the consideration for the assignment and other two-way terms of the deal.

A recordable assignment, because it lacks such confidential business terms, is suitable for recordation in public registries such as the assignment branch at the U.S. Patent and Trademark Office or the Library of Congress, or the equivalent public agencies in other countries. Such registries are publicly accessible, like the registries of deeds for real estate. If the assignee fails to record an assignment, the assignor may assign rights to someone else, who may record the other assignment and obtain superior rights. The rules for recordation vary by country and depend on the type of IP right being assigned. When someone buys an IP asset, it is advisable to conduct a title search, checking to be sure that appropriate assignments are publicly recorded. However, this can be an arduous procedure, requiring investigation in many different countries.

A contractual obligation to assign future inventions and copyright is frequently found in employment and consulting agreements. These contracts, in essence, trade the benefits of employment for a promise to assign rights in the future. An employee agrees that if in the future she produces a patentable invention or trade secret, she will assign to the employer all related IP rights. If that happy event occurs, then after the patent application is filed, the employee is asked to sign a recordable assignment to fulfill the obligation, and the assignee records the document to complete the assignment process.

In some assignments, the assignee pays nothing additional, as with corporate employment agreements. In others, the assignee may pay money up front, as with any purchase and sale contract. Occasionally, an assignor arranges to be paid by the assignee over time. If the assignee fails to pay, then the question arises whether title should revert back to the original owner. Because an assignment transfers title, generally the only relief the original owner will find will be for payment of the money owed.

In some countries, university faculty members own any IP rights they create, but in many countries, including the United States, the institution acquires ownership by assignment. The university assignee generally agrees to pay a generous share of any royalties received to the faculty inventor assignors – generally between 25 percent and 50 percent of what the university receives, after expenses. University ownership and an inventor's share are both mandated in the United States by the Bayh-Dole Act (discussed in Chapter 2) for federally funded research, and this has stimulated extensive involvement by faculty members in commercializing their inventions, and some antipathy.

Instead of granting an assignment, the owner of an IP asset may grant a security interest, known as a lien. This is, in effect, an obligation to assign. An investor or a creditor may take a security interest in a company's IP rights as collateral for a loan. If the loan is not repaid, the creditor takes title, by assignment. The approach is similar to the rights that a homeowner gives to the bank when taking out a mortgage. The owner still holds legal title to the asset (the patent), but the security holder has the right to take title in the event of nonpayment.

Unlike real estate mortgages, there is little consistency in the procedures in various countries for recording security interests in patents, copyrights, trademarks, and other IP assets. For U.S. patents, a document assigning a security interest can be recorded in the state where the owner is incorporated, and in the USPTO. To streamline the system, there have been proposals for a unified international registry for security interests in IP assets.[2] It would be helpful, indeed, to have a single international registration office for assignments and security interests. This would reduce the need for IP investors to search the national registries in every relevant country, and would help create a liquid market for IP assets.

Licenses and related transfers

A license is a contract that grants less than all of the rights to one or more intellectual property assets, without transferring ownership. This principle holds true for many different types of licensing agreements covering many different kinds of assets. The best practice is for each right to be specified and thereby conveyed separately, though in a single document. The mix of assets differs depending on the type of license, as does the knowledge of the industry required to negotiate these agreements.

- Technology licenses generally include a transfer of patent rights (including pending applications and patentable inventions), trade secrets (including "know-how," confidential information and materials), and copyright (for technical material – e.g., computer software, databases, and instruction manuals). Rights to use trademarks may also be conveyed.
- Publishing and entertainment licenses focus on copyrights in creative works such as books, music, and movies.
- Trademark licenses cover trademarks, trade names, and trade "dress" in products, typically consumer products, and may also include design patents. In

---

[2] Howard Knopf, "Security Interests In Intellectual Property: An International Comparative Approach," 9th Annual Fordham Intellectual Property Law And Policy Conference (New York, 2001), available at http://www.ulcc.ca/en/cls/security-interests.pdf, accessed December 17, 2006.

merchandising licenses, owners of well-known trademarks such as "Coke" and "Eddie Bauer" license their trademarks for use outside their fields, such as "Coke" sweatshirts or "Eddie Bauer" SUVs.

- Franchise licenses, for restaurants, auto rental agencies, and so on, typically combine a license to use the franchise trademark and licenses to use trade secret processes and materials as well as any associated patented inventions.

- Technology "barter" or cross-license agreements help competitors exchange valuable IP. The first owner licenses IP rights to the second, and the second owner cross-licenses other IP rights to the first. The rights may be the same or different, and money may change hands or not, depending on how the parties value their assets. A future oriented cross-license is a "grant back" where the licensee agrees to license back to the licensor any improvements that the licensee makes while using the licensor's innovation.

- Sublicenses are essentially like any other license, except that the sublicensor does not own the IP asset, but rather holds licensed rights received from the owner. A close analogy is to a real estate tenant who rents an apartment out to a subtenant. Any IP asset can be sublicensed, if the terms of the license permit it.

- Open access licenses based on copyright began with software and have expanded to website content, journals, and scientific materials.

- Biodiversity access and benefit sharing agreements permit a "bioprospector" to acquire biological materials and possibly traditional knowledge on condition that certain benefits will be shared with representatives of the source country. The benefits may include direct payments, training, equipment, professional recognition, and royalties if there is a commercial product.

Generally, licenses can be categorized as *exclusive*, meaning the licensor gives only one license, or *nonexclusive*, meaning the licensor can give multiple licenses. Licenses can be formal written documents signed by both parties. Or they can be oral agreements. For example, a simple trade secret license is established in a conversation when one person says "What I'm telling you is confidential, between you and me," and the other person says "OK."

Licenses can be electronic. Increasingly, with the Internet, end user license agreements (EULAs) for software and data are entered into by clicking "I agree" to the terms of a small-print agreement scrolled on a webpage. These are sometimes called "clickwrap" agreements, in reference to their predecessor "shrinkwrap" licenses. Shrinkwrap licenses, pioneered in the 1980s, are agreed to merely by tearing open the shrinkwrap on a box containing a floppy or compact disk containing a computer program.

The preceding types of licenses all involve an explicit agreement, whether written or not. Some licenses are implied, the parties never specifically referring to a transfer by license. For example, if someone hires a consultant to design a webpage or write a jingle without any explicit agreement, they will generally receive an implied license to use the webpage, jingle, or data – but not ownership.

Also, the transfer of a tangible object implicitly transfers a license to the IP rights embodied within it. When someone buys (or leases) a computer, that person receives an implied license to use all the patented hardware within it, and all the copyrighted software, except as may be specified on explicit agreements for some of the components.

Similarly, IP rights may be transferred implicitly when one person borrows a tangible thing from someone else. Lawyers refer to this as a bailment.

Biological material transfer agreements (BMTAs or MTAs) are sometimes structured as bailments.[3] The owner of plant samples, or microbes, or DNA, or human tissue, provides the physical material to a recipient – generally for research purposes – along with an agreement that specifically limits the rights that are transferred with it. The recipient may have to promise to destroy the material when finished, not to transfer the material to anyone else, to pay royalties on any revenue derived from the material, or not to make commercial use of it at all. A MTA is somewhat like a trade secret license, because the owner provider access to the material (like secret information) under certain limited conditions.[4]

An MTA can also operate like an open access agreement, as with the regime established under the 2004 International Treaty on Plant Genetic Resources for Food and Agriculture (ITPGRFA). The ITPGRFA established a two tiered system for 64 food and forage crops, whereby plant breeders and researchers can access plant genetic materials for public unrestricted use, so long as they do not seek proprietary rights in any new plants deriving from the accessed material. Any one who wants IP protection on such derivatives must enter into a separate agreement.

Similar to implied licenses, rights can be transferred "by operation of law," even in the absence of an explicit or implicit agreement, depending on the circumstances. Such transfers are in effect built in to the legal definitions of intellectual property. For example an employer in the U.S. is generally entitled to a "shop right" by operation of law. This is a nonexclusive right to use any inventions by its employees (even without an assignment or license). An employer in the United States is also entitled to own the copyright of works produced by employees in the ordinary scope of their employment.

The Bayh-Dole Act automatically gives the U.S. government certain license rights to patents on inventions made with U.S. funding, by operation of law. Similarly, compulsory licenses can also transfer rights by operation of law, without the consent of the transferring party. A U.S. government contractor working for the U.S. has the statutory right to infringe patents, in exchange for paying a reasonable royalty under 28 U. S. C. §1498.

Another example relates to genetic resources, which prior to the 1992 Convention on Biological Diversity (CBD) were considered to be either private property or the common heritage of humanity. The CBD established a principle in international law that genetic resources are subject to the sovereign rights of the nation in which they are found. Thus, quasi-IP rights in biological materials were established in the nation in which they are found by operation of law.

[3] Michael Gollin, "Biological Materials Transfer Agreements." *Bio/Technology* 13:243 (1995).

[4] Michael Gollin, "Elements of Commercial Biodiversity Prospecting Agreements," in Sarah Laird (ed.), *Biodiversity and Traditional Knowledge: Equitable Partnerships in Practice.* (Earthscan, 2000), annexes available at http://peopleandplants.org/whatweproduce/Books/biological/annexes2.htm, accessed February 4, 2007.

Unlike a transfer by operation of law, illegal transfers are not recognized by law even if the parties agree to them. For example, a contract to purchase an illegally downloaded copy of the latest movie would generally not be enforceable – most such merchandise is sold hand to hand in cash transactions. A Coca-Cola employee was arrested for trying to sell secret documents to Pepsi, including information about a new soda recipe. The Pepsi officials wisely reported the incident to Coca-Cola and law enforcement officials.

There is generally no requirement to record licenses publicly. License terms are often kept confidential because they include sensitive business and technical information that may help a competitor. Some licenses are made public, for example in public annual reports by publicly traded companies. And some companies may choose to record licenses at the appropriate registration office (for example the USPTO for patents and trademarks, or the Library of Congress for copyrights).

Assignment vs. license

In theory, an assignment conveys more rights and a license conveys fewer. But in practice, there are exceptions to this rule, and these exceptions can be used to advantage by either the owner or the person seeking access to the innovation protected by IP rights.

The difference between assignments and licenses is not always readily apparent. Assignments generally need to be in writing, but not all written IP transfer agreements are assignments – not even those captioned "Assignment." As the U.S. Supreme Court observed long ago, classifying an agreement concerning patent rights as an assignment or a "mere license" depends on the provisions in the body of the contract rather than on its heading.[5] A key issue is the right to sue. If a document grants exclusive rights, including the right to sue infringers, then it may be considered an assignment even if it calls itself a license. In the same way, a licensee sometimes enters into a contract granting certain rights in a document called an "Assignment," but this does not assign the underlying licensed patent or copyright, because of the rule that you can't give what you don't have.

In many situations, two or more individuals or organizations may have joint ownership over an IP asset, as happens with joint inventors with different employers, or with joint authors. Joint ownership has perils because, by operation of law, the rights and obligations of both parties may be different than one of them may wish, absent a contract between them. This is analogous to a partnership agreement, whereby the partners enter into an agreement about how to manage the partnership. Likewise, with IP assets, it is best for joint owners to spell out who will control the process of obtaining and enforcing IP rights, who will pay, who will receive income, and who has the rights to sublicense.

Surprisingly, it may be better for one joint owner to grant sole ownership (legal title) to the other party in exchange for strong contractual license rights, including control over the asset and the right to profit from it. This fundamental distinction between legal title and contractual control is often misunderstood. Most people do

---

[5] *Waterman v. Mackenzie*, 138 U.S. 255 (1891).

not realize that mere legal title may not be very beneficial, although it looks good on paper. Often one party insists on "owning" a patent, either out of ego, pride, or ignorance, and has no other concerns. If so, then it is possible to negotiate an agreement giving that party ownership (mere legal title), while the other party gets the more valuable rights.

Here is how, in practice, it is possible to convey more rights by license than assignment. For example, a transfer will be considered an assignment if it conveys legal title ("ownership") to the recipient. But if mere legal title is transferred from A to B, while B transfers to A all control over the invention, and all royalties, and rights to sublicense, and the right to decide when to enforce the IP right and when to settle an enforcement action, then B, the licensee, holds more practical rights than A, the owner.

All that A holds then is the right to be called the owner, with an eggshell-thin right of reversion, meaning that if the license terminates for some reason, or B dissolves (if B is an organization), or dies (if B is a person), then A regains control. But until that time, if ever, B is in control and holds the much more valuable bundle of rights, the egg white and yolk, if not the eggshell.

Transfer of particular IP assets

Trade secrets

Trade secrets often exist in process technology, marketing infomation, and generalized know how, and these are frequently licensed along with patents and copyrights. A trade secret comes into being when a creative person conceives of the idea, discovers the thing, collects the information, or gains the relevant know-how to benefit gainfully from a market advantage. It remains in existence so long as it's kept confidential, meaning that it is not made public, especially to competitors.

For a trade secret to survive when passed from one person to another there must be some form of nondisclosure agreement, whether express or implied. If confidential information is provided to a government agency, the information may remain confidential under government regulations. If there is no confidentiality agreement, express, implied, or by operation of law, then the disclosure is not confidential, and any rights accruing to the trade secret evaporate.

It is generally difficult to partition trade secrets by geography or field of use. It is also difficult to manage an exclusive license to exploit that secret. Transferring a thing like a biological material, or a secret machine, may in effect transfer the trade secrets it embodies, especially if the recipient can extract the secret information from it via reverse engineering. A stated obligation not to reverse engineer may therefore be necessary.

Patents

Patent rights are created initially by the act of invention, and ownership differs from country to country. In the United States, the inventor is the initial owner and applicant for patent rights, until rights are assigned to someone else such as an employer. If an invention has more than one inventor, they share rights. There is no obligation to share revenues under U.S. law. Inventor rights differ from country to country.

The patent rights held in each country can be transferred separately. The right to make, have made, use, sell, offer for sale, or import an invention can be transferred separately, as can the right to exploit the invention within stipulated geographical regions within the United States, and in different fields of use (ways in which the invention can be used). Because of the cost of obtaining a patent, control over patent prosecution and responsibility for the costs of prosecution may become a significant issue.

Patent licensing is a vast and specialized topic. Because patents can be extremely valuable, financial valuation can be important, and the financial terms of a deal can be complex. Negotiating patent licenses is often a time consuming task not susceptible to form agreements.

Copyright

Copyright attaches to original works of authorship, expressed in a tangible medium (which can include radio waves or digital media). The owner at creation is either the author or the author's employer (if the work was created within the scope of employment). The Berne Convention provides that authors have the "moral right" to be identified as such, but in the United States, the one who commissions a work may be considered its author, like an employer under a work for hire agreement. A ghost writer of an "autobiography" is an employee under contract merely, copyright being retained by the ostensible author and subject of the work.

Once copyright has been created, it may be transferred by assignment or license. If a U.S. copyright is jointly owned, the owners must share any revenues.

Consulting agreements should generally provide that the consultant's copyright will be transferred to the commissioning party, whether as a work for hire, or by assignment. Typically, only those rights that are specified are transferred. An author can readily assign or license all, or less than all, of the "arrows in the quiver" of a work. For example, a book author may transfer the right to make print copies, but not oral recordings, translations, adaptations, or electronic versions. In the *Tasini* case, the U.S. Supreme Court confirmed that freelance authors for the *New York Times* who signed contracts applicable to the print versions of their work before the emergence of the Internet, did not give to the New York Times the right to post electronic copies of their work at the Times' website.[6] Publishers thereafter have authors sign agreements transferring electronic rights in their works.

Copyright is a legal right that is separate from material objects embodying the copyright work. If I purchase a DVD movie recording, I own the DVD, but I have only a limited license to use the DVD to play the movie – I do not own the copyright, and cannot make further copies. If I receive or purchase a letter from a famous author, I own the letter, but the author or her estate retains all rights to reproduce and adapt the words.

"Open access" licensing deserves some special discussion. The open source approach to software licensing developed in 1998. In open source licensing, the software copyright owner makes the source code for the program available by license o the public (instead of keeping it secret, as with most software), and permits copying,

---

[6] *New York Times Co. v. Tasini*, 533 U.S. 483 (2001).

modification, and redistribution by the user community without fees. Most open source licenses are so-called "copyleft" (a play on the word copyright, implying its opposite), which means that if the work is modified, then that derivative work must be made available on the same terms as the originally licensed work. A copyleft license may be referred to as viral, in the sense that it infects all downstream modifications.

A copyleft license actually promotes greater access to the licensed work than if the work were published in the public domain. With a public domain work, anybody may modify it to make a derivative work and then exclude others from using the derivative work, thus privatizing the modification. With an open source copyleft license, the downstream user cannot privatize the derivative work in that fashion, and so, counterintuitively, greater public access results.

Many organizations, such as Wikipedia and the Creative Commons, both founded in 2001, extend the use of open source licensing beyond software. Wikipedia uses something called the GNU Free Documentation License as the framework for its collaborative encyclopedia built from user generated text.[7] Creative Commons, a nonprofit group promoting shared access to information, has pioneered a variety of form copyright licenses, each of which requires attribution of the author and may include combinations of copyleft requirements along with the right to copy, make derivative works, make commercial use, or even to make an explicit dedication of work to the public domain. The concept of open source licensing has moved further into science, leading to the Science Commons project, which develops open access licensing models for scientific publications and biological materials.

Trademarks

Where trademark rights arise from use, in the United States and some other countries, exclusive rights are owned by the person or organization initially using them. To apply for a U.S. registration of a trademark, the applicant needs to be using it, or have an intent to use it. In countries requiring registration, the applicant is the owner, regardless of use or intent to use.

A naked assignment of a U.S. trademark – the mark itself, with nothing else – can invalidate it. The assignor must transfer at least the good will associated with the mark, for example the business associated with it. A naked license can invalidate a trademark just like a naked assignment. The licensor needs to retain quality control over the licensee's goods or services, or at least the right of review.

Trademark licenses can be limited by geography or the types of goods or services that are permitted (fields of use), like "Cambridge University" clothing, or books. Often when two trademark owners have marks that closely resemble each other, or whose products become more and more similar over time, or who expand into the same countries, they negotiate coexistence agreements that limit both parties to specific uses so as to avoid confusion.

Reasons for an IP owner to license out

To implement an IP management strategy, the owner of an IP asset may choose to (a) abandon the exclusive rights that come with ownership, (b) hold onto the right,

---

[7] Wikipedia: Text of the GNU Free Documentation License (2002), available at http://en.wikipedia.org/wiki/Wikipedia:Text_of_the_GNU_Free_Documentation_License, accessed December 10, 2006.

exclude others, and try to meet market demand, (c) sell all rights to others, or (d) license out part of the rights. The choices are analogous to ownership of real estate. A landowner, for various reasons, may abandon the property to the state, live on the land, farm the land, sell the land, or rent it out (in IP terms, "license" it out) to others. Here, we consider when licensing is the best choice.

First, by licensing rights instead of selling or abandoning them, the owner maintains the underlying ownership interest. This includes rights into the future, which provides the potential for further innovation and enhanced value. Licensing is also appropriate if the owner can not meet market demand. Universities are generally expected or required to retain ownership of their patents, not to commercialize the inventions, and so they license.

Likewise, an owner that can not reach multiple market opportunities in different sectors may decide to license another company that has access to those markets and experience with them. Licensing out provides leverage by adding the licensee's business resources to the licensor's innovative strength, sales force, distribution channels, and so forth. Recording companies learned how to sell songs direct to consumers on vinyl records, then compact discs, but they have licensed Internet sales to Apple's iTunes and other companies rather than do their own on-line publishing. Disney retains ownership and control over its trademarks while licensing them out prolifically to merchandisers.

Licensing to companies with established product lines helps to increase market penetration. Such complementary products can enhance reputation and goodwill for both companies.

Licensing can help inexpensively broaden geographic reach. It is easier to license a distributor than to enter foreign markets by establishing a national subsidiary.

Licensing is also well-suited for collaborations where people and organizations team up to research, develop, or market a product. For example, two companies may form a joint venture, with each one licensing rights to the joint venture. This is similar to straightforward licensing except that the joint venture structure may give the owner more control over the management of the innovation and its marketing.

An alternative to collaboration through licensing in these circumstances is to "do it yourself." This would require an investment in the staff and infrastructure necessary to develop, distribute, and promote products and services in all available markets, or it would require outsourcing to a company that would do all that for a fee. These approaches may require too much capital, as compared to licensing, where the licensee takes on the cost burden.

Licensing is a good option for a patent owner seeking to create an ongoing revenue stream, without the need for investment. IBM receives over $1 billion per year by licensing its patents. This is equivalent to many billions of dollars in product sales, because royalties are almost pure profit after the overhead of licensing staff and costs of acquiring and maintaining the patents. Numerous companies that do not sell products have made fortunes licensing patents and other IP. Even though one of Jerome Lemelson's patents on machine vision (bar codes) was ultimately struck down, he obtained about 600 patents and received over $1 billion in license fees, his main overhead being the cost of enforcement litigation. Ronald Katz has licensed his patents on computer-telephone interfaces for what is expected to exceed $1 billion before the patents expire, and NTP obtained over $600 million in settlement from Research in Motion for the Blackberry device. Licensing, coupled with enforcement, has proved to be a lucrative business for these people. They are sometimes called patent trolls because they are not themselves the innovators of the patents they've acquired, but they can also be called patent entrepreneurs, depending on your perspective.

Disadvantages of licensing out

Licensing is not without costs and risks. First, the licensor loses much control over the ways in which the innovation is developed and commercialized. For a manufacturing license, the licensor may lose all control over the manufacturing process and the quality of the products. For a marketing and distribution license, the licensor may lose control over advertising, promotion, distribution channels, or pricing. In both cases, the licensor loses contact with customers, who are often the greatest source of feedback fueling future innovation.

Second, the licensor loses the incentive to expand into new product and service lines, and into new geographical markets. The licensor organization also loses the incentive to develop itself and its innovations further when it lets others take over marketing, and may lose new business opportunities.

Third, the licensor becomes dependent on others for revenue. Licensees may fail to pay the promised royalty, leaving a lawsuit as the licensor's only recourse.

Fourth, a licensee may stop innovating in the areas that are licensed. This leads to a loss of the technological edge necessary to further innovation.

Fifth, the licensor may lose opportunities to gain public recognition for the licensed product. For example, the licensee of a patent may sell products under a trademark and gain the goodwill associated with the product, while the licensor gains nothing. This is the problem Intel seeks to avoid with its "Intel inside" licensing campaign, attempting to associate its trademark with those of the computers carrying Intel's chips.

Finally, licenses carry a heavy risk of loss of IP rights. Once the licensee learns how to make the innovative product and market it, there is a strong temptation to use the IP rights to compete directly. For example, if companies are not careful when contracting with a foreign distributor, the distributor may take out a trademark registration in that country. Then, if the licensor terminates the distributorship, the distributor is in a position to exclude the licensor from using its own trademark in that country. Trademark owners see this problem repeatedly when expanding trademark rights worldwide, and may have to file a lawsuit or pay a nuisance settlement to the distributor.

PIVOTAL TERMS FOR IP TRANSACTIONS

As explained in previous chapters, assessment and implementation of IP strategies requires evaluation of the nonfinancial aspects of the IP assets but also a financial valuation. This holds true with assignments and licenses. Most people focus on the economic terms but especially with a license, the noneconomic terms may be just as important. So we shall consider them first.

Noneconomic terms

The scope of an assignment or license can be visualized in three dimensions, as when assessing IP assets themselves. For IP assets, the three dimensions are (1) the types of IP and their legal strengths (exclusivity), (2) the duration of the IP rights, and (3) the geographic extent of the exclusive rights conferred by the asset.

With an assignment, all the rights in any particular asset are transferred, although they can be limited. For example, one can assign patents, retaining trade secrets and copyrights. Or one can assign all patent, copyright, and trademark rights in Europe, retaining rights to Asia and America.

But assessing a license requires an extra step. First, the three-dimensional strength of the underlying IP asset is considered. Then any further limitations found in the license are identified.

Granting clause

Although the format for a license can vary widely, the most important term in an effective licensing agreement is the granting clause, specifying what IP rights are being granted. It should also identify what rights, if any, are reserved by the licensor.

The party granting the license must, of course, own the relevant intellectual property. In the case of a sublicense, the sublicensor must have authority from the owner to grant the license. One cannot license rights that one neither owns nor controls.

Moreover, the IP asset must actually be protected by law as intellectual property, or be eligible for legal protection. One cannot license public information as a trade secret. If a patent application never matures into a patent, there can be no patent license. A work that is not original cannot be protected by copyright. A generic name like "escalator" cannot be licensed as a trademark.

Although licenses often lump all IP rights together into a single granting clause, it is easiest if there is a separate granting clause for each type of IP asset, specifying the special requirements for each. A trade secret licensee must maintain confidentiality. A patent licensee must mark products with the patent number. A trademark licensee must submit products or services to the licensor for approval of their quality.

The scope of each grant may be different as well. The grant may be as large as the licensor's rights, or smaller. It is an act of infringement if a licensee strays outside the limited scope of the license.

Exclusivity

The grant may be exclusive, such that the licensee is the only one who is permitted to practice the innovation, effectively replacing the owner. In a limited exclusive license, the licensor retains the right to use the innovation, but not to license any one else. In a nonexclusive license, such as with consumer software, there may be no limit to how many other parties are permitted to practice the innovation.

Field of use

The scope of a license may encompass all conceivable types of activities, or the field of use may be limited. Typically, different industrial sectors may be defined and licensed separately. A biological method like the polymerase chain reaction method for amplifying DNA may be licensed to an instrument company to make a laboratory device, to a pharmaceutical company to find drugs, to an agricultural company to find pesticides, and to universities for noncommercial research.

Patents are limited to their claims but include the right to make, use, sell, offer, or import the invention, and these rights may be divided up. Copyright includes a bundle of rights that can be separately licensed, including the right to copy, to perform, and to make derivative works (such as electronic versions and foreign language translations). Trademark rights may be limited to particular goods or services, but these too can be divided into different fields.

Sublicensing
Some licenses permit the licensee to transfer some or all of the licensed rights forward to a third party. For example, a computer maker obtains licenses with the right to sublicense use of software and hardware to its customers. Other licenses preclude sublicensing, and require personal performance by the licensee. A composer may license a band to record her song, without the right to sublicense other bands to perform and record the song as well.

Duration
The license may extend to the full term of the IP asset, or be limited to a specific term of years. Trademark and trade secret licenses may be perpetual, while a copyright or patent license can not extend past the term of the asset.

Territory
The licensor may grant all worldwide rights in each asset or a limited territory for one or more of them. Copyright and trade secret rights may be granted worldwide, while patent and trademark rights are limited to those countries where the legal requirements have been satisfied.

Transferability
Transferability is related to sublicensing. The issue here is whether the license holder is permitted to assign the license to someone else, instead of (but not in addition to) the licensee. Transfer is generally permitted if the licensee is being acquired by another company.

Termination
Termination clauses relate to license duration. Most licenses can be terminated if one of the parties breaches the agreement. Some licenses can by terminated by one party or the other after a certain period of time, or if certain milestones are not met. In effect, such licenses may have a shorter duration than might appear from the duration clause. Historically, patent licensees in the U.S. needed to terminate their license before they could challenge the validity of the patent. But the Supreme Court's 2007 *MedImmune* decision[8] held that a licensee may challenge a patent without terminating the license. Thus, in principle, a licensee can take a license,

---

[8] *Medimmune, Inc. v. Genentech, Inc.*, 127 S.Ct. 764 (2007).

challenge the patent, and if successful, stop paying royalties, or if unsuccessful, continue paying them.

Improvements

The way in which rights in improvements are allocated is often a point of contention in negotiation of licenses and other agreements calling for collaborative research. It is also a frequent source for disputes after an improvement has been made. The problem is that it is very difficult to predict exactly what innovations will result from the work.

There are several different ways in which rights to future innovations can be allocated. (See Figure 15.1.) As a starting point, the parties generally define a joint scope of work, based on the project and their individual goals. Each party (or that party's employees) can be expected to make some innovations jointly (working together) and some independently (working apart) within the joint scope of work. Next, it is usually straightforward that each party should own all rights in future innovations that it will make independently outside the joint scope of work. Such innovations are beyond the scope of the agreement and neither party seeks rights to the other's IP assets beyond that scope.

Within the scope of the project, there are essentially five possible allocations of future rights. In the two extremes, one party owns all IP assets produced by either party within the joint scope of work (A), or the other one does (E). In the two more moderate allocations of improvements, each party owns the innovations made solely by its own employees within the scope of work, and one or the other owns any improvements arising from joint work (B and D). In the fifth arrangement, popular in simple agreements because it seems fair, each party owns its own independent innovations, and they both jointly own joint innovations (C).

The fifth approach (C), although elegant in its simplicity, can be problematic for two reasons. First, allowing each party to have sole control over its independent inventions or works of authorship may thwart the common objectives of the collaboration. (A different approach would solve this problem – both parties have joint ownership of all innovations within the joint scope of work.) Second, joint ownership without any clear allocation of control and exclusivity invites discord between the parties. So the intermediate arrangement is often superior, with each party holding the rights that are most important to its own ongoing mission. They can then grant each other by license any rights that each one needs to enjoy the benefits of the collaboration.

Policing/Enforcement

Although various arrangements are possible, most licenses provide that the licensee should inform the licensor of any infringement by a third party and the licensor should then enforce the underlying IP assets. If the licensor does not enforce, the licensee can then enforce the IP rights against the infringer. The costs, control, and sharing of any damages or settlement can be arranged however the parties see fit.

Warranties/Indemnities etc.

A licensee will generally seek a warranty that the IP asset's rights are indeed in force. A licensor generally seeks an indemnity against any liability from acts of the

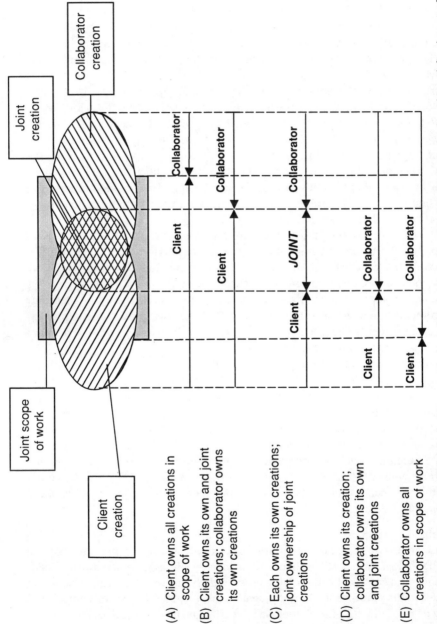

(A) Client owns all creations in scope of work

(B) Client owns its own and joint creations; collaborator owns its own creations

(C) Each owns its own creations; joint ownership of joint creations

(D) Client owns its creation; collaborator owns its own and joint creations

(E) Collaborator owns all creations in scope of work

Figure 15.1. Allocating rights in future innovations. With two collaborators working jointly and independently within a defined scope of work, each can (1) allocate all rights to one party or the other (A and E), or (2) own its independent innovations with one of them owning joint innovations (B and D), or (3) own its independent innovations with both jointly owning the joint innovations (C).

licensee. These terms are generally highly negotiable. Other terms that are standard in any contract may vary widely from country to country, such as the controlling law, mechanisms for dispute resolution, and so on.

Economic terms

A license agreement stipulates the consideration being provided in exchange for the grant of a license. The consideration may include up front, milestone, royalty, and minimum payments.

"Royalty" refers to a payment (a percentage of sales or per unit) depending upon the productivity or use of the licensed IP right. In the U.S., there is generally no restriction on the amount of royalty that a licensor may charge or receive. For patents, royalties may range from 0.1 percent (or lower) to 25 percent (or higher) of the manufacturer's net revenue from sales of the patented product (often 3–10 percent).

Many factors affect the royalty rate. (See Chapter 12.) The principle factors relate to the scope of rights transferred and to the ability of the licensee to use those rights to generate revenue. For example, with patents, some of the key questions are as follows. For each, the first option drives the royalty up and the second drives the royalty down.

- Does the patent control a pioneering invention or an incremental improvement?
- Does the scope of the patent claims encompass all or substantially all of the revenue generating activities or merely a part of them?
- Is the patent likely to be held valid or invalid if challenged in court?
- Is it difficult or easy to "design" around the patent?

In the extreme case, a pioneering patent covering all revenue generating activities, likely to be held valid and hard to design around, is worth much more than an incremental patent covering only a part of revenue generating activities, likely to be invalidated, and easy to design around.

The details for calculating payments are set out in various clauses. One is the basis for calculating royalties. Typically, royalties are defined in terms of net sales, the amount of revenue the licensee obtains from using the licensed IP asset, minus taxes, shipping, and so on. Alternatively, royalties can be based on a fixed fee per month or year, or per unit sold. Sales figures are easily verifiable. Sometimes royalties are based on profit, but this is a more complex calculation because it requires data about marginal cost, overhead, and other costs. With sublicenses, the license may provide that the licensor is entitled to a share, for example 25 percent, of any sublicensing revenue. There are endless variations on these fundamental concepts.

Licenses may also include complex terms for foreign currency calculations, the timing of payment, and so on. Auditing provisions are common when royalties are based on sales or profits, permitting the licensor to check the licensee's books to ensure honest reporting.

Exclusive licenses usually state minimum performance standards requiring the licensee to develop and market the product or service, and to pay minimum royalties. If the licensee does not pay a minimum amount then the license reverts to nonexclusive, or it terminates.

Finally, the economic and noneconomic terms of licenses need to be considered carefully to see if they present any unfair anticompetitive effects or violate antitrust laws. The United States and Europe have sophisticated laws against anticompetitive activities, and IP agreements sometimes run afoul of them. Generally IP owners have substantial latitude about how to parcel out the bundle of rights they own in a legitimate IP asset. However, certain circumstances can give rise to strong antitrust challenges.

For example, an innovator may hold a patent on a computer printer, but not on ink cartridges. It could be an improper use of the patent if the innovator licenses another party to manufacture the patented printer, and prohibits the manufacturer from using any competitor's ink cartridge. Such prohibitions improperly extend the exclusive rights provided by a patent to unpatented products, and may be considered to be improper monopolistic tying arrangements.

Also, generic companies routinely challenge the patents for branded pharmaceuticals. Branded and generic companies have increasingly been entering into settlement agreements in the United States in which the patent holder licenses the generic company to use the patent in exchange for a payment. In a variation, the patent holder pays the generic company, and the generic company stays off the market – the opposite of a usual licensing payment to the patent holder. The rationale for such agreements is that this is a fair bargain for a generic company, whose challenge to the patent has an uncertain outcome. Under the Hatch-Waxman Act, generic companies have certain rights, such as six months exclusivity for the first to challenge a patent, and (the argument goes), the generic company is entitled to some compensation for giving up those statutory rights. However, the economic result is to delay the lower prices due to generic competition, and this has led the Federal Trade Commission to try to block such agreements, even as the courts uphold them.

One deal may involve a simple assignment of all rights for a set fee. Another deal may involve a complex series of financial terms, with an up-front payment, annual payments, milestone payments when certain successes are achieved, a running royalty on sales of products, a step up (or down) over time or as sales increase. Licensing is an extremely complex topic that goes well beyond these few examples. There are few "standard forms." Every party to a license should engage an IP professional to ensure that its needs are met. But, as with enforcement, IP dealmaking is best viewed as a tool for strategic IP management.

DOING DEALS

For many people, licensing and technology transfer is a profession and a way of life. Licensing executives, technology transfer personnel, and business development officers spend their time assembling the resources to support innovation and at the same time building the relationships and negotiating agreements to acquire or transfer IP assets elsewhere, where they will be used. Each industry has its own IP transfer specialists, and the demands on these people are likely to grow as IP becomes more and more valuable in the global economy.

Thus, a few words about negotiating IP agreements are in order. First, IP is a human creation, and negotiating transfers of IP rights is a human endeavor. One can better understand the larger implications of IP transfers when one grasps its place within the operation of the innovation cycle, and understands IP's role in driving it forward.

Second, a negotiator should have an IP strategy in mind before beginning the IP transfer process. Focusing on a specific outcome can help improve the chances of success. Focusing on strategy also helps simplify the process, by avoiding the complexity that arises if one tries to negotiate every term of an agreement with equal vigor. Likewise, dealing with strategic principles rather than bargaining positions can create opportunities for creative solutions that might create a win-win outcome.

Third, as with all strategic management, and all negotiations, it is important to conduct research. Both negotiators should learn as much as possible about their own firm's IP assets, and also find out the other side's strategy and bottom line. How to assess IP was discussed previously. A negotiator who knows her own bottom line deal killers will be more able to judge when it is time to walk away from a negotiation, and when to continue. A negotiator who has figured out the other side's bottom line will be able to push harder for a better deal.

Fourth, it is crucial to keep in mind that economic terms, as important as they are, are only one piece of the puzzle. A negotiator must also master the noneconomic terms, such as the scope of the grant, future improvements, and termination.

Fifth, a negotiator should be flexible, and able to trade off economic terms against noneconomic terms, to bargain for all three dimensions of the IP rights being transferred and to be specific about patents, trade secrets, trademarks, and copyrights.

Sixth, almost all terms are negotiable. However, a good IP negotiator avoids acting like a junk yard dog fighting over every term and phrase. This can lead to a situation I have seen where parties take over a year to negotiate, and spend a fortune on legal fees arguing about each clause. Rather, the best approach is to find a way to get the rights one wants, giving up rights one is willing to part with. Ultimately if the parties approach the negotiation process as an opportunity for discovering mutual strategic advantages, not as antagonists, then they may find ways to build a relationship that will survive the particular agreement being negotiated at the moment. With the goodwill such an approach creates, most agreements can be easily amended later, if need be. If the parties later have a falling out, then the record will be clear about what each party really wanted from the deal, and what each deserves.

The goal of good negotiating is, in essence, for both parties to be able to achieve their own strategic goals, or to come as close as possible, one giving and the other gaining access to an innovation. Deals structure the many dynamic relationships with suppliers, collaborators, consultants, employees, customers, and investors. More broadly, doing deals with IP rights is a central part of the innovation cycle, and the process of trading away exclusivity, so that innovations can be handed off, improved, and adopted by society. IP transactions are therefore important both to organizations implementing their own IP management plans, and to societies seeking to promote the public interest through innovation.

SUMMARY. Transferring IP rights is part of implementing a strategic plan. IP transactions, like any other deals, involve agreement and an exchange of consideration. For IP assets, the consideration involves intangible rights and often a promise not to sue.

IP rights can be acquired by operation of law (as with an author's copyright), or by contract – by assignment, license, gift, or otherwise. The dynamics of acquiring, holding, and transferring ownership differ for each type of IP asset, and there are further differences based on the particular interests of the parties in each situation. In transferring trade secrets, confidentiality is required. For patents, rights must be transferred country by country. For copyright, a written agreement is generally required. When trademarks are transferred, the owner must have control over the quality of the goods or services. The reasons for an owner to license rights out to others include expanding the reach of an innovation into new markets, to obtain additional revenue or achieve social impacts. Disadvantages of licensing out include loss of control, dependency, a possible reduction in innovation, and the risk of creating a competitor. Despite the many differences, there are some common pivotal terms and conditions in IP transfer agreements. Noneconomic terms include the granting clause, degree of exclusivity, field of use, possibility of sublicensing and transfer, duration, geographical territory, allocation of rights in improvements, enforcement terms, and warranties. Economic terms depend on valuation calculations as discussed in Chapter 12, and include up front, milestone, royalty, and minimum payments. IP deals are part of strategic management, and negotiation should be approached in that light – with a plan and comprehensive knowledge about the subject of the deal and the broader environment. As in any negotiation, focusing on the desired outcome increases the chance of success. Making IP transactions simpler to complete will improve the performance of individual organizations trying to implement their plans, and will ultimately help the innovation cycle operate efficiently in society at large.

PART FOUR

STRATEGIES ON A GLOBAL STAGE

16 Organization-Specific Strategies

Having described the innovation cycle, the dynamics of the intellectual property system, and the steps of strategic management, the last part of the book addresses strategies on a global stage. This chapter illustrates how strategy tools and practices can be applied in different situations. First, we consider how IP management practices change with the growth stage of an organization, from start-up to large multinational corporations. Second, we review how IP management differs by industry and innovation community, including life sciences, electronics, consumer products, entertainment, and nonprofit research institutions, and public performances. Third, we summarize differences between the practices suitable for particular technologies – biological materials, electromechanical equipment, and software. A strategic approach leads to IP management practices specific to each of these situations.

$$* \quad * \quad * \quad * \quad * \quad *$$

DIFFERENT GROWTH STAGES

IP practices change with the age of an organization. Early on, organizations protect just a few key assets with IP rights, relying on informal protection where possible. A middle sized organization expands its portfolio. Later, the organization has several portfolios of patents, trademarks, trade secrets, and copyrights, and a specialized intellectual property team to manage them. As shown in Table 16.1, the basic tools described earlier are used to produce different results for early, mid-, and late stage companies.

A startup or emerging company tends to depend heavily on trade secrets rather than patents and typically takes the simplest, least expensive measures to protect its trade secrets, using employee confidentiality agreements and nondisclosure agreements with outsiders. It may have no patents, because of the cost of acquiring them. If there is a key technology, an early stage company may protect the most valuable aspects with just one or two broad patent applications that have not matured into patents. The organization uses simple copyright notices, without registration, and seeks to find one or two strong trademarks for the company name and lead product. There is no specialized IP management, and the CEO is the innovation chief and IP manager by default.

As the company grows to several dozen employees, with product revenues, its IP management practices typically grow as well. With trade secrets, the most valuable

Table 16.1. IP strategies change with the stage of an organization

Stage IP Type	Early	Mid	Late
Trade Secrets	Nondisclosure agreements, employment agreements	Document control	Diverse portfolio and special practices such as sequestering "crown jewels"
Patents	0–2 broad applications for key inventions	Expanding globally in relevant countries	Diverse portfolio in various technologies, with pioneering and improvement patents
Copyright	Notices/registration, assure title	Registrations	Licensing, enforcement
Trademark	1–2 on the company name, lead product, domain name	Expanding global family	Brand variations, renewals, new markets
IP Management	CEO	General counsel	IP counsel with team of professionals

ones are sequestered, and relevant documents are marked carefully. As for patents, the portfolio expands globally as pending applications are filed in foreign countries, and new applications are filed in the home country to cover improvements and new products. Key copyright works are registered and trademark registrations are obtained in the home country, with new variations and slogans being protected as well. Most organizations hire a general counsel by this time, and delegate the IP management task to that person. The general counsel often needs to rely on outside patent and trademark lawyers and consultants for specialized expertise in dealing with IP. The IP Chief may have numerous IP managers.

For larger companies with several hundred employees, practices begin to diversify widely between different industries. Special practices may be developed for trade secrets. The Coca-Cola Company claims that only two executives know the entire formula for the fabled soft drink, although skeptics believe that talk about the company's trade secret practices is more of a media stunt at this point, given the technical abilities of analytic chemists to do reverse engineering. The Guinness brewery advertises that it keeps a fresh reserve supply of its heirloom yeast locked in the director's safe in its headquarters in Dublin.

Patents are the dominant form of IP in the portfolios of many mature companies. A multinational corporation typically has a large portfolio with hundreds of patents and applications around the world, grouped into different families. There are also copyright registrations for important works, and a diverse array of trademarks for various products, services, and slogans, with logos evolving over time.

There are wide variations in these categories between industries, and between corporations and public organizations (as described in the next section). But the

Table 16.2. IP practices differ by industry

Industry IP Type	Life sciences (biotechnology, pharmaceuticals)	Electronics (computer, imaging, telecom)	Consumer products and services	Entertainment	Academia
Trade Secrets	Biological materials, formulations, collaborative agreements, business secrets	Circuits and, source code, business secrets	Market plans, internal systems, recipes, business secrets	Limited, except works in progress and business secrets	Very limited (imperative to publish)
Patents	Many, on basic research and specific products	Very many, on methods and hardware, some on software	Moderate, incremental, design patents	Few, underlying hardware and business methods	Moderate, basic research, early stage inventions, active licensing
Copyright	Databases, bioinformatics, publications	Software products licensed to users, instruction manuals	Packaging, ads, design features	Heavy use for content	Generally left to faculty
Trademark	Few strong marks	Many marks	Heavy, strongly advertised marks, trade dress, slogans, licensing	Characters and shows	Names of universities, researchers, and awards

general rule for all companies and nonprofit groups is that the size and complexity of IP portfolios and the sophistication of IP management increases with the size of the organization.

DIFFERENT INDUSTRIES AND SECTORS

As should be clear to any reader by now, there can be great differences in IP management practices in different industries and sectors. But some concepts remain the same, and people in one industry can learn from the different practices of others.

Several industries are highlighted in Table 16.2. They are, broadly considered, biotechnology, information technology, consumer products, entertainment, and academia (research universities). These five examples cover a range of scenarios in which IP is important.

Life sciences

Life science industries include medical and biotechnology and pharmaceutical companies. The industries are characterized by long term investments in research projects including laboratory research, clinical research for regulatory approval for medical products, and field tests in agriculture. A convergence of biology, information science, and materials technology is driving major technical innovations, and life sciences companies manage their IP aggressively.

Often the chief science or R&D officer is involved in managing IP and integrating it with the research agenda, along with an in-house and outside IP counsel. In pharmaceutical companies, IP management often centers on the battle between the innovator who first gains market approval from regulators, and follow-on generic competitors who seek to sell the same drugs for less, as discussed in Chapter 17.

Business trade secrets exist in all industries, including lists of customers and suppliers, and financial information. In the life science industries in particular, trade secrecy can protect biological materials such as genetic material, isolated animal cells, plant extracts, and microorganisms. Because of their unique biochemical characteristics, access to these materials is often crucial to be able to duplicate research or results. Biological materials are typically exchanged under a contract that limits how the recipient can use and disclose the materials, regardless of whether they are patentable. Some companies build their entire business model on supplying biological and other materials, such as the catalog companies – Sigma-Aldrich and others – and the nonprofit organizations American Type Culture Collection and U.S. Pharmacopeia. Trade secrets also apply for product formulations. There are many research collaborations in the life sciences, and so confidentiality agreements are crucial to protect trade secrets from disclosure.

Patents are crucial to the life science industries, particularly because most products have a long lead time requiring expensive research before there is a marketable product. Patents are ideally suited to protect large, long term investments. There tend to be fewer patents in the life science industry than in other industries, but they often encompass more subject matter than in the electronics or mechanical fields. The value of one or two patents on a blockbuster drug may be enormous. Ranbaxy recently challenged two Pfizer patents on LIPITOR, the world's top selling drug, and in a recent decision by the U.S. Court of Appeals, one patent was invalidated but the other upheld.[1] That one patent helps protect Pfizer's profit on $13 billion of annual sales. Novartis challenged the constitutionality of a section of the Indian patent law that was used to reject its patent application for a crystalline form of the leukemia drug Gleevec, facing a 2007 loss at the High Court and public outrage over the single patent application. In other industries, one single patent is rarely that significant.

Copyright is less important to the life science industries because biotechnology contains only limited amounts of creative written expression. Company reports and databases may be valuable and worth protecting, as are marketing materials and label designs.

Trademarks, too, are not as important as patents, because biotechnology companies tend to have a small number of products and the number of their trademarks tends not to be significant compared with consumer products. However, the value of one brand name may be enormous, such as Pfizer's LIPITOR. The names of the major pharmaceutical companies themselves are important trademarks, invaluable for distinguishing their products from generic versions. Trademarks on products are less important to generic pharmaceutical companies (which sell generic products), and yet the company names are increasingly important in global competition. The leading generic drug manufacturers seek to promote

---

[1] *Pfizer Inc. v. Ranbaxy Laboratories*, 457 F.3d 1284 (Fed. Cir. 2006).

themselves as more reliable than other companies that may have poorer quality control.

All legitimate drug manufacturers, innovators and generics, share a concern to block the rise of counterfeit drugs sold by illegitimate sources. Counterfeit drugs can kill, by being ineffective or toxic, and no company wants its brands associated with a patient's death due to counterfeit.

Electronics

Electronics companies (including computer, imaging, and telecommunications) have a shorter product development cycle than life sciences companies, and regulatory approval is rarely required before products can be sold on the market. This also makes it easier for competitors to enter a market. So IP management in electronics companies is market-driven.

Electronics companies tend to build and hold significant trade secrets in their electronic hardware and software. For example, circuit designs and software source code are generally maintained subject to trade secrets, except in an open-source system like Linux. Yet patents are the dominant IP right in this industry. According to statistics maintained by the Intellectual Property Owners organization, in 2002 the top 35 patent owners in the United States were mainly multinational electronics companies, with IBM, Hitachi, and Canon at the top of the list. (Automaker Honda and auto parts suppliers were also high on the list. In contrast, the top chemical and pharmaceutical manufacturers were way down the list, ranking at 36, 44, and 46, respectively, with about 400 new patents each.)

The availability of patent protection for software is uneven around the world, but where it is available it is very valuable, as with the *NTP v. RIM* Blackberry case. Copyright is well-suited to protecting software used in electronic products around the world, but has limited relevance to hardware. Of course, software piracy is a huge concern of software companies, and the existence of copyrights is no guarantee that they will be enforced.

Trademarks are also quite important in electronics companies. Many companies have strong brands protected worldwide by large international trademark portfolios. (Think of IBM, Sony, Hewlett-Packard, Canon, Intel, Microsoft, Texas Instruments, and so on).

Consumer products and services

The consumer product and service industry includes house wares, clothing, groceries, food and beverages, delivery services, hotels, restaurants, and some sectors of electronics. You find these products when you open your refrigerator, cabinets, and closets, or go shopping, or go out to a chain restaurant. Common features include rapid product development and integrated marketing, distribution, and sales efforts reaching a broad marketplace, coupled with fierce competition. IP management in consumer product companies may demand strong input from the marketing department. Rapid decisions may be required to protect rights or avoid infringing the rights of others.

One of the easiest ways to gain insights into IP management basics is by studying consumer product packaging and labels. Packaging will frequently refer to patent numbers, include copyright notices, and identify various words and logos as registered and unregistered trademarks. Trade secrets will not be visible on the label (of course), and are not often found in consumer products anyhow because of the ease of reverse engineering. However, trade secrets are important behind the scenes, in the methods used to make the products, in internal management systems, and in marketing plans. Patents can be important too, but because the innovations in consumer products are often less consequential than those in the life sciences and electronics, the patents may be narrow. This is the industry in which product design patents are most important.

Packaging, advertisements, and some product design features themselves can be subject to copyright protection, and may involve extensive licensing arrangements. Radio and television advertisements often use famous songs to reach consumers, for example, and such use requires a copyright license.

Trademarks are most important in the consumer products industry, which is characterized by creative marketing – the integrated use of all available channels of publicity, promotion, advertising, and distribution. Direct marketing and the Internet continue to increase opportunities for innovation in marketing. The launch of a new product generally includes selecting a trademark, making sure it is clear of infringement in all relevant markets, protecting the trademark, and launching the product. Franchises (think McDonald's) are based on the licensing of trademarks as well as trade secrets, patents, and copyright. Starbucks, in contrast, is a company that owns its stores, and therefore does not need to license its trademarks.

The lines between copyright, trademark, and design patents can become quite blurry when considering the configuration (shape) of a product, which may be functional, or artistic. This is a ripe area for litigation, as illustrated by three U.S. Supreme Court decisions. In 1954, the Supreme Court held that copyright can exist in a lamp base that was a statuette of a dancing figure.[2] More recently, the Supreme Court ruled that the configurations of a designer's line of children's dresses were not subject to trademark protection, and that my firm's client, Wal-Mart, was free to make similar products (using different names).[3] Copyright protection was not an issue before the court in the *Samara* decision. Finally, the court held that there was no trademark or trade dress right in the distinctive shape of traffic signs mounted on springs (to keep them from tipping over in the wind) because the configuration was functional, as evidenced by utility patents that had expired.[4] The lesson is that trade dress, product configuration, packaging, and labeling are rich areas for IP to protect, and also for challenging others who assert their rights.

There are intellectual property issues in memorable foods. Trade secrecy protects the best hot fudge sauce in the world (according to my family and friends), made at the Four Seas Ice Cream parlor in Cape Cod, Massachusetts. For years we tried to

[2] *Mazer v. Stein*, 347 U.S. 201 (1954).

[3] *Wal-Mart Stores, Inc. v. Samara Brothers, Inc.*, 529 U.S. 205 (2000).

[4] *Traffix Devices, Inc. v. Marketing Displays, Inc.* 532 U.S. 23 (2001).

reverse engineer the formula, asking the staff, looking at the containers of ingredients in the kitchen, and experimenting with different recipes, but with no success. The owner Dick Warren, published a fudge recipe in "The Complete Idiot's Guide to Home Made Ice Cream," but it was not the same fudge. So the Four Seas fudge recipe remains a trade secret, although, because it has been on sale, it is too late to patent it.[5]

Entertainment industry

The entertainment industry includes all of the creators, producers, and administrators of recreations intended to amuse people and occupy their leisure time. It includes both for profit and nonprofit organizations in the performing arts, sports, movies, music recordings, publishing, television and radio broadcasting, video and computer games, theme parks, casinos, art museums, and increasingly, Internet websites. IP managers in all these enterprises can exert control over the experience of their audiences, to widen their reach and/or improve their financial performance.

Here, the emphasis is on public displays, not secrets, and so trade secrecy would seem to be of little importance. In Hollywood, Bollywood (the film industry in India, the largest in the world in numbers of feature-length films produced), Nollywood (Nigeria) and in the Chinese cinemas based in Hong Kong or Xian, it is hard to keep the latest big movie concept pitch from the public eye and in fact early publicity preparing the way for the film's release depends on "leaked" stories about the film. But confidential financial information is always important.

Also, many innovations in entertainment – new movies, new television shows, or new theme parks – begin as confidential concept proposals, which can be extremely valuable. In the 1990s, a baseball umpire and an architect designed a fantasy sports theme park and disclosed it to Walt Disney Co. under a confidentiality agreement. Disney turned down the proposal, but went ahead and built its Wide World of Sports theme park in Florida anyway. In 2000, a jury found Disney liable for misappropriating the proposal and ordered Disney to pay the umpire and architect damages of $240 million. According to SEC filings, Disney settled the case in 2002, for an undisclosed sum.

Patents do not apply to the content produced by artists and entertainment organizations. However, the media involve technology-rich hardware, and there are many patents on recording, editing, duplication, transmittal, and display equipment and devices. A string of patented innovations may link a singer's voice to the digital recording to the listener's loudspeaker. Video games are also increasingly subject to patent disputes. And business method patents can cover entertainment business models, especially those with an electronic component, both in the U.S. and other countries.

---

[5] Perhaps patent issues arise in the bizarre ice cream concoctions I have sampled at other restaurants over the years – olive oil ice cream, balsamic vinegar ice cream, mustard ice cream, and even lobster ice cream, loaded with frozen chunks of the crustacean. One could combine those four recipes to produce a seafood salad ice cream, but if that is patentable, I hereby dedicate the invention to the public!

Copyrights, of course, are tailor-made for the content-rich entertainment industry. Copyright does not attach to creative ideas themselves but to their expression in a tangible medium – to recordings, movies, and publications, to game software or paintings. In the context of the innovation cycle, an artist's creative idea is not subject to copyright protection (although it may be a secret). But once recorded, the idea can become distributed and adopted broadly in society.

The principle value of an entertainment-based organization may be in its copyright portfolio – its library of music recordings, movies, television shows, or books. Entertainment organizations are wise to dedicate much of their attention to enforcing and licensing their copyrights, as described in Chapter 14.

Copyright and star power can make a potent IP mix, as David Bowie showed in 1997, when he made financial history by working with entrepreneur David Pullman to sell $55 million in bonds backed by future royalties in his 25 record albums. (See Chapter 17.) Since then, many musicians have used this technique to turn IP assets into liquid securities, turning future revenue into present day cash.

IP law and practice shapes the availability of entertainment in many ways, both in for profit and nonprofit organizations, and in developing countries. In the current paradigm, recording artists sell their copyright to a major recording company, which in turn burns discs, and sells them to distributors, who sell them to retailers, and ultimately to consumers. The record company pays the artist a royalty, which may be shared with studio musicians and a manager. The record company also pays the music's author (if different from the recording artist) to license the song, and pays the cost of producing, manufacturing, and distributing the recording.

Alternatively, in a model increasingly common with independent musicians, the recording artist steps into the foreground, retaining copyright, making independent recordings, and distributing the music independently on the Internet. The artist sells directly to the market, and keeps the net profit after paying a royalty to the music's author, and a fee to session musicians, producer, and distributors. With this model, piracy causes a direct loss to the artists, whether in rich or poor countries. For example, piracy in Trinidad and Tobago was estimated to cost local musicians $3 million in 1997.[6]

The technology for duplicating and distributing digital music, and now video, via computer has caused almost uncontrollable proliferation worldwide, leading to displacement in the entertainment business. As happened before with vinyl recordings, audiotape recorders, videotape recorders, and compact disc burners, Internet file swapping has forced new forms of marketing and distribution into existence. Audiences will still pay for convenient access to a work, and for live concerts by the more famous of their creators, so artists can still benefit from their creations. IP laws are reformed to catch up with technological change. For example, Article 11 of the 1996 WIPO Copyright Treaty calls for legal remedies against the circumvention of technical measures used to prevent unauthorized access and copying. Implementing

---

[6] Vanus James (ed.). "The Caribbean Music Industry Database (CMID)," Report Prepared for The United Nations Conference on Trade and Development (UNCTAD) and World Intellectual Property Organization (WIPO, 2000), p. 27, available at http://www.wipo.int/about-ip/en/studies/pdf/study_v_james.pdf, accessed December 28, 2006.

laws, such as the U.S. Digital Millennium Copyright Act of 1998, make it illegal to hack through the encryption that prevents a listener from playing an iTune recording on any MP3 player other than an iPod.

Recording artists and music labels, movie actors and studios, authors and publishers can each have strong trademark rights. Likewise, trademarks can attach to characters and shows. The Superman and Spiderman characters are trademarks of their publishers, DC and Marvel comics, respectively, and those trademark rights apply to all of their derivative books and movies. The trademark rights coexist with copyright.

For example, Superman's teenage creators Joe Shuster and Jerry Siegel sold their rights for $130 during the 1930s, and later became paupers, while Superman enjoyed success in comic books and on television. When the 1978 hit Superman movie came out Siegel began a publicity campaign about the creators' plight, and the Warner company ultimately gave them modest lifetime pensions and acknowledgment as Superman's creators. Both men died in the 1990s. Siegel's heirs continue legal battles to repossess copyright, and have been awarded partial ownership of the copyright to Superboy.[7] But the publisher still owns the Superman trademark and many derivative rights and after almost 70 years, absent a settlement, it could take continued litigation to sort out who controls which rights.

Nonprofit research institutions

Universities, nonprofit research institutions, and government research agencies have learned to use intellectual property to further their missions. Rather than making profit for shareholders, the goals of these organizations involve expanding knowledge, improving access to it, and helping society reap the benefits. Accordingly, the IP management of such organizations should, and does, differ from that of profit-making corporations.

Generally, in nonprofits, IP management is handled by a technology transfer and licensing office, which may be located in the general counsel's office but is often linked with the institution's management of research grants. These offices are staffed by professionals with scientific, business, and/or legal educations.

University and nonprofit researchers in the sciences and humanities can create as many innovations as researchers in for-profit ventures, but rather than pooling them and channeling them into commercial products, the approach is generally to publish and spread what they have learned, to add it to the accessible domain of knowledge directly without maintaining any of it as a long-term secret. Nonprofit organizations do of course maintain trade secrets in their admissions records and the usual financial information.

Academic research results are often kept secret long enough for patent applications to be filed first. Since the passage of the Bayh-Dole Act in 1980, U.S. universities have actively obtained and licensed many patents (with my firm's client the

[7] Robert Vosper, "The Woman of Steel," Inside Counsel.com, available at http://www.insidecounsel.com/issues/insidecounsel/15_159/profiles/191-1.html.

University of California at the top of the list). They also maintain strong trademarks in their names and logos, and license them.

Because of their public mission and public scrutiny, universities tend to be more open about their IP assets and management practices than for profit industries. According to the 2004 Association of University Technology Managers Licensing Survey, 195 U.S. university respondents handled a total of over 16,000 invention disclosures, filed over 10,000 patent applications, and received over 3600 issued patents. These numbers are over double what they were a decade before. Responding universities issued almost 4000 licenses, and 32 hospitals issued more than 600 licenses, with total revenue of almost $1.4 billion. Canadian institutions had smaller but still active patenting and licensing programs. Some government agencies, such as the US National Institutes of Health, also build patent portfolios and license them out. IP management is very important in the funding of these nonprofit organizations, and more importantly, in managing external relations of faculty members with industry researchers.

Despite the impression given by such huge numbers, universities and research centers continue to place a priority on publishing over secrecy, in contrast to industry. According to a survey by the American Academy for the Advancement of Science, 44 percent of industry respondents reported choosing not to publish their work, compared to only 6 percent for academic scientists.[8] Interestingly, for both groups, the primary reason for publishing was to disseminate their results, with prestige and timeliness being secondary. The survey documented the increasing use of open access journals.

The drive to publish is not necessarily inconsistent with patenting, but can lead to emergency patent filings on occasion. A university or government research agency client may call patent counsel at the last minute to announce that a faculty member is about to publish a paper or deliver a speech on a valuable invention. The general approach such clients adopt is not to delay the publication or speech but to file a patent application immediately, before publication or on the same day, to preserve its patent rights. A provisional application might be prepared in such a case in a matter of hours, rather than the more typical one to two months.

Academic freedom is a topic that comes up in patenting decisions. Faculty members usually have a high degree of control and choice over whether to file a patent application, because their IP managers do not like to proceed unless the faculty member will take the lead. Because U.S. faculty members typically earn 25 percent to 50 percent of any licensing revenues, they have a strong motivation to participate in the patenting process. Ironically, the individual incentives for academic researchers to pursue patent protection are even greater than in industry because corporate employees typically receive no direct financial stake in their inventions.

The numbers of patents and licenses are lower in most foreign universities. In some, innovation is not as rapid. In many countries universities are not entitled to own the inventions of faculty, and so arrangements to allocate faculty inventor rights

[8] "Effects of intellectual property protections on the conduct of scientific research," Project on Science and Intellectual Property in the Public Interest (SIPPI), available at http://sippi.aaas.org/Symposium_US/Symposium_Brief.pdf, accessed January 28, 2007.

are made as circumstances arise. In one project I handled, a university in Thailand agreed to a 50/50 co-ownership arrangement with the faculty member inventor of an agricultural technology.

Copyrights can be important to faculty, who retain title to their own works according to the policies of most universities. This applies to books as well as software.

Trademarks are important in protecting the name of a university. Licensing the trademarks for use on merchandise such as clothing can be a very big business, given the popularity of university names and emblems. Strong trademarks can also help other nonprofit organizations distinguish themselves in their communities. The Smithsonian Institution has a very active trademark licensing program intended to help build recognition for the organization and its mission. Weak trademarks of relatively unknown institutions do not have this advantage.

Nonprofit pharmaceutical companies, otherwise known as product development partnerships (PDPs), have proliferated since 2000. They are a new type of hybrid organization with characteristics both of a pharmaceutical company and a research institution. They are public-private partnerships. A PDP may establish a vertically integrated virtual network to conduct basic research, product development, and clinical research, to gain regulatory approval, to manufacture, and to distribute drugs that would not be otherwise available. They focus on so-called neglected diseases that affect millions of people in developing countries but that do not receive much research investment by profit-making pharmaceutical companies.

For example, the Institute for One World Health focuses on leishmaniasis and other diseases, and Aeras Foundation focuses on tuberculosis. PDPs build their IP portfolios both by in-house research, and by acquiring rights in patented inventions from others, by donation or otherwise.

The Bill & Melinda Gates Foundation has become a major force in imagining, proposing, shaping, funding, and following up with PDPs and other models for nonprofit healthcare innovation. The BMGF Global Health Program is charting the new field of venture philanthropy, creating synergies in the discovery and delivery of new diagnostics, vaccines, and therapies for neglected diseases. These models use novel IP management approaches to harness innovation both in nonprofit and for profit organizations, such as commitments for sharing information and materials, and to make inventions available in developing countries, whether they are patented or not. Combining access and exclusivity can drive the innovation cycle for neglected diseases.

Public performances and IP

Theater companies, symphony orchestras, dance troupes, music bands, comedians, and political parties are nonprofit creative communities in which IP shapes innovation in ways beyond financial incentives. Each strengthens our cultural backbone through live performances. At first glance, it is hard to see how performances are susceptible to IP protection. On closer inspection, intellectual property plays a crucial role in supporting and shaping the innovation cycle in theater, music, dance, and speeches.

Theater is largely a nonprofit activity in the US, with local and regional theaters run by nonprofit troupes, and only a few of the biggest Broadway theaters being run for profit (many of them at a loss). Market economy profit is not the prime motive for most playwrights, producers, directors, and actors. There is a steady stream of new plays, in addition to the out-of-copyright classics (Shakespeare, in particular). Playwrights create new plays either to "hold a mirror to society," to engage in a cathartic act of self-expression, or because they just enjoy the creative act. Some try to entertain the audience, some try to communicate a message, some try to change the way people perceive their world. But copyright is crucial to making the system work properly. Although they are usually eager to have their plays staged, copyright gives authors the control necessary to choose which theater will produce their work. Authors with more successful plays, dealing with larger regional theaters, may agree to limit productions so multiple productions of the same play do not compete within a given region. Playwrights can prevent their work from being performed without their permission, or from being rewritten or produced in a way that would conflict with their original artistic purposes. Playwrights can also retain the right to make a movie or television productions, for the exceptional play that makes it that far.[9]

Trademark also plays a role in theater. Theater companies are well known by their names, which serve as trademarks. Many theater-goers will trust the selection, production, direction, and acting talents of their local company, and will attend plays based on the reputation of the company as much as the playwright.

If there was no IP control over plays, chaos would result, and the innovation cycle would be blocked. The original creative purposes of the playwrights would be thwarted. Fewer playwrights would make the effort to write plays, not just because there would be less money, but because they would be frustrated in their purpose of controlling their art. The possibility of expanding the number of productions of a given play would diminish. Fewer plays would be written and produced, and fewer theater companies would survive.

The innovation cycle for symphony orchestras is slightly different. While new pieces continue to be written, much of the repertoire is older music, generally in the public domain and readily available. With such works, creativity is found in the expression of the musicians bringing such pieces to the modern audience, with the interpretation of their conductor.

Copyright protection in a work of creative expression requires that it must be fixed in a tangible medium. This presents special challenges for performing artists. Actors memorize lines, musicians memorize their scores, dancers memorize their moves, and public speakers may speak from notes.

A symphony may broadcast its performance on radio, or make a sound recording, which helps fulfill the nonprofit mission of reaching more listeners. However, orchestra members continue to debate whether such recordings should be distributed freely in an open access model, distributed directly via Internet web sites, or subject to conventional terms of purchase and payment.[10] The same issue confronts popular musicians. They now have the option of touring with mobile recording units (such

---

[9] Personal communication from Mark Lerman, producer/director of 140 productions at the Perishable Theatre in Providence Rhode Island.

[10] Personal communication from Daniel Armstrong, bassist with the Chicago Symphony Orchestra.

as DiscLive and Real Image Recording) that can mix, master, copy, and package CDs to sell to concertgoers as they leave a concert as well as those who were not able to attend. By fixing the concert in a digital medium, the performers are able to assert copyright over their creative expressions.

Symphony conductors, like theater directors, have no easy way to protect their creative role in staging performances. Few IP rights attach to live performances. In the dance world, the U.S. 1976 Copyright Act allows protection for choreography. This law shifted the balance for later works from the public to the private domain, and has been valuable for famous names like George Balanchine.[11] Play directors and symphony conductors have no analogous rights. However, like other celebrities, the successful ones may have high value associated with their names, which can serve as trademarks both for them and the organizations with which they are associated.

Comedians have taken note of IP management. At Edinburgh's Fringe Festival in 2006, classes were given on how to stop jokes from being stolen by rivals. One piece of advice was to insert a copyright notice on written copies of whatever is performed. But written copies of jokes make it easier for those not present to learn and tell them.

IP issues affect political figures giving public speeches. In 1963, Martin Luther King, Jr. delivered his famous "I have a dream" speech to a huge crowd at the Lincoln Memorial in Washington, DC. King's speech was recorded and he later registered copyright in the speech. CBS News later claimed that the speech was in the public domain and could be freely reproduced and rebroadcast. However, almost 40 years later, a court ruled that there was a valid copyright in the speech, so the estate was entitled to restrict broadcast of recordings of the speech.[12]

Public office holders are generally not permitted to assert copyright of their speeches. Candidates for public office may assert copyright for their speeches for example at political conventions, but they usually do not (perhaps because so many political speeches are so dull!). US copyright records include several registrations for reports and speeches by UN Secretary General Kofi Annan, Senator Edward Kennedy, and former Cardinal Ratzinger, now Pope Benedict XVI. Journalistic use of political speeches is generally permissible under doctrines of fair use. However, the copyright owner can restrict printing and sale in commerce.

DIFFERENT TECHNOLOGIES

Many different types of technology converge in the individual industries discussed above. Life sciences companies use biological materials, electronics, and computer software, as well as data, mechanical devices and special materials such as nanotechnology. Electronics companies use hardware and software, data, and special materials, and they may use creative media content as well (e.g., sounds and images). Consumer products and services companies employ a wide range of machines,

---

[11] Joi Michelle Lakes, "A Pas de Deux for Choreography and Copyright," *New York University Law Review*, 80:1829 (2005).

[12] *Estate of Martin Luther King, Jr., Inc. v. CBS, Inc.*, 194 F.3d 1211 (11th Cir. 1999).

Table 16.3. IP practices for different technologies

Technology IP type	Biological materials	Electromechanical equipment	Software
Trade Secrets	Unique genetic and chemical information accessible only from particular material	Only if components can be hidden by technical means ("black box")	Source code
Patents	If manipulated to be new, not "natural"	Readily available	Technical effects can be claimed in most countries
Copyright	No	No	Readily available
Trademark	Not much used	Yes	Yes
Other IP	Material transfer agreements	Leasing	EULA, open source licenses

materials, electronic parts, and, for food and cosmetics, biological materials – vegetable oils, proteins, starches, nutrients, and other extracts, additives and chemicals obtained from plants, animals, and microbes. Academic research relates to every technology and creative sector, from nanotechnology to poetry.

There are certain common issues that arise when managing IP for each type of technology, and these IP management approaches transcend industries. For example, the types of IP available for protecting software are largely the same for a biotechnology company, a computer company, a recording studio, or a university.

The following discussion provides a few highlights about the types of IP protection available for biological materials, electromechanical equipment, and software. (See Table 16.3.) These ideas illustrate the concepts of access and exclusivity, and suggest how an IP manager can design a strategy suited to a particular organization, based on the types of innovation it produces.

Biological materials

Biological materials are susceptible to strong protection with trade secrecy and patents. Trade secrecy can be used to maintain exclusivity over methods of processing biological materials. It can also be used for innovative biological materials when the material itself is required to gain access to the innovation. Making plant-based medicines typically requires access to the plant itself, to prepare an active extract, although many compounds can be made by synthetic organic chemistry, and more will be possible with synthetic biology. In agriculture, a published description of a new plant variety does not permit other people to propagate the plant unless they gain physical access to it. With access, it becomes possible to grow unlimited numbers of the plant. The plant itself embodies a form of trade secrecy. Likewise, with microbes, a published report that a particular bacterial strain produces a useful new antibiotic does not enable anyone to produce the antibiotic without access to a sample of the bacteria.

Until recently the same was true for DNA sequences as for plants and microbes. That is, a biological sample was required to make use of the DNA contained in it, and publishing a sequence for a particular gene did not make it publicly available for reproduction. As of 2005, however, synthetic biology had advanced to the point that scientists using chemical techniques could routinely synthesize gene-sized DNA sequences hundreds of bases long, virus-sized sequences thousands of bases long (e.g., the 1918 human influenza virus). Thus, due to technical innovation, publishing a genetic sequence now makes the gene itself available to the public. The only option for protecting such a sequence is to keep it completely secret (not common in the culture of open publication of DNA sequences) or else to patent it. As this example shows, the innovation cycle has progressed from Watson and Crick's discovery of the TCAG "alphabet" of life found in the coding structure of DNA, to the ability to efficiently "read" the entire genomic sequences of humans and other organisms, to the ability to "write" increasingly larger sequences of DNA. Craig Venter's team announced in 2007 that they had successfully transplanted a genome into a bacteria, and would soon use the technique to insert a synthetic chromosome, designed and "written" entirely from its nucleotide bases. This research is being conducted by Venter's Institute and his company, Synthetic Genomics, Inc.[13]

Biological materials are well suited to patenting, provided they meet the legal standards in various countries. First, to be patentable, a material must be new, in the sense that it is different from what occurs naturally without human intervention. Examples include a plant extract, an isolated bacterial cell, an isolated human gene, and a recombinant organism in which new genetic material was inserted. An invention must also be different from other similar man-made materials.

Second, there must be an inventive step over prior materials, such that the differences are nonobvious. Third, the material must be adequately described so that others can have access to it. In particular, most patent laws require inventors of patents involving microorganisms to provide a sample of the biological material necessary to practice the invention to a publicly accessible depository, which serve as gene banks. Several dozen such depositories are recognized for international patenting under the 1977 Budapest Treaty on the International Recognition of the Deposit of Microorganisms for the Purposes of Patent Procedure. Fourth, the claims must be written in a definite manner so it is clear what they encompass, such as "a DNA molecule having the following sequence . . . ."

Finally, the biological materials must also fall within one of the categories of patentable subject matter under national laws consistent with the international TRIPS Agreement. (See Appendix A.) According to TRIPS Article 27(3)(b), extracts of plants and animals, including genetic material, are patentable in all TRIPS countries, as are microorganisms. Plants may either be patented or subject to a form of *sui generis* plant variety protection. Animals may or may not be patentable.

Also, inventions which are contrary to *ordre public* or morality can be excluded from patentability under TRIPS Article 27(2). IP rights in some biological materials are more controversial on moral as well as scientific and legal grounds. Generally, the hierarchy of moral controversy is as follows:

---

[13] J. Craig Venter, *A Life Decoded: My Genome, My Life* (Viking Penguin 2007), pp. 353–357.

- Extracts are less controversial than whole organisms.
- Nonreplicating materials like small chemicals are less controversial than replicating materials like DNA or microbes.
- Plants are less controversial than animals.
- Nonhuman animals are less controversial than human materials.

Patentability of biological materials is least controversial for small molecules isolated from plants. At the other extreme, all countries, including the United States, have explicitly prohibited patents on "Frankenstein's monsters," genetically engineered or surgically modified humans.

Historically, copyright has been inapplicable to biological materials. Because they are objects and not symbolic constructs, biological materials have offered no possibility of expressing an idea in a tangible medium of expression. However, synthetic biology may be changing that rule. Students in Drew Endy's International Genetically Engineered Machines competition at Massachusetts Institute of Technology have produced biological cameras in which a crude photographic image is recorded on a bacterial Petri dish. The photosensitive material is not silver on a plastic film or a light sensitive digital sensor, but rather a specially engineered bacterial culture that reacts to light by changing its growth pattern. A bio-photo could be protected by copyright. Intriguingly, there is also the possibility that copyright might extend to novel DNA sequences written and synthesized by scientists, if different from those in nature, just as copyright applies to software code.

Commercial products based on biological materials are subject to conventional trademark principles. However, there are special nuances, for example with naming new plant varieties. A plant breeder who develops a new plant variety can choose its name when registering the variety with an international authority. That name cannot serve as a trademark, but rather is regarded as a generic description of the variety, so that anyone growing or selling that variety must call it by that name. A different name must be selected to serve as a trademark – such as the name of the breeding company.

Finally, other forms of quasi-IP apply to biological materials. The owner of biological material (a cell, a plant, or an extract) holds a combination of tangible property rights (like owning a potted houseplant), and trade secrets (information about the material, like where it came from, how to cultivate it, and what to do with it). There may also be national sovereign rights in genetic resources under the Convention on Biological Diversity. When the owner of biological materials wants to give them to someone else, the transfer typically takes place under a material transfer agreement (MTA). When the transfer takes place from within one country to a researcher in another country, an MTA providing access to the material typically requires the sharing of any benefits that result from the transfer. This type of transfer of biological material is generally referred to as an access and benefit sharing (ABS) agreement.

Electromechanical equipment

It is relatively straightforward to apply IP rights to electromechanical devices, including electronic components (in computers and cell phones), robotic devices used in manufacturing and research, and larger counterparts such as automobiles and airplanes. Methods of making such equipment can be kept secret, as can their design and use, if access is restricted. For publicly available products, the circuitry and design of electronic circuits can often be readily reverse engineered by competitors. However, manufacturers have devised ways to conceal components within a "black box" that can not easily be reverse engineered because it is built in such a way that a competitor can not identify the circuits or components.

Patents apply well to electrical and mechanical equipment, compared to biological material, because none of these devices exist in nature in any form and they are all, inevitably, human-made. Patenting mechanical devices goes back over 500 years to the Venetian patent law of 1474, so the principles are well established. The companies who hold the most patents all make electronic hardware, and there are more patents in this field than in others.

Copyright does not apply to functional mechanical or electronic devices themselves, but it can apply to information encoded in memory chips. This is discussed below under software.

A special form of IP protection was created in the 1980s to prevent reverse engineering and copying of integrated circuits, the microscopic electronic components laid out by photolithography on a silicon wafer. An innovator can register such designs, and obtain copyright-like protection. See TRIPS Agreement, Articles 35–38. Such protection has not been used much, presumably because the threat it addressed can be met in other ways. Chip makers tend to use patent protection instead. This is an example of an innovation in IP law that was not very successful.

Finally, trademark rights are well suited to electrical and mechanical devices. Finished products typically bear the trademark of the company marketing them, either well known or an "off" brand. Often the marketing companies also design the product, but not necessarily. The components within a product are often branded with the mark of the different manufacturers that supply those components to the company that assembles and markets them. The consumer typically looks first to the brand of the marketer for quality assurance, and secondly to the component manufacturer. There are exceptions. Many people are comfortable buying computers from less well known companies, so long as the components are from major suppliers, as reflected for example in the "Intel Inside" logo for processors.

As to licensing, device makers implicitly give a license to all IP rights when they sell a product, under the first sale doctrine. It is possible to avoid that loss of rights, either by placing explicit terms in the sales agreement, restricting access to the underlying copyright, trade secrets, and patent rights, or by leasing the equipment with such restrictions.

Software

Software *object code* (the digital electronic commands used to run a computer) can in principle be protected as a trade secret by use of confidentiality agreements. A mass manufacturer will not pursue a confidentiality approach with consumers, but this approach can work for small volume specialty software, like that used in laboratories and factories. Software *source code* (the logical instructions written by a human in a programming language) is not immediately apparent from object code, and so it can be kept as a trade secret, and often is. Data can also be kept secret by restricting access to it.

Software can be patented to different degrees in the United States, Europe, and other countries. The digital bits encoded in computer readable memory (like a CD or hard drive) are not patentable per se, but what these bits tell the computer to do can be patented. Software inventions can often be summarized in a flow chart showing the steps of entering data into a programmable device, processing that data, and displaying or outputting data from the device. The steps shown in such a flow chart could be patentable, but they are not protectable with copyright.

U.S. courts have liberalized the definition of patentable subject matter to encompass computer programs used in industrial processes, and also computers with programs running on them, and programs as data structures on computer readable media necessary to operate computers, such as hard drives or memory cards. The trend toward expanding patent protection for software is controversial and is not universal. Amazon.com's 1-click patent on a method of concluding an online purchase by clicking on a single icon was upheld in the United States but rejected in the EPO, and has been the subject of boycotts and criticism.

In Europe, an invention is patentable if it provides a new and nonobvious technical solution to a technical problem. Computer programs as such are not patentable subject matter, but patents are granted for programs in terms of their technical effect, such as how they make the computer operate ("a method for displaying X, Y, and Z on a computer screen"). Business methods without a technical effect are not patentable. In the United States, the *State Street* decision[14] opened the door for patents on business methods provided they produce a useful, concrete, and tangible result. Most business methods are embodied in computer programs that can satisfy the test in the USPTO. Drafting patent claims that satisfy such legal requirements is a highly specialized skill.

Copyright applies readily to software – to both object code and source code, no matter how published – hard drive, CD, or website. Data itself can not be protected by copyright, but may be subject to database protection in Europe. Copyright on software makes duplication illegal, but does not prevent someone else from writing a new program to do the same thing, although software patents can restrict such new programs.

The ease with which anyone can copy digital information perfectly, repeatedly, and inexpensively, puts great pressure on copyright enforcement mechanisms worldwide. There is a saying that only one licensed copy of software is sold in many countries, all the other bootleg copies being made from that one legitimate copy. Problems with software copyright infringement underlie many of the international controversies over piracy and enforcement. Likewise, popular music has a history of being duplicated without authorization, first via tapes, now with digital recording media and over the Internet.

Trademarks are quite appropriate for software programs. For example, a video game company may obtain all the following types of IP protection: trademark

---

[14] *State Street Bank & Trust Company v. Signature Financial Group, Inc.*, 149 F.3d 1368 (Fed. Cir. 1998).

registration on the game's title and fanciful characters or locations; copyright on the program as stored on a memory card, as a literary and a visual work; trade secrecy for the source code; and patents on methods for running the game and for the controllers. An infringer that sells duplicate copies of the program would infringe all these types of IP rights, and would be subject to damages under each one.

A typical approach to commercializing software is an end user license agreement, or EULA. EULAs are presented to the user when loading or running a new computer program or downloading material from a website. A EULA is a form of blanket license where the IP right owner offers a license to anyone who wants it. By clicking "I agree" or "I accept" we have all entered into numerous EULAs, generally without troubling to read what their terms are. As a general matter, EULAs restrict the user's right to duplicate the program, to modify it, to export it, or perform various other acts which would be authorized only by an outright sale. Another approach is an open source license, discussed elsewhere.

SUMMARY. This chapter provides examples of how the tools and practices of IP strategy are used in different organizations and situations, from start-ups to mature corporations, and including the life sciences, communications, consumer products, and entertainment industries, nonprofit research institutions, and in the arts – public performances of music, drama, and dance, and by extension in all creative human endeavors. The specific IP management strategies differ in each situation. The final portion summarizes differences between the practices suitable for particular technologies – biological materials, electromechanical equipment, and software. The many examples help show people how to put intellectual property to work in their own organizations to achieve their goals, and how to analyze IP management in other organizations.

17 A Comparison of National Intellectual Property Systems

This chapter turns to national IP laws, focusing on differences as opposed to the many similarities and trends toward convergence under the TRIPS agreement. The differences relate to language, standards for obtaining patents and trademarks, intensity of patenting activity, negotiation, litigation and enforcement, alternate dispute resolution, criminal liability, the extent of counterfeiting and piracy, compulsory licensing, and other limits on enforcement. A brief tour highlights some of the IP systems in particular countries. The United States, Europe, and Japan have the strongest, oldest IP systems, with the regional character of the European countries adding a layer of complexity. The BRIC countries (Brazil, Russia, India, and China) share some similarities as their economies grow rapidly and the IP systems struggle to keep up with rampant infringement. China and Korea have jumped into the top tier of patent and trademark activity. The least developed countries present a unique set of practices, with IP rights difficult to protect, and local innovation at a lower level than more affluent countries. IP strategies need to take into consideration these different legal systems.

* * * * * *

SIMILARITIES AND DIFFERENCES AMONG NATIONS

The TRIPS agreement has led to significant convergence of national IP laws and the establishment of an international IP regime whose fundamental principles apply worldwide. Yet significant differences remain. Each country has the sovereign right and responsibility, subject to the TRIPS agreement and other international agreements, to promulgate IP laws that fit within its legal history and suit the needs of its citizens. Consequently IP laws and practices differ in narrow but significant ways from country to country, and national IP laws are dynamic, changing constantly at least in subtle ways. National IP systems, and the practices followed by individual organizations operating within them, will inevitably remain diverse as countries pursue their own national goals. Such diversity can be viewed as a manifestation of sovereign and individual choice and freedom. Whether one favors greater harmonization or diversity in IP laws, anyone dealing with innovation should recognize that legislative autonomy in the many different countries of the world leads to differences and changes in IP laws and practices. These differences add complexity to the task of managing IP rights worldwide.

The general strategies and good practices for managing intellectual property – protecting and accessing innovations, obtaining, transferring, and enforcing rights – are similar in most of the world. First, most people (individuals, corporations, nongovernmental organizations, and governments) seek to protect their innovations, and to control the dissemination of their products out into the world, using the legal tools available to them. Corporations expend great efforts to use the exclusive rights conveyed by IP laws to control their valuable products, technology, brands, and domain names, allowing customers access, but restricting competitors. Because of the TRIPS Agreement, increasingly, the statutory options for protecting IP rights in innovations are similar in the most advanced countries (such as the United States, Europe, Japan), and the intermediate countries (such as India, China, Brazil, and Russia). IP-rich countries use international diplomacy to pressure IP-poor countries to enforce IP rights more strongly.

Second, individuals, organizations, and countries seek to obtain access to innovations and products of others that are protected by IP rights. Corporations may take licenses or sue to invalidate patents. Individuals may download unlicensed files on the assumption their use is fair, or they will not be caught. Some nonprofit organizations try to take advantage of safe harbors such as fair use and research exceptions. Some developing countries use compulsory licensing proceedings to obtain access to essential medicines.

Meanwhile certain important specifics vary from country to country. In the poorer nations the TRIPS Agreement has not been fully implemented, not all types of IP protection are available, and enforcement is difficult or impossible. The numerous remaining differences in the specific details of IP laws and practices in each country can be confirmed by even a casual glance at a multivolume compendium of national intellectual property laws such as *World Intellectual Property Rights and Remedies*.[1]

In addition to the country-by-country differences in IP laws, there are very different patterns of innovation in science, technology, and cultural activities, due to differences in education, economic markets, and political and judicial systems. Education and expertise are high in the wealthier countries, are growing in expanding economies, and are lacking in poor countries. Consequently, specific approaches to managing intellectual property can vary widely depending on the countries involved. All these national differences make it challenging to generalize about IP strategies, but it is important to do so, to extract fundamental principles that hold true around the globe, meanwhile identifying which IP laws and practices vary the most.

The basics for protecting innovations with IP rights were laid out in Chapters 1 and 14, and these are generally true in most countries. Copyright, trademarks, patents, and trade secrets can be protected to some extent in almost every country. Most countries have means for enforcing intellectual property rights against infringers, but private enforcement may be inadequate, government enforcement may be lacking, and the courts may be overwhelmed or otherwise slow in dealing with civil actions. Some of the areas that differ most, country to country, include the following:

---

[1] Dennis Campbell (ed.), *World Intellectual Property Rights and Remedies* (Oceana Publications, 1999).

Language. Most countries require patent and trademark applications, and lawsuits, to be presented in the national language. As with any international business dealings, translations can add cost, delay, and confusion.

Standards for obtaining patents. The TRIPS Agreement established some consistency between countries, but there is no international patent, and there are many specific but important differences between countries. It requires consultation with experts in each country to determine how any particular application will be handled. But as a general strategy, in order to protect an invention with national patents in the countries with largest markets, an inventor should prepare an application that complies with the strictest rules that apply in *any* of those countries. Here are some examples:

- The United States requires inventors to describe the "best mode" of carrying out the invention, and so foreign applicants seeking a U.S. patent have learned to include information about the best mode in applications filed in their countries, too, even though it is not required there.
- The U.S. requires inventors to submit an information disclosure statement listing any prior art they are aware of, and so this too has become a de facto international standard.
- The United States, Japan, and Australia allow informal provisional patent applications, but they only protect what is described and so most practitioners try to make even provisional applications as complete as possible.
- Prior publication of an invention destroys patentability immediately in most countries, so most applicants file an application before any publication, even though there is a one-year grace period in the United States and in other countries.
- Different types of publications and activities constitute prior art in different countries. In particular, countries with a one-year grace period do not consider publications within that year to be prior art. Although patentability is determined country by country, it is best to focus on inventive subject matter that is patentable in view of all prior art, globally.
- The European Patent Office (EPO) requires applicants to disclose aspects of an invention with more specificity than in the United States, for example, with regard to the technical character of a software invention, and specific examples of pharmaceutical formulations, so that careful applicants from other countries write their applications with EPO standards in mind.
- Most countries require strict examination of patent applications to ensure they comply with the substantive requirements of patentability. Others, like South Africa, grant patents with minimal examination of formalities only. Some countries, like South Africa and Europe, permit members of the public to oppose a patent in an administrative proceeding. Other countries, like the United States, allow patents to be challenged in court. Most applicants therefore assume their patents will be subject to challenge in every country, by an examiner, by an opposer, or in court.
- The patentability of inventions in the life sciences varies significantly from country to country. Genetic material, microbes, plants, and animals may be patented in the United States. According to TRIPS Article 27(3) (b), microbes are patentable

in all WTO countries. Plants and animals and genetic material and other isolated and purified extracts of plants and animals may or may not be patentable. Surgical and other medical procedures are not subject to protection in most countries. IP counsel must consider all available types of protection, including the possibility of avoiding patent applications altogether and keeping the invention secret,

- Biological materials need to be deposited in a public gene bank under the terms of the Budapest Treaty to satisfy disclosure requirements in most countries. In the United States, the deposit is not required until patent issuance, but in most countries it is required at the time of filing, so most applicants make the biological deposit prior to patent filing.
- Brazil and South Africa passed biopiracy laws requiring patent applicants to certify that any indigenous genetic material or traditional knowledge obtained from those countries and used in the invention was obtained with permission. Other countries are pursuing such legislation. Disclosure of origin requirements for genetic materials went from concept to law over the past decade, and even though only a few countries have similar requirements, for practitioners, these laws now establish an international standard.

In summary, a wise patent practitioner learns the strictest rules in effect in all countries in which protection is desired, and tries to comply with them all, following an evolving international best practice for patent applications. Sometimes the rules conflict, and choices must be made. Despite even the best efforts to coordinate international patent examination, the different national rules result in patents with different scope in different countries.

Intensity of patenting. There are great differences in the numbers of patents filed in different countries, by inventors from different countries. According to WIPO's 2006 statistical report of patenting activity, 75 percent of the 1.6 million patent applications filed in 2004 were filed in the patent offices of Japan, United States, Korea, China, and the European Patent Office. Other countries among the top 20 include Canada, Australia, Russia, Brazil, India, Mexico, Singapore, and Argentina. Adjusted for population, Japanese inventors top the list of patenting intensity, followed by Korea, United States, Germany, and Australia. The greatest number of filings by non-residents, an indicator of market strength and perceived patent value by foreigners, was in the United States, followed by Europe, China, Japan, and Canada. The "big three" – Europe, United States, and Japan – topped the list of 135,000 PCT international applications, and had the greatest number of patents granted.

Professional certification. The criteria needed to qualify to prepare and prosecute patent applications differs from country to country. In the United States, one who passes the patent bar can practice either as a patent agent or a patent attorney if the person is separately admitted to the bar as an attorney. Europe established a certification process for European Patent Attorneys, who are not attorneys. Most developed countries require certification for patent practitioners. In many countries, any attorney may practice before the patent office.

Standards for obtaining trademarks. The popularity of different trademark offices varies, with China having taken the lead in trademark filings in 2004. Most countries grant rights to the first to file an application, so early filing is recognized as the best global practice, even though rights arise from use without registration in some countries. Countries differ in the specificity with which goods and services must be described in an application. Countries extend different types of protection for geographical indications of origin (such as Champagne, or Florida oranges). There are many variations in the protection given to atypical trademarks such as trade dress (general product appearance), celebrities' right of publicity, and marketing features such as sound and color. Countries also differ in whether they give famous trademarks special broad rights against dilution.

Copyright standards. The duration of copyright varies, as do the formalities for enforcing a copyright against an infringer, such as registration. The availability of fixed statutory damages varies, as do other measures of damages. Moral rights – including the right of an author to control the integrity of a work even after it is sold – are stronger in some countries, weaker in others. Fair use standards are country-specific, as are standards for defamation and freedom of speech. Databases may be protected under copyright in some countries, or under special legislation in others, like Europe.

Negotiation. As elaborated for example in Chapters 5 and 15, deal making is a central part of IP management. IP professionals, worldwide, work together as local counsel for each other when registering patents and trademarks, and we increasingly belong to the same professional societies. An international standard for IP contracts is emerging from such interactions. The strategic approach – proceeding from goals to assessment, from strategies to tactical implementation – works anywhere in the world. Nonetheless, although the legal basics are consistent, and the final documents may have a common structure, negotiation styles differ radically from region to region, country to country. The pace, role of personal relationships, importance of verbal agreements, and other aspects of negotiation in my home country have little relevance in different cultures such as Brazil, China, or Saudi Arabia.[2] The ability to conclude a technology transfer agreement or to settle an enforcement action may be limited by negotiation differences. Also, copyright licensing organizations active in most developed countries allow for negotiation of a single blanket license for many properties, whereas in other countries, individual agreements must be negotiated for each copyright work.

Litigation/Enforcement. Significant differences include the ability to obtain discovery of evidence from the opponent, the measure of damages available against an infringer, injunctive relief, the cost of litigation, possibility of recovering attorney fees from the loser, the time to a decision, the availability of cross-border enforcement, and the possibility of proceeding in a specialized court system familiar with IP law, as opposed to appearing before judges who are ignorant of (or hostile to) disputes involving intellectual property. There are also differences in the interaction between the courts and the administrative agencies responsible for patents, copyrights, and trademarks. In some countries an accused patent infringer can challenge the patent at the patent office instead of in court. In some countries, a government agency may provide the court with an advisory opinion on the merits of a particular case.

---

[2] Frank Acuff, *How to Negotiate Anything with Anyone Anywhere in the World* (AMACOM, 1997).

A topic of increasing relevance worldwide is cross-border enforcement of IP rights. For example, if a software company writes a program in the United States, ships a single "golden master disc" overseas, and then reproduces and installs hundreds of thousands of copies in computers outside the United States, is there any infringement of U.S. patent rights? In the *AT&T v. Microsoft* case, the U.S. Supreme Court said "No."[3] Similar issues apply to biological replicating materials removed from one country and replicated in another. Different standards for patentability make such cross-border disputes ever more likely, and create a need for international coordination.

On the one hand, a software patent is not worth much unless it covers software writing activity and the commercial fruits of that activity. On the other hand, court judgments in one country cannot be easily enforced overseas, and there is a risk of multiple lawsuits with overlapping damages in different countries. U.S. software companies argue that they may need to relocate their software research facilities outside of the United States to avoid such extraterritorial liability. The same issues will be addressed increasingly in national courts in many countries.

Alternate dispute resolution. Given the vagaries of enforcement in courts around the world, some organizations are attracted to mediation and arbitration, two forms of alternative dispute resolution. Both can be quick and relatively simple compared to court proceedings. The parties agree to submit their dispute to a private party, according to rules established by the parties or an impartial body, with the parties paying for the dispute resolution services. The agreement may come in advance, such as in a license, or it may come after a dispute arises.

In mediation, the results are not binding, and the mediator's role is to help the parties explore the possibility of settlement. In arbitration, the result is binding on the parties. Arbitration can be carried out under the auspices of many different organizations, such as the International Chamber of Commerce, the American Arbitration Association, or WIPO's Arbitration and Mediation Center. The WIPO Center has been extremely active in resolving Internet domain name disputes under the Uniform Domain Name Dispute Resolution Policy, with about 10,000 disputes resolved between 1999 and 2007. ADR is most appropriate in commercial disputes where the public interest is less significant than the private rights of the parties.

Counterfeiting and piracy. The total economic value of counterfeit and pirated products may exceed $150 billion per year. But the economic value of IP infringement in a particular country is only one factor in the overall perception of whether IP rights are respected there. Although some critics object to overstrong patent and copyright systems as a general matter, few would argue in favor of permitting counterfeit drugs and mechanical parts that can endanger lives. According to reports by WIPO and the U.S. Trade Representative, the countries with the highest amount of piracy are China and Russia, despite their increased prosecution of infringers under criminal sanctions, followed by India, Brazil, Israel and Indonesia.

---

[3] *Microsoft Corp. v. AT&T Corp.*, 127 S.Ct. 1746 (2007).

Criminality. Most countries treat some infringements of IP rights as criminal matters, such as large-scale counterfeiting of goods (trademark infringement) or pirating recordings of music, movies, or software (copyright infringement). Criminal liability requires a high degree of intent, in contrast with civil liability for IP infringement, which often applies regardless of intent. In Russia, copyright infringement can lead to up to 5 years in jail, patent infringement or "usurpation of inventorship" can lead to up to 2 years in jail. In Egypt, all infringement of IP rights begins as a criminal matter to be pursued by the relevant government agency, with the involvement of the IP owner, and after the infringement is established, the owner may commence a civil action for damages.[4]

Criminalization of IP infringement may be a rising trend. The prospect of a non-democratic government imprisoning citizens for unknowing IP violations without due process of law is disturbing. Selective prosecution of those whose activities threaten government officials is one foreseeable problem. We can imagine the need for criminal defenders to learn the basics of intellectual property law in order to keep falsely accused people out of jail.

Compulsory licensing. Compulsory licensing procedures vary from country to country. In the United States, government use of patented inventions may be subject to the constitutional fifth amendment prohibition against government takings of property without due process of law. Canada used to have a standardized compulsory licensing procedure for generic pharmaceutical companies, but eliminated it in 1993. The TRIPS Agreement allows countries to grant compulsory licenses to domestic companies. South Africa, Brazil, Thailand, and Taiwan have used the threat of compulsory licensing proceedings as leverage in drug price negotiations with pharmaceutical manufacturers, as has the United States. The WTO's Doha Declaration went further, suggesting that compulsory licenses could be granted for countries to export drugs to countries that could not make them domestically. Some drug producer countries (Canada, India, Korea, and Norway) have passed laws permitting export of patented drugs to developing countries that could not make them. This is a very high stakes issue for developing countries that distribute the drugs for free, and for the patent owners who make them. In 2007, Thailand issued a compulsory license for Abbott's AIDS drug Kaletra, prompting Abbot to withdraw its new drugs from the country after negotiations over price reductions failed. Brazil's health minister likewise threatened compulsory licensing and negotiated a price reduction of about 50 percent from the approximately $100 million per year paid to Abbott.

Other limitations to enforceability. Most countries have laws that exempt some sorts of research from patent infringement liability, but these vary widely. The United States was the first to enact a so-called Bolar provision entitling a pharmaceutical company to practice any invention for the purpose of gaining regulatory approval for a drug, and some countries such as Japan and Spain have similar provisions. Other countries permit researchers to use an invention for academic purposes or to improve on the invention. As to copyrights, standards for fair use differ from

---

[4] Nemlen Al-Ali and Robert Mihail, "Egypt: Renewed Enthusiasm for IP Protection," in *IP Value 2007: Building and enforcing intellectual property value, An International Guide for the Boardroom* (Globe White Page, 2006), p. 245.

country to country. Overarching the different types of IP rights, competition law may also restrict enforceability. For example in the European Commission, Article 81(1) outlaws any agreements that would prevent, restrict, or distort competition, and Article 81(3) provides a safe harbor for intellectual property licensing agreements so long as they result in an improvement in production or technical progress, while allowing consumers a fair share of the resulting benefit.

A BRIEF TOUR OF IP SYSTEMS AROUND THE WORLD

The following summary highlights special concerns in different countries. The intent is to provide examples of the types of differences that exist, not to characterize each and every one.

United States. The United States, in general, allows the greatest amount of IP protection on the broadest range of innovations, and has very strong enforcement. Because many of the examples in this book and others come from the United States, we can touch on just a few points here. The United States is a litigious country. The monetary damages for infringing IP rights can be astronomical, including about $1 billion for Kodak's infringement of the Polaroid instant photograph technology in the 1980s, the 2006 $600 million settlement for RIM's Blackberry sales, and awards of $500 million (for Eolas) and $1.5 billion (for Alcatel-Lucent) against Microsoft (both of which went on to continued litigation). Business method patents, patents on genetic materials, and other novel forms of IP are available and enforceable in the United States, although recent Supreme Court decisions are weakening patent rights. The U.S. Patent and Trademark Office, like its counterparts around the world, is backlogged and is seeking ways to streamline patent examination.

Copyright term has been expanded to 70 years after the author's life, or 95 years after publication of works made for hire, longer than most countries. The volume of trademark filings and litigation reflects the dynamic economy. The costs of obtaining protection in the United States are relatively low in comparison to the huge market size. It is not unusual for companies from two different countries to litigate over their IP rights in the United States. Professional expertise among innovators, lawyers, and business people is high. Licensing is active.

Europe. In Europe, the level of IP protection is high. Patents are somewhat more limited than in the United States, with a high degree of specificity required. Software and business method patents must demonstrate a technical character. Animal patents are disfavored. Copyright is readily enforceable, and the European Community has recognized rights in databases that are lacking in most countries. European countries are generally less litigious than the United States, but IP owners can obtain injunctions and win substantial damage awards in European courts. There is a large and sophisticated IP legal profession familiar with obtaining, trading, and enforcing IP rights.

One of the peculiarities of Europe is the overlap of regional and national law, which affects patent and trademark law in particular. As to patents, most inventors obtain a unitary European patent through the EPO, and then formalize it with translations in each country, rather than filing individual patents in each country. However, enforcement remains a creature of national law, and a patent owner may need to commence a patent infringement suit in each country where a remedy is desired, although some cross-border enforcement is possible. It is not unusual for a patent owner to succeed in enforcing a patent in one country, but to fail in another, on the same patent, against the same defendant, for the same acts. Efforts to establish a less expensive, more consistent cross-border enforcement system have so far been unsuccessful, although a centralized patent court remains a possibility.

For trademarks, many applicants now seek a unitary European trademark registration under the Community trademark (CTM) system, which covers a market of 350 million consumers. An international trademark applicant under the Madrid Protocol may seek a Community Trademark as well as individual trademarks in the European countries. For various reasons it can be desirable to obtain both a CTM Community trademark and a national or international trademark as well. Substantive standards vary – a star logo may not be protected by a European Community trademark, while France's national trademark system permits registration of an asterisk.[5] Moreover, it is not possible to obtain a Community trademark if someone else has a prior registration in even one of the member countries. In that situation, a common approach is to seek individual trademarks in each of the other countries where registration is still available. For example, a client had a trademark application in France that was opposed based on a vaguely similar registration by another, much larger, company. But because the client had prior applications in other European countries that would have blocked the opposer there, we were able rapidly to negotiate a favorable settlement permitting both companies to continue their nonoverlapping use.

Japan. Japan, like Europe, has relatively high levels of IP protection, and a culture that favors settlement over litigation. The value of IP rights can give rise to legal disputes such as an $8 million settlement for damages claimed by the inventor of the blue light emitting diode. The level of professional expertise is high.

Japan established an IP High Court in 2005 to hear appeals from the JPO and district courts on all IP matters. This should streamline resolution of disputes in Japan. However, the success rate of patent owners is very low. The government has proposed a shared patent examination process in the Asia-Pacific region, which would help speed patent examination in Japan. In 2007, Japan and the United States agreed to standardize patent application formats and to exchange information to help both countries improve examination.

The global dominance of Japanese industry in automobiles, electronics, pharmaceuticals, and other fields correlates to the leadership of Japanese inventors in patents filed around the world. Likewise, court proceedings in the U.S. and other countries are populated by Japanese IP owners.

The "BRIC" countries. Brazil, Russia, India, and China, have intermediate economies, and intermediate levels of IP protection. Each of these countries has been strengthening IP laws and enforcement mechanisms over the last decade in compliance with the TRIPS Agreement. It is now possible to obtain patents in each of these countries for all the technologies stipulated in TRIPS. However, it remains difficult to stop infringement of intellectual property rights in each of these countries.

---

[5] J. F. Bretonniere and Cecile Cailac, "The National Trademark Versus the Community Trademark," in *IP Value 2007*, p. 156.

Foreign technology companies file patent and trademark applications, and pursue copyright and confidentiality agreements, but some remain reluctant to introduce technology for fear it will be copied without serious consequences. As local innovation becomes more important in these countries, the local advantages of strong IP rights can be expected to increase popular support for stronger rights. As described in Chapter 3, the evidence suggests that countries tend to keep their levels of IP protection low, which facilitates faster internal development, until their domestic innovation and creativity reach a level where local innovators want increased protection.

Brazil. Brazil, like many other developing countries, strengthened its IP laws in accordance with the 1995 TRIPS agreement. There has been an increase in trademark and patent filings, and a growing backlog of patent applications awaiting examination, and overburdened courts. Punitive damages are available in Brazil for trademark infringement. An international group of electronics and computer companies formed a coalition called the Brazilian Legal Institute to share information about counterfeiting and piracy, and to coordinate enforcement actions regarding unlicensed computers, software, cell phones, cameras, and clothing are common.

As noted above, Brazil passed a law requiring patent applicants to identify any Brazilian genetic resources or traditional knowledge used in the invention, and to demonstrate that the Ministry of the Environment has authorized such use. Provisional Measure No. 2,186-16/01. This measure is intended to prevent biopiracy, the unauthorized expropriation of biological materials and associated traditional knowledge. In addition to aggressively protecting its domestic biodiversity resources, Brazil has pushed hard to access AIDS medicines through use of compulsory licensing.

Russia. Russia has no special courts for IP litigation, but the full range of compensatory remedies and injunctions may be pursued in the commercial court system. Penalties and fines are relatively low. However, Russia has criminal provisions that apply to all types of IP infringement (patent, copyright, and trademark), with violations being punishable by up to five years in jail. Reportedly a Russian student was jailed for one year for commercially installing unlicensed Microsoft operating systems on computers. In a different case, President Putin spoke out in defense of a school official charged with criminal infringement because of a school computer whose software was unlicensed.

Russia faces peculiar problems deriving from the breakdown of the Soviet Union. Stolichnaya vodka was protected by several USSR-owned trademarks that were licensed to PepsiCo in 1992, and a Russian government agency successfully consolidated trademark rights in many countries. However, when the Russian agency challenged the ownership of U.S. rights acquired by distributor Allied Domecq in U.S. court, its action was dismissed.

India. India has overhauled its IP laws since joining the WTO in 1995, and it is moving quickly to become an innovation leader in software, pharmaceuticals, and biotechnology. In 2005, India amended its patent laws to protect food, drugs, and chemical products, allowing the 250 large and 22,000 small and medium sized pharmaceutical companies to obtain patents on their commercial products. Before, only the methods of synthesizing drugs and agrochemicals were patentable, so the Indian industry became masters of chemical synthesis. Now, however, Indian companies are learning to protect their own innovations with patents, and to gain access to patented drugs from innovators. Foreign companies are more inclined to establish Indian subsidiaries. This has led to a boom in research investment, climbing from about $40 million in 2000 to about $1.7 billion in 2004.[6] The new model of generic company innovation is leading to extensive patent portfolios and extensive inter-generic patent litigation by Indian and other generic companies in India, the United States, and elsewhere.

India's new laws also expanded the patent office, improved examination, and began to address a backlog in court cases. Trademark and patent infringement damages have increased dramatically, into the millions of dollars, with punitive damages available. The Delhi High Court has blocked parallel imports of gray market goods including dehumidifiers and printer ink cartridges. Parallel imports are those that are purchased legitimately in one country, but then shipped to another country without permission. Concerns arise because of differences in safety regulations, instructions and other labeling, warranties, and the availability of service.

India boasts a strong university system that has adopted guidelines for university ownership and management of intellectual property. The emerging system is similar to the Bayh-Dole Act in the United States.

India laws recognizing geographical indications came into effect in 2003, and protect Indian products such as Basmati rice and Darjeeling tea. Foreign geographical indications are also protected, so that the Scotch Whisky Association was able to block use of the name "Scotch" for whisky from outside Scotland.

Concern for traditional knowledge is very high in India. In 1995, a government agency successfully challenged a U.S. patent held by the University of Mississippi for using turmeric for wound healing, on grounds that this use was well-known in the Ayurvedic literature. The Traditional Knowledge Digital Library was created thereafter, in part to prevent improper patenting of Indian traditional knowledge around the world.

China. China, since modernizing its IP laws in 1985, has moved very quickly to a leadership position, characterized by extremes. The Chinese trademark office became the most popular in the world in 2004, and the number of filings continues to increase by double digits, as do domain name registrations. Patent filings by local and foreign companies are increasing rapidly, too, with more applications filed in China than in the European Patent Office.

Foreigners estimate that 20 million citizens are engaged in making, distributing, or selling infringing goods, and complain that penalties and fines are so small as to pose no real deterrent. The government proclaims statistics showing increased enforcement by the Administration for Industry and Commerce (AIC), with about 40,000 cases, and the Public Service Bureau police, which jails about 2000 people annually for IP crimes. New laws are intended to streamline enforcement of IP rights. China outlawed uploading and downloading of copyright material without permission, and copyright owners have won some suits against websites that facilitated such downloads. Computers sold in China must include licensed operating systems, and government offices and enterprises are required to use licensed software.

---

[6] Pravin Anand and Keshav Dhakad, "India: Key Milestones for Intellectual Property," in *IP Value 2007*, p. 266.

Chinese litigation over IP rights is becoming more complex and sophisticated. A court invalidated Pfizer's Viagra patent, but it was restored on appeal. Later, a Chinese company successfully barred Pfizer from using the "Wei Ge" trademark for Viagra due to a prior registration. Damages for infringement are increasing into the multimillion dollar range. Trademark owners have had some success in suing the landlords of counterfeit vendors, such as Beijing's Silk Street Market.

Public leaders routinely speak in support of IP rights, and President Hu Jintao proclaimed the importance of a strong intellectual property system to promote self-innovation as the backbone of China's growth. Over time, such attitudes and increasing domestic innovation are likely to lead, gradually, to greater interest in protecting IP rights in China.

Taiwan. Taiwan's intellectual property system is separate from mainland China, and due to Taiwan's special status, it is not a member of many international IP treaties. However, it has joined the WTO, and so patent applications filed in Taiwan enjoy the right of priority when counterpart applications are filed elsewhere, and vice versa. Taiwan has been aggressive with compulsory licensing, granting two. A conditional compulsory license was granted to ensure an adequate stockpile of Tamiflu, an avian influenza medicine patented by Roche and Gilead. A second license was granted to a Taiwan manufacturer of recordable compact disks, based in part on arguments that the patent owner had refused to provide a license at a reasonable royalty rate.

Korea. Korea is a leader in electronics and software, and joins Japan and China with the fastest growth in patent filings. It strengthened its IP laws prior to the TRIPS agreement, and by 1995 the number of patent applications filed in Korea by Koreans exceeded those filed by foreigners, showing that domestic technological innovation was already strong by then. Korea continues to strengthen its civil and criminal copyright enforcement provisions. There is a growing expertise in management of IP assets in Korea. For example, LG Industries is a company that follows international standards of research and development and IP management.

Least developed countries. The poorest countries present special problems for protecting, enforcing, and licensing IP rights. Local innovators may not be able to obtain protection for their creations. For example, in Haiti, there is concern over infringement of the copyright of local artists. In many countries, musicians are unable to prevent duplication of their songs, and textile makers can not prevent duplication of new patterns. Tropical nations are concerned about biopiracy, meaning the misappropriation of biological resources from the country, and use without permission and without benefit to the source country.

Foreigners are confronted with local infringement, as with the BRIC countries, although the economic stakes are smaller. A universal problem is software duplication, because the technology is so widely available. The poorest countries have little or no domestic biotechnology, pharmaceutical, chemical, or electronics industries, and there is little basis for foreigners to invest in establishing these companies if they face the risk that their advanced technologies will be taken and used by a local competitor. Of course, weak intellectual property systems are not the only reason for a lack of innovation in the poorest countries, or for limited access to medicines and other technology. Other serious economic problems are involved, including a lack of skills to manage technology, as recognized by international initiatives to promote innovation in the least developed countries, relating to biotechnology[7] and health.[8]

South Africa. Commercial practices in Southern Africa demonstrate the challenge of cross-border trademark protection. Many individuals and microenterprises trade goods from South Africa into neighboring countries such as Namibia, Botswana, Lesotho, and Swaziland. Hence, a manufacturer should register trademarks in all the bordering countries, because it is likely that goods in one country will pass to the others.[9] Meanwhile, at least one South African practitioner argues that the pendulum has swung too far in favor of large trademark owners, with small used parts dealers being prohibited from identifying the brands of the automobiles for which the parts may be used, leading to a public perception that the IP system is becoming a tool of anti-competitive economic repression.[10]

Sierra Leone. Sierra Leone is a member of the African Regional Industrial Property Organization (ARIPO). It is still recovering from the effects of a civil war. According to the patent and trademark administration, in the first half of 2006, about 18,000 trademarks were issued. Only about 250 patents were issued. Although over 8000 patents were submitted through ARIPO, Sierra Leone's current patent law does not enable the granting or enforcement of patent rights in Sierra Leone through ARIPO or the Patent Cooperation Treaty (PCT). So the great majority of patents are without effect. According to Beatrice Dove-Edwin of the Ministry of Trade and Industry, Sierra Leone is losing significant revenue that it could receive from foreign patent filing fees.

Mexico. Although strong IP systems promote local innovation, systems with weak IP rights, including broad fair use, experimental use, and other limits on exclusivity, may invite use of foreign technology. It has been suggested that countries with weak intellectual property regimes like Mexico may be attractive for research and development,[11] although this is somewhat counterintuitive. First, there are many fewer PCT international patents filed in Mexico than in the EPO, Japan, Korea, the United States, or China, so there are fewer patents to infringe. Second, there is an experimental use exception so that noncommercial research use of an invention is not an infringement. Third, Mexico gives prior user rights to one who used an invention before someone else filed a patent application on it.

Likewise, in the Andean Community (ANCOM), it is not an infringement to use a patent for noncommercial purposes. The costs of infringement are much lower, too. In Venezuela, a patent enforcement action may cost up to $30,000 to trial, and up to $25,000 to appeal, in contrast to several million dollars in the United States, and damages are small.

---

[7] Calestous Juma and Ismail Serageldin, "Freedom to Innovate: Biotechnology in Africa's Development," Report of the High-Level African Panel on Modern Biotechnology (2007), available at http://www.nepadst.org/doclibrary/pdfs/biotech_africarep_2007.pdf, accessed August 24, 2007.

[8] World Health Organization, Intergovernmental Working Group On Public Health, Innovation And Intellectual Property, "Draft Global Strategy and Plan of Action on Public Health, Innovation and Intellectual Property," Report by the Secretariat A/PHI/IGWG/2/2 (31 July 2007).

[9] Vanessa McPhee, "Cross-Border Brand Protection in Southern Africa," in *IP Value 2007*, p. 238.

[10] Ron Wheeldon, "South Africa Trademark Law: Where Is It Heading," in *IP Value 2007*, p. 255.

[11] Juan Carlos Amaro and Hector Chagoya, "Mexico: Providing a Safe Harbour for Research and Development," in *IP Value 2007*, p. 147.

Increasingly, organizations in even the poorest countries are learning how to use IP laws to their advantage. For example, in Kenya, the word "kikoi" describes a particular kind of woven cloth and, by association, a sarong type of clothing worn by the majority of Kenyan women. An importer of Kenyan crafts filed a trademark application with the UK Patent and Trademark Office for "kikoy" for clothing. A Kenyan fair trade coalition, with the assistance of an attorney identified by PIIPA, opposed the trademark, so that Kenyan craftspeople could continue to sell their products in the UK.

SUMMARY. The fundamental concepts of the innovation cycle, the growth and flow of IP rights, and the strategies for protecting innovations and accessing those of others apply globally, but there are important national differences. Indeed, the very existence of such differences is one of the fundamental concepts presented in this book. Each country around the world struggles to improve its IP legal system and practices consistent with its domestic economic and political situation. Consequently, organizations must grapple with the dynamics of local differences and continuous change as they work to meet their objectives locally and around the world. Fortunately the legal and practical differences fall into a finite number of categories: language, standards for obtaining patents and trademarks, intensity of patenting activity, negotiation, litigation and enforcement, alternate dispute resolution, criminal liability, the extent of counterfeiting and piracy, compulsory licensing, and other limits on enforcement. Countries may be grouped into several categories in which similarities are greatest. The United States, Europe, and Japan have the strongest, oldest IP systems, although levels of protection differ, as do litigiousness, and the combined national and regional character of European laws is complex. The fast growing economies of China, Korea, India, and Brazil, and other countries share some similarities as the scope of IP rights expand faster than the ability of the judicial systems to keep up with infringement. As people in these countries turn from copying foreign innovations towards increasing domestic innovation, they will likely strengthen enforcement and increase the value of IP rights. In the least developed countries, IP rights are also being strengthened, but given political instability, economic problems, judicial weakness, and poor education, local innovation is at a lower level and IP rights are less relevant than in wealthier countries. As a result of Internet commerce and globalization, it is no longer sufficient to learn the laws and practices in only one country. Except for the smallest, least innovative organizations, IP managers must consider the range of different laws and practices around the world, including the established economies of Europe, the United States, and Japan, the fast-growing economies, and the poorest, least-developed countries.

18 Global Challenges for Managing Intellectual Property

In this chapter, we focus on five global challenges for communities and organizations where innovation is swift, and IP rights are a driving force. The first challenge is to create a financial market in IP rights, by increasing liquidity and reducing transaction costs. The second challenge is to promote sustainable innovation in medicine by harnessing the competition between branded and generic pharmaceutical companies as they compete around the world across the boundaries of time and geography. A third challenge is how to drive innovation in response to demands created by the rise of international terrorism. A fourth challenge is to promote environmentally beneficial innovation by effectively integrating IP laws and environmental regulation. Fifth, we outline the strange alliances formed around intellectual property between supporters and opponents of biotechnology. Finally, we consider several possible scenarios of what global IP systems might look like in the future.

* * * * * *

SECURITIZATION OF IP RIGHTS

Entrepreneurs are beginning to link intellectual property to capital markets. Intellectual property lacks many of the attributes required for a successful financial market, which have been characterized as follows:[1]

Liquidity – ease of trading, with a narrow spread between buy and sell prices
Transparency – availability of prompt and complete information about trades and prices
Reliability – trades completed quickly and accurately
Enforceability – contract disputes can be readily resolved
Investor protection – regulations inspire confidence, without overregulation
Low transaction costs – trading costs, regulatory costs, and taxes.

IP rights are not liquid. There is very little transparency, and reliable information about transfers of IP rights is hard to get due to confidentiality. Transactions can take a very long time to complete, enforcement is uncertain, there are few regulations establishing a trading system, and transaction costs are high. IP auctions, still in

---

[1] Marc Levinson, *The Economist Guide to Financial Markets* (Economist, 2003), chapter 1.

Table 18.1. Examples of IP securitization[2]

Company	Industry	IP Asset	$(M)	Year	Underwriter
David Bowie	Music recordings	Copyright	55	1997	Pullman Group
Yale Univ.	Drugs	One patent	100	2000	RoyaltyPharma
Candies	Apparel	TM license	20	2002	UCC Capital
Dreamworks	Films	Copyright	1000	2002	FleetBoston etc.
Guess?	Apparel	TM licenses (12 US, 2 non)	75	2003	JP Morgan
Athlete's Foot	Shoes	Franchise TM and trade secrets	30–50	2003	UCC Capital
Various	Biologic drugs	13 patent pool	225	2003	RoyaltyPharma
Tokiwa Seiki	Machinery parts	Patents		2005	UFJ Trust Bank (Japan)
Dr. Reddy's	Generic drugs	FDA applications	55	2005	ICICI (India)
Emory U	HIV drug	Patent	525	2005	RoyaltyPharma
Marvel	Characters	TM/copyright	525	2005	Merrill Lynch
Dunkin'	Food	TM/franchise	1700	2006	

their infancy, are not linked to capital markets. Hence, there is no financial market in IP assets.

But a new business model is changing this situation – securitizing IP assets. Securitization is a process for aggregating individual assets which are difficult to sell and have unclear value, and using them to back securities that can be sold in financial markets. Securitization accelerates the ability of innovators to obtain ready money for their IP assets.

Converting IP assets into securities is a mechanism that has been used in numerous transactions, with the total value of IP-backed securities about $10 billion as of 2005. The transactions involved entertainment (copyright), consumer products (trademark), and pharmaceuticals/biotechnology (patents). (See Table 18.1.)

In a typical transaction, the owner of an IP asset transfers legal title to a Special Purpose Vehicle (SPV), and receives money (and optionally a share of the SPV). The owner can retain equitable rights to the IP asset, or sell it outright. The SPV issues asset-backed securities to capital market bond investors through private placement, at a market-based yield and term. The SPV may manage the IP asset and sell products, or the owner may do so. Consumers buy products protected by the IP asset, and payments and royalties flow to the SPV. The SPV makes contractual payments to the

---

[2] John S. Hillery, Securitization of Intellectual Property: Recent Trends from the United States (March 2004), available at http://www.iip.or.jp/e/paper.html; Jay Eisbruck, "Royal(ty) succession: the evolution of IP-backed securitization," in *IP Value 2007*, p. 17.

bond holders, and with any excess money either builds a reserve fund or pays it back to the owner of the IP asset.

In 1997, David Bowie issued $55 million of bonds with the Pullman Group, based on existing and future copyright in his recordings, in order to pay a tax debt. Reportedly the bonds were downgraded to junk rating but there was sufficient funding to pay the bondholders. Pullman has done similar deals with other musicians.

As shown in Table 18.1, other underwriters have issued securities based on apparel trademarks, franchise trademark and trade secret assets, and machinery parts. Dreamworks issued securities based on its existing movie copyrights to pay for new films. RoyaltyPharma rolled up pharmaceutical patent royalty interests from Yale University, Emory University, and various other institutions and corporations, in a portfolio valued at about $1 billion. RoyaltyPharma provides liquidity to patent holders who do not want to wait to collect royalties, and RoyaltyPharma leverages its portfolio as security for its investments in financial markets. Indian investor ICICI arranged to fund Dr. Reddy's Abbreviated New Drug Applications to the U.S. Food and Drug Administration (FDA), trading support of the research and patent litigation costs for a share of revenues from any approved generic drugs.

The growth of IP asset-backed securitization is driven by several forces. First, IP assets represent an increasing percentage of enterprise value relative to tangible assets. Second, IP assets are a new source of liquidity, and can help the owner settle debt or make investments. Third, the credit rating for an IP asset can be higher than that of the overall company. Fourth, experience is mounting with IP due diligence and valuation, legal models, and business models. Fifth, there are limited options for IP monetization, such as sale, licensing out, entering into a joint venture or alliance, spinning out an asset, donating an asset, or selling the royalty stream, and the transaction costs for these arrangements are very high. Sixth, the owner can shield other corporate assets from the securitized IP assets. Seventh, the owner can retain equity in the IP asset. Finally, investors can invest in a special technology or creative niche rather than a whole company having a different overall risk profile.

Some of the obstacles to growth of IP securitization are as follows. It is a novel approach to investment, requiring experienced teams. There is ongoing uncertainty about the value of IP assets globally. There is no streamlined legal framework and no centralized registry of IP asset security information.[3] There are no "Generally Accepted Accounting Principles" (GAAP) for IP securitization. Securitization is time consuming, expensive, and complex. It requires careful due diligence, financial valuation, and risk assessment for IP assets, done by experts. The demand for a product might drop off. Infringers may undercut sales. These risks are not easily insurable, although intellectual property infringement enforcement insurance may pay for the cost of enforcing an IP asset.

Ultimately, the buyers of IP-asset backed securities drive the business forward. Financial markets, for example institutional investors in the bond markets, cannot buy a unique, custom-made, illiquid asset like a patent, for which buyers are generally

---

[3] William J. Murphy, "A Proposal for a Centralized and Integrated Registry for Security Interests in Intellectual Property." *IDEA* 41:297 (2002).

unavailable or extremely difficult to find, and for which asset transfer requires a complex, custom-made license agreement which can take a year and cost $100,000 to negotiate. But they will invest in a liquid asset that can be bought and sold in the gigantic flow of financial markets worldwide. By pooling or selecting IP assets carefully, the party offering IP securities can reduce the transaction cost per asset, and can define a risk level and rate of return that are attractive to investors.

Linking IP assets to financial markets increases the force that the IP system exerts on the innovation cycle, for good or ill. The financial incentive to acquire an IP asset increases if innovators can sell their rights quickly to generate ready money. That money could be returned into innovation. Alternatively, critics would be concerned that the drive of the financial markets could push innovation into efforts that can produce strong IP rights but are socially unproductive, and could create an "IP bubble" boom-and-bust effect.

Companies that issue IP asset-backed securities have not been subjected to the criticism faced by so-called patent trolls, companies that buy patent rights and enforce them against others. Most patent enforcement companies are privately held and do not create or trade IP assets. But over time, it is likely that these two business models will overlap in a company that buys IP assets to enforce them, and issues securities based on the portfolio of IP assets and the revenue to be generated from enforcement actions. To avoid political pressures, that company will need to convince the public that trading in IP assets is good for innovation and good for society.

BRANDED AND GENERIC DRUG COMPANIES: COMPETING AT BOUNDARIES OF TIME AND GEOGRAPHY

The pharmaceutical industry is divided into two camps – the branded (or innovator) companies that develop and patent new drugs, building exclusivity; and the generic companies that seek access to duplicate the drugs once patents expire. Locked in a struggle over markets, branded and generic companies constantly fight legal battles about IP rights across boundaries of time and geography. For the individual companies, these battles are costly, and to hear the lobbyists, each side is poised to destroy the other and harm the public. My view is more optimistic. The fierce competition between the companies can be seen as a sign of a robust IP system at work balancing exclusivity and access to achieve social benefit.

From a social perspective, the public interest is served by promoting basic research, applied research, development; and commercialization of safe and effective drugs; and by expanding access to these drugs for all who need them. The IP system can help achieve these goals by providing exclusive rights as incentives for innovation and investment, but limiting that exclusivity and fostering generic competition for each drug at the end of its patent term. The desired balance would be one of "sustainable innovation," where today's medicines are broadly available, while innovation continues to improve medicines for tomorrow.[4]

---

[4] Michael Gollin, "Sustainable Innovation for Public Health," *Food and Drug Law Institute Update Magazine* (January/February 2002). See Gollin, "Generic Drug Companies: Competing at Boundaries of Time and Geography," in *TRIPS and Global Pharmaceutical Industry: Perspectives and Implications*, ch. 16, Manish Adhiya, ed. (Lefai University Press 2007).

Medicine later vs. medicine now

At the core of the struggle are two fundamental human desires, which create what we can call the dilemma of "medicine later vs. medicine now." This problem of intergenerational equity may be framed as follows:

> How can society balance the needs of today's patients for today's medicine with the needs of future patients to have new medicine?

On the one hand, people want new and better medicines in the future, to make us and our children healthier and therefore happier. Our societies reward medical researchers, but only a few can win the Nobel Prize or other awards. IP laws have a broader more universal reach, giving all inventors the possibility of obtaining a patent and to be rewarded with limited exclusive rights over the invention.

Meanwhile, sick people want the best medicine they can get, now. This leads to the populist argument that patents keep the cost of medicine too high for poor patients. It follows that governments should weaken exclusive patent rights to help improve access, for example by granting compulsory licenses and importing less expensive generic drugs in order to protect the public health. This approach supports the generic industry.

The branded drug industry argues that these steps weaken patents and reduce research, development, and improvements in health care, in effect robbing future innovation from future patients. This argument is based on economics and is lost on people who frame the issue as a populist choice of 'patients vs. patents.'

The IP system plays a central role in striking the intergenerational balance, by defining the specific boundaries of drug patents in terms of their strength, geographic scope, and duration. That is, the exclusive rights of the branded company give way to generic competition at a crucial temporal boundary – when a patent expires. But there is an appalling lack of guidance on the core issue – what is the optimum strength and duration of drug patents to achieve this balance?

Finding the right balance must also take into consideration the broader pharmaceutical "ecosystem," which is not just a bipolar world of patented pharmaceutical companies vs. generic companies, but rather a diverse innovation community with many stakeholders. They include biotechnology companies, inventors, nonprofit research institutions, governmental regulators (patent offices and food and drug and health agencies), health care providers (patients, doctors, nurses, and hospitals), and funders (investors, insurers, and philanthropic donors). All these groups operate within the innovation cycle for pharmaceuticals. (See Figure 18.1.)

Many innovations come from publicly funded research, some of which benefit private corporations simply by being published. Public sector IP rights can also be transferred exclusively to a pharmaceutical company which develops the early stage research into potential products. Private research then progresses to the clinical stage, and a drug is developed and approved for market, thus beginning the patentee commercialization phase shown in Figure 18.1. Pharmaceutical innovations eventually return to the accessible domain when patents expire or are ruled invalid. This is where generic competition begins, often accompanied by litigation

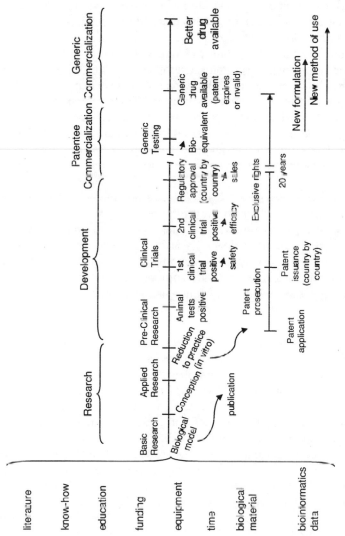

Figure 18.1. The innovation cycle for pharmaceuticals. The various inputs of accessible knowledge go into research and discovery of a drug lead, which proceeds through development (preclinical and clinical trials) to market approval, beginning the patentee's commercialization stage, while patent rights are being secured; after patent expiration, generic competition occurs, while new research produces variations and eventually replacement drugs, starting the cycle again.

about whether the innovator's patent is valid, and whether the generic company's product infringes.

In most countries the government sets the price of new drugs. In the United States, the Hatch-Waxman Act allows generic companies to develop their manufacturing capability and conduct clinical trials prior to patent expiration, so that competition can begin immediately when the relevant patent expires. Generic companies are also allowed to rely on the patent holder's clinical trial data, and need only show that the generic drug is bioequivalent to the patented drug – a much less expensive requirement than for new drugs.

There is currently no analogous system to balance the end of exclusivity with "biologic" drugs such as therapeutic proteins. Examples are erythropoietin, human growth hormone, insulin, and interferon. The Hatch-Waxman Act does not apply to these drugs. It is harder for generic companies to enter the market for biologic drugs, so there may be less incentive for the original innovator to keep making improvements to existing drugs. Also, if generic companies have to redo all the clinical trials, to regenerate clinical data, there will be great cost, with no social benefit except to clinical research organizations. It would be better to invest in other more valuable projects.

All companies – branded pharmaceuticals, generics, and biotechnology companies – engage in extensive skirmishing around the boundary of patent expiration. The first-moving branded companies innovate and patent new dosage forms, formulations, and chemical variants on successful drugs, bringing a stream of improvements to patients. These improvements may be more modest than a new blockbuster, but are nonetheless important. The most common approaches taken by branded companies include making new formulations, making a next-generation product, finding new medical indications for a drug, or combining multiple, active ingredients into one dosage form.[5]

Generic companies have an incentive to enter the marketplace quickly when a patent expires, and even to challenge a weak patent so they can enter the market earlier. Generic companies increasingly innovate to develop new chemical synthesis processes, and to produce new analogs, crystal forms, dosages, salts, and formulations, even some new drugs, and they obtain patents on these innovations.

Ultimately the distinction between branded and generic pharmaceutical companies is something of a false dichotomy. Generic companies hold patents and innovate, and branded patent-holders challenge other innovators and also sell generic drugs. Generic companies innovate and patent their inventions in areas such as chemical synthesis, new methods of use, and new delivery systems, and as they grow they even do basic research. Branded companies compete with each other by producing alternatives to other blockbuster products – such as Cox-2 inhibitors (Vioxx by Merck and Celebrex by Pfizer), and PDE5 inhibitors (Viagra, Cialis, and Levitra). Some branded drug companies also run their own generic operations to take advantage of the separate generic market niche (as with Novartis and its generic subsidiary Sandoz).

[5] Cutting Edge Information, *Combating Generics: Pharmaceutical Brand Defense for 2007, Executive Summary* 12 (2006), available at www.cuttingedgeinfo.com/pharmagenerics/PH76_Download.asp#body, accessed October 15, 2006.

Some examples of the skirmishes at the temporal boundaries illustrate the significance of litigation and legal and political challenges in making the system work.

Schering Plough owned a patent on a metabolite of the antihistamine Loratidine. The patent was ruled invalid in a challenge by Teva and other generic companies. As a result, generic drugs entered the market before the end of the patent's full term, at lower cost. Claritin lost most of its market share, and faced huge price erosion. Because of its trademark it still sells at a price premium over equivalent generic products, but at a much lower sales volume.

GlaxoSmithKline's Paxil (paroxetine hydrochloride) was patented as a particular "polymorph" or crystal form. The patent was ruled invalid, and generic company Apotex immediately launched sales of the antidepressant. GlaxoSmithKline then launched a controlled release tablet to compete with the generic version.

Bayer's ciprofloxacin was in high demand during the U.S. anthrax scare in 2001. U.S. Secretary of Health and Human Services Thompson briefly threatened that the United States might assert a compulsory license to gain access to Cipro at below market prices. A reduced price purchase agreement was reached.

A 1958 U.S. National Cancer Institute study led to the discovery of paclitaxel, an organic molecule in Pacific yew tree bark. The biological mechanism of action was discovered in the 1970s, and in the 1980s NIH researchers developed a method of producing the drug in high volume. The technology was transferred by license to Bristol-Myers Squibb (BMS) in 1991, which developed paclitaxel into Taxol, a leading drug for ovarian, breast, and other cancers, and obtained patents on aspects of its synthesis and formulation, and related methods of treating patients. Taxol went on the market in the U.S. in 1993, and worldwide sales by 2002 were more than $9 billion, making it the most successful cancer drug ever. Competitors around the world sought to undercut the BMS patents, and many organizations mounted legal and political challenges to agreement with NIH, saying it was too generous – reportedly NIH had invested almost $500 million in research but received only $35 million in royalties from BMS.[6] Eventually a generic product was approved in 2000. The price dropped dramatically, of course. Innovation involving paclitaxel has remained intense. Between 1994 and 2006, 539 patents with claims referring to paclitaxel were issued in the United States, including those on the paclitaxel-coated coronary stent, a block buster medical device.

The U.S. Federal Trade Commission has sought to block what are arguably anti-competitive agreements between generic drug companies and patent holders, whereby the patent holder pays the generic company to stay off the market. The FTC's goal is to maintain robust competition benefiting patients now, without sacrificing future innovations.

International equity – Medicine here vs. medicine elsewhere

A second issue in the competitive relationship between branded and generic pharmaceutical companies is international equity, or "medicine here vs. medicine elsewhere." The question may be framed as follows:

[6] "Technology Transfer: NIH-Private Sector Partnership in the Development of Taxol," General Accounting Office Report to the Hon. Ron Wyden, U.S. Senate (June 2003), available at http://www.wyden.senate.gov/leg_issues/reports/taxol.pdf, accessed January 27, 2007.

How can society balance the needs of patients in rich countries like the United States with those of poor countries?

The IP system plays an important role in striking such a balance. Increasingly, there are global markets for making and selling drugs, and patent-holding companies seek markets in all corners of the world. However, patients in poor countries are at a disadvantage because of the small markets, low purchasing power, lack of incentive for development of drugs for their worst public health problems (e.g., malaria, tuberculosis, leishmaniasis), and the absence of intellectual property expertise, which is concentrated almost entirely in the rich countries.

One solution has been to promote a globalization of the generic industry. A drug may be patented in some countries but not in others. A generic version of the drug can be made and/or sold in any country where there is no patent in force. Competent patent professionals can readily identify countries in which there is no patent blocking access to a drug – see the decision process described in Chapter 13. But as patenting expands under the WTO agreement on Trade Related Aspects of Intellectual Property (TRIPS), the number of countries where drug patents are obtained may increase.

A second way to promote globalization of the generic industry is via compulsory licensing consistent with the TRIPS Agreement. There has been competition at the geographical borders with respect to antiretrovirals in South Africa and Brazil. A country may choose between exercising a compulsory license to make the drug domestically, or to import from a generic company in another country, or to seek price concessions from the original patent holder. The latter seems to be the most common outcome. Here, limits on exclusivity result in wider access at lower prices.

Countries such as India, Brazil, South Africa, and Thailand are building local generic industries for domestic use and export. This endeavor can serve many national development goals. India's generic companies have become important players in the global pharmaceutical market, due to recent investments and their longstanding skills and technology in pharmaceutical chemical synthesis. International generic competition will increase supplies of drugs at reduced cost, and may reduce any need or interest in price controls.

Another approach has been to establish public, nonprofit, public-private drug development partnerships and consortia. This is the path selected by the Bill & Melinda Gates Foundation. The IP system (patents, trademarks, and trade secrets) is unable to provide private companies with sufficient market incentives because poor patients have little money to pay for medicine. Philanthropic and government funding is used to pay for research and production of drugs for malaria, leishmaniasis, tuberculosis, and other diseases whose main victims are in poor countries.

The need for medical technology is not completely one sided. Wealthier countries sometimes find themselves in need of health-related innovation from poorer countries. Bird flu, the H5N1 avian influenza virus, causes poultry epidemics in Asian countries and occasionally kills people. The viral DNA mutates rapidly in Asian countries and the variants are important to vaccine research. Indonesia and other countries have suggested an embargo against sharing access to the viral mutant DNA unless they receive preferential treatment on access to resulting vaccines and drugs. Taiwan instituted compulsory licensing proceedings for Tamiflu, a medicine to treat the disease. The World Health Organization, recognizing a threat to the global influenza surveillance network established decades ago, initiated measures to ensure reciprocity, so that viruses and information continue to flow from poorer countries, with vaccines and vaccine technology flowing from developed countries.[7]

These examples show that the competition at temporal and geographical boundaries is intense and complex. Society should support both those who innovate in medicine and those who disseminate the best medical innovations now. Social benefit is maximized by a framework that rewards innovator drug companies with patent rights that are limited by specific boundaries of time and geography, while encouraging generic drug companies to compete vigorously outside those boundaries.

The inevitable consequence of this system is a furious policy battle over the optimal strength of medicine patents in general, and specific legal battles at the temporal and geographical boundaries. These challenges are an inherent part of balancing the IP system. By confronting them, society can promote sustainable innovation, balancing our desire for the best medicines here and now with the desire for better drugs everywhere tomorrow. Better knowledge of how to manage these challenges and access to people with IP expertise will lead to better and more just results.

HOMELAND SECURITY TECHNOLOGY

Nations turn to innovation to help them confront threats due to terrorism and military invasion. In the United States, the Homeland Security Act of 2002 promoted innovation in technologies for detecting, preventing, protecting against, and responding to attacks involving chemical, biological, radiological, nuclear, and related weapons and material.[8] Others relate to law enforcement, such as the interoperability of voice and data public safety communications between police, fire, and military forces. Border control technology includes screening and detection equipment. Computer hardware and software innovations can be used to protect the Internet and financial and other corporate and public networks. Monitoring systems can promote security in transportation infrastructures.

Any organization involved with homeland security technology can implement an IP management plan as discussed in the previous chapters, to deal with the intellectual property rights involved – patents, trademarks, copyrights, and trade secrets – and how these assets can be used to further the organization's strategic goals.[9] There are a few special aspects of dealing with these technologies.

---

[7] World Health Organization, Sixtieth World Health Assembly, "Pandemic influenza preparedness: sharing of influenza viruses and access to vaccines and other benefits," WHA60.28 (23 May 2007), available at http://www.who.int/csr/don/archive/disease/influenza/A60_R28-en.pdf, accessed August 24, 2007.

[8] 6 U.S.C. 182(b) and 182(5).

[9] Michael Gollin, James Jatras, Thomas Madden, Richard Schmidt, and Stuart Smith, "Science, Technology, and Intellectual Property," in Venable LLP (eds.), *Homeland Security Deskbook: Private Sector Impacts of the War Against Terrorism* (Matthew Bender, 2004, revised 2005), chapter 15.

For example, patent applications relating to homeland security technology can benefit from expedited examination in the United States, upon petition.[10] The United States imposes export restrictions on international transfer of certain technologies for national security reasons.[11] Many homeland security technologies would be considered dual use exports regulated by the Department of Commerce because they have primarily civilian uses, but some military application. Defense exports are subject to licensing by the Department of State. Transfers to certain countries are subject to embargo.

Patent owners need to be aware of the Tucker Act, a compulsory licensing provision that permits government contractors to infringe patents upon payment of a "reasonable royalty," shielding them from injunctive relief, enhanced damages, and lost profits for patent infringement if the patented product or method is being used "by or for" the federal government.[12] Much homeland security technology falls into this category. Likewise, state governments and agencies may be able to infringe patents, copyrights, and trademarks with impunity, under the sovereign immunity guaranteed to states under the Eleventh Amendment to the U.S. Constitution.[13] Municipalities and local governments are not protected by the Tucker Act or the Eleventh Amendment, and so are in the same category as private parties, who may not use innovations protected by IP rights absent a license from the owner.

As a practical matter, although federal and state public agencies have advantages over a private party in procuring homeland security (or other) technologies, an innovator company selling a product will still usually have an advantage due to trade secrets, know-how, and manufacturing capacity. That is, the government agency will not want to independently produce the product or provide the service itself, and will choose to buy or license it. The innovator's problem arises if the government agency decides to ask another company to make a competitive bid to provide the innovator's technology. Such a situation may be resolved by an enforcement action in the federal or state court of claims.

Homeland security technology, like most others, is part of a global innovation business. In 2002, the Bush administration called for bids to provide a new smallpox vaccine. The number of vaccine manufacturers is small. Danish company Bavarian Nordic (BN) obtained two patents on its vaccine, and entered into licensing discussions with rival, UK company Acambis. Both companies entered competing bids to supply the U.S. government. BN sued Acambis in federal district court for misappropriation of trade secrets, and filed a patent action at the International Trade Commission (ITC), seeking to block import of Acambis' vaccine. BN lost both cases, with the ITC ruling that the patents are invalid, and a district court ruling that there was no misappropriation of trade secrets. But ultimately, BN won the contract to supply the U.S. government with smallpox vaccine, and the IP dispute was settled.

---

[10] 37 Code of Federal Regulations § 1.102(c)(2)(iii).

[11] *Homeland Security Deskbook*, § 15.05[4][c].

[12] 28 U.S.C. § 1498.

[13] *Florida Prepaid Postsecondary Education Expense Bd. v. College Savings Bank*, 527 U.S. 627 (1999); *College Savings Bank v. Florida Prepaid Postsecondary Education Expense Bd.*, 527 U.S. 666 (1999).

IP rights affecting national security innovations illustrate the delicate balance inherent in IP law. National laws generally limit the exclusive rights of innovators in favor of the national government, which for policy reasons retains access to any technology that is important for national security.

CULTIVATING OUR GARDEN: PROMOTING ENVIRONMENTAL TECHNOLOGY WITH INTELLECTUAL PROPERTY

Paradoxically, technology innovation both hurts and helps the environment. Therefore, intellectual property, by promoting innovation, can be good or bad for the environment.[14] Although some people suggest that IP laws should be adapted to screen good from bad technologies, my view is that is better to leave that role to environmental law, so that intellectual property and environmental law can work together to promote beneficial innovation.

Voltaire's *Candide* ends with one of my favorite lines:

Well said, but we must cultivate our garden.

Gardeners promote plant growth with good soil and fertilizer, but then weed out undesired plants. By analogy, we can promote growth of good and bad innovative technology with the IP system, but restrict harmful technology with environmental regulation. This leads to sustainable innovation.

Environmental technology innovation is a worldwide phenomenon. Like other sectors, it involves government, nonprofit researchers, and industry, working in the US and other wealthy developed countries, and in developing countries. In all countries, energy supply and efficiency are major concerns. Local water and air pollution are poorly regulated in many countries, and greenhouse gas emissions everywhere create the shared problem of global warming. Biodiversity is being lost rapidly, especially in the tropics. There are wide discrepancies between the effectiveness of different countries and regions in promoting sustainable development.

Environmental regulation has progressed through the decades in the United States. The 1960s saw the rise of environmental impact review in public decision-making. The "environment" was defined broadly, including social and health impacts, aesthetics, and ecosystems. In the 1970s, the emphasis shifted to reducing air and water pollution, using pollution control and prevention equipment. In the 1980s, the emphasis moved to cleaning up pollution, with remediation technologies promoted through the Superfund program. In the 1990s, there was a new emphasis on the international issues of climate change and biodiversity loss, as well as genetically modified organisms. In the 2000s, we will see increased attention to energy efficiency and nanotechnology.

An important legacy of environmentalism is the practice of considering environmental impacts before taking action. Today's environmental problems were yesterday's technology solutions (as with polychlorinated biphenyls, asbestos, chlorinated fluorocarbons, and energy use producing carbon dioxide emissions). From that past,

---

[14] Michael Gollin, "Patent Law and the Environment/Technology Paradox." *Environmental Law Reporter*, 20:10171 (1990).

we can predict that today's innovation may become tomorrow's environmental problem. In that light, a goal for environmental technology innovation is to solve today's problems while preventing tomorrow's.

Beneficial environmental technology innovation is that which provides a net environmental benefit compared to existing technologies in terms of resources consumed, wastes produced, and risks to human health and the environment. Here are some examples:

- Industrial processes which minimize resource consumption and waste production
- Consumer products which are environmentally benign throughout their life cycles
- Recycling equipment and processes
- Waste management technologies for solid and hazardous waste
- Pollution control devices
- Products and methods for cleaning up pollution.

Governments try to stimulate "good" technology, to replace "bad" technology. One way is to pass laws requiring new beneficial technologies, in so-called technology-forcing regulations.[15] Organizations have a strong legal incentive to adopt these technologies if they reduce the costs of environmental compliance and reduce the risk of environmental liability. They also have a microeconomic incentive to reduce the costs of materials and production, increase production, and increase the attractiveness of products in the marketplace.

Some efforts to promote environmental technology innovation use market forces.

- With energy independence a priority in many countries, innovation in sustainable energy sources can create millions of jobs, lower utility bills, increase productivity and competitiveness and result in cleaner air and water, improve public health, and reduce dependence on foreign energy sources. Research investments provide a technology "push" for innovation. New standards for fuel efficiency, tax benefits for hybrid vehicles, and other government action such as procurement decisions can produce a market "pull" as well.
- The Stockholm Convention on Persistent Organic Pollutants, finalized in 2000, banned the most damaging chemicals, such as PCBs, dioxin, DDT, and chlordane. This ban creates a technology "pull" that promotes innovation to provide more benign chemicals.
- The 1992 Convention on Biological Diversity (CBD) promotes conservation and sustainable use of biological resources. The CBD established sovereign rights over biological resources, and requires those who obtain biological resources to share benefits with those who provide the resources, creating a mechanism that promotes conservation. The CBD creates a market "pull," an economic force favoring conservation.

---

[15] Michael Gollin, "Using Intellectual Property to Improve Environmental Protection," *Harvard Journal of Law and Technology* (1991), available at http://jolt.law.harvard.edu/articles/pdf/v04/04HarvJLTech193.pdf, accessed January 27, 2007.

Intellectual property can play an important role in driving environmental technology innovation, just as it drives innovation in other sectors. Because innovation can have positive or negative effects on the environment, suggestions have been made to bias intellectual property law toward environmentally beneficial technology, and away from harmful technology. This seems desirable but may be difficult or impossible in practice, with a few exceptions.

Patents. The patent system, as discussed, provides incentives, rewards innovation, creates assets for further investment and development, and promotes disclosure. It is technology neutral, treating software, machines, chemicals, biological components, and methods the same way, and producing a market pull for successful innovations. Nonetheless, it is exceedingly complex already. Giving special treatment to environmental technology innovation under patent laws is unlikely to have much positive impact on innovation, and would complicate the system. Environmental technologies have the possibility of expedited patent examination in the United States, but this is trivial. Regulations requiring a new technology, and financial incentives like tax reductions for hybrid cars, more directly encourage technology innovation, and related IP activity.

Trademarks. Trademark law can help environmental innovators capture goodwill in "green" brands, those that are valued by consumers for being environmentally sound. Individual efforts can be amplified by certification of environmental benefits by third parties like the German Blaue Engel (Blue Angel) program. Conversely, the risk of a bad environmental reputation can disincentivize bad behavior. This market force is the basis for Rainforest Action Network's successful publicity campaigns to "shame" the timber, paper, banking, and automobile industries into adopting more sustainable practices.

Trade Secrets. Government disclosure requirements increase risk of loss of trade secrets. Laws that require disclosure of "bad" technology reduce its value. For example, a company that must list pollutants emitted by its factories faces the risk that competitors can use that list to deduce the chemical processes being used. Conversely, laws that minimize the disclosure burden for beneficial technology provide an incentive to adopt it.

Technology transfer. The CBD, the Intergovernmental Panel on Climate Change, the Kyoto Protocol, and other international environmental arrangements, call for technology transfer from wealthy to poorer countries, to further the goal of sustainable development. In many cases, environmental technology transfer requires careful licensing of IP rights. Innovators may be concerned about transferring their technology to a country where it will be difficult or impossible to prevent immediate copying and competition. Companies are more willing to transfer their technology into another country when they have some confidence that they can enforce their patents and copyrights and maintain their trade secrets there.

In summary, societies that pursue short-term economic development at any cost, with weak environmental regulation, can not achieve beneficial innovation. Systems with weak incentives and rewards will also fail to promote innovation of any kind. It is a complex task to integrate the incentives of IP laws and practices with environmental regulation to produce environmentally beneficial innovation. In the practical approach outlined above, the IP system can be applied to promote domestic innovation and importation of foreign innovations, while other legal structures, particularly environmental law, are used to restrict damaging technology and activities.

REGULATING BIOTECHNOLOGY WITH INTELLECTUAL PROPERTY LAW

The biotechnology revolution of the past few decades and the forces of globalization have increasingly focused the world's attention on intellectual property law as a tool of public policy. At first glance, the political positions seem clear and consistent: Industrialists are opposed to regulation of biotechnology and support intellectual property to stimulate continued innovation. Environmental advocates, consumer groups, and some developing country organizations favor restrictions on genetic engineering and are opposed to "life patents." However, despite the temptation to accept such a simple view, upon closer inspection, the picture is much more complex.

Ironically, there is a movement among biotechnology researchers for open access research, without IP protection, in seeming alliance with anti-technologists. Meanwhile, environmentalists and opponents of globalization have sought to expand IP rights to protect biological diversity and traditional knowledge in developing countries. So, people who are "for" biotechnology may be "against" patents and people who are "against" biotechnology may be "for" intellectual property.

Given these strange alliances, one can reasonably conclude that IP law is subject to different political forces than biotechnology regulation, and that the policies and laws relating to patent law and to regulation should remain independent. Those forces can be understood by asking the rationale of each of the four interest groups.

Why do most biotechnology innovators favor strong IP protection? The rationales are as discussed above – incentives and control over the innovation process, the possibility of investing and earning a return on investment, and so on.

Why do some public interest advocates favor strong IP protection? Some see IP rights as a way to promote biological diversity and traditional knowledge – to conserve what we already have and what we create. The Convention on Biological Diversity subjected biological resources to sovereign national rights, and required states to support the role of traditional knowledge in maintaining and using those resources. The combination of national rights and traditional knowledge formed the basis for novel quasi-intellectual property rights. It also established a trading system, in which innovators seeking access to those resources must agree to share resulting benefits, and those benefits can be used to conserve biodiversity. The innovators can obtain patent rights, indirectly helping secure benefits to share with the source countries.

To strengthen compliance with that trading system, some countries have passed laws requiring patent applicants to disclose where biological materials were obtained, and to certify that the materials were obtained lawfully, that is, under an agreement providing access to the materials in exchange for benefit sharing. For example, in Brazil and South Africa, patent applicants are required to certify that any indigenous genetic material or traditional knowledge that was used in the invention was obtained with permission. With such laws, the patent system is being used to strengthen rights in biological resources under the CBD. But such measures may be too cumbersome, or unfair, or expensive to manage, or impossible for patent examiners to handle. They may violate the principle of technology neutrality in patent law (the treating of biotechnology, electrical, and mechanical inventions all the same way), and impose a burden on innovations involving biological resources. Other sanctions outside the patent system might be used to ensure that researchers follow procedures for obtaining permission to use biological resources, such as civil or criminal penalties for violations.[16]

Human rights advocates also have reason to support IP protection. Article 27 of the 1948 UN Universal Declaration of Human Rights characterizes as human rights both access to and exclusive rights in innovations:

Article 27 (1) Everyone has the right freely to participate in the cultural life of the community, to enjoy the arts and to share in scientific advancement and its benefits.

(2) Everyone has the right to the protection of the moral and material interests resulting from any scientific, literary or artistic production of which he is the author.

Why do many public interest groups oppose "life patents?" One reason is concern about biopiracy – the misappropriation by people from wealthy countries of traditional knowledge and biological diversity in poorer countries. Another concern is biocolonialism, the perpetuation of biotechnology in wealthy countries, and its absence in poor countries. Environmentalists also complain about unhealthy incentives that reduce crop diversity, such as pesticide resistant crops that may derive from a small number of varieties. Patient advocates favor increased access to medicine. Developing country agricultural advocates favor better crop varieties in developing countries, more conservation of varieties, and the ability of developing country farmers to export their crops into Europe, the United States, and other wealthy countries.

Still other groups raise morality issues. As noted in Chapter 16, there is a hierarchy of moral concern for biological materials, which can be stated in order of most concern to least:

Human > animal > plant > isolated tissue > microorganism > DNA > other chemical compounds.

Why do some biotechnology innovators also oppose strong IP protection? Many of these issues have been discussed before. Academic researchers fear closure and restriction of their ability to conduct research, and favor open access. Some businesses have decided open access suits them in noncore areas, too. Businesses complain about the risk of patent trolls, people who do not innovate, but speculate by buying patents. There is a concern about junk patents, the extremely high cost of litigation, and risk of liability.

Intellectual property drives innovation, but its relevance in shaping biotechnology is more limited than some might fear. Patent law reforms cannot restrict the damage

---

[16] Michael Gollin, "Feasibility of National Requirements for Disclosure of Origin," in M. Chouchena-Rojas, M. Ruiz Muller, D. Vivas, and S. Winkler (eds.), *Disclosure Requirements: Ensuring Mutual Supportiveness Between the WTO TRIPS Agreement and the CBD* (IUCN and ICTSD, November 2005), available at http://www.iucn.org/en/news/archive/2005/12/disclosure_requirements_publication.pdf, accessed January 27, 2007.

caused by existing technologies or practices. IP law reform will not have any direct impact on the risks most commonly argued in connection with biotechnology – genetic pollution, reduction of biodiversity, allergic reactions, and so on.

Arguments that biotechnology patents should be weakened to promote innovation may also be overstated. The key issue is access. Although there is little data, overbroad patents need not limit access, not if they are rejected, abandoned, re-examined, invalidated, or licensed at acceptable rates, and if they eventually expire, allowing for generic competition. As I outlined in Chapter 13, innovators can often find ways to avoid patents, to achieve the same results. Of course, such access may carry a cost or require delay.

Arguments that biotechnology patents should be eliminated to deter harmful innovation miss the point. Patent offices and examiners are poorly equipped to determine the environmental and health effects of technology, or to handle moral questions. Moral standards differ from country to country.

If there is an environmental, health, or moral reason for blocking a particular kind of harmful or offensive technology, an outright ban or restriction is a much more efficient deterrent approach than a subtle change in IP policy. For example, human cloning is banned in many countries, as is nuclear technology innovation. But a ban on patents would have only an indirect effect on such innovation. On the other hand, if the benefits of a particular type of research are unclear or mixed, as with most innovations, then it makes more sense to allow research and subsequent patenting to proceed, and to rely on environmental or health regulations to sort the good from the bad.

FUTURE IP SCENARIOS

As the previous examples show, polarized debates based on the narrow interests of a particular group are not the best way to help society shape the future. Unfortunately there are few comprehensive reports that examine the underlying assumptions of the various interest groups, and fewer still that review the potential consequences of their recommendations. One of the most innovative and thorough of these reports was completed in 2007 by the European Patent Office (EPO) in its Scenarios for the Future report ("EPO Report").[17]

Based on extensive interviews with a broad range of stakeholders, the EPO Report identified several plausible holistic long-range IP scenarios – complex stories about the consequences of the decisions countries and organizations are being asked to make today. The simplistic scenario of a world without any IP laws at all was not analyzed in detail because it is simply not plausible in view of the history of IP law and practice as it has evolved over the past several centuries.

Five driving forces were identified as particularly influential. First, power relationships are in flux due in part to globalization and cross-cutting alliances formed between and among multinational corporations, global networks of civil society

[17] European Patent Office, *Scenarios for the Future: How Might IP Regimes Evolve by 2025? What Global Legitimacy Might Such Regimes Have?*, available at http://www.epo.org/focus/patent-system/scenarios-for-the-future/download.html accessed August 24, 2007.

special interest organizations, and international bodies and trade blocs, so it is not clear who will have authority over the IP system in the future. Second, the flattening of the world creates a global jungle of competition, among local communities and countries, companies and industry groups, market sectors and workforces, making it hard to say which will survive and which will not. Third, a faster rate of change in technology and economics contrasts with slower changes in human psychology, culture, and the environment. Fourth, interdependence creates massive systemic risks and threat of regional, ethnic, and cultural conflicts. Fifth, there is a paradox between the increasing use of IP rights to restrict innovation, and the increased availability of knowledge around the world. The EPO Report refers to this fragmented but interconnected world with dramatic demographic shifts as a Kaleidoscope Society, one in which no trends dominate and accurate predictions are impossible. These forces affect both the legal system and the practices organizations use to operate within them.

The EPO Report imagined four separate scenarios that could result from these driving forces. The assumptions in each overlap, and there are few bright line distinctions between them. However, following the analysis out 20 years in each case leads to very different futures.

Market Rules

Business has its way in this scenario, which is the most familiar one. Projecting forward, new forms of technology become patentable, and more people seek patent protection. Corporations use patent portfolios to dominate particular technologies. Patents are traded as financial assets. Given the sheer volume of patent applications, a global patent treaty is finally implemented. Market forces predominate, with anti-competition laws the principle tool for curbing abuse of the system and problems such as boom-bust economic cycles. Successful business lobbying would indicate a trend in this direction, where success would be defined by speed and efficiency.

Whose Game?

In this scenario, geopolitics dominates the IP agenda. Players in wealthy countries fail to maintain technical superiority with strong IP rights, and some developing countries catch up, while others migrate to a communal use paradigm. Differences among IP systems are increasingly used as weapons in trade wars between nations and trade blocs. Global enforcement becomes more difficult in an even more fragmented world. A trend in this direction would be signaled by assertiveness by new entrants such as China, Brazil, and India, and success would be defined in terms of "my society wins."

Projecting forward in this scenario, weak economies and reduced investment in research in the developed countries could lead many scientists to move to intermediate countries like China and India, raising levels of innovation in those countries dramatically, and leading to a bipolar world: a bloc of North America and Europe, and an Asian-South American bloc.

Trees of Knowledge

Social groups are the dominant force in this scenario. Politics comes to dominate research and innovation, rather than science and market forces. Heightened criticism and distrust lead to an erosion of the IP system. In an increasingly kaleidoscopic society, fleeting alliances form around specific issues and crises, such as health, knowledge, food, and entertainment. Popular movements and the media drive toward dominance of an A2K (access to knowledge) approach, with reward for innovation being secondary. A rise in discussion of environmental, philosophical, and religious implications of IP systems would signal a move in this direction, where success is measured by broad social acceptance.

Tension between private property and public goods is high in this scenario, where the open access movement weakens rights in the entertainment industry and scientific research. A global pandemic pushes society toward a centralized grant/prize/purchase system for medical innovation instead of the decentralized patent system. Global blights on key crops lead to centralized agricultural research. Patents are restricted to mechanical and chemical inventions, not genetics and software. Patent offices evolve to serve as knowledge agencies implementing various incentive programs. Secrecy and branding are the dominant IP rights, and some areas of innovation whither, like biotechnology.

Blue Skies

In this scenario, technology is the main driver in a fragmented world. Special IP practices apply to integrative technologies in biotechnology, information technology, and nanotechnology, viewed as crucial to overcoming challenges like disease and hunger. Novel licensing practices such as open source systems, patent pooling, and compulsory licensing promote collaboration and diffusion and use of these critical technologies. These practices are formalized in international arrangements providing access in exchange for mandatory payments, in environmental climate change technology, and in telecommunications. Patent offices are tasked with administering these complex licensing systems, with an international IP court resolving some disputes. Growing tension between new and classic technology sectors would signal a trend in this direction, where success is measured in terms of technology diffusion and resilience.

The EPO Report's set of four "challenging, relevant and plausible scenarios" is an excellent and inspiring example of creative thinking by a government agency. Its ultimate conclusion – that the IP system status quo is likely to change dramatically – is forcefully presented. The scenario planning approach is promising, and the PIIPA organization is extending it to deal with emerging and least developed countries.

It will be a challenge for different countries, organizations, and private companies to participate in efforts to modify the IP system, and to influence which of these scenarios plays out. The dynamics of the innovation cycle are at stake. Knowledgeable IP professionals will be crucial participants in this process.

SUMMARY. The concepts and strategies presented in this book enable a fresh look at the larger dynamics of intellectual property, and the tensions between different countries, regions, and industries. Five illustrations involve innovative communities and organizations for whom IP rights are a driving force. First, the emerging financial market in IP rights is increasing liquidity and reducing transaction costs. Eventually IP trading companies are likely to emerge. Second, sustainable innovation in medicine can be promoted by maintaining a balance between branded and generic pharmaceutical companies. The balance can be struck so that today's patients can have adequate access to existing medicines, while tomorrow's patients can have better medicines in the future; and so that patients in all countries can have access to the medicines they need most. Third, the U.S. response to the rise of international terrorism included measures promoting innovation. The role of IP assets in commercializing homeland security technology is different when the customer is a national, state, or local government, or a private party. Fourth, intellectual property laws and environmental protection laws each have weaknesses in promoting environmental technology innovation, but the two can be applied together to promote sustainable innovation. Fifth, controversies over biotechnology have led to surprising alignments on intellectual property issues. Some antitechnologists and human rights activists ironically favor stronger IP rights protecting genetic resources in developing countries, while some biotechnology researchers favor open access models for their research results, publishing DNA sequence information freely. Finally, the EPO scenarios planning report looks to several potential innovation futures and shines light on what the world might look like, depending on which social force predominates in shaping the IP system.

19 Intellectual Property, Innovation, and Freedom

This concluding chapter looks at the relationship of innovative individuals and their societies, the significance of innovation to freedom, and the role of intellectual property in maintaining that freedom. The concepts and strategies presented in this book can help individuals, organizations, and nations improve the world through the power of innovation.

* * * * * *

Innovation plays a central role in social welfare, and intellectual property has developed as a tool for driving and channeling innovation, by balancing access and exclusivity. How that balance is struck affects both individual organizations and larger communities and nations.

Intellectual property remains controversial. Yet it is and has long been a fundamental instrument of innovation and even personal freedom, and its crucial role will surely continue well into the future.

Nobel laureate economist Amartya Sen argues that national development goes beyond economics or technological progress, and should be seen "as a process of expanding the real freedoms that people enjoy,"[1] including facilities for education and health care as well as political and civil rights. Sen points to freedom of expression and action, freedom to exchange words, goods, and gifts, as basic liberties, part of the way human beings interact with each other unless prevented from doing so. Economic wealth is only one means for achieving freedom in a long and healthy and happy life. Freedom is increased by political liberties, social opportunities, and the enabling conditions of good health, basic education, protective security, and the encouragement and cultivation of initiative. Even a rich person who lacks these freedoms is deprived. Development should be directed at increasing such freedoms.

Sen suggests that we should see humans as beings leading lives of choice, not merely as human capital, instruments of production.[2] I believe that, by extension, intellectual property, often viewed as a tool of human capital, can be seen instead as an instrument by which innovators express choices regarding their creations. In this light, intellectual property contributes not just to economic development, but also to the development of freedom – of personal choice, of individual responsibility, of free expression, and free trade.

---

[1] Amartya Sen, *Development as Freedom* (Anchor/Random House, 1999), p. 6.
[2] *Id.*, chapter 12.

The IP system, in driving the innovation cycle, serves at least in part as an instrument of individual freedom and choice. Creators choose whether to give their innovations away or to restrict access with IP rights. For example, the individual freedom inherent in the IP system gave rise to open access communities in software, science, and entertainment, which are expressions of choice by many individuals. The owner of IP rights can trade these assets with others, and acquire more in the process of pushing an innovation out into society.

On the other hand, the exclusivity of IP rights restricts the freedom of choice of those who seek access to an innovation. A creator or competitor who lacks access to an innovation lacks the freedom to use it as she chooses. A Russian school teacher who is threatened with jail for unwittingly using pirated computer software does not feel free. The freedom of an IP owner to exclude others has limits.

So there must be a balance between the freedom of an IP owner to exclude others, and the freedom of others to access the IP-protected innovation. The balance between exclusivity and access has been apparent throughout this book – in the rise of intellectual property, in the basic structure of the modern system, in the detailed practical choices required to manage intellectual property in organizations, and in the global dynamic of intellectual property reform. From these discussions about control over innovation, we may conclude that the inherent need for balance between exclusivity and access in the IP system fits well within Sen's idea of development as freedom.

This analysis also suggests that the intellectual property system can provide a higher degree of individual freedom than a centralized system of grants, incentives, and prizes awarded by governments and philanthropies. Such "top-down" incentive systems may have the desired effect of driving innovation in particular directions, but at the cost of individual choice and flexibility.

It is not a new idea to proclaim that intellectual property is an instrument of freedom. Long ago, Abraham Lincoln recognized that physical labor and intellectual pursuits together drive civilization forward, and that ill effects are best avoided by the moral acts of free hardworking people in a democratic state. Lincoln repeatedly argued that innovation helps end a "slavery of the mind," and "emancipates the mind," so that people "get a habit of freedom of thought."[3]

Lincoln was concerned with a Young America benefiting from global trade in goods, and from slavery. He proclaimed the superiority of physical work over capital. One reason was that innovative work contributes to happiness, not just profitability: "I know of nothing so pleasant to the mind," he said, "as the discovery of anything which is at once *new* and *valuable* – nothing which so lightens and sweetens toil, as the hopeful pursuit of such discovery."[4]

This was the context for Lincoln's famous praise for the patent system as adding "the fuel of interest to the fire of genius." It is remarkable that 150 years ago, on the eve of the Civil War, at a time when the nation's attention was focused on

---

[3] Abraham Lincoln, *Complete Works*, John Nicolay and John Hay, eds. (Century, 1907), pp. 525–227 (also discussed in Chapter 2).

[4] Eugene Miller, "Democratic Statecraft and Technological Advance: Abraham Lincoln's Reflections on 'Discoveries and Inventions.'" *Review of Politics*, 63.405–515 (2001); see, especially, p. 514.

slavery, Lincoln was also actively grappling with the issues of globalization, innovation, intellectual property, and freedom that are front page news today.

One may ask whether the horrors of the Civil War shook Lincoln's faith in the positive social effects of creative work fueled by intellectual property. War and oppression persist today, and peace and social harmony sometimes seem elusive. Economic forces can be destructive, too (if not as violent).

But creative human endeavor continues. Every day, people write new books, sing new songs, make new movies, develop new drugs, find new energy sources, and improve electronics and communications.

The concept of creative destruction suggests that an evolutionary model applies to innovation in a market economy. Life itself proceeds by destroying life. In a forest, oak trees produce billions of pollen grains; thousands of acorns, hundreds of saplings, and dozens of trees. The rest die off. On a coral reef, millions of fish eggs are laid, thousands of minnows hatch, but most are eaten and only a few reach maturity. These ecosystems are healthy, in balance, if new life emerges at least as quickly as life is destroyed. The health of the system as a whole balances out the loss of the many individuals that are destroyed. Likewise, with innovation, only a few new ideas mature and survive, and the rest are lost or left undeveloped. There are winners and losers. But because innovation is a human endeavor, the health of the larger system may bring little comfort to an individual, a company, an industry, or a nation left behind by a newcomer. Winners are happy, losers are not.

No one is free in the sense that they can escape the larger system of competition and the innovation cycle, but we can seek to ensure that the system is fair. The intellectual property system can play a role in promoting fairness, by balancing the innovator's freedom to exclude against the public's freedom to use the innovation. The IP system promotes both individual independence and community interdependence.

We can not predict what is over the horizon, who will win, and who will lose, but we continue to innovate, by trial and error, and hope for the best, just like our ancestors before us. Inevitably some will do better than others, and the best we can hope for is a system in which people and nations compete fairly, with the freedom to pursue their creative endeavors.

Modern debates about intellectual property have old roots, but they are fresh, intense, and important. The opportunities and challenges presented by the IP system have never been greater. The outcome is uncertain. But it is clear that nations and organizations and individuals within them should strive for higher levels of sophistication about the intellectual property system. They should consider how the system affects them and their goals, and then put their insights to work.

SUMMARY. This book reflects my effort to describe the fundamental concepts and dynamics of the IP system and how it shapes our world, and to derive a practical approach that can be used by for-profit corporations and nonprofit organizations in different industries and cultural pursuits, in rich and poor countries, working within the system to make it work better. Having reached the end of that task, I can summarize the lessons I have learned as follows. The intellectual property system is messy and complex, but like organizations, governments, and human societies themselves, it is necessary. We would have to invent intellectual property if it did not already exist. Indeed, those of us working with intellectual property and the innovation cycle know that in trying to find the balance between exclusive rights and access, we reinvent the system in many small ways every day.

The concepts and examples presented in this book illustrate why there is a need for competent IP management, and careful weighing of the implications of any proposed legal reform to the IP system. Some basic principles emerge.

- The need for advice about IP law and practice is strong and growing.
- The lack of access to IP expertise is particularly acute in developing countries.
- The basic skills required to manage intellectual property can be learned by most people.
- IP laws and practices are complex, and it requires experience and professional expertise to fully understand and apply them.
- The IP system is global in reach, and local in impact, and working within it requires a broad network of talent.
- Debates about IP laws are polarized, but a balanced approach can establish a common ground free of fear and ignorance, and lead to productive reforms.

All countries, and all organizations within them, can benefit from an improved understanding of how intellectual property drives the innovation cycle, how innovation changes the IP system, and how organizations and societies can manage intellectual property to further their goals in this changing world. The innovation cycle will continue into the future, and those who can best work within it, or change it, will benefit the most.

Excerpts from TRIPS Agreement
Agreement on Trade-Related Aspects of Intellectual Property Rights

The TRIPS Agreement (Trade-Related Aspects of Intellectual Property Rights) is Annex 1C of the Marrakesh Agreement Establishing the World Trade Organization, signed in Marrakesh, Morocco on April 15, 1994. Relevant portions are reproduced here. The full text is available at http://www.wto.org/english/docs_e/legal_e/27-trips.pdf.

* * * * * *

PART I. GENERAL PROVISIONS AND BASIC PRINCIPLES

PART II. STANDARDS CONCERNING THE AVAILABILITY, SCOPE, AND USE OF INTELLECTUAL PROPERTY RIGHTS
1. Copyright and Related Rights
2. Trademarks
3. Geographical Indications
4. Industrial Designs
5. Patents
* * *
7. Protection of Undisclosed Information
8. Control of Anti-Competitive Practices in Contractual Licences

PART III. ENFORCEMENT OF INTELLECTUAL PROPERTY RIGHTS
1. General Obligations
2. Civil and Administrative Procedures and Remedies
3. Provisional Measures
* * *
5. Criminal Procedures

PART IV. ACQUISITION AND MAINTENANCE OF INTELLECTUAL PROPERTY RIGHTS AND RELATED INTER-PARTES PROCEDURES

PART V. DISPUTE PREVENTION AND SETTLEMENT

Members,

Desiring to reduce distortions and impediments to international trade, and taking into account the need to promote effective and adequate protection of intellectual property rights, and to ensure that measures and procedures to enforce intellectual property rights do not themselves become barriers to legitimate trade;

Recognizing, to this end, the need for new rules and disciplines concerning:

(a) the applicability of the basic principles of GATT 1994 and of relevant international intellectual property agreements or conventions;

(b) the provision of adequate standards and principles concerning the availability, scope and use of trade-related intellectual property rights;

(c) the provision of effective and appropriate means for the enforcement of trade-related intellectual property rights, taking into account differences in national legal systems;

(d) the provision of effective and expeditious procedures for the multilateral prevention and settlement of disputes between governments; and

(e) transitional arrangements aiming at the fullest participation in the results of the negotiations;

Recognizing the need for a multilateral framework of principles, rules and disciplines dealing with international trade in counterfeit goods;

Recognizing that intellectual property rights are private rights;

Recognizing the underlying public policy objectives of national systems for the protection of intellectual property, including developmental and technological objectives;

Recognizing also the special needs of the least-developed country Members in respect of maximum flexibility in the domestic implementation of laws and regulations in order to enable them to create a sound and viable technological base;

Emphasizing the importance of reducing tensions by reaching strengthened commitments to resolve disputes on trade-related intellectual property issues through multilateral procedures;

Desiring to establish a mutually supportive relationship between the WTO and the World Intellectual Property Organization (referred to in this Agreement as "WIPO") as well as other relevant international organizations;

Hereby agree as follows:

PART I. GENERAL PROVISIONS AND BASIC PRINCIPLES

Article 1. Nature and Scope of Obligations

1. Members shall give effect to the provisions of this Agreement. Members may, but shall not be obliged to, implement in their law more extensive protection than is required by this Agreement, provided that such protection does not contravene the provisions of this Agreement. Members shall be free to determine the appropriate method of implementing the provisions of this Agreement within their own legal system and practice.

2. For the purposes of this Agreement, the term "intellectual property" refers to all categories of intellectual property that are the subject of Sections 1 through 7 of Part II.

* * *

Article 3. National Treatment

1. Each Member shall accord to the nationals of other Members treatment no less favourable than that it accords to its own nationals with regard to the protection[1] of intellectual property. . . .

* * *

Article 7. Objectives

The protection and enforcement of intellectual property rights should contribute to the promotion of technological innovation and to the transfer and dissemination of technology, to the mutual advantage of producers and users of technological knowledge and in a manner conducive to social and economic welfare, and to a balance of rights and obligations.

Article 8. Principles

1. Members may, in formulating or amending their laws and regulations, adopt measures necessary to protect public health and nutrition, and to promote the public interest in sectors of vital importance to their socio-economic and technological development, provided that such measures are consistent with the provisions of this Agreement.
2. Appropriate measures, provided that they are consistent with the provisions of this Agreement, may be needed to prevent the abuse of intellectual property rights by right holders or the resort to practices which unreasonably restrain trade or adversely affect the international transfer of technology.

PART II. STANDARDS CONCERNING THE AVAILABILITY, SCOPE, AND USE OF INTELLECTUAL PROPERTY RIGHTS

SECTION 1: COPYRIGHT AND RELATED RIGHTS

Article 9. Relation to the Berne Convention

1. Members shall comply with Articles 1 through 21 of the Berne Convention (1971) and the Appendix thereto . . .
2. Copyright protection shall extend to expressions and not to ideas, procedures, methods of operation or mathematical concepts as such.

Article 10. Computer Programs and Compilations of Data

1. Computer programs, whether in source or object code, shall be protected as literary works under the Berne Convention (1971).

---

[1] For the purposes of Articles 3 and 4, "protection" shall include matters affecting the availability, acquisition, scope, maintenance and enforcement of intellectual property rights as well as those matters affecting the use of intellectual property rights specifically addressed in this Agreement.

2. Compilations of data or other material, whether in machine readable or other form, which by reason of the selection or arrangement of their contents constitute intellectual creations shall be protected as such. Such protection, which shall not extend to the data or material itself, shall be without prejudice to any copyright subsisting in the data or material itself.

* * *

Article 12. Term of Protection

Whenever the term of protection of a work, other than a photographic work or a work of applied art, is calculated on a basis other than the life of a natural person, such term shall be no less than 50 years from the end of the calendar year of authorized publication, or, failing such authorized publication within 50 years from the making of the work, 50 years from the end of the calendar year of making.

Article 13. Limitations and Exceptions

Members shall confine limitations or exceptions to exclusive rights to certain special cases which do not conflict with a normal exploitation of the work and do not unreasonably prejudice the legitimate interests of the right holder.

Article 14. Protection of Performers, Producers of Phonograms (Sound Recordings) and Broadcasting Organizations

1. In respect of a fixation of their performance on a phonogram, performers shall have the possibility of preventing the following acts when undertaken without their authorization: the fixation of their unfixed performance and the reproduction of such fixation. Performers shall also have the possibility of preventing the following acts when undertaken without their authorization: the broadcasting by wireless means and the communication to the public of their live performance.
2. Producers of phonograms shall enjoy the right to authorize or prohibit the direct or indirect reproduction of their phonograms.
3. Broadcasting organizations shall have the right to prohibit the following acts when undertaken without their authorization: the fixation, the reproduction of fixations, and the rebroadcasting by wireless means of broadcasts, as well as the communication to the public of television broadcasts of the same. Where Members do not grant such rights to broadcasting organizations, they shall provide owners of copyright in the subject matter of broadcasts with the possibility of preventing the above acts, subject to the provisions of the Berne Convention (1971).

* * *

SECTION 2: TRADEMARKS

Article 15. Protectable Subject Matter

1. Any sign, or any combination of signs, capable of distinguishing the goods or services of one undertaking from those of other undertakings, shall be capable of constituting a trademark. Such signs, in particular words including personal names, letters, numerals, figurative elements and combinations of colours as well

as any combination of such signs, shall be eligible for registration as trademarks. Where signs are not inherently capable of distinguishing the relevant goods or services, Members may make registrability depend on distinctiveness acquired through use. Members may require, as a condition of registration, that signs be visually perceptible.

* * *

3. Members may make registrability depend on use. However, actual use of a trademark shall not be a condition for filing an application for registration. An application shall not be refused solely on the ground that intended use has not taken place before the expiry of a period of three years from the date of application.
4. The nature of the goods or services to which a trademark is to be applied shall in no case form an obstacle to registration of the trademark.
5. Members shall publish each trademark either before it is registered or promptly after it is registered and shall afford a reasonable opportunity for petitions to cancel the registration. In addition, Members may afford an opportunity for the registration of a trademark to be opposed.

Article 16. Rights Conferred

1. The owner of a registered trademark shall have the exclusive right to prevent all third parties not having the owner's consent from using in the course of trade identical or similar signs for goods or services which are identical or similar to those in respect of which the trademark is registered where such use would result in a likelihood of confusion. In case of the use of an identical sign for identical goods or services, a likelihood of confusion shall be presumed. The rights described above shall not prejudice any existing prior rights, nor shall they affect the possibility of Members making rights available on the basis of use.

Article 17. Exceptions

Members may provide limited exceptions to the rights conferred by a trademark, such as fair use of descriptive terms, provided that such exceptions take account of the legitimate interests of the owner of the trademark and of third parties.

Article 18. Term of Protection

Initial registration, and each renewal of registration, of a trademark shall be for a term of no less than seven years. The registration of a trademark shall be renewable indefinitely.

Article 19. Requirement of Use

1. If use is required to maintain a registration, the registration may be cancelled only after an uninterrupted period of at least three years of non-use, unless valid reasons based on the existence of obstacles to such use are shown by the trademark owner. Circumstances arising independently of the will of the owner of the trademark which constitute an obstacle to the use of the trademark, such as import restrictions on or other government requirements for goods or services protected by the trademark, shall be recognized as valid reasons for non-use.

2. When subject to the control of its owner, use of a trademark by another person shall be recognized as use of the trademark for the purpose of maintaining the registration.

Article 20. Other Requirements

The use of a trademark in the course of trade shall not be unjustifiably encumbered by special requirements, such as use with another trademark, use in a special form or use in a manner detrimental to its capability to distinguish the goods or services of one undertaking from those of other undertakings. This will not preclude a requirement prescribing the use of the trademark identifying the undertaking producing the goods or services along with, but without linking it to, the trademark distinguishing the specific goods or services in question of that undertaking.

Article 21. Licensing and Assignment

Members may determine conditions on the licensing and assignment of trademarks, it being understood that the compulsory licensing of trademarks shall not be permitted and that the owner of a registered trademark shall have the right to assign the trademark with or without the transfer of the business to which the trademark belongs.

SECTION 3: GEOGRAPHICAL INDICATIONS

Article 22. Protection of Geographical Indications

1. Geographical indications are, for the purposes of this Agreement, indications which identify a good as originating in the territory of a Member, or a region or locality in that territory, where a given quality, reputation or other characteristic of the good is essentially attributable to its geographical origin.
2. In respect of geographical indications, Members shall provide the legal means for interested parties to prevent:
   (a) the use of any means in the designation or presentation of a good that indicates or suggests that the good in question originates in a geographical area other than the true place of origin in a manner which misleads the public as to the geographical origin of the good. . . .

    * * *

SECTION 4: INDUSTRIAL DESIGNS

Article 25. Requirements for Protection

1. Members shall provide for the protection of independently created industrial designs that are new or original. Members may provide that designs are not new or original if they do not significantly differ from known designs or combinations of known design features. Members may provide that such protection shall not extend to designs dictated essentially by technical or functional considerations.
2. Each Member shall ensure that requirements for securing protection for textile designs, in particular in regard to any cost, examination or publication, do not unreasonably impair the opportunity to seek and obtain such protection. Members shall be free to meet this obligation through industrial design law or through copyright law.

Article 26. Protection

1. The owner of a protected industrial design shall have the right to prevent third parties not having the owner's consent from making, selling or importing articles bearing or embodying a design which is a copy, or substantially a copy, of the protected design, when such acts are undertaken for commercial purposes.
2. Members may provide limited exceptions to the protection of industrial designs, provided that such exceptions do not unreasonably conflict with the normal exploitation of protected industrial designs and do not unreasonably prejudice the legitimate interests of the owner of the protected design, taking account of the legitimate interests of third parties.
3. The duration of protection available shall amount to at least 10 years.

SECTION 5: PATENTS

Article 27. Patentable Subject Matter

1. Subject to the provisions of paragraphs 2 and 3, patents shall be available for any inventions, whether products or processes, in all fields of technology, provided that they are new, involve an inventive step and are capable of industrial application.[2] Subject to [transitional measures] ... and paragraph 3 of this Article, patents shall be available and patent rights enjoyable without discrimination as to the place of invention, the field of technology and whether products are imported or locally produced.
2. Members may exclude from patentability inventions, the prevention within their territory of the commercial exploitation of which is necessary to protect *ordre public* or morality, including to protect human, animal or plant life or health or to avoid serious prejudice to the environment, provided that such exclusion is not made merely because the exploitation is prohibited by their law.
3. Members may also exclude from patentability:
   (a) diagnostic, therapeutic and surgical methods for the treatment of humans or animals;
   (b) plants and animals other than micro-organisms, and essentially biological processes for the production of plants or animals other than non-biological and microbiological processes. However, Members shall provide for the protection of plant varieties either by patents or by an effective *sui generis* system or by any combination thereof. The provisions of this subparagraph shall be reviewed four years after the date of entry into force of the WTO Agreement.

Article 28. Rights Conferred

1. A patent shall confer on its owner the following exclusive rights:
   (a) where the subject matter of a patent is a product, to prevent third parties not having the owner's consent from the acts of: making, using, offering for sale, selling, or importing[3] for these purposes that product;

---

[2] For the purposes of this Article, the terms "inventive step" and "capable of industrial application" may be deemed by a Member to be synonymous with the terms "non-obvious" and "useful" respectively.

[3] This right, like all other rights conferred under this Agreement in respect of the use, sale, importation or other distribution of goods, is subject to the provisions of Article 6.

(b) where the subject matter of a patent is a process, to prevent third parties not having the owner's consent from the act of using the process, and from the acts of: using, offering for sale, selling, or importing for these purposes at least the product obtained directly by that process.

2. Patent owners shall also have the right to assign, or transfer by succession, the patent and to conclude licensing contracts.

Article 29. Conditions on Patent Applicants

1. Members shall require that an applicant for a patent shall disclose the invention in a manner sufficiently clear and complete for the invention to be carried out by a person skilled in the art and may require the applicant to indicate the best mode for carrying out the invention known to the inventor at the filing date or, where priority is claimed, at the priority date of the application.

2. Members may require an applicant for a patent to provide information concerning the applicant's corresponding foreign applications and grants.

Article 30. Exceptions to Rights Conferred

Members may provide limited exceptions to the exclusive rights conferred by a patent, provided that such exceptions do not unreasonably conflict with a normal exploitation of the patent and do not unreasonably prejudice the legitimate interests of the patent owner, taking account of the legitimate interests of third parties.

Article 31. Other Use Without Authorization of the Right Holder

Where the law of a Member allows for other use[4] of the subject matter of a patent without the authorization of the right holder, including use by the government or third parties authorized by the government, the following provisions shall be respected:

(a) authorization of such use shall be considered on its individual merits;

(b) such use may only be permitted if, prior to such use, the proposed user has made efforts to obtain authorization from the right holder on reasonable commercial terms and conditions and that such efforts have not been successful within a reasonable period of time. This requirement may be waived by a Member in the case of a national emergency or other circumstances of extreme urgency or in cases of public non-commercial use. In situations of national emergency or other circumstances of extreme urgency, the right holder shall, nevertheless, be notified as soon as reasonably practicable. In the case of public non-commercial use, where the government or contractor, without making a patent search, knows or has demonstrable grounds to know that a valid patent is or will be used by or for the government, the right holder shall be informed promptly;

(c) the scope and duration of such use shall be limited to the purpose for which it was authorized, and in the case of semi-conductor technology shall only be for public non-commercial use or to remedy a practice determined after judicial or administrative process to be anti-competitive;

---

[4] "Other use" refers to use other than that allowed under Article 30.

(d) such use shall be non-exclusive;

(e) such use shall be non-assignable, except with that part of the enterprise or goodwill which enjoys such use;

(f) any such use shall be authorized predominantly for the supply of the domestic market of the Member authorizing such use;

(g) authorization for such use shall be liable, subject to adequate protection of the legitimate interests of the persons so authorized, to be terminated if and when the circumstances which led to it cease to exist and are unlikely to recur. The competent authority shall have the authority to review, upon motivated request, the continued existence of these circumstances;

(h) the right holder shall be paid adequate remuneration in the circumstances of each case, taking into account the economic value of the authorization;

(i) the legal validity of any decision relating to the authorization of such use shall be subject to judicial review or other independent review by a distinct higher authority in that Member;

(j) any decision relating to the remuneration provided in respect of such use shall be subject to judicial review or other independent review by a distinct higher authority in that Member;

(k) Members are not obliged to apply the conditions set forth in subparagraphs (b) and (f) where such use is permitted to remedy a practice determined after judicial or administrative process to be anti-competitive. The need to correct anti-competitive practices may be taken into account in determining the amount of remuneration in such cases. Competent authorities shall have the authority to refuse termination of authorization if and when the conditions which led to such authorization are likely to recur;

(l) where such use is authorized to permit the exploitation of a patent ("the second patent") which cannot be exploited without infringing another patent ("the first patent"), the following additional conditions shall apply:

  (i) the invention claimed in the second patent shall involve an important technical advance of considerable economic significance in relation to the invention claimed in the first patent;

  (ii) the owner of the first patent shall be entitled to a cross-licence on reasonable terms to use the invention claimed in the second patent; and

  (iii) the use authorized in respect of the first patent shall be non-assignable except with the assignment of the second patent.

Article 32. Revocation/Forfeiture

An opportunity for judicial review of any decision to revoke or forfeit a patent shall be available.

Article 33. Term of Protection

The term of protection available shall not end before the expiration of a period of twenty years counted from the filing date.[5]

---

[5] It is understood that those Members which do not have a system of original grant may provide that the term of protection shall be computed from the filing date in the system of original grant.

Article 34. Process Patents: Burden of Proof

1. For the purposes of civil proceedings in respect of the infringement of the rights of the owner referred to in paragraph 1(b) of Article 28, if the subject matter of a patent is a process for obtaining a product, the judicial authorities shall have the authority to order the defendant to prove that the process to obtain an identical product is different from the patented process. Therefore, Members shall provide, in at least one of the following circumstances, that any identical product when produced without the consent of the patent owner shall, in the absence of proof to the contrary, be deemed to have been obtained by the patented process:
   (a) if the product obtained by the patented process is new;
   (b) if there is a substantial likelihood that the identical product was made by the process and the owner of the patent has been unable through reasonable efforts to determine the process actually used.
2. Any Member shall be free to provide that the burden of proof indicated in paragraph 1 shall be on the alleged infringer only if the condition referred to in subparagraph (a) is fulfilled or only if the condition referred to in subparagraph (b) is fulfilled.
3. In the adduction of proof to the contrary, the legitimate interests of defendants in protecting their manufacturing and business secrets shall be taken into account.

* * *

SECTION 7: PROTECTION OF UNDISCLOSED INFORMATION

Article 39

1. In the course of ensuring effective protection against unfair competition as provided in Article 10bis of the Paris Convention (1967), Members shall protect undisclosed information in accordance with paragraph 2 and data submitted to governments or governmental agencies in accordance with paragraph 3.
2. Natural and legal persons shall have the possibility of preventing information lawfully within their control from being disclosed to, acquired by, or used by others without their consent in a manner contrary to honest commercial practices[6] so long as such information:
   (a) is secret in the sense that it is not, as a body or in the precise configuration and assembly of its components, generally known among or readily accessible to persons within the circles that normally deal with the kind of information in question;
   (b) has commercial value because it is secret; and
   (c) has been subject to reasonable steps under the circumstances, by the person lawfully in control of the information, to keep it secret.
3. Members, when requiring, as a condition of approving the marketing of pharmaceutical or of agricultural chemical products which utilize new chemical entities, the submission of undisclosed test or other data, the origination of which involves

---

[6] For the purpose of this provision, "a manner contrary to honest commercial practices" shall mean at least practices such as breach of contract, breach of confidence and inducement to breach, and includes the acquisition of undisclosed information by third parties who knew, or were grossly negligent in failing to know, that such practices were involved in the acquisition.

a considerable effort, shall protect such data against unfair commercial use. In addition, Members shall protect such data against disclosure, except where necessary to protect the public, or unless steps are taken to ensure that the data are protected against unfair commercial use.

SECTION 8: CONTROL OF ANTI-COMPETITIVE PRACTICES IN CONTRACTUAL LICENCES

Article 40.

1. Members agree that some licensing practices or conditions pertaining to intellectual property rights which restrain competition may have adverse effects on trade and may impede the transfer and dissemination of technology.
2. Nothing in this Agreement shall prevent Members from specifying in their legislation licensing practices or conditions that may in particular cases constitute an abuse of intellectual property rights having an adverse effect on competition in the relevant market. As provided above, a Member may adopt, consistently with the other provisions of this Agreement, appropriate measures to prevent or control such practices, which may include for example exclusive grantback conditions, conditions preventing challenges to validity and coercive package licensing, in the light of the relevant laws and regulations of that Member.

* * *

PART III. ENFORCEMENT OF INTELLECTUAL PROPERTY RIGHTS

SECTION 1: GENERAL OBLIGATIONS

Article 41

1. Members shall ensure that enforcement procedures as specified in this Part are available under their law so as to permit effective action against any act of infringement of intellectual property rights covered by this Agreement, including expeditious remedies to prevent infringements and remedies which constitute a deterrent to further infringements. These procedures shall be applied in such a manner as to avoid the creation of barriers to legitimate trade and to provide for safeguards against their abuse.
2. Procedures concerning the enforcement of intellectual property rights shall be fair and equitable. They shall not be unnecessarily complicated or costly, or entail unreasonable time-limits or unwarranted delays.
3. Decisions on the merits of a case shall preferably be in writing and reasoned. They shall be made available at least to the parties to the proceeding without undue delay. Decisions on the merits of a case shall be based only on evidence in respect of which parties were offered the opportunity to be heard.
4. Parties to a proceeding shall have an opportunity for review by a judicial authority of final administrative decisions and, subject to jurisdictional provisions in a Member's law concerning the importance of a case, of at least the legal aspects of initial judicial decisions on the merits of a case. However, there shall be no obligation to provide an opportunity for review of acquittals in criminal cases.
5. It is understood that this Part does not create any obligation to put in place a judicial system for the enforcement of intellectual property rights distinct from that

for the enforcement of law in general, nor does it affect the capacity of Members to enforce their law in general. Nothing in this Part creates any obligation with respect to the distribution of resources as between enforcement of intellectual property rights and the enforcement of law in general.

SECTION 2: CIVIL AND ADMINISTRATIVE PROCEDURES AND REMEDIES

Article 42. Fair and Equitable Procedures
Members shall make available to right holders[7] civil judicial procedures concerning the enforcement of any intellectual property right covered by this Agreement. Defendants shall have the right to written notice which is timely and contains sufficient detail, including the basis of the claims. Parties shall be allowed to be represented by independent legal counsel, and procedures shall not impose overly burdensome requirements concerning mandatory personal appearances. All parties to such procedures shall be duly entitled to substantiate their claims and to present all relevant evidence. The procedure shall provide a means to identify and protect confidential information, unless this would be contrary to existing constitutional requirements.

Article 43. Evidence
1. The judicial authorities shall have the authority, where a party has presented reasonably available evidence sufficient to support its claims and has specified evidence relevant to substantiation of its claims which lies in the control of the opposing party, to order that this evidence be produced by the opposing party, subject in appropriate cases to conditions which ensure the protection of confidential information.
2. In cases in which a party to a proceeding voluntarily and without good reason refuses access to, or otherwise does not provide necessary information within a reasonable period, or significantly impedes a procedure relating to an enforcement action, a Member may accord judicial authorities the authority to make preliminary and final determinations, affirmative or negative, on the basis of the information presented to them, including the complaint or the allegation presented by the party adversely affected by the denial of access to information, subject to providing the parties an opportunity to be heard on the allegations or evidence.

Article 44. Injunctions
1. The judicial authorities shall have the authority to order a party to desist from an infringement, *inter alia* to prevent the entry into the channels of commerce in their jurisdiction of imported goods that involve the infringement of an intellectual property right, immediately after customs clearance of such goods. Members are not obliged to accord such authority in respect of protected subject matter acquired or ordered by a person prior to knowing or having reasonable grounds to know that dealing in such subject matter would entail the infringement of an intellectual property right

---

[7] For the purpose of this Part, the term "right holder" includes federations and associations having legal standing to assert such rights.

2. Notwithstanding the other provisions of this Part and provided that the provisions of Part II specifically addressing use by governments, or by third parties authorized by a government, without the authorization of the right holder are complied with, Members may limit the remedies available against such use to payment of remuneration in accordance with subparagraph (h) of Article 31. In other cases, the remedies under this Part shall apply or, where these remedies are inconsistent with a Member's law, declaratory judgments and adequate compensation shall be available.

Article 45. Damages

1. The judicial authorities shall have the authority to order the infringer to pay the right holder damages adequate to compensate for the injury the right holder has suffered because of an infringement of that person's intellectual property right by an infringer who knowingly, or with reasonable grounds to know, engaged in infringing activity.
2. The judicial authorities shall also have the authority to order the infringer to pay the right holder expenses, which may include appropriate attorney's fees. In appropriate cases, Members may authorize the judicial authorities to order recovery of profits and/or payment of pre-established damages even where the infringer did not knowingly, or with reasonable grounds to know, engage in infringing activity.

Article 46. Other Remedies

In order to create an effective deterrent to infringement, the judicial authorities shall have the authority to order that goods that they have found to be infringing be, without compensation of any sort, disposed of outside the channels of commerce in such a manner as to avoid any harm caused to the right holder, or, unless this would be contrary to existing constitutional requirements, destroyed. The judicial authorities shall also have the authority to order that materials and implements the predominant use of which has been in the creation of the infringing goods be, without compensation of any sort, disposed of outside the channels of commerce in such a manner as to minimize the risks of further infringements. In considering such requests, the need for proportionality between the seriousness of the infringement and the remedies ordered as well as the interests of third parties shall be taken into account. In regard to counterfeit trademark goods, the simple removal of the trademark unlawfully affixed shall not be sufficient, other than in exceptional cases, to permit release of the goods into the channels of commerce.

Article 47. Right of Information

Members may provide that the judicial authorities shall have the authority, unless this would be out of proportion to the seriousness of the infringement, to order the infringer to inform the right holder of the identity of third persons involved in the production and distribution of the infringing goods or services and of their channels of distribution.

* * *

SECTION 3: PROVISIONAL MEASURES

Article 50

1. The judicial authorities shall have the authority to order prompt and effective provisional measures:
    (a) to prevent an infringement of any intellectual property right from occurring, and in particular to prevent the entry into the channels of commerce in their jurisdiction of goods, including imported goods immediately after customs clearance;
    (b) to preserve relevant evidence in regard to the alleged infringement.

* * *

SECTION 5: CRIMINAL PROCEDURES

Article 61

Members shall provide for criminal procedures and penalties to be applied at least in cases of wilful trademark counterfeiting or copyright piracy on a commercial scale. Remedies available shall include imprisonment and/or monetary fines sufficient to provide a deterrent, consistently with the level of penalties applied for crimes of a corresponding gravity. In appropriate cases, remedies available shall also include the seizure, forfeiture and destruction of the infringing goods and of any materials and implements the predominant use of which has been in the commission of the offence. Members may provide for criminal procedures and penalties to be applied in other cases of infringement of intellectual property rights, in particular where they are committed wilfully and on a commercial scale.

PART IV ACQUISITION AND MAINTENANCE OF INTELLECTUAL PROPERTY RIGHTS AND RELATED INTER-PARTES PROCEDURES

Article 62

1. Members may require, as a condition of the acquisition or maintenance of the intellectual property rights provided for under Sections 2 through 6 of Part II, compliance with reasonable procedures and formalities. Such procedures and formalities shall be consistent with the provisions of this Agreement.
2. Where the acquisition of an intellectual property right is subject to the right being granted or registered, Members shall ensure that the procedures for grant or registration, subject to compliance with the substantive conditions for acquisition of the right, permit the granting or registration of the right within a reasonable period of time so as to avoid unwarranted curtailment of the period of protection.

* * *

4. Procedures concerning the acquisition or maintenance of intellectual property rights and, where a Member's law provides for such procedures, administrative revocation and *inter partes* procedures such as opposition, revocation and cancellation, shall be governed by the general principles set out in paragraphs 2 and 3 of Article 41.

5. Final administrative decisions in any of the procedures referred to under paragraph 4 shall be subject to review by a judicial or quasi-judicial authority. However, there shall be no obligation to provide an opportunity for such review of decisions in cases of unsuccessful opposition or administrative revocation, provided that the grounds for such procedures can be the subject of invalidation procedures.

PART V DISPUTE PREVENTION AND SETTLEMENT

Article 63. Transparency

1. Laws and regulations, and final judicial decisions and administrative rulings of general application, made effective by a Member pertaining to the subject matter of this Agreement (the availability, scope, acquisition, enforcement and prevention of the abuse of intellectual property rights) shall be published, or where such publication is not practicable made publicly available, in a national language, in such a manner as to enable governments and right holders to become acquainted with them. Agreements concerning the subject matter of this Agreement which are in force between the government or a governmental agency of a Member and the government or a governmental agency of another Member shall also be published.

Article 66. Least-Developed Country Members

2. Developed country Members shall provide incentives to enterprises and institutions in their territories for the purpose of promoting and encouraging technology transfer to least-developed country Members in order to enable them to create a sound and viable technological base.

Intellectual Property Non-Policy

Warning: This Is a Parody

This is not a legal form and should not be confused with legal advice. This document sets forth the policy an organization has in place by default if it does not have suitable intellectual property provisions in its employment and consulting agreements. The Non-policy is written tongue-in-cheek as if the organization had affirmatively decided to accept only the minimum duties imposed by law, without any of the typical obligations companies impose on employees by agreement.

NONMISSION STATEMENT

The Organization is **opposed** to managing intellectual property a matter of principle. In a spirit of generosity to its employees and competitors, and courage in the face of daunting liability, the Organization has established the general policy of not requiring employees and consultants to contribute to the strength of the Organization's intellectual property position.

This employee intellectual property non-policy is consistent with the Organization's overall intellectual property goals, which are:

(1) The Organization will not seek a return on its investments in innovation, despite its duty to its shareholders to do so, and will not use intellectual property tools to help it fulfill its mission.
(2) The Organization will depend on its insurance to cover liability for mismanagement of intellectual property.
(3) The Organization will permit competitors to use the Organization's intellectual property in research, development, and marketing of products and services.
(4) The Organization will allow free-riders to enjoy the fruits of the Organization's efforts without sharing the benefits.
(5) The Organization will not respect the intellectual property rights of others and will bravely face exposure to liability for infringement.
(6) The Organization will ignore the legal avenues available to expand its intellectual property portfolio, and will rely instead on whatever the common law implies.

In short, the Organization invests resources in innovation for the benefit of its employees and competitors, not for itself. The Organization wants others to grow their businesses using the

Organization's intellectual property without any charge, recognition, or obligation beyond the minimum that the law imposes on them.

NONMANAGEMENT OF INTELLECTUAL PROPERTY ASSETS

The Organization recognizes that it invests enormous financial and human resources in its intellectual property assets, and that these assets could be used to help the Organization accomplish its mission. Also, the Organization recognizes that its competitors have intellectual property rights that, if infringed, can create catastrophic liability for the Organization. The Organization's employees and consultants could play a pivotal role in maximizing these assets and minimizing these liabilities.

However, the Organization has decided not to assign someone to manage its intellectual property assets. The Organization prefers to lose track of such assets so that we may inadvertently lose our rights, leaving them in the public domain. By avoiding the need for reporting, tracking, and protecting intellectual property, this policy also frees up employee time for gossip or other personally fulfilling activities. We feel that it is important to share our assets with other companies for no charge, and to allow other companies to enforce their rights in their intellectual property against us, imposing charges for our use of their property or preventing us from using their assets.

CONFIDENTIALITY NONPROGRAM

The Organization has developed a substantial body of information, which if maintained as trade secrets, could give the Organization a significant advantage over its competitors. The information includes (1) technical information such as formulas, processes, and specifications; and (2) business information such as customer lists, supplier lists, pricing information, salaries, and benefit packages for employees. The Organization has decided not to require employees to maintain secret information as secrets, and indeed will not even inform our employees of the need for maintaining Organization secrets, because we do not want to make the employees nervous or burden their ability to share what they learn here with our competitors, or to use it for themselves.

We recognize that state laws may impose an implied duty of confidentiality on employees with regard to some information, but the Organization does not want to use direct enforceable contractual language to strengthen or clarify the implied obligations, or make them consistent for our employees in all states. For example, although we could, by contract, keep employees from disclosing nonsecret information about customers, we choose not to, so that they are free to disclose and use such information as they wish. Additionally, we do not want to put up unnecessary roadblocks to prevent our employees from leaving our Organization and taking our trade secrets to our competitors because we do not want to keep our competitors at a disadvantage. This is our small contribution to our local economy.

We do not mark trade secret documents as "confidential," or segregate them from public information, or follow any other procedures to avoid accidental disclosure, because the only reason for such actions would be to help restrict our employees from publicly divulging such information. As we have no intention of enforcing trade secret rights, we need not protect them.

When new employees arrive, we do not require them to represent that they will avoid using confidential information from their former employers, because we are well-insured and assume that if the employee steals secret information from our competitor and uses it for the Organization's benefit, the competitor will share our generous view toward intellectual property. If we do get sued, we hope our insurance will pay for our liability.

Likewise, we do not remind departing employees of any obligations of confidentiality the law might impose on them, because that might interfere with the employee's success at taking market share away from us. We do not require or request return of confidential and proprietary information of the Organization because we hope that the employee's primary objective in leaving us to join our competitor is the Organization's well-being. When applied to key employees, these policies are especially effective in disposing of the Organization's intellectual property.

COPYRIGHT NONPROGRAM

We invest a great deal of resources in the development of copyrighted works (software and graphic designs in such things as web pages). Unfortunately, the law gives us copyright ownership in our employees' works. However, no such rule applies to independent contractors and consultants, and in the absence of a written agreement, they own copyright in their works. We have at most a limited nonexclusive license. Therefore, when we do not require consultants to transfer their copyrights to us, we are supporting our general policy of avoiding intellectual property protection. We would not want to impede a consultant's creative energy, and we want the consultant to have the right to sell the works and to prevent us from using or selling the works.

PATENT NONPROGRAM

The Organization recognizes that patents can serve as revenue-generating assets and as protection against other parties utilizing or appropriating the Organization's inventions. We do not require our employees to sign agreements assigning ownership of inventions to the Organization. Therefore, for many employees, all the Organization has as a matter of law is a limited "shop right" to practice the invention – but no right to preclude others from using it, and no right to license the invention to others. We pay the employee, provide the employee with a place to work and with other resources to enable the employee to create patentable inventions, and are happy when the employee can exploit his or her inventions for personal gain, to ensure sufficient revenue to fund a lavish vacation home and early retirement. We are content to have limited shop rights in the invention, while our employee has unlimited rights to the invention.

The Organization desires to leave its rights of ownership to the vagaries of state laws that differ from jurisdiction to jurisdiction, rather than having a consistent, strong position.

Further, we feel that it is not advantageous to have a patent portfolio. This policy saves our employees time because they need not prepare invention disclosures for consideration by the Organization (and we have no one to review them anyway). The employees are also spared the burden of working with patent counsel to prepare and prosecute patent applications.

A patent portfolio might inhibit our competitors from copying our inventions, which would be unfortunate for them. Also, we might be tempted into the distraction of seeking licensing revenues, or suing companies that use inventions that we spent much time and money creating. We also do not want to have any leverage with other companies to cause them to cross-license their patent portfolio to us, preferring to face exposure to patent infringement bravely, as with trade secret liability. As long as we do not have a patent portfolio, we hope other companies will not feel threatened by us and we certainly do not want to cause our competitors any anxiety.

TRADEMARK AND MARKETING NONPROGRAM

Generally, the law confers on the Organization all rights to trademarks used by the Organization, so that it is not as easy as we would like to lose trademark rights to employees. However, if we have foreign employees, they may be free to register our trademarks in their own names in their own countries. Also, when we hire consultants to create logos and marketing copy for our Organization and our products, they hold the copyrights (see Copyright Nonprogram, above). We make sure that all this original work is performed by consultants who are not subject to agreements which assign their rights to the Organization. We feel that it is important that the consultants own the logos and that they have the right to restrict the way we use or modify the logos. Although the Organization invests substantial time, effort, and expense in building a reputation signified by logos and advertising copy, we want outsiders to be able to restrict the Organization's right to modify the logos or update them later.

NONCOMPETITION NONCOVENANTS

We do not require our employees to sign noncompetition agreements. We feel that it is important that our employees have complete freedom to work anywhere they choose. We believe that it is important to train employees so that they can leave to work for our competitors and jump right in with minimum interruption to help the competitors put us out of business.

In sum, the Organization has decided that managing intellectual property is not a priority. The Organization is content to operate at a disadvantage in relation to its employees and other organizations who make reasonable efforts to manage their own intellectual property.

Intellectual Property Assessment Questionnaire

Name: _____

Title: _____

Organization: _____

Location: _____

E-mail: _____

Phone: _____

Date Completed: _____

Background. This information will help focus on which of the following questions are most pertinent to you.

0.1 Identify the principal products and services of your group (program, project, or regional office, as applicable), checking off as many as apply:

printed publications by the Organization   ____

publications published by others   ____

software programs   ____

databases   ____

materials posted on websites (e.g., publications, databases, software)   ____

research data   ____

grant proposals   ____

scientific material   ____

other equipment   ____

tests or analysis for others   ____

graphic designs and images   ____

music or video content   ____

other (list)   ____

0.2 Identify the principal technologies used in your group, checking off as many as apply:

specialized software   ____

specialized computer hardware   ____

laboratory instruments and equipment   ____

reagents and other materials   ____

scientific research techniques and methods   ____

management techniques   ____

indigenous knowledge —
scientific publications —
online databases —
mechanical/electrical equipment —
other —

0.3 List examples of the principal collaborations of your group involving creating or using intellectual property (those with significant time and money involved) and briefly describe the subject matter. Provide copies of any standard or representative collaborator agreements for your group (e.g., Letter of Agreement or Memorandum of Understanding).

0.4 List examples of the principal research grants (government and other) and identify any provisions specifically relating to ownership or disclosure of software, patents, data, confidentiality, or other intellectual property issues. Provide copies of standard or representative agreements or documents.

0.5 If you have any immediate pressing concerns about the organization's intellectual property or that of outside parties, please mention them here, or discuss them with the audit project coordinator.

Copyrights. Copyrights exist in many forms of expression, including writings, photographs, drawings, software, web pages, and any other work which is "fixed" in a tangible medium.

1.0 [For publications unit] Provide a list of all categories of books, journals, reports, articles, training materials, and other writings, created in whole or in part by organization employees (including works published by others) during the past several years. Please identify and send examples of (a) the most requested and (b) the most widely distributed works.

1.1 [For others] Do you know of any books, journals, reports, articles, training materials, electronic postings on web sites or other writings, created in whole or in part by organization employees (including works published by others) that would not be known by the publications unit?

Yes – the details are:
No

1.2 Do you know of any photographs, slides, films, videos, music, drawings or other graphic works made by you or any other organization employees or used by the organization and which are important to the organization or its mission?

Yes – the details are:
No

1.3 Do you know of any web pages made by you or other persons employed by the organization or web pages concerning the organization?

Yes – the details are:
No

1.4 If you answered yes to Question 1.1, 1.2 or 1.3, did any outsiders including consultants contribute to creating the works, and if so, under what terms and conditions or agreement?

    Yes – the details are:
    No
    Do not know.

1.5 If you answered yes to Question 1.1, 1.2 or 1.3, have applications for copyright registration been filed in any countries? Have copyright registrations been issued?

    Yes – the details are:
    No
    Do not know.

1.6 If you answered yes to Question 1.1, 1.2 or 1.3, have any rights in the works been given to an outsider (completely or jointly with the organization)? For example, has ownership of the work been sold or given to an outsider, or has an outsider been given the right to copy or distribute the work, or has an outsider been given the right to modify the work?

    Yes – the details are:
    No
    Do not know.

1.7 If you answered yes to Question 1.1, 1.2 or 1.3, have any approvals or other rights in the works been received from an outsider?

    Yes – the details (restrictions and other terms and conditions) are:
    No
    Do not know.

1.8 Does the organization (or your group) have a policy or guide regarding approvals, photo credits, copyright notices, etc. on works which it publishes? If so, please describe the policy.

    Yes – the details are:
    No
    Do not know.

1.9 Does the organization (or your group) get written permission from the authors of articles, images, music, videos, and software to publish them, post them on its website or otherwise disseminate them?

    Yes – the details are:
    No
    Do not know.

1.10 Does the organization (or your group) get approvals from people whose images the organization publishes or otherwise uses?

    Yes – the details are:
    No
    Do not know.

1.11 Does the organization (or your group) use any proprietary software or databases (including operating systems and applications) from an outsider or have the such software or databases resident on its systems or websites?

> Yes – the details are:
> No
> Do not know.

1.12 If you answered yes to Question 1.11, does the organization own the software or has it obtained a license to use the software?

> Yes – the details are:
> No – please discuss the details with your project coordinator.
> Do not know.

1.13 With respect to any software developed at the organization, do you know of any other people who may claim rights in the software such as the right to use or sell the software, or a right to a royalty on the use or sale of the royalty?

> Yes – the details are:
> No

Trade secrets. Trade secrets are valuable confidential information of the organization. Trade secrets include unpublished data, formulas, methods of doing something, source code, composition of materials, mailing lists, supplier information, employment records, and other information that is not available to the public and is not generally known outside of the organization.

2.1 Do you know of any formulas, methods, compositions, lists, records or any other information that you believe are confidential information and of the highest importance to the organization and its mission?

> For example:
>
> Databases ___
> Employment data ___
> Source code for software ___
> Mailing lists ___
> Scientific formulas ___
> Other ___
> Do not know ___
> Please provide details as to any items checked:

2.2 Do you know of any circumstances where confidential information of the organization was disclosed to an outsider under a confidentiality agreement?

> Yes – the details are:
> No

2.3 Do you know of any circumstances where confidential information was used by outsiders in a manner that was not authorized by the organization?

> Yes – the details are:
> No

2.4   Have any rights in confidential information been given to an outsider? For example, has any third party or government been given a license to use the confidential information?

   Yes – the details are:
   No
   Do not know.

2.5   During collaborations between the organization or organization personnel and outsiders, is or was any highly confidential information (i.e. trade secrets) disclosed?

   Yes – the details are:
   No

2.6   During training sessions which are conducted by the organization or organization personnel, is or was any highly confidential information disclosed?

   Yes – the details are:
   No

2.7   Is confidential information marked as such, is access restricted to those who need to know, and is confidential information kept in locked offices or cabinets?

   Yes
   No – the details are:

2.8   Is confidential information disposed of in a manner to prevent disclosure?

   Yes – the details are:
   No – the details are:

2.9   Has the organization received confidential information of outsiders?

   Yes – the details are:
   No – the details are:

2.10 If you answered yes to Question 2.9, does the organization take measures to keep outsiders' confidential information secure and confidential?

   Yes – the details are:
   No – the details are:

2.11 If you answered yes to Question 2.9, has the organization used the outsiders' confidential information to develop or improve machines, processes, or other scientific material?

   Yes – the details are:
   No – the details are:

Trademarks. Trademarks and trade dress help to identify the work and materials provided by the organization. Trademarks can be words, colors, symbols, logos, or designs. Trade dress is the ornamental design or shape.

3.1 Do you know of any names, acronyms, words, colors, symbols, logos, packaging shapes, or designs by which the organization and its programs are known? If so, please list them.

> Yes – the details are:
> No

3.2 Do you know of any names, words, colors, logos, packaging shapes, or designs under which any books, reports, other information, or other material or service is or may have been released by the organization?

> Yes – the details are:
> No

3.3 Do you know if any of the trademarks have been registered in any countries?

> Yes – the details are:
> No
> Do not know.

3.4 Do you know if any outsiders use trademarks that are similar to the organization's trademarks?

> Yes – the details are:
> No
> Do not know.

3.5 If you answered yes to Question 3.1 or 3.2, have any rights in the trademarks been given to an outsider for endorsement, sponsorship, or the like?

> Yes – the details are:
> No
> Do not know.

3.6 Do you know of any trademarks of outsiders used by the organization, and if so, is the organization's use pursuant to agreement?

> Yes – the details are:
> No

3.7 Does the organization (or your group) have a policy or guide regarding adoption and use of names and logos on publications and in connection with new varieties, devices, projects, and other products and services? If so, please describe the policy or provide a written copy.

> Yes – the details are:
> No – the details are:
> Do not know.

Patents. Patents may be issued to protect inventions. Inventions may take the form of machines, compositions, methods or processes, and sometimes plants.

4.1 Does the organization or its collaborators own any patents, or has the organization or its collaborators filed any patent applications on work done in part by the organization?

> Yes – the details are:
> No

4.2 If you answered yes to Question 4.1, are there any people or entities other than the organization who have rights to the patent?

> Yes – the details are:
> No

4.3 If you answered yes to Question 4.1, were all the people and entities who helped to create the invention which is being protected subject to written agreements which assigned all their rights in the invention to the organization?

> Yes
> No – the details are:

4.4 Do you know of any unpatented inventions or ideas for inventions, beyond those of Question 4.1, created in whole or in part by you or any other persons employed by or collaborating with the organization?

> Yes – Please complete an invention disclosure form
> No

4.5 Are there any new or improved useful laboratory equipment, reagents, materials or techniques which were developed at the organization and which are not yet known about outside of the organization?

> Yes – the details are:
> No

4.6 Does the organization or your group have any policies or processes in place regarding the identification of inventions?

> Yes – the details are:
> No

4.7 Does the organization require all personnel routinely to fill out invention disclosure forms?

> Yes – the details are:
> No

4.8 Does the organization take steps to evaluate the patentability of all inventions and to patent those inventions which may have value to the organization or to others?

> Yes – the details are:
> No

4.9 Are you aware of any technology of outsiders that is or may be patented and is used by the organization?

> Yes – the details are:
> No

4.10 If you answered yes to Question 4.9, is the use permitted pursuant to license or otherwise?

> Yes – the details are:
> No – please discuss the details with your audit project coordinator.
> Do not know.

Employment issues. Depending on the laws of the country in which an employee works and the employee's work status, the employee may have rights in intellectual property developed for the organization by that employee. It is important to identify those situations.

5.1 Are all employees subject to employment agreements which assign ownership of inventions, copyrightable works, and all other confidential information and trade secrets to the organization, provide for non-disclosure of trade secrets and/or limit conflicts of interest?

> Yes – the details are:
> No

5.2 Do you know of any employees who are not subject to employment agreements as in Question 5.1?

> Yes – the details are:
> No

5.3 With respect to any inventions you listed in Questions 4.1 and 4.4, or copyrights in Questions 1.1, 1.2, and 1.3, do you know if the people who created or modified the inventions or copyrighted materials were subject to organization employment agreements at the time of the creation or modification?

> Yes – the details are:
> No

5.4 Regarding those who created or contributed to the creation of the inventions or copyrights you listed in Questions 1.1, 1.2, 1.3, 4.1 and 4.4, are or were any of them consultants or independent contractors?

> Yes – the details are:
> No
> Do not know.

5.5 If so, what agreements are there with the independent contractors and consultants regarding intellectual property?

5.6 When considering the work of employees of the organization, are there any projects which are likely to involve know-how, technology, and information obtained from the employees' previous employers? If so, please discuss.

> Yes – the details are:
> No
> Do not know.

5.7 Does the organization interview new employees before they start performing work for the organization to inquire as to whether there is any work or knowledge that they are restricted from using at the organization, whether the employees are subject to any covenants not to compete with former employers or any agreements which assign rights in their work to the former employers?

> Yes – the details are:
> No
> Do not know.

5.8 Does the organization perform exit interviews, for when employees leave the employ of the organization to request the disclosure and return of all intellectual property to the organization, and to advise the employee of the organization's rights in its intellectual property?

> Yes – the details are:
> No
> Do not know.

5.9 Are officers and directors subject to agreements or policies limiting use of confidential information and trade secrets of the organization, and/or limiting conflicts of interest?

> Yes – the details are:
> No

5.10 Please list all existing policies covering the following activities and attach if written or describe if not written.

- use of logos
- use of trademarks
- publications policy

Agreements. License agreements and other agreements are very important to the organization.

6.1 Please list on Exhibit I all written Licenses, Material Transfer Agreements, Material Acquisition Agreements, software license agreements, and other agreements with outsiders to (a) take, borrow, purchase, or use; (b) give, sell, lend, or otherwise transfer intellectual property rights into or out of the organization (regarding e.g. patents, copyrights, trademarks or trade secrets).

6.2 Do you know of any other agreements by which the organization has (a) obtained from or (b) transferred to outsiders the following, with restricted rights:

> Patent rights   ___
> Copyrights   ___
> Permission to use copyrighted material   ___
> Trademark rights   ___
> Rights to confidential information   ___
> Mechanical/Electrical equipment   ___
> Reagents   ___

Other intellectual property rights   ——
Please provide details   ——
No   ——

6.3 If the organization received funding for the research, development, or creation of the copy-righted works listed in Questions 1.1, 1.2 or 1.3, or the inventions listed in Question 4.1 and 4.4, did the person or entity which provided the funding obtain any intellectual property rights in return for the funding?

Yes – the details are:
No
Do not know.

6.4 Does the organization have any standard form agreements relevant to intellectual property?

Yes
No – the details are:

6.5 Does the organization (and your group) obtain prior informed consents from appropriate governmental authorities authorizing the transfer of material into and out of the organization?

Yes – the details are:
No because consents were not required.
No – the details are:.

6.6 Has the organization committed to indemnify any outsider against losses of any kind, or to defend an outsider against suits claiming losses of any kind?

Yes – the details are:
No

6.7 Has the organization made any disclaimers against liability in distributing scientific material, software, creative media, or other products or committed to indemnify any outsider against losses of any kind, or to defend an outsider against suits claiming losses of any kind?

Yes – the details are:
No

6.8 With respect to all of the agreements you have listed or referenced in this Questionnaire, please return one copy of each agreement with this Questionnaire. Will you provide copies of all of the agreements to us?

Yes
No, I am unable to give you copies of the following agreements for the following reasons:

Other concerns. This Questionnaire may not have covered all of the issues that you believe are important to the organization's mission and use of intellectual property. This section provides you with an opportunity to point such matters out to us.

7.1 Do you have any issues or concerns regarding the organization's development and protection of its intellectual property, the use of outsiders' intellectual property, or any other matters related to patents, copyrights, trademarks, trade secrets, and confidential information?

> Yes – please provide details or contact the audit project coordinator.
> No

7.2 Are there any other matters related to the issues covered by this Questionnaire which were not addressed by the questions but which you believe we should know?

> Yes – the details are:
> No

EXHIBIT I

List of Agreements

Please list all agreements and other documents which you identified in the Questionnaire, and provide copies.

Memoranda of understanding
Letters of intent   ____
Employment contracts   ____
Consultant agreements   ____
Material transfer agreements   ____
Acquisition agreements   ____
License agreements   ____
Collaboration agreements
Research agreements   ____
Research grant documents   ____
Management agreements   ____
Database agreements   ____
Supply contracts for critical software and equipment (leases etc.) ____
Assignments   ____
Releases   ____
Other agreements   ____

Research Tools for Obtaining Intellectual Property Information

Note: Search websites are routinely updated, so these links and detailed steps may become outdated. The basic information resources should remain available, and will likely be enhanced over time.

PATENTS

To search U.S. patents:
Go to www.uspto.gov
Click "Search" under the "Patents" heading on the left side.
Click "Quick Search" under "Issued Patents" on the left side.
Select Term 1: [e.g. company name] Field: [select e.g. Name or All Fields].
Select Date Range: [1976 to present].
·Hit search button.
You will get a list of patents. Clicking the number will pull up the patent text.

To search U.S. published patent applications since March 2001:
Go to Search page as above.
Click on "Quick Search" under "Published Applications" on the right side.
Select Term 1: [e.g. company name] Field: [e.g. Assignee Name or All Fields].
Select Years: [2001 to present].
Hit search button.

To see if a U.S. patent has been cited by others:
Go to www.uspto.gov.
Click the "Patents" button on the left side.
Click the "Search patents" button under "Services."
Click the "Quick Search" button.
Select Term 1: [X,XXX,XXX] Field: [select References Cited or All Fields].
Select Date Range: [to present].
Click search button.

You will get a list of patents. Clicking the number will pull up the patent text.

To review public patent prosecution documents at USPTO Public PAIR:

Go to http://portal.uspto.gov/external/portal/pair and type in the application number (e.g., 10/123,456) or the publication number (e.g., 2004-0000567).

Click the "Transaction history" tab to list all documents filed and actions taken within the USPTO or mailed out.

Click the "Image File Wrapper" tab to access all documents in the file, for review or download.

International patent information

The World Intellectual Property Organization (WIPO), www.wipo.org, provides many types of information and links. Links to searchable patent databases in various countries are at http://ipdl.wipo.int/.

For international published applications (not patents), go to http://ipdl.wipo.int/. Click on "Guest Access" and use "All Dates" and in the query box put pa/[company name] to search by owner.

Foreign patents from 50 countries may be searched via the European Patent Office website at http://www.european-patent-office.org/espacenet/info/access.htm then to http://ep.espacenet.com/, follow directions

Many specialized IP websites and blogs have appeared, including:

The National Agricultural Library: www.nal.usda.gov
The Life Science Web: www.sciweb.com/features/patents.cfm
Patent cafe http://www.ipbookstore.com/index.asp
Bust patents http://www.bustpatents.com

Paid commercial databases provide comprehensive coverage for patents. Some of the most broadly used are:

Dialog: www.dialog.com
Faxpat/Optipat: www.faxpat.com
Recdfax: www.recdfax.com
Lexis/Nexis: www.lexis.com
Westlaw: www.westlaw.com
Delphion: www.delphion.com

TRADEMARKS

To find trademark registrations by a company:
U.S. trademarks
Go to www.uspto.gov.
Hit the "Trademarks" button on the left side.
Hit the "Search trademarks (TESS)" button.
Hit the "New User Form Search (Basic)" button.
Enter Search Term: [made up mark] Select Field [Combined Work Mark].

Hit search button.

You should see similar registered marks. You can click on each item to get more information.

International trademarks:

WIPO provides links to online trademark databases for many countries at http://ecommerce.wipo.int/databases/trademark/output.html. Choose a country, click on the link, and type in the appropriate name to search. OHIM searches European Community trademark records. Each site, search engine, and way to search assignee (owner, proprietor) and mark is different and reliability is inconsistent.

To research domain name protection

Go to http://www.register.com, use "I am looking for" [WHOIS lookup] and put company name for "domain name" and search various tld addresses (.com,.org,.edu). Click on "Taken" to see WHOIS ownership information.

COPYRIGHT

To find U.S.copyright registrations:

Go to http://www.loc.gov/copyright/search.

Choose the type of publication, enter the name of the company, and follow through with various results.

GENERAL BUSINESS INFORMATION

(with information about major IP licenses, litigation)

U.S. Securities and Exchange Commission (SEC) for filings listing company IP assets: www.sec.gov.

Local Government sites for corporate information, usually filed with the Secretary of State.

For example, Maryland provides corporate data at the site for the Department of Assessment and Taxation, http://www.dat.state.md.us/sdatweb/datanote.html.

Bibliography

Publications:

Aalbersberg, William. "The Development of Bioprospecting Agreements in Fiji." BCNet (1999). http://www.worldwildlife.org/bsp/bcn/whatsnew/biosprosfiji.htm (accessed August 13, 2007).

Acuff, Frank. *How to Negotiate Anything With Anyone Anywhere in the World.* AMACOM, 1997.

Agiato, Joseph. "The Basics of Financing Intellectual Property Royalties." In *From Ideas to Assets: Investing Wisely in Intellectual Property*, ch. 19. Bruce Berman, ed. Wiley, 2002.

Aharonian, Gregory. "Patent/Copyright Infringement Lawsuits/Licensing Awards." http://www.patenting-art.com/economic/awards.htm (accessed December 4, 2006).

American Intellectual Property Law Association. Report of the Economic Survey (2007).

Anson, Weston, ed. *Fundamentals of Intellectual Property Valuation: A Primer for Identifying and Determining Value.* American Bar Association, 2005.

Arrow, Alexander. "Managing IP Financial Assets." In *From Ideas to Assets: Investing Wisely in Intellectual Property*, ch. 5. Bruce Berman, ed. Wiley, 2002.

Australian Academy of Technological Sciences and Engineering. "The Innovation Cycle." *Australia Innovates.* http://www.powerhousemuseum.com_australia_innovates/?behaviour = view_article&Section_id = 30 (accessed January 4, 2007).

Barton, John. "Adapting the Intellectual Property System to New Technologies." In *Global Dimensions of Intellectual Property Rights in Science and Technology.* National Academy of Sciences, 1993.

Barton, John, and Siebeck, Walter. "Intellectual Property Issues for the International Agricultural Research Centers, What are the Options." *Issues in Agriculture* 4 (1992).

Bayh, Birch. "Bayh-Dole: Don't Turn Back the Clock." *LES Nouvelles* (December 2006). http://www.venable.com/publications.cfm?action = view&publication_id = 1621&publication_type_id = 2 (accessed August 14, 2007).

BayhDole25. "The Bayh-Dole Act at 25: A Survey of the Origins, Effects, and Prospects of the Bayh Dole Act" (2006). http://www.bayhdole25.org/resources (accessed January 13, 2007).

Bellman, Christophe, Dutfield, Graham, and Meléndez-Ortiz, Ricardo, eds. *Trading in Knowledge: Development Perspectives on TRIPS, Trade and Sustainability.* Earthscan, 2003.

Ben-Menachem, Gil, Ferguson, Steven, and Balakrishnan, Krishna. "Beyond Patents and Royalties: Perception and Reality of Doing Business with the NIH." *Journal of Biolaw and Business* 9:4 (2006).

Berman, Bruce, ed. *From Ideas to Assets: Investing Wisely in Intellectual Property.* Wiley, 2002.

Bouchie, Aaron. "Roche and Igen in Shotgun Wedding." *Nature BioTechnology* 21:958 (2003).

Brown, Glenn. "Out of the Way: How the Next Copyright Revolution Can Help the Next Scientific Revolution." PLoS Biology 1:30–31 (2003).

Brownlee, L.M. *Intellectual Property Due Diligence in Corporate Transactions: Investment, Risk, Assessment, Management.* West, 2002.

Bryer, Lanning, and Simensky, Melvin, eds. *Intellectual Property Assets in Mergers and Acquisitions.* Wiley, 2002.

Bugbee, Bruce. "Genesis of American Patent and Copyright Law. In *Foundations of Intellectual Property*, pp. 12–13. Robert Merges and Jane Ginsburg, eds. Foundation Press, 2004.

Burge, David. *Patent and Trademark Tactics and Practice*, 3d ed. Wiley, 1999.

"Calling Innovation Insurgents: Efforts on to Transform 50,000 Grassroots Ideas into Applications." *Sunday Times of India*, New Delhi, February 19, 2006, available at http://www.sristi.org/anilg/.

Center for International Environmental Law. "The Ayahuasca Patent Case." http://www.ciel.org/Biodiversity/ayahuascapatentcase.html.

Chapman, Audrey, ed. *Perspectives on Genetic Patenting: Religion, Science, and Industry in Dialogue.* American Association for the Advancement of Science, 1999.

Chisum, Donald, and Jacobs, Michael. *Understanding Intellectual Property Law,* § 1(C). Matthew Bender, 1992.

Christenson, Clayton, Anthony, Scott, and Roth, Erik. *Seeing What's Next: Using the Theories of Innovation to Predict Industry Change.* Harvard Business School, 2004.

Collins, Kimberly. "Profitable Gifts: A History of the Merck Mectizan Donation Program and Its Implications for International Health." *Perspectives in Biology and Medicine* 47:1 (2004).

Commission on Intellectual Property Rights. *Integrating Intellectual Property Rights and Development Policy.* CIPR, 2002. http://www.iprcommission.org/graphic/documents.htm.

Commission on Intellectual Property Rights, Innovation, and Public Health. *Public Health Innovation and Intellectual Property Rights.* CIPIH, 2006. http://www.who.int/intellectualproperty/en/.

Committee on Innovative Remediation Technologies, National Research Council. *Innovations in Ground Water and Soil Cleanup: From Concept to Commercialization.* National Academy Press, 1997.

Committee on Intellectual Property Rights in Genomic and Protein Research and Innovation, National Research Council. *Reaping the Benefits of Genomic and Proteomic Research: Intellectual Property Rights, Innovation and Public Health.* National Academy Press, 2005.

Correa, Carlos. *Intellectual Property Rights, the WTO and Developing Countries: The TRIPS Agreement and Policy Options.* Zed Books and Third World Network, 2000.

Cutting Edge Information. "Combating Generics: Pharmaceutical Brand Defense for 2007." Executive Summary 12. (2006). http://www.cuttingedgeinfo.com/pharmagenerics/PH76_Download.asp#body (accessed October 1, 2006).

Davila, Tony. *Making Innovation Work: How to Manage It, Measure It, and Profit from It.* Wharton School Publishing, 2005.

da Vinci, Leonardo. "The Vitruvian Man." Public domain image available at http://en.wikipedia.org/wiki/Image:Vitruvian.jpg (accessed August 1, 2007).

Davis, Julie, and Harris, Suzanne. *Edison in the Boardroom: How Leading Companies Realize Value from Their Intellectual Assets.* Wiley, 2001.

de Soto, Hernando. *The Mystery of Capital: Why Capitalism Triumphs in the West and Fails Everywhere Else.* Basic Books, 2000.

Developing an IP Strategy for Your Company: Leading Lawyers on Intellectual Property Portfolio Capitalization. Aspatore, 2005.

Diamond, Jared. *Guns, Germs, and Steel: The Fates of Human Societies.* Norton, 1997.

Dinwoodie, Graeme, and Dreyfuss, Rochelle Cooper. "Patenting Science: Protecting the Domain of Accessible Knowledge." In *The Future of The Public Domain in Intellectual Property.* Lucie Guibault and PB Hugenholtz, eds. Kluwer Law International, 2006.

Drucker, Peter. *Innovation and Entrepreneurship: Practice and Principles.* HarperBusiness, 1985.

Dutfield, Graham. *Intellectual Property Rights, Trade and Biodiversity.* Earthscan 2000.

Dutfield, Graham, and Suthersanen, Uma. "Harmonisation or Differentiation in Intellectual Property Protection? The Lessons of History." *Anuario Andino de Derechos Intelectuales* II(2): 61–79 (2005).

"Effects of Intellectual Property Protections on the Conduct of Scientific Research." Project on Science and Intellectual Property in the Public Interest (SIPPI). 2007. http://sippi.aaas.org/Symposium_US/Symposium_Brief.pdf (accessed January 28, 2007).

Egelyng, Henrik. "Evolution of Capacity for Institutionalized Management of Intellectual Property at International Agricultural Research Centers: A Strategic Case Study." *AgBioForum* 8(1): 7–17 (2005). http://www.agbioforum.org/v8n1/v8n1a02-egelyng.htm (accessed November 29, 2006).

Eisbruck, Jay. "Royal(ty) Succession: The Evolution of IP-Backed Securitization." *IP Value, 2007,* pp. 17–21. http://www.buildingipvalue.com/07intro/p.17–21%20Intro,%20Moody.pdf (accessed March 31, 2007).

Elon, Menachem, ed. *The Principles of Jewish Law.* Keter Publishing House, 1975.

European Patent Office. *Scenarios for the Future: How Might IP Regimes Evolve by 2025? What Global Legitimacy Might Such Regimes Have?* EPO, 2007. http://www.epo.org/focus/patent-system/scenarios-for-the-future/download.html.

Evans, David, and Schmallensee, Richard. "Some Aspects of Antitrust Analysis in Dynamically Competitive Industries." In *Innovation Policy and the Economy*, vol. 2. Adam Jaffe, Josh Lerner, and Scott Stern, eds. National Bureau of Economic Research. MIT Press, 2002.

Evenson, Robert. "Survey of Empirical Studies." In *Strengthening Protection of Intellectual Property in Developing Countries: A Survey of the Literature*, Discussion Paper 112. Walter Siebeck, ed. World Bank, 1990.

Finger, J. Michael, and Schuler, Phillip, eds. *Poor People's Knowledge: Promoting Intellectual Property in Developing Countries*. World Bank, 2004.

Fink, Carsten, and Maskus, Keith, eds. *Intellectual Property and Development: Lessons From Recent Economic Research*. World Bank, 2005.

Finkelstein, William, and Sims, James, III, eds. *The Intellectual Property Handbook: A Practical Guide for Franchise, Business and IP Counsel*. American Bar Association, 2005.

Fishman, Ted. "Manufaketure." *New York Times*, January 9, 2005.

Fitzsimmons, Chris, and Jones, Tim. *Managing Intellectual Property*. Capstone Publishing, 2002.

Frame, J. D. "National Commitment to Intellectual Property Protection: An Empirical Investigation." *Journal of Law and Technology* 2:209 (1987).

Friedman, Thomas. *The World Is Flat: A Brief History of the Twenty-First Century*. Farrar, Straus & Giroux, 2005.

Frumkin, Maximilian. "Early History of Patents for Invention." *Transactions of the Newcomen Society* 26:47–56 (1947–1949).

———. "The Origins of Patents." *Journal of the Patent Office Society* 27:1433–1449 (March 1945).

———. *Transactions of the Chartered Institute of Patent Agents* 66:20–69 (1947–48).

Gibbs, Andy, and DeMatteis, Bob. *Essentials of Patents*. Wiley, 2003.

Glazier, Stephen. *Patent Strategies for Business*, 3d ed. Law & Business Institute, 1997.

Gollin, Michael. "Answering the Call: Public Interest Intellectual Property Advisors," *Washington University Journal of Law and Policy* 17:187–224 (2005), http://www.piipa.org/library_asp (accessed October 31, 2007).

———. "Biological Materials Transfer Agreements." *Bio/Technology* 13:243 (1995).

———. "Carving Property Rights Out of the Public Domain to Conserve Biodiversity." Paper presented at the 3rd Common Property Conference of the International Association for the Study of Common Property (Washington, DC, September 18, 1992).

———. "Commentary on Tropical Genetic Diversity." In *Conservation of Plant Genes II: Utilization of Ancient and Modern DNA*. R. P. Adams et al., eds. Missouri Botanical Garden, 1994.

———. "Developing a Strong Patent Strategy." In *Developing a Patent Strategy: Leading Lawyers on Infringement, Litigation, and Protection for Businesses*. Aspatore, 2005.

———. "Elements of Commercial Biodiversity Prospecting Agreements." In *Biodiversity and Traditional Knowledge: Equitable Partnerships in Practice*,

Sarah Laird, ed. Earthscan, 2000. http://www.rbgkew.org.uk/peopleplants/manuals/biological/annexes2.htm.

———. "Feasibility of National Requirements for Disclosure of Origin." In *Disclosure Requirements: Ensuring mutual supportiveness between the WTO TRIPS Agreement and the CBD*. M. Chouchena-Rojas, M. Ruiz Muller, D. Vivas and S. Winkler, eds. IUCN and ICTSD, 2005.

———. "Generic Drug Companies: Competing at Boundaries of Time and Geography." Paper presented at Intellectual Property and International Public Health, IPPI. (Georgetown University, October 2003), Chapter 16 in TRIPS and Global Pharmaceutical Industry: Perspectives and Implications. Icfai University Press, 2007.

———. "How to Manage Intellectual Property in Dealing with Africa." Paper presented at the International Society of African Scientists, 13th Annual International Technical Conference. (Wilmington, DE, August 14, 1998).

———. "An Intellectual Property Rights Framework for Biodiversity Prospecting" and "The Convention on Biological Diversity." In *Biodiversity Prospecting: Using Genetic Resources for Sustainable Development*, edited by Walter Reid, Sarah Laird, Carrie Meyer, Rodrigo Gámez, Ana Sittenfeld, Daniel Janzen, Michael Gollin, and Calestous Juma. World Resources Institute, 1993.

———. "Introduction." In *World Intellectual Property Rights and Remedies*. Dennis Campbell, ed. Oceana Publications, 1999.

———. "Linking Intellectual Property Rights with Traditional Medicine." In *Ethnomedicine and Drug Discovery*, ch. 18, Maurice Iwu and Jacqueline Wootton, eds. Elsevier Science, 2002.

———. "Managing the Cost of Intellectual Property." *California Lawyer* (November 2002).

———. "New Rules for Natural Products Research." *Nature Biotechnology* 17:921 (September 1999). http://www.venable.com/tools/ip/naturalproducts.html and http://www.actionbioscience.org/biodiversity/gollin.html.

———. "Patent Law and the Environment/Technology Paradox." *Environmental Law Reporter* 20:10171 (1990).

———. "Patenting Recipes From Nature's Kitchen." *Bio/Technology* 12:406 (1994).

———. "Probing the Human Genome: Who Owns Genetic Information." *Boston U. Journal of Science and Technology Law* 4:2 (1997). http://www.bu.edu/law/scitech/OLJ4.htm.

———. "Protecting Bioinformatics' Value." *Modern Drug Discovery* (October 2004).

———. "Protecting Intellectual Property, Parts I and II." *Inventors' Digest* (March/April and May/June 1996).

———. "Sustainable Innovation for Public Health." *Food and Drug Law Institute Update Magazine* (January/February 2002).

———. "Using Intellectual Property to Improve Environmental Protection." *Harvard Journal of Law and Technology* 4:193 (1991).

Gollin, Michael, Jatras, James, Madden, Thomas, Schmidt, Richard, and Smith, Stuart. "Science, Technology, and Intellectual Property." In *Homeland Security*

Deskbook: Private Sector Impacts of the War Against Terrorism, ch. 15. Venable LLP, eds. Matthew Bender, 2004, rev. 2005.

Gollin, Michael, and Laird, Sarah. "Global Policies, Local Actions: The Role of National Legislation in Sustainable Biodiversity Prospecting." *Boston University Journal of Science and Technology Law* 2:16 (1996).

Gollin, Michael, and Taylor, Ronald. "Protecting Your Company's Intellectual Property." (Venable LLP, 1999). http://www.venable.com/publications.cfm?action/view&publication_id = 549&publication_type_id = 2 (accessed April 15, 2007).

Gollin, Michael, and Yu, Jianyang. "Patent Strategies in China." *Managing Intellectual Property* (November 1997).

Gollin, Richard. *A Viewer's Guide to Film: Arts, Artifices, and Issues.* McGraw-Hill, 1992.

Grant, Robert. *Contemporary Strategy Analysis: Concepts, Techniques, Applications.* Blackwell, 2002.

Grubb, Philip. *Patents for Chemicals, Pharmaceuticals and Biotechnology: Fundamentals of Global Law, Practice and Strategy.* Oxford University Press, 1999.

Hamilton, Marci. "The TRIPs Agreement: Imperialistic, Outdated, and Overprotective." *Vanderbilt Journal of Transnational Law* 29:613 (1996).

Hansen, Hugh, ed. *US Intellectual Property Law and Policy.* Edward Elgar Publishing, 2006.

Hansen, Stephen, and VanFleet, Justin. *Traditional Knowledge and Intellectual Property: A Handbook on Issues and Options for Traditional Knowledge Holders in Protecting Their Intellectual Property and Maintaining Biological Diversity.* American Association for the Advancement of Science, 2003. http://shr.aaas.org/tek/handbook/handbook.pdf (accessed January 28, 2007).

Hardin, Garrett. "The Tragedy of the Commons." *Science* 162:1243–1248 (1968).

Heller, Michael, and Eisenberg, Rebecca. "Can Patents Deter Innovation? The Anticommons in Biomedical Research." *Science* 280:5364 (1998).

Hillery, John S. "Securitization of Intellectual Property: Recent Trends from the United States." Washington | CORE, 2004. http://www.iip.or.jp/summary/pdf/WCORE2004s.pdf.

Hughes, Justin. "The Philosophy of Intellectual Property." *Georgetown Law Journal* 77:287 (1988).

Imparato, Nicholas, ed. *Capital for Our Time: The Economic, Legal, and Management Challenges of Intellectual Capital.* Hoover Institution Press, 1999.

"Intellectual Property: A Balance." *The British Library Manifesto.* 2006. http://www.bl.uk/news/pdf/ipmanifesto.pdf (accessed October 7, 2006).

Intellectual Property Owners Association. "Top 300 Organizations Granted U.S. Patents in 2006." IPO, 2006.

Inside the Minds: The Art and Science of Patent Law. Aspatore Books, 2004.

Intellectual Property Rights: Designing Regimes to Support Plant Breeding in Developing Countries. World Bank, 2006.

International Policy Network. *Civil Society Report on Intellectual Property, Innovation and Health* (2006). http://www.policynetwork.net/main/content.php?content_id = 47 (accessed August 24, 2007)

IP Value 2007: Building and Enforcing Intellectual Property Value, An International Guide for the Boardroom. Globe White Page, 2006.

James, Vanus, ed. "The Caribbean Music Industry Database (CMID)." Report prepared for The United Nations Conference on Trade and Development (UNCTAD) and World Intellectual Property Organization (WIPO) (2000). http://www.wipo.int/about-ip/en/studies/pdf/study_v_james.pdf (accessed December 28, 2006).

Johnson, Stephen. "Digital Maoism." *New York Times,* December 10, 2006.

Juma, Calestous. *The Gene Hunters: Biotechnology and the Scramble for Seeds.* Princeton University Press, 1989.

Kaufman, Joshua. "Want the Pride of IP Ownership? Get it in Writing." *Legal Times,* January 17, 2000.

Kelly, Kevin. "Scan This Book!" *The New York Times,* May 14, 2006.

Kimbrell, Andrew. *The Human Body Shop.* HarperSanFrancisco, 1995.

Knight, H. Jackson. *Patent Strategy for Researchers and Research Managers.* Wiley, 1996.

Knopf, Howard. "Security Interests in Intellectual Property: An International Comparative Approach." 9th Annual Fordham Intellectual Property Law and Policy Conference (New York, 2001). http://www.ulcc.ca/en/cls/security-interests.pdf (accessed December 17, 2006).

Koch, Richard. *FT Guide to Strategy: How to Create and Deliver a Winning Strategy,* 3d ed. FT Prentice Hall, 2005.

Krattiger, Anatole, and Mahoney, Richard. "Intellectual Property Management in Health and Agricultural Innovation: A Handbook of the Best Practices." Oxford Center for Innovation, 2006.

Krattiger, Anatole, Mahoney, Richard, Nelson, Lita, Thompson, Jennifer, Bennett, Alan, Satyanarayana, Kanikaram, Graff, Gregory, Fernandez, Carlos, and Kowalski, Stanley, eds. *Intellectual Property Management in Health and Agricultural Innovation: A Handbook of Best Practices.* MIHR:Oxford, U.K. and PIPRA: Davis, U.S.A., 2007

Lakes, Joi Michelle. "A Pas De Deux for Choreography and Copyright." New York University Law Review 80:1829 (2005).

Lanier, Jaron. "Digital Maoism: The Hazards of the New Online Collectivism." *Edge* (May 30, 2006). http://www.edge.org/3rd_culture/lanier06/lanier06_index.html (accessed December 31, 2006).

Ledford, Heidi. "IP: Ideas for Purchase?" *Berkeley Science Review* (Spring 2006).

Lev, Baruch. *Intangibles: Management, Measurement, and Reporting.* Brookings Institution Press, 2001.

Lev, Baruch; Flignor, Paul, and Orozco, David. "Intangible Asset & Intellectual Property Valuation: A Multidisciplinary Perspective." IPThought.com, June 2006.

Levinson, Marc. *The Economist Guide to Financial Markets,* ch. 1. Economist, 2003.

Levitt, Steven. *Freakonomics: A Rogue Economist Explores the Hidden Side of Everything.* Wm. Morris/HarperCollins, 2005.

Lincoln, Abraham. *Complete Works.* John Nicolay and John Hay, eds. Century, 1907.

Long, Pamela. "Invention, Authorship, 'Intellectual Property' and the Origin of Patents: Notes Toward a Conceptual History." *Technology and Culture* 32:846–884 (1991).

———. *Openness, Secrecy, Authorship: Technical Arts and the Culture of Knowledge from Antiquity to the Renaissance.* Johns Hopkins University Press, 2001.

Machlup, Fritz, and Penrose, Edith. "The Patent Controversy in the Nineteenth Century." *Journal of Economic History* 10:1–29 (1950).

Maskus, Keith. *Intellectual Property Rights in the Global Economy.* Institute for International Economics, 2000.

Maskus, Keith, and Reichman, Jerome,. eds. *International Public Goods and Transfer of Technology Under a Globalized Intellectual Property Regime.* Cambridge University Press, 2005.

Matsui, Akihiro. "Intellectual Property Litigation and Foreign Sovereign Immunity: International Law Limit to the Jurisdiction over the Infringement of Intellectual Property." Institute of Intellectual Property (2002). http://www.iip.or.jp/e/summary/pdf/detail2002/e14_20.pdf (accessed December 10, 2006).

Meinzen-Dick, Ruth, and Di Gregorio, Monica, eds. "Collective Action and Property Rights for Sustainable Development." *Intellectual Food Policy Research Institute.* Focus 11 (February 2004).

Meland, Marius. *IP Litigation Yielded $3.4 Billion in 2006: Survey* (IP Law 360, December 29, 2006.

Merges, Robert, and Ginsburg, Jane, eds. *Foundations of Intellectual Property.* Foundation Press, 2004.

Mgbeoji, Ikechi. *Global Biopiracy: Patents, Plants and Indigenous Knowledge.* Cornell University Press, 2006.

Miller, Eugene F. "Democratic Statecraft and Technological Advance: Abraham Lincoln's Reflections on 'Discoveries and Inventions.'" *Review of Politics* 63:485–515 (2001).

Moore, Adam. *Intellectual Property and Information Control: Philosophic Foundations and Contemporary Issues.* Transaction Publishers, 2004.

Moussa, Farag. "The Role of Innovation." International Federation of Inventors' Associations. IFIA, 2002. http://www.invention-ifia.ch/role_of_innovation.htm (accessed August 24, 2007).

Muir, Albert. *The Technology Transfer System: Inventions, Marketing, Licensing, Patenting, Setting, Practice, Management, Policy.* Latham, 1997.

Murphy, William. "A Proposal for a Centralized and Integrated Registry for Security Interests in Intellectual Property." *IDEA* 41:297 (2002).

Narin, Francis, Thomas, Patrick, and Breitzman, Anthony. "Using Patent Indicators to Predict Stock Market Performance." In *From Ideas to Assets: Investing Wisely in Intellectual Property*, ch. 14. Bruce Berman, ed. (Wiley, 2002).

Naughton, John. "Intellectual Property Is Theft. Ideas Are for Sharing." *The Observer*, February 9, 2003.

Newman, Pauline. "Speech to ABA-IPL Section," *Patent Trademark & Copyright Journal* 48:277 (1994).

Nickols, Fred. "Strategy Definitions and Meanings." 2006. http://home.att.net/~discon/strategy_definitions.pdf (accessed December 27, 2006).

O'Rourke, Maureen. "Toward a Doctrine of Fair Use in Patent Law." *Columbia Law Review* 100:5 (June, 2000).

Pike, Christopher. *Virtual Monopoly: Building an Intellectual Property Strategy for Creative Advantage: From Patents to Trademark, from Copyrights to Design Rights.* Nicholas Brealey Publishing, 2001.

Poltorak, Alexander, and Lerner, Paul. *Essentials of Intellectual Property.* Wiley, 2002.

Posey, Darrell, and Dutfield, Graham. *Beyond Intellectual Property: Toward Traditional Resource Rights for Indigenous Peoples and Local Communities.* IDRC, 1996.

Prager, Frank. "The Early Growth and Influence of Intellectual Property." *Journal of the Patent Office Society* 34:106–40 (1952).

Price, Andrew. "Corporate Trademark Portfolios: Ten Steps to Effective Management." *Intellectual Property Today* (December 2002), p. 32.

Primo Braga, Carlos. "The Developing Country Case For and Against Intellectual Property Protection." In *Strengthening Protection of Intellectual Property in Developing Countries: A Survey of the Literature*, Discussion Paper 112, Walter Siebeck, ed. World Bank, 1990.

Public Interest Intellectual Property Advisors. *Resource Manual for Bioprospecting.* PIIPA. 2003. http://www.piipa.org/library.asp (accessed January 28, 2007).

Razgaitis, Richard. *Early-Stage Technologies: Valuation and Pricing.* Wiley, 1999.

Reichman, Jerome. "Charting the Collapse of the Patent-Copyright Dichotomy: Premises for a Restructured International Intellectual Property System." *Cardozo Arts and Enertainment Law Journal* 13:475 (1993).

Rivette, Kevin. *Rembrandts in the Attic.* Harvard Business School, 2000.

Rockman, Howard. *Intellectual Property Law for Engineers and Scientists.* Wiley/IEEE, 2004.

Rosmerduc, Serge. Stele C-14. Hieroglyphic texts. http://www.iut.univ-paris8.fr/~rosmord/hieroglyphes/hieroglyphes.html (accessed January 28, 2007).

Ryan, Michael. *Knowledge Diplomacy: Global competition and the politics of intellectual property.* Brookings Institution Press, 1998.

Sachs, Jeffrey. *The End of Poverty: Economic Possibilities for Our Time.* Penguin London, 2005.

Sathe, Vijay. *Corporate Entrepreneurship: Top Managers and New Business Creation.* Cambridge University Press, 2003.

Satterthwaite, Janet "New Dilution Law." *Venable IP News and Comment,* November 2006.

Shulman, Seth. *Owning the Future.* Houghton Mifflin 1999.

Scalise, David G., and Nugent, Daniel. "International Intellectual Property Protections for Living Matter: Biotechnology, Multinational Conventions and the Exception for Agriculture." *Case Western Reserve Journal of International Law* 27:83 (1995).

Schumpeter, Joseph. "Capitalism, Socialism and Democracy." Harper, 1975 [orig. pub. 1942].

Scotchmer, Suzanne. *Innovation and Incentives.* MIT Press, 2005.

Sen, Amartya. *Development as Freedom.* Anchor Random House, 1996.

Sherman, Brad, and Bently, Lionel. *The Making of Modern Intellectual Property.* Cambridge University Press, 1999.

Shipman, Ross L. "Samuel Maverick: John Howland's Texas Legacy." Pilgrim John Howland Society. http://www.pilgrimjohnhowlandsociety.org/john_howland_texas_legacy.shtml (accessed January 13, 2007).

Shreeve, James. *The Genome War: How Craig Venter Tried to Capture the Code of Life and Save the World.* Knopf, 2004.

Smith, Gordon, and Parr, Russell. *Intellectual Property: Licensing and Joint Venture Profit Strategies,* 2nd ed. Wiley, 2000.

Stiglitz, Joseph. "Scrooge and Intellectual Property Rights." *British Medical Journal* 333:1279–1280 (2006).

Sullivan, Patrick. *Protecting Intellectual Capital: Extracting Value from Innovation.* Wiley, 1998.

Swanson, Timothy, ed. *Intellectual Property Rights and Biodiversity Conservation: An Interdisciplinary Analysis of the Values of Medicinal Plants.* Cambridge University Press 1995.

Taylor, Michael, and Cayford, Jerry. "American Patent Policy, Biotechnology, and African Agriculture: The Case for Policy Change." Resources for the Future (2003).

"Technology Transfer: NIH-Private Sector Partnership in the Development of Taxol." General Accounting Office Report to the Hon. Ron Wyden, U.S. Senate (2003). http://www.wyden.senate.gov/leg_issues/reports/taxol.pdf (accessed January 27, 2007). (See Appendix A.)

ten Kate, Kerry, and Laird, Sarah, *The Commercial Use of Biodiversity: Access to Genetic Resources and Benefit Sharing.* Earthscan, 2000.

ten Kate, Kerry; Touche, Laura, and Collis, Amanda. "Benefit-Sharing Case Study, Yellowstone National Park and the Diversa Corporation, Convention on Biological Diversity" (1998). http://www.biodiv.org/doc/case-studies/abs/cs-abs-yellowstone.pdf (accessed December 31, 2006).

The TRIPS Agreement. Trade-Related Aspects of Intellectual Property Rights. Annex 1C of the Marrakesh Agreement Establishing the World Trade Organization. Signed in Marrakesh, Morocco April 15, 1994. See Appendix A.

Thoreau, Henry David. *Walden, or Life in the Woods* (1854). Available at http://publicliterature.org/books/walden/xaa.php.

Toobin, Jeffrey. "Google's Moon Shot: The Quest for the Universal Library." *New Yorker,* February 2, 2007.

UNCTAD-ICTSD. *Resource Book on TRIPS and Development.* Cambridge University Press 2005.

Van Mele, Paul, and Zakaria, A.K.M. "The Innovation Tree: a New PRA Tool to Reveal the Innovation Adoption and Diffusion Process." Participatory Learning and Action, PLA notes 45 (2002). http://www.iied.org/NR/agbioliv/pla_notes/documents/plan_04511.pdf.

Venter, J. Craig. *A Life Decoded: My Genome, My Life.* Viking Penguin, 2007.

Vito, Christine, and Weidemier, Jean. "In the Beginning, There is a License." IP Frontline.com, October 19, 2005. http://www.ipfrontline.com (accessed January 3, 2007).

Vosper, Robert. "The Woman of Steel." *Inside Counsel*, February 1, 2005. http://www.insidecounsel.com/issues/insidecounsel/15_159/profiles/191–1. html.

Waltersheid, Edward. "The Early Evolution of the United States Patent Law: Antecedents (Part 1), Journal of the Patent and Trademark Office Society 76:697 (1994), through Part 5, Journal of the Patent and Trademark Office Society 78:615 (1996).

Willamette Management Associates. *Insights: Focus on Intellectual Property Economic Damages/ Lost Profit Analysis.* 2006.

Wilson, Edward. *Consilience: The Unity of Knowledge.* Knopf, 1998.

WIPO. "How Can Patent Offices Encourage Inventive and Innovative Activities?" WIPO-IFIA International Symposium. 2000. WIPO/IFIA/BUE/00/11 (2000). www.wipo.int/edocs/mdocs/innovation/en/wipo_ifia_bue_00/wipo_ifia_bue_00_11.doc (accessed January 4, 2007).

CASES:

ABKCO Music Inc. v. Harrisongs Music, Ltd., 722 F.2d 988 (2d Cir. 1983).

Bright Tunes Music Corp. v. Harrisongs Music, Ltd., 420 F.Supp. 177 (S.D.N.Y. 1976).

College Savings Bank v. Florida Prepaid Postsecondary Education Expense Bd., 527 U.S. 666 (1999).

Davoll v. Brown, 1 Woodbury & Minot 53, 57 (1st Cir. 1045)

eBay Inc. v. MercExchange, L.L.C., 127 S.Ct. 1837 ((2006)).

Estate of Martin Luther King, Jr., Inc. v. CBS, Inc., 194 F.3d 1211 (11th Cir. 1999).

Florida Prepaid Postsecondary Education Expense Bd. v. College Savings Bank, 527 U.S. 627 (1999).

Georgia-Pacific Corp. v. U.S. Plywood Corp., 318 F. Supp. 1116 (S.D.N.Y. 1970).

KSR International Co. v. Teleflex Inc., 127 S. Ct. 1727 (2007).

Mazer v. Stein, 347 U.S. 201 (1954).

MedImmune, Inc. v. Genentech, Inc. 127 S.Ct. 764 (2007).

Microsoft Corp. v. AT&T Corp., 127 S.Ct. 1746 (2007).

New York Times Co. v. Tasini, 533 U.S. 483 (2001).

Polaroid Corp. v. Eastman Kodak Co., 16 U.S.P.Q.2d 1481 (D. Mass. 1990), *as corrected*, 17 U.S.P.Q.2d 1711 (D. Mass. 1991).

State Street Bank & Trust Company v. Signature Financial Group, Inc., 149 F.3d 1368 (Fed. Cir. 1998).

Symbol Technologies, Inc. v. Lemelson Medical, Education & Research Foundation, LP, 422 F.3d 1378 (Fed. Cir. 2005).

Traffix Devices, Inc. v. Marketing Displays, Inc. 532 U.S. 23 (2001).

Wal-Mart Stores, Inc. v. Samara Brothers, Inc., 529 U.S. 205 (2000).

Waterman v. Mackenzie, 138 U.S. 255 (1891).

Index

LaVergne, TN USA
24 September 2010
198258LV00009B/1/P